GEL PLATE PRINTING

A Guide to Making Beautiful Layered Art

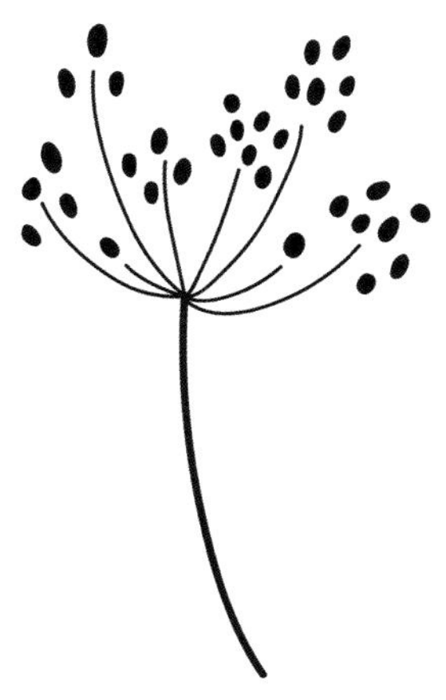

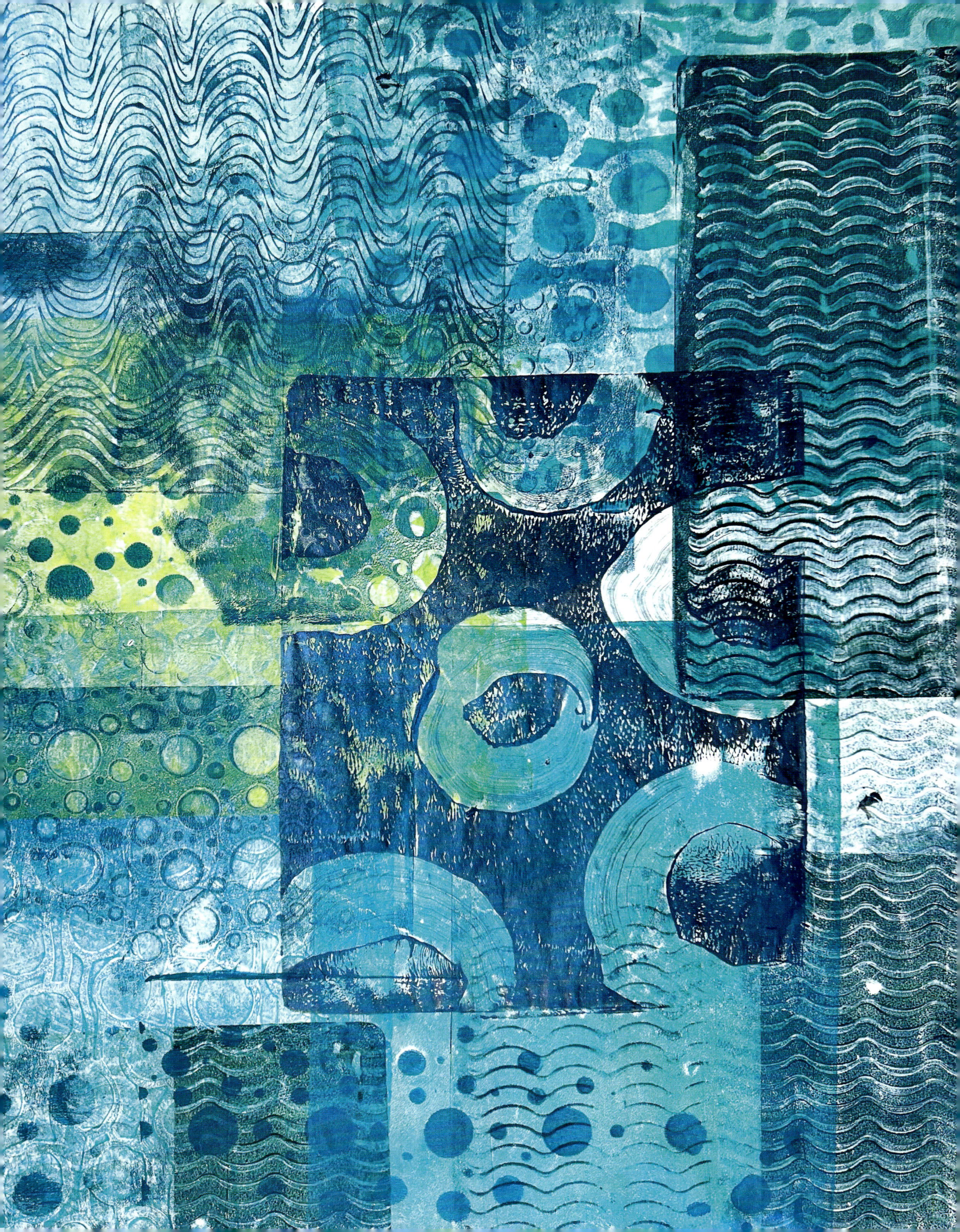

GEL PLATE PRINTING

A Guide to Making Beautiful Layered Art

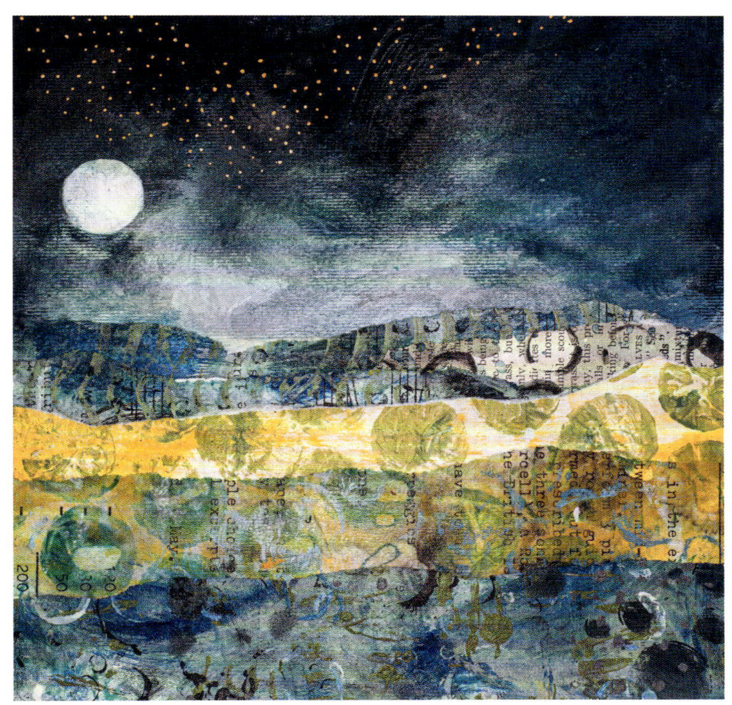

Susan McCreevy

H E R B E R T   P R E S S

LONDON · OXFORD · NEW YORK · NEW DELHI · SYDNEY

HERBERT PRESS
Bloomsbury Publishing Plc
50 Bedford Square, London, WC1B 3DP, UK
Bloomsbury Publishing Ireland Limited
29 Earlsfort Terrace, Dublin 2, D02 AY28, Ireland

BLOOMSBURY, HERBERT PRESS and the Herbert Press logo are trademarks of Bloomsbury Publishing Plc

First published in Great Britain in 2026

A catalogue record for this book is available from the British Library
Library of Congress Cataloguing-in-Publication data has been applied for

ISBN: 978-1-78994-338-2; eBook: 978-1-78994-337-5

2 4 6 8 10 9 7 5 3

Design and layouts by Lorraine Inglis Design
Printed and bound in Türkiye by Imak Ofset

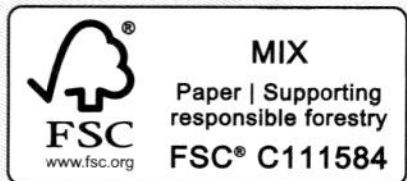

To find out more about our authors and books visit www.bloomsbury.com and sign up for our newsletters
For product safety related questions contact productsafety@bloomsbury.com

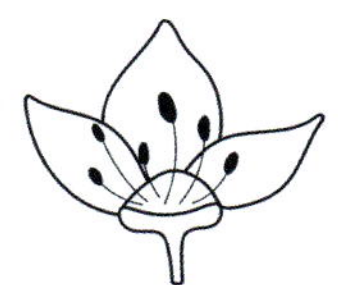

CONTENTS

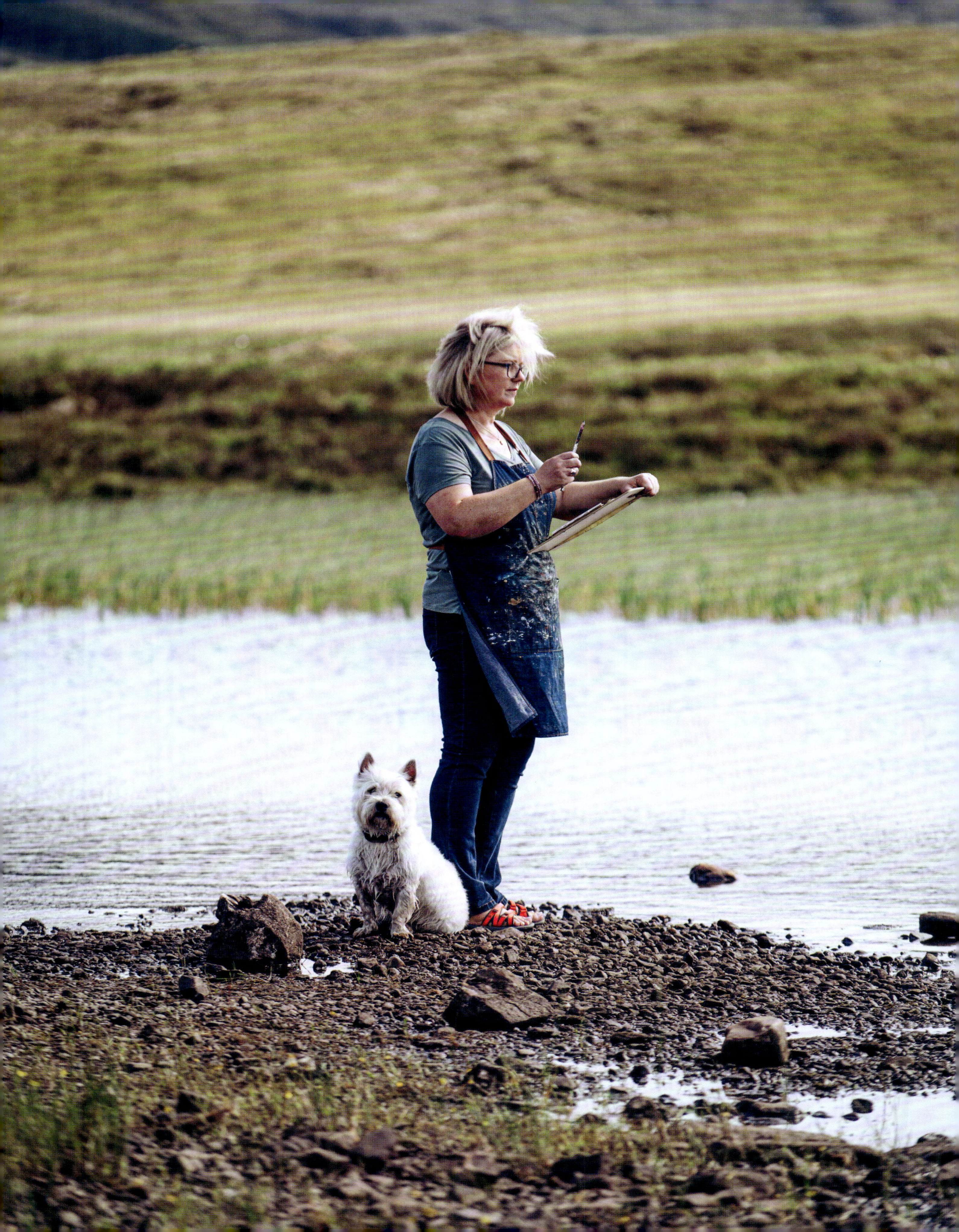

INTRODUCTION

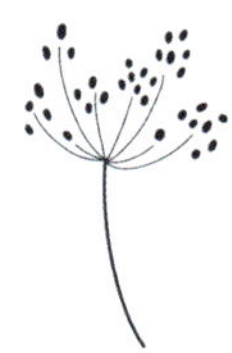

Hi, I'm Susan, a mixed-media artist and printmaker, living in Inverness in the north of Scotland with my two teenage daughters and our West Highland Terrier, Toby.

I have a studio in Wasps Creative Academy in Inverness, which is lovely, as I am part of an artist community. I studied textile design and printmaking at Duncan of Jordanstone College of Art & Design.

During my time at art college, I focused mainly on etchings, linocuts and monoprints. After graduating, I continued as a printmaker and joined a printmaking studio in London, where I sold my prints at Portobello Market and Spitalfields.

Years later, after having my daughters, I became a member of the Highland Print Studio in Inverness. It was there I would spend a few precious hours each week making art just for myself. As a single parent, this creative time became a lifeline. In 2008, I began exploring collagraphs, which marked an exciting new chapter in my creative journey.

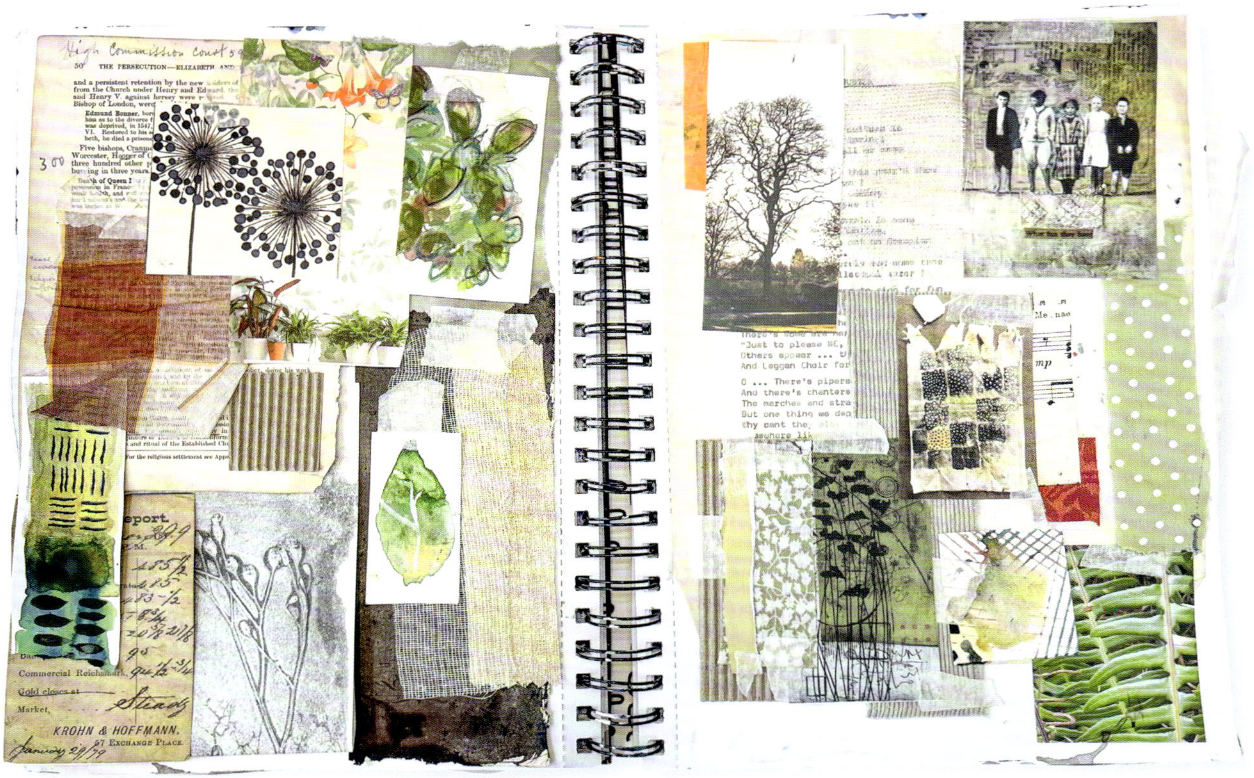

As time went on, attending the print workshop became more challenging, and our home was too small to have a dedicated art space, so I stopped creating for a few years. When the desire to create eventually returned, I began exploring designs that inspired me and discovered the world of mixed-media art. I took as many online courses as I could and learned many new techniques.

In March 2020, I posted on Instagram for the very first time. Little did I know where this platform would lead me! I began by posting paintings produced

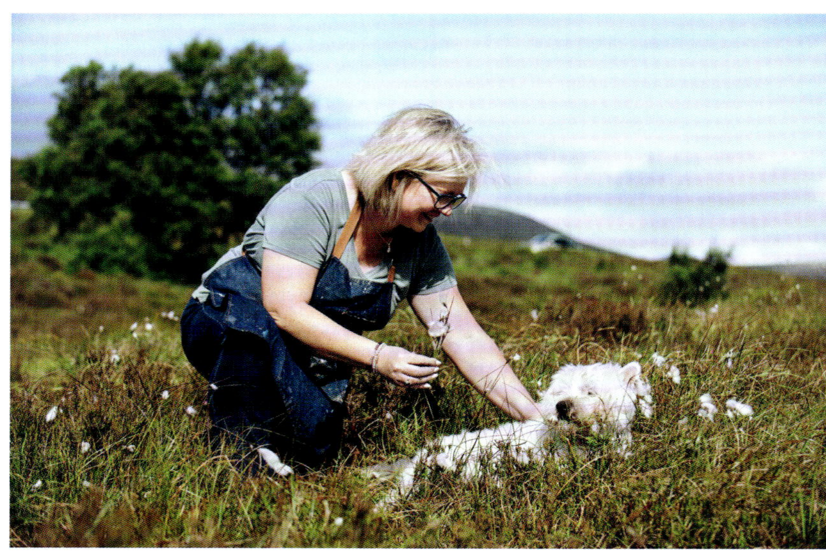

from the online classes I had been taking. I was gaining momentum and my confidence was beginning to grow. My art supplies were also multiplying and so we invested in a home studio, and I soon purchased my first gel plate. I could then continue printmaking without the need for a printing press.

I had heard about #The100DayProject – a challenge to work on a personal project every day for 100 days. It's a great way to explore creativity, try new ideas and build creative habits through small daily acts. Many people share their progress online, creating a supportive and inspiring community. I thought this challenge would be a great way to learn how to combine this new tool with my mixed-media artworks. People seemed to like what I was creating and my followers began to grow. I started to experiment with filming reels and discovered that I enjoyed creating video content too.

I shared tips about what I was learning along the way, which people seemed to enjoy and find helpful. The online community is great; I discovered private Facebook groups that specialised in gel printing and I realised that thousands of people out there were loving it too. They were so happy to share their tips and the successes and many failures they were having with the gel plate.

In August 2021, I did my first test run of a gel print workshop, after being asked by my friend if I would host it in her gallery in Maud, Aberdeenshire. I packed up all my kit and headed off to with much trepidation. As soon as I began teaching, my nerves left me. I loved seeing all the artwork created by the students. I taught several workshops over the course of my three days in Maud, and that was the beginning of my teaching journey. Since then, artists have travelled from as far afield as the Caribbean and Norway to take part in in-person workshops with me.

My online teaching journey began when I was approached by my art mentor, Ivy Newport, to see if I would like to teach a lesson on her platform, Studioworks Creative Academy. I felt that this would be a nurturing way to dip my toe in the water of the online teaching business. It turned out to be a great decision. It was a huge learning curve but I was encouraged to keep going because of the amazing feedback from students.

The art that I was creating using the gel plate combined with my mixed-media techniques began to gain attention, and many people asked me, 'Will you be making an online course to teach your process?' This was my cue to develop the Botanical Gelli Print Course, which has been enjoyed by hundreds of students. I am now a full-time artist with a new larger studio in Wasps Creative Academy. I feel like I am living the artist dream!

My art reflects the beauty around me. Living in this stunning part of the world, I find inspiration in flowers, leaves, trees, birds and seascapes – my favourite subjects to paint. Coming from a textile design background, I often infuse patterns into my work. Nature itself provides a wealth of unique patterns waiting to be discovered. Once you start noticing them, you'll see patterns everywhere, turning the ordinary into something extraordinary.

Susan McCreevy

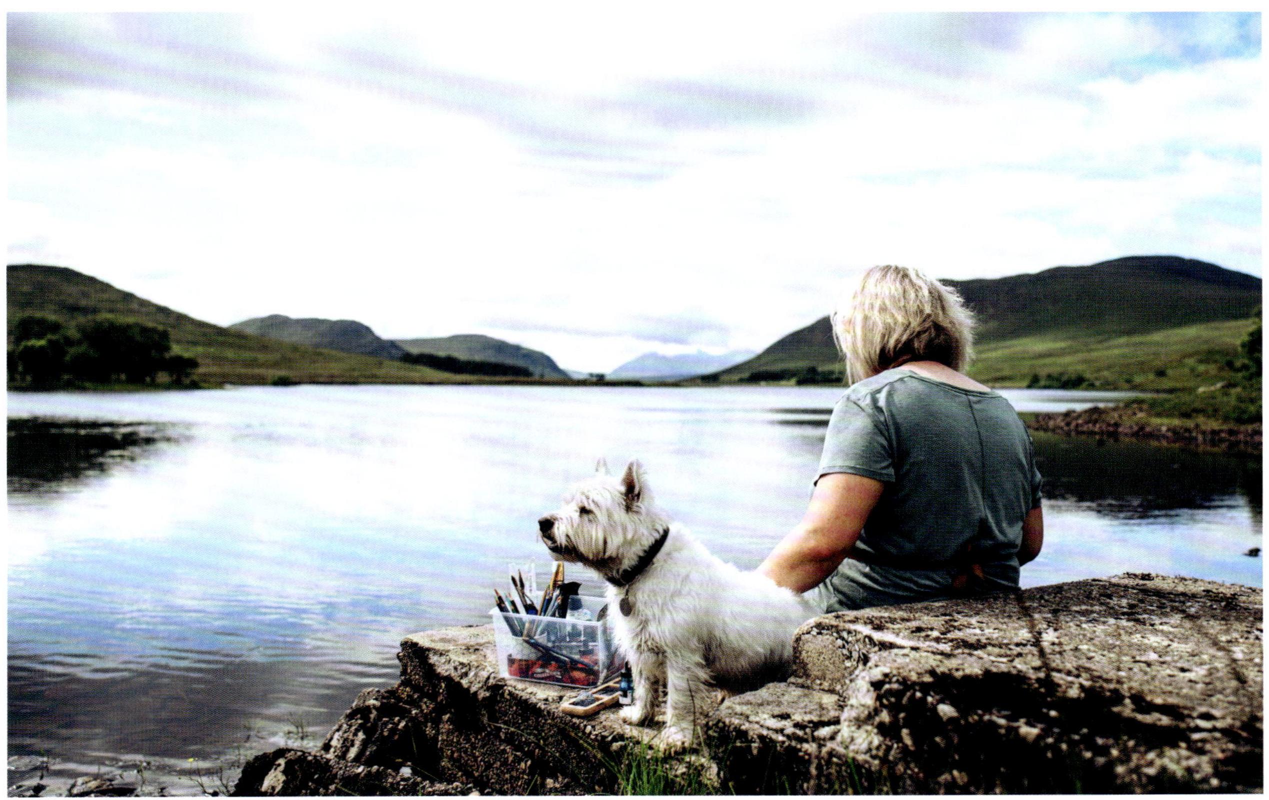

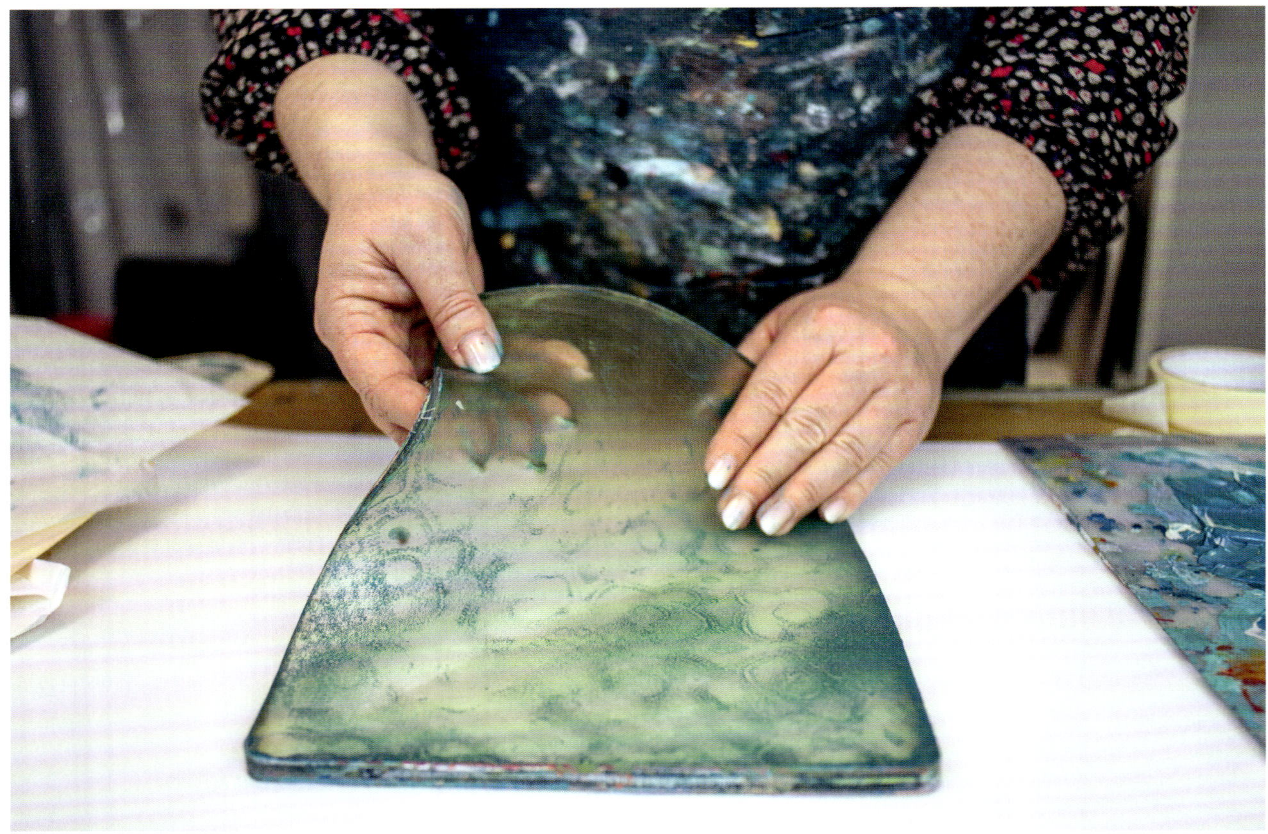

Reusable gel plate.

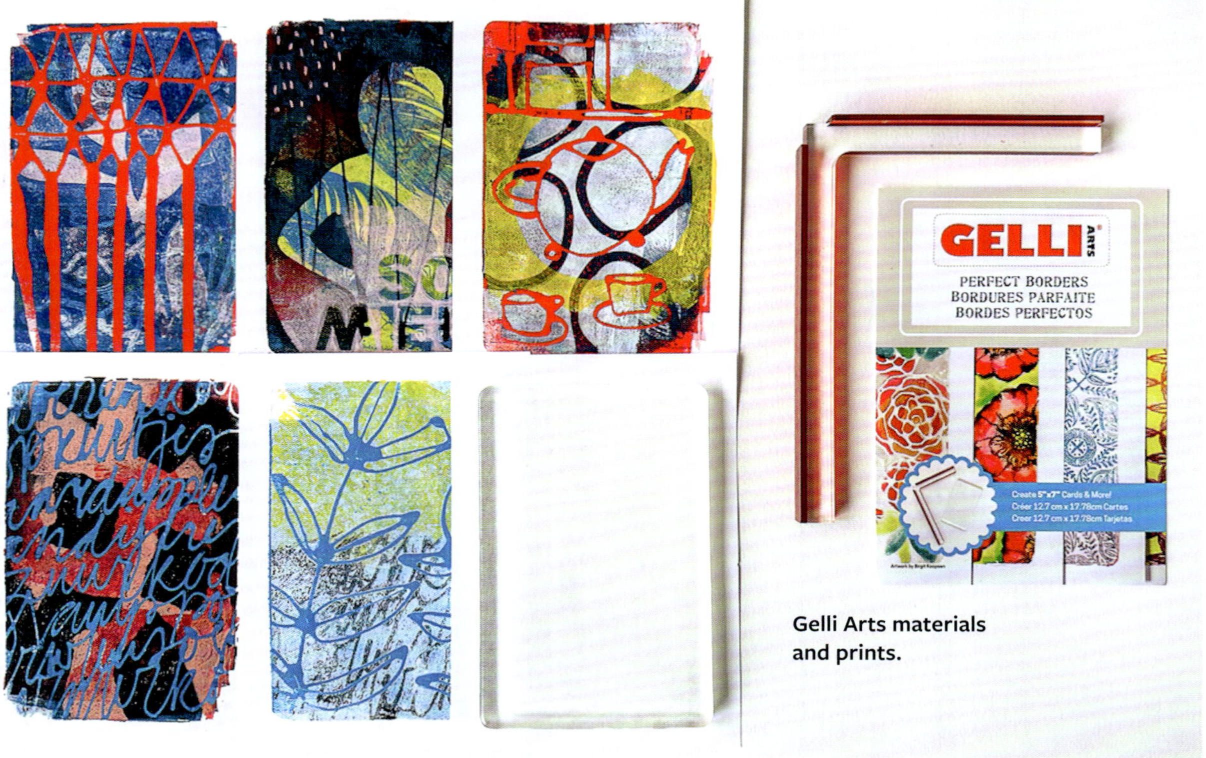

Gelli Arts materials
and prints.

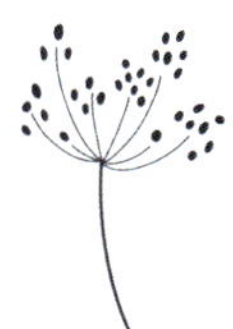

THE HISTORY OF THE GEL PLATE

Everything that I learnt to do as a printmaker at art college required a printing press, which is very costly and takes up a huge amount of space. I wanted to be a printmaker, but how could I do this from the comfort of my small home studio? After extensive research, and trial and error of home printing methods, I decided to invest in a gel plate.

Gel plates have gained in popularity over the past few years. They are reusable, durable printing plates that allow you to monoprint without a press. A monoprint is basically a single print, as opposed to a print from an etching plate where the design on the metal plate can be cleaned and used again many times. The plates look and feel like gelatin plates, but there is no gelatin or animal products in them. Let's go back a little to explain their origins.

The first gel plate was called a Hectograph, invented in 1869. The Hectograph is a flat box filled with a layer of jelly-like mass (a mixture of gelatin, glycerine and water). The text and illustrations are put onto paper by means of a special ink, then the resulting copy is pressed onto the surface of the gel, producing a copy of the text and illustrations. Each layer of gel and ink could produce 100 copies, hence the name 'Hectograph'.

Where did the idea to create a gel printing plate come from?

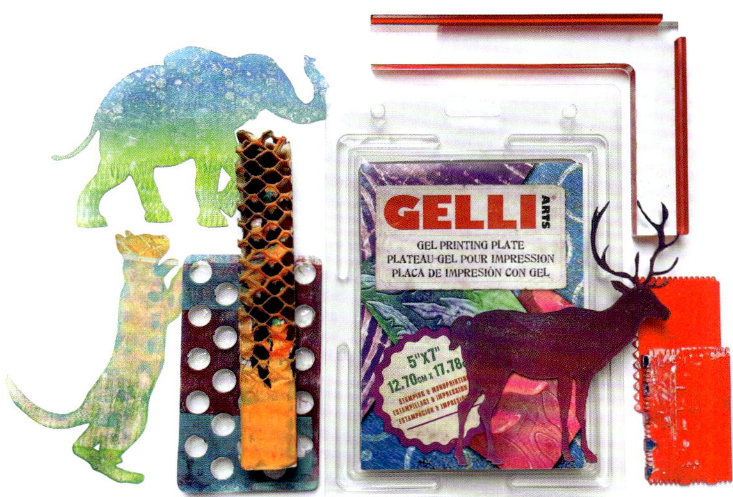

Joan Bess, co-founder of Gelli Arts, came up with the idea of a reusable gel plate. She loved to print on gelatin but never seemed to have a real gelatin plate on hand when inspiration struck.

Joan and her colleague, Lou Ann Gleason, spent a year developing and testing a gel plate that was durable, non-toxic and easy to clean and store. They tested the design in many focus groups before finally launching the gel plate in 2011, so it's a relatively new product on the market. The product is loved by fine artists and crafters of all ages!

CARING FOR YOUR GEL PLATE

To make the most out of your gel plate, you must take good care of it. Here are five key points worth remembering:

1. When your gel plate arrives, remove the plastic sheets. Storing it with the plastic sheets on can lead to air bubbles imprinting on the plate and affecting your prints.

2. Gently wash your gel plate after use with soapy water or baby oil and kitchen paper to clean stubborn marks or paint from it. It is safe to use vegetable, olive or baby oil, and it also helps to condition the plate.

3. Keep the clamshell to protect the gel plate and reuse the plastic sheets later.

4. Place a piece of paper, cut to the size of the plate, on top before storage. This will keep your gel plate safe and free from any potential imprints.

5. Store your gel plate in its clamshell, without any heavy objects on top, to prevent dents.

I hope you find these reminders helpful as you dive into using your gel plate. Remember: the more you care for it, the longer its lifespan will be.

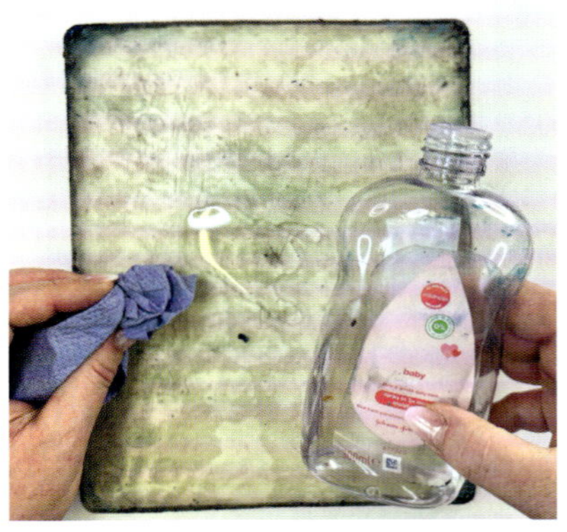

Remove stubborn marks with baby oil.

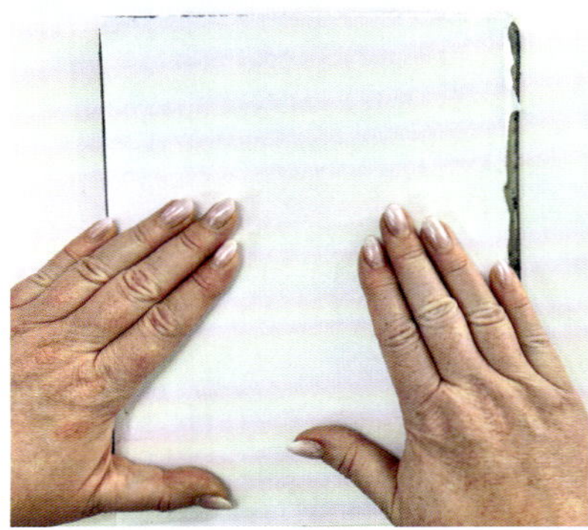

Carefully smooth the paper to prevent any air bubbles being trapped.

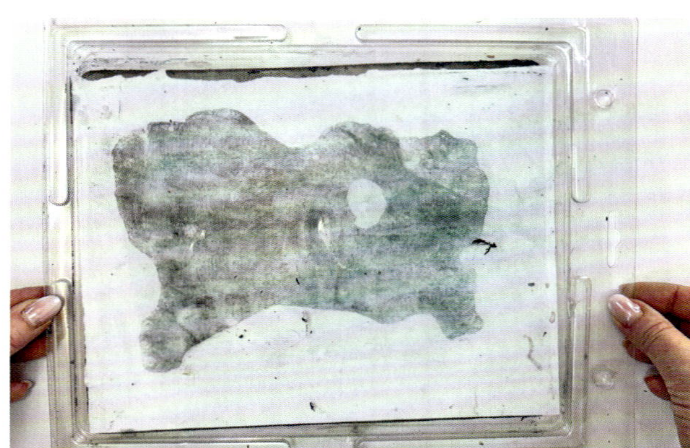

Gel plate stored in the clamshell.

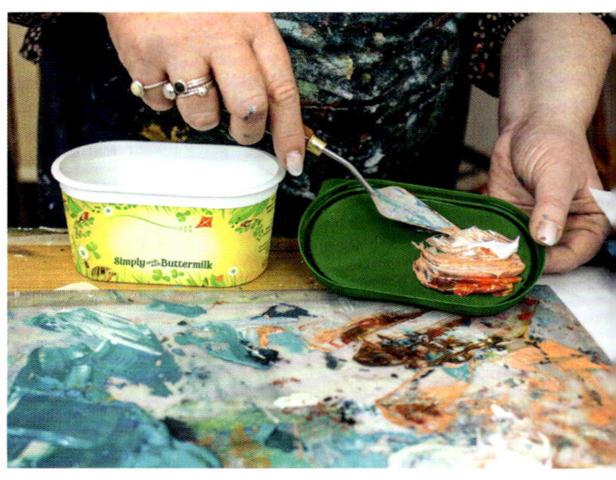

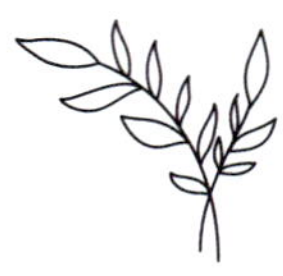

Tip

If you find yourself with extra paint on your palette after a session, gently scrape off the excess with a palette knife and transfer it onto the inside of a margarine tub lid. Place the bottom of the tub on top of the lid, creating a seal which keeps the paint usable for about a week or so. Just give it a quick spray with water when you're ready to use it again.

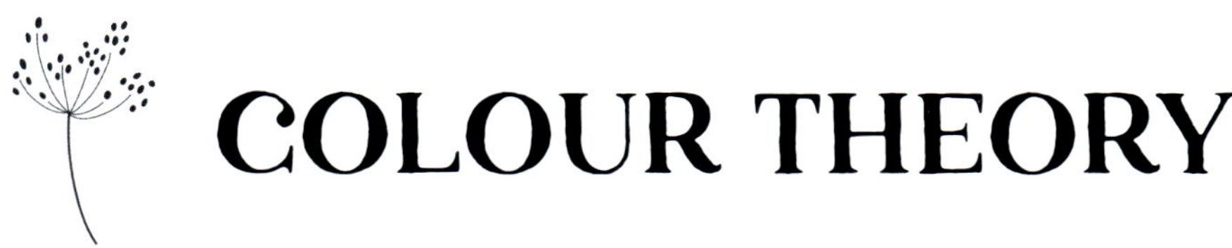

COLOUR THEORY

Colour theory helps us to understand how colours work together – which ones complement each other and how to use them to create the right mood in your work. By knowing how to mix colours, use warm and cool tones, and balance different shades, you can make your art more interesting and powerful.

Below, you'll find the basics of colour theory, including a colour wheel, mixing hues and understanding colour temperature.

Colour wheel

The colour wheel separates colours into cool tones, such as blues, greens and violets, and warm tones, including yellows, reds and oranges. When you mix two colours, the resulting colour will be located between them on the wheel; for example, mixing yellow and blue will produce green.

Many people learn to mix using red, yellow and blue, but it can be hard to create bright shades like turquoise or lime green with these colours. I would recommend using CMYK colours to achieve more vibrant mixes.

To determine whether you'll get a bright or dull green when mixing, identify whether your base colour is warm or cool – look closely to see if there's more blue, yellow or red in the colour. For instance, a green can lean towards yellow, creating a warm green, or towards blue, resulting in a cool green.

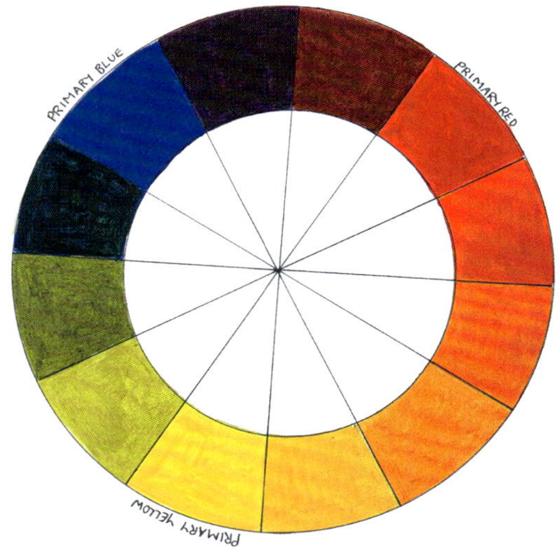

RGB colour wheel.

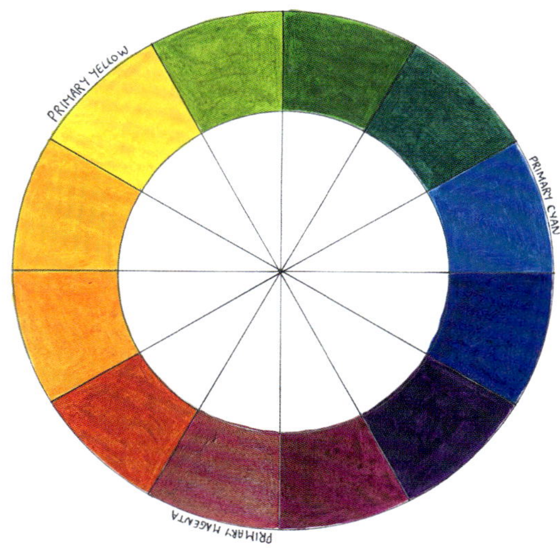

CMYK colour wheel.

Colour hue

Hue refers to the pure state of a colour – such as red, blue or yellow – without any black, white or grey added.

Complementary colours

Complementary colours are pairs of colours that are directly opposite each other on the colour wheel. When placed next to each other, they create contrast and make each other appear more vibrant. Examples include blue and orange, red and green, and yellow and purple.

Value

Value refers to the darkness or lightness of an object. Objects that are further away appear lighter due to atmospheric moisture and dust.

Remember: dark colours come forward and light colours recede.

Colour temperature

An object that is further away from you also tends to shift towards the cool side as it recedes into the distance. You can still have warm colours in the distance but they will have to be cooler than the colours in the foreground. Cool colours, such as blue, green and violet, push elements back, whereas warmer colours, such as yellow, red and orange, will bring elements to the foreground.

Remember: warm colours come forward and cool colours recede.

Intensity of colour

The intensity of the colour refers to how bright it is. You can grey down your colour (reduce its brightness) by adding a small amount of its complementary colour. So, if you want to grey down a bright red, add a little green into the mix.

Remember: bright colours come forward and dull colours recede.

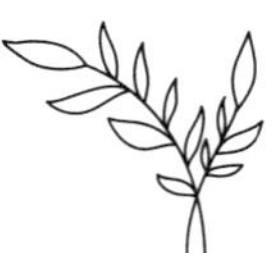

Tip

For more vivid colours, use cyan, magenta and yellow instead of red, yellow and blue. Look for paints labelled Primary Cyan, Primary Magenta and Primary Yellow.

These colours blend beautifully to create bright greens, turquoise, warm reds, oranges, deep purples and blues. Although you can easily buy pre-mixed colours for convenience, understanding colour mixing will really help you to develop as an artist.

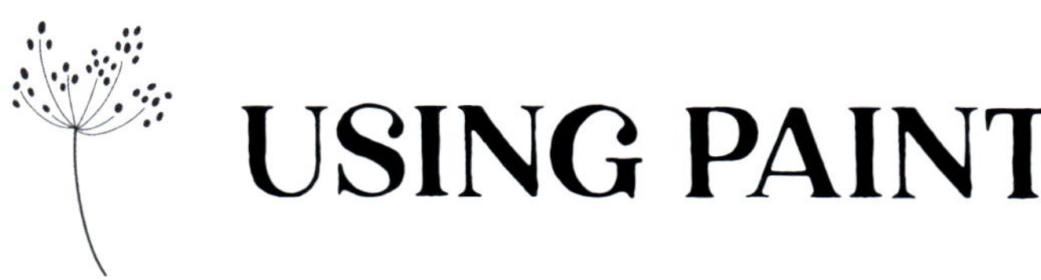

USING PAINT

Transparent paints allow light to pass through them. This means that when you layer transparent colours over one another, the colours beneath can still be seen, creating depth and richness.

Opaque paints are the opposite of transparent paints. They block light from passing through, so when you layer opaque colours, the colours beneath are completely covered.

Metallic paints can range from semi-transparent to opaque, depending on how they are applied. Thinner layers might allow the underlying surface to show through, while multiple layers provide solid, metallic coverage.

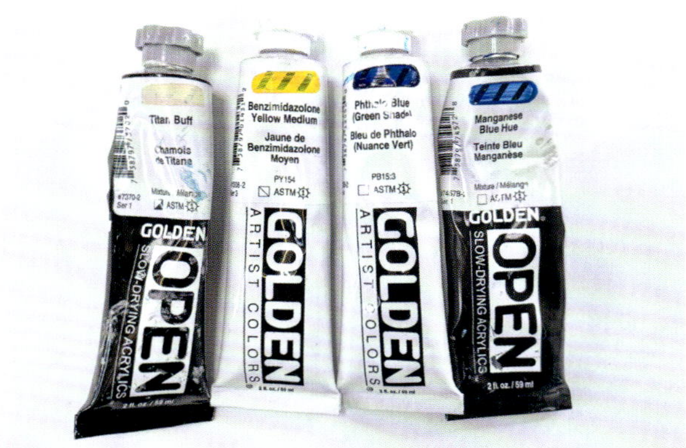

Transparent and semi-transparent Golden acrylics.

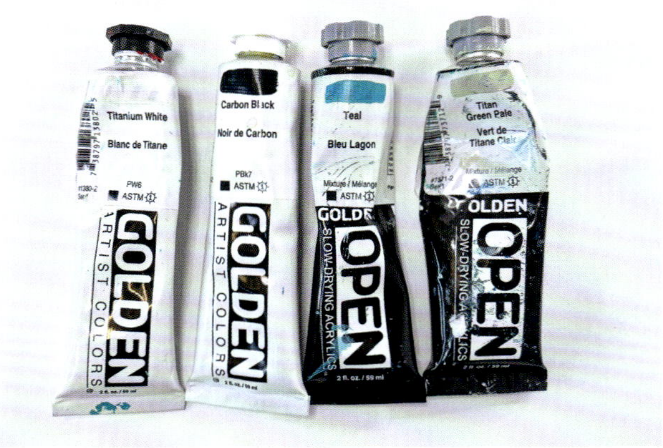

Opaque Golden acrylics.

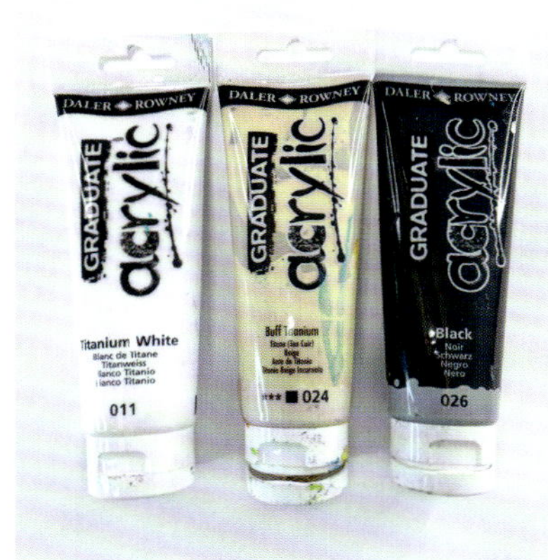

Opaque Graduate Daler Rowney acrylics.

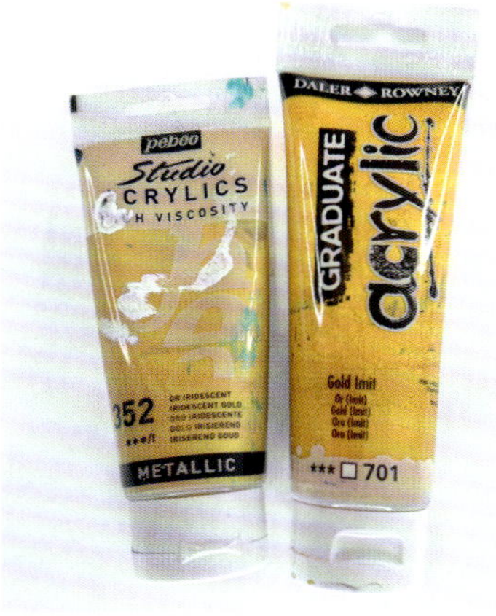

Semi-transparent metallic gold acrylics.

Pébéo DYNA acrylic paints are some of my favourites for printing. They're iridescent and change colour when viewed from different angles, which creates a shimmering, eye-catching effect. These paints are semi-opaque, so they partially cover the surface beneath, and their colours stand out best on dark backgrounds. They are great for adding layers to your prints.

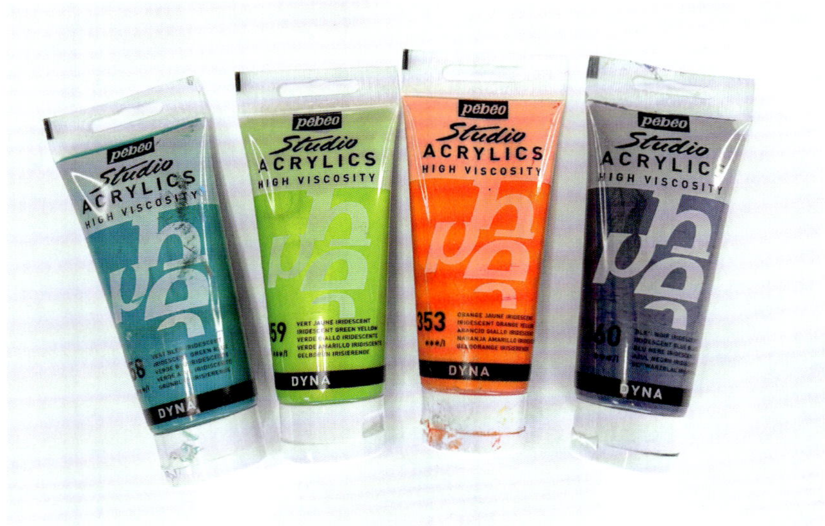

Semi-opaque Pébéo DYNA iridescent acrylics.

Understanding transparent paint

Understanding the transparency of your acrylic paint is crucial for layering techniques and achieving desired visual effects in your artwork.

Identifying the transparency of acrylic paint can be done using the symbols and information on the paint tube or container. Here's how to interpret them:

- **Transparency symbol:** Look for a symbol that resembles a square with one side shaded or a diamond shape. This indicates the paint's level of transparency.

- **Information label:** Some tubes may explicitly state the paint's transparency level as 'transparent', 'semi-transparent' or 'opaque'.

- **Pigment information:** Check the pigment information on the tube; some pigments are naturally more transparent than others, and paints made from transparent pigments will generally be see-through.

It is also useful to think about the lightfastness of paint, i.e. how it will fade over time if exposed to bright sunlight. Identifying the lightfastness of paint is via the asterisk/star system on the paint tube:

**** Permanent
*** Normally permanent
** Moderately permanent
* Fugitive

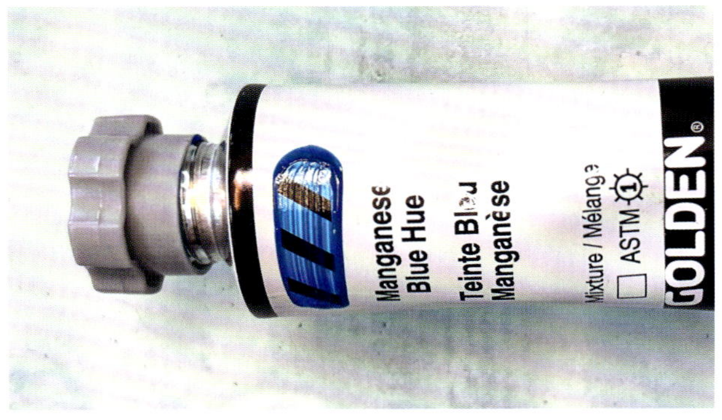

Here, the black lines are visible underneath this transparent paint.

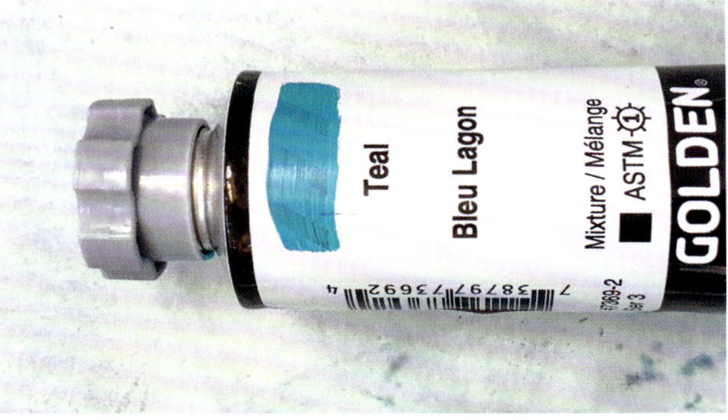

Here, the lines are covered completely as this teal is opaque.

Extending the drying time of acrylic paint

If you are based in a country with hot or dry weather, you may find that your paints dry on the plate before you have had time to get to work. Slowing down their drying time can be achieved through various methods, including the following:

- **Using retarders:** Acrylic retarders are additives specifically designed to slow down the drying time of acrylic paint. They are available at art supply stores and can be mixed directly into your paint or applied to the surface before painting.

- **Adding a few drops of water:** Acrylic paints are made up from a mixture of pigment, binder and water. The more expensive the paint, the less water it will contain.

- **Using 'open' acrylics:** Some brands such as Golden offer 'open' or 'slow-drying' acrylic paints, which have a longer drying time compared to regular acrylics. These paints are formulated to stay wetter for a longer period, allowing for more blending and workability.

- **Adding a painting medium:** Adding a painting medium, such as gel medium or glazing medium, to your acrylic paint can alter the consistency and drying time of the paint without significantly changing its colour or opacity.

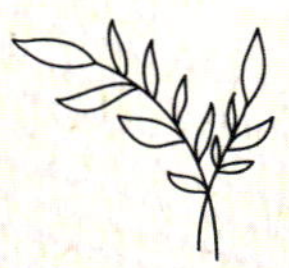

Tip

Daler Rowney offers a free downloadable PDF that provides a comprehensive reference for all their acrylic paints, which I have linked on page 172.

Materials master list

Below I've laid out a master list of tools and supplies which you will need throughout the projects. It might seem a little overwhelming, but you will likely find that you have a few of these things lying around the house! I've also recommended a few places to buy key supplies from on page 174 but do visit your own local craft shops.

PRINTING SUPPLIES
- Gel plate – I usually use a 20 x 25cm (8 x 10in) gel plate (Gelli Arts is a popular brand)
- Baren or flat lid (such as a Pringles lid)
- 15cm (6in) brayer or roller

PAPER
- Mountboard or stiff card
- 300gsm watercolour or mixed-media paper
- Tracing paper or carbon paper
- Printed images of landscape in colour and black and white
- Regular copy paper
- Wet-strength tissue paper
- Old prints or book pages for collages

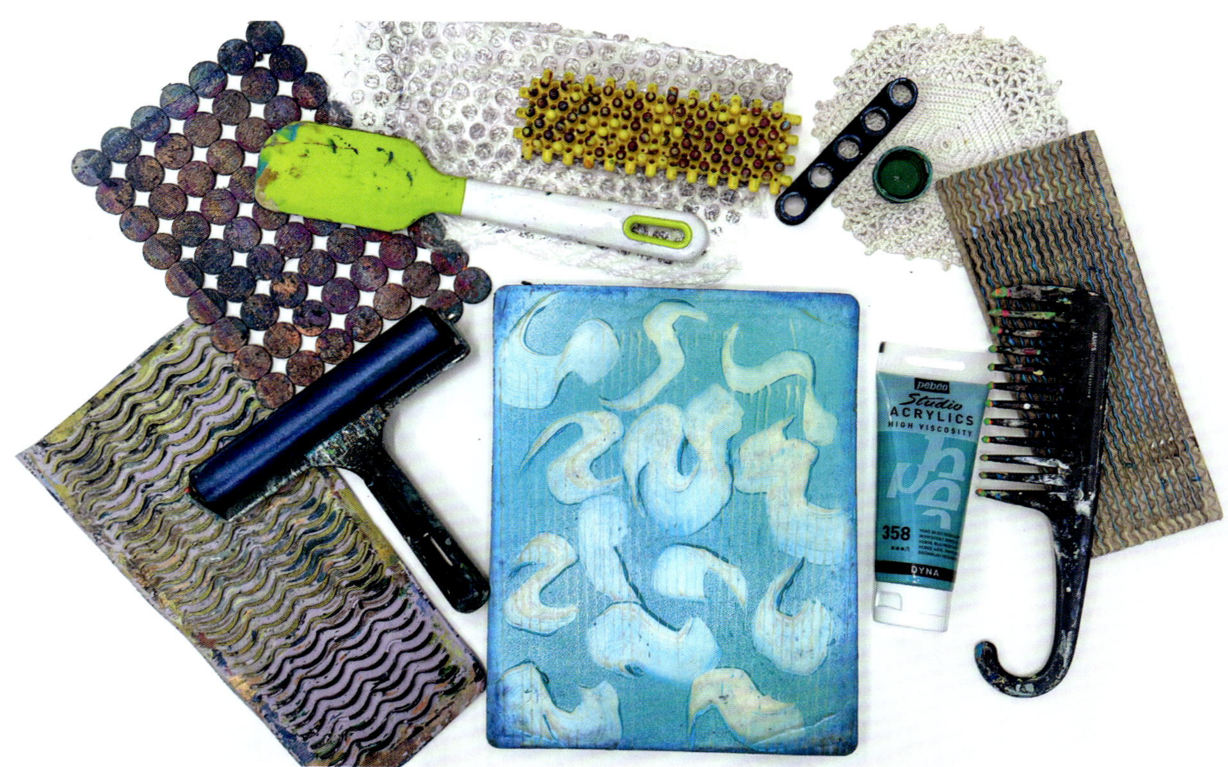

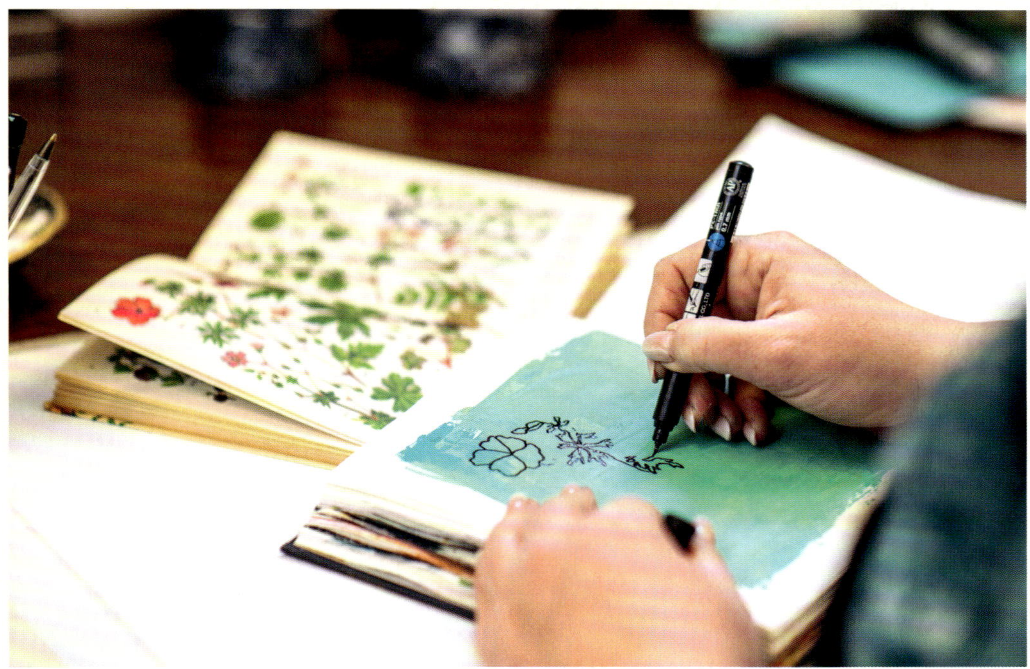

PAINT AND MEDIUMS

- Acrylic paint: Titanium White, Indigo, Turquoise Blue and Black are my favourites, but each project lists the specific colours used
- Gloss gel medium
- Matte medium
- White gesso
- Neocolor® II pastels, fine liners, Posca pens, Uni-ball Signo bronze gel pen

TOOLS

- Metal ruler, scissors, pencil
- Cutting mat and craft knife
- Masking tape
- Hairdryer or heat gun
- Palette knife
- Baby wipes
- PVA glue

OPTIONAL

- String, rubber bands, jute fabric, carborundum or fine sand for collagraph plates
- Various sizes of paintbrush and decorator's brush
- Silicone spatula
- Old credit card or catalyst wedge
- Metal ball stylus sculpting tool, wide-toothed plastic comb
- Hole punch, pre-made stencils, sponges
- Mixed media spray varnish (optional)

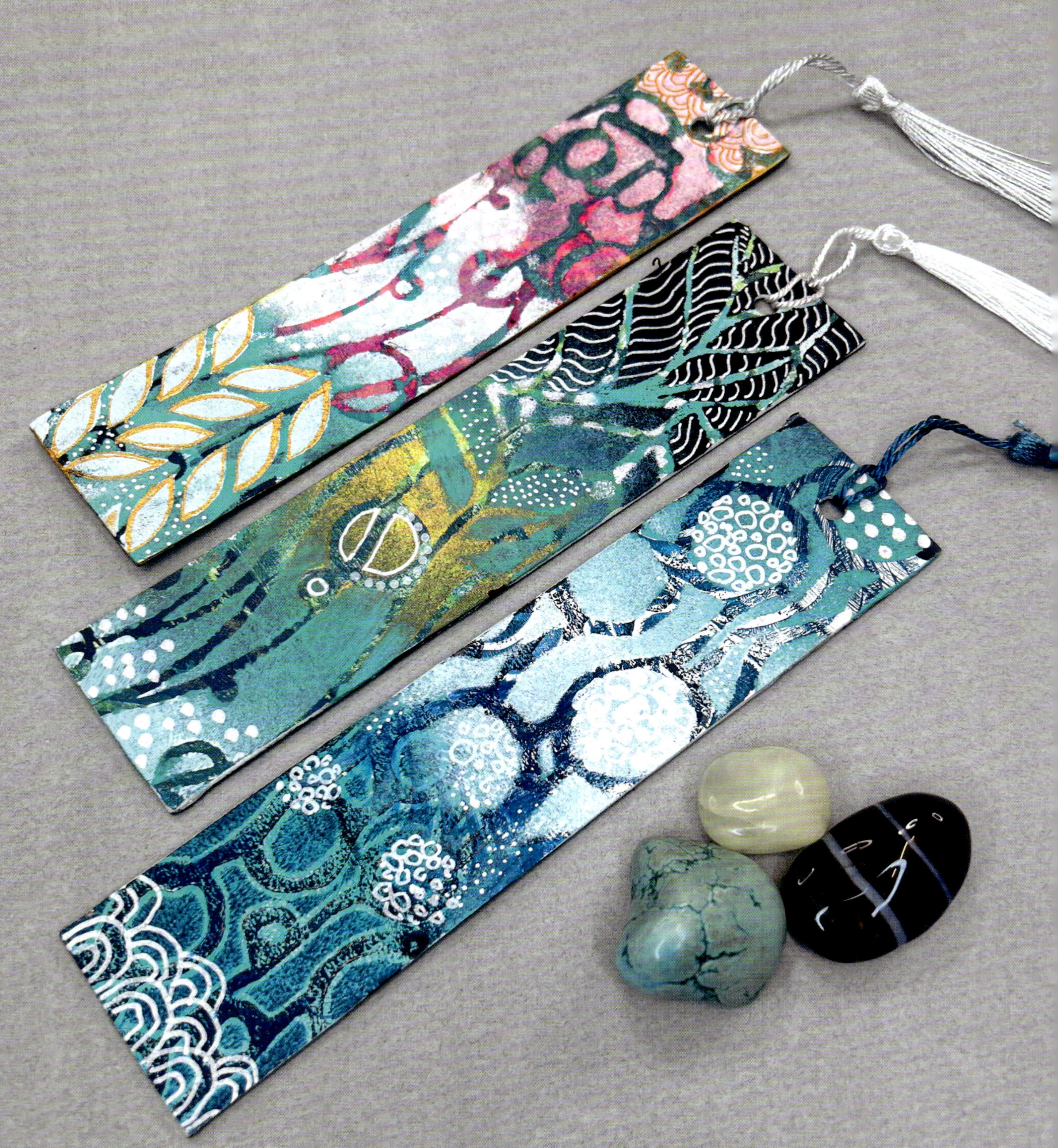

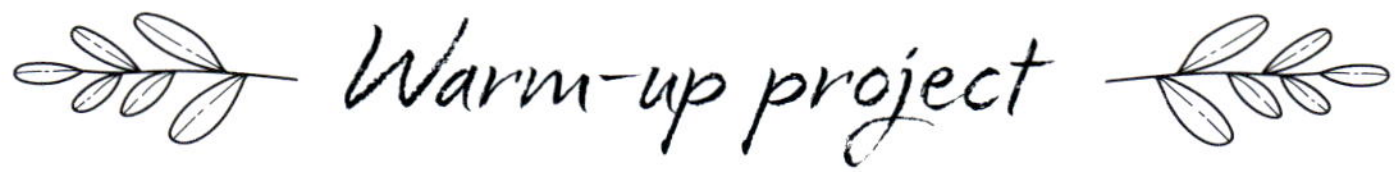

BOOKMARKS AND ABSTRACT COMPOSITIONS

Let's ease into the creative process with this simple warm-up. Start with an A2 sheet of paper, take out your gel plate, set up your workspace and begin experimenting. If you don't have any large pieces of paper, just tape a few A4 sheets together on the back with masking tape to make your own. Make sure to use the entire page!

Once you've filled your paper with overlapping prints, shapes and marks, you can use a viewfinder to pick out sections that work as small abstract designs. This isn't about making a perfect print, it's about playing with the process. You'll know you're in the creative flow when you're surrounded by prints and time seems to fly by.

This warm-up project is all about getting into the creative rhythm – have fun!

MATERIALS

Refer back to the master list on page 18 for the essential items.

- Acrylic paint: Turquoise Blue, Indigo, Iridescent Blue, Iridescent Orange, Iridescent Gold, Iridescent Green, Titanium White, Fluorescent Pink, Prussian Blue and Black
- Gel plate – 20 x 25cm (8 x 10in)
- 4 large sheets of thin A2 sketchbook paper – 42 x 59.4cm (16½ x 23½in)

- 1 sheet of A3 mountboard or card – 29.7 x 42cm (11¾ x 16½in)
- Wooden cradleboard – 15 x 15cm (6 x 6in)
- Tassels
- Plastic sleeves
- Mixed media spray varnish (optional)

Adding paint to the gel plate

For this project, I'll be using some of my favourite colours, including Turquoise Blue, Indigo, Iridescent Orange and a hint of Iridescent Gold. I'll work with my 20 x 25cm (8 x 10in) gel plate, but this process works just as well with a 12.5 x 17.5cm (5 x 7in) plate or sections of a larger 41 x 50cm (16 x 20in) plate.

Start by squeezing a small amount of Turquoise acrylic paint onto the plate (a) and rolling it out into a smooth, even layer (b).

Dragging a comb through wet paint

I've started with one corner, to ensure I can fill the whole page with prints. I use a plastic comb to drag a design through the paint (c) – the plate will not be damaged easily by the comb if it is a plastic one. Depending on how much paint you add to the plate you can pull two or three prints from the plate (d).

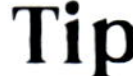

Tip

I like to use face paint sponges and cut them in half. You can reuse them if they are washed after use.

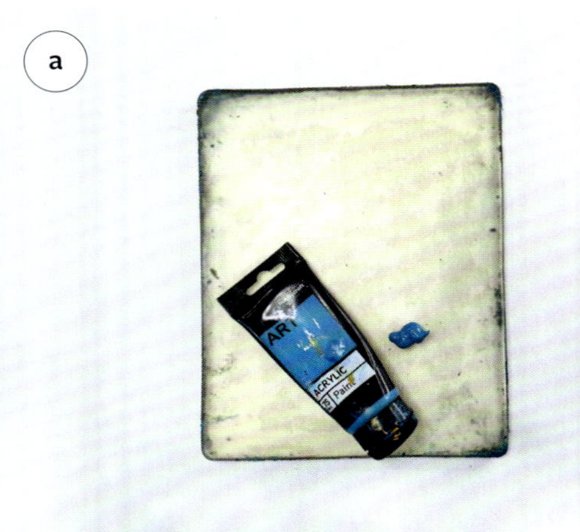

a

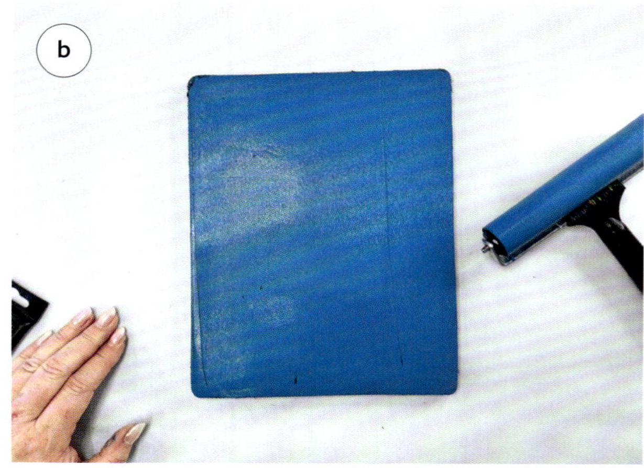

b

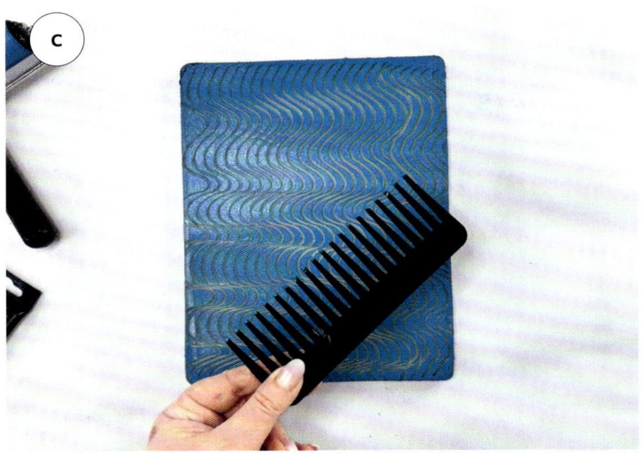

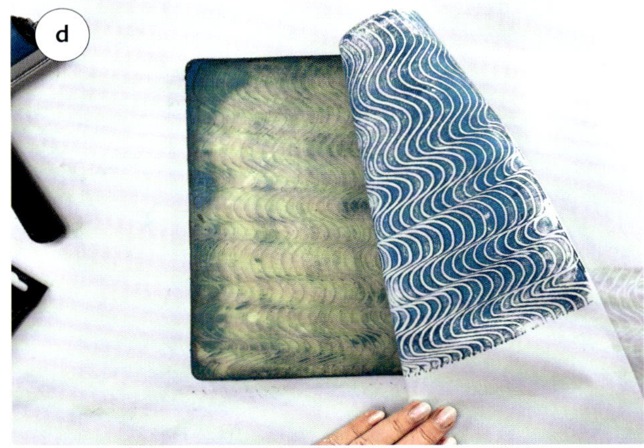

Pulling a lighter layer

There was a faint design still on the plate (e), so I rolled a thin layer of Iridescent Blue over it (f). After firmly pressing the paper onto the plate and letting it sit for about a minute, I then pulled the print, overlapping my comb print slightly (g).

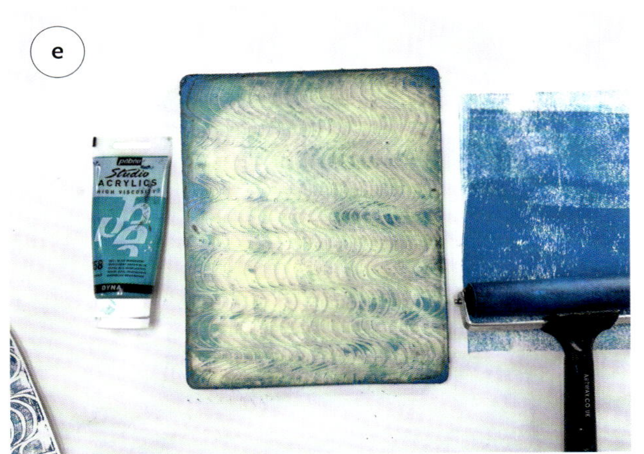

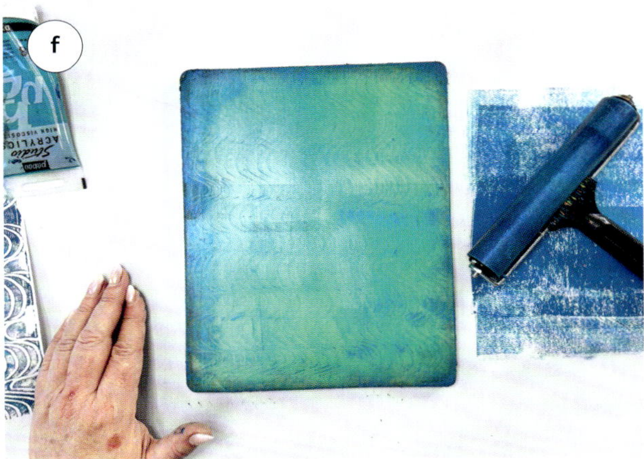

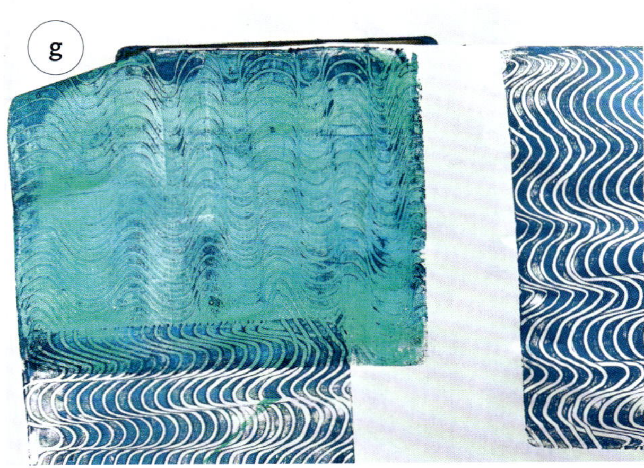

Using stencils on the gel plate

For this next print, I rolled a thin layer of Turquoise paint onto the plate and placed a stencil over it (a). Then I used a glue spreader to add a small amount of a darker shade of Indigo on top of the stencil, rolled the paint over it and positioned a section of paper with lighter Iridescent Blue over the stencil and plate (b). The result was beautiful (c).

To add more depth, I applied more Indigo over the stencil and then removed it (d). I pressed the paper onto different sections of the plate to create varied print sizes, adding interesting layers and texture (e).

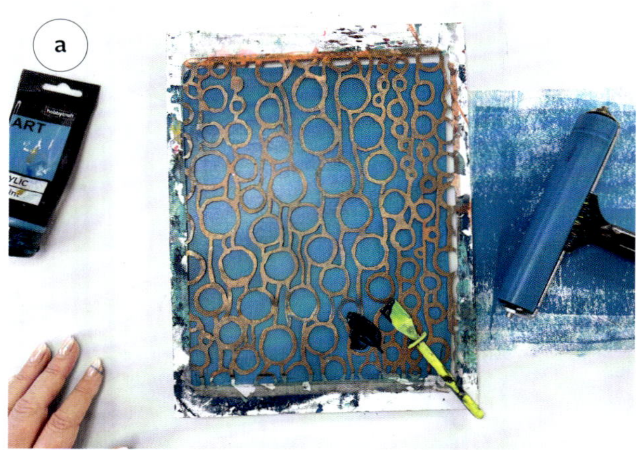

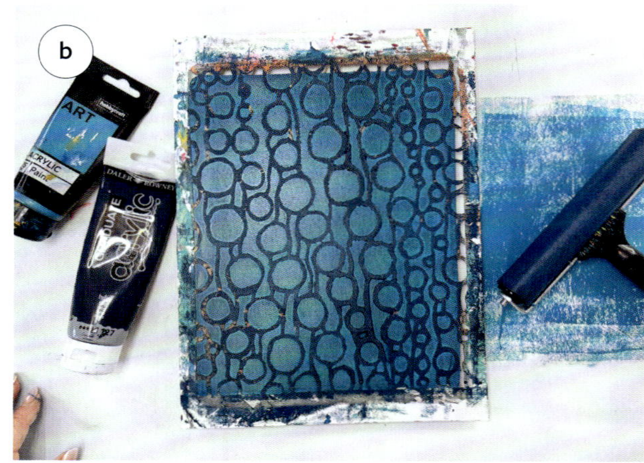

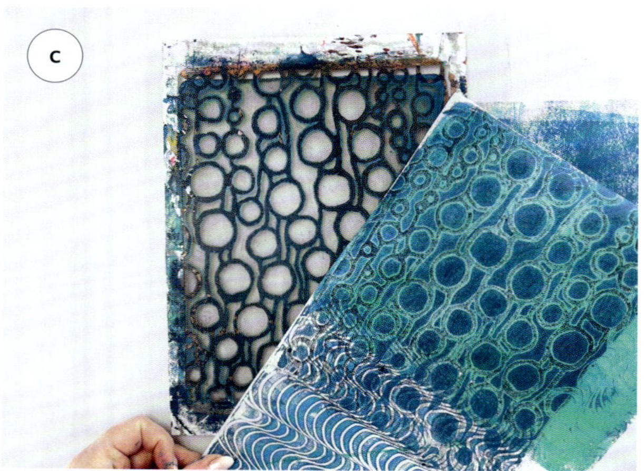

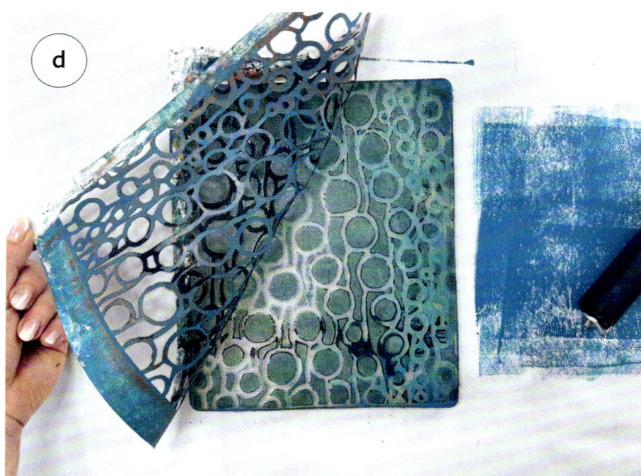

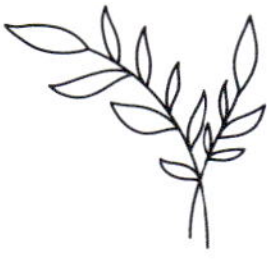

Tip

Make sure you're not adding too much paint to the plate. Rolling the paint should be relatively silent, so listen out for a tacky noise and check that there isn't a raised layer or texture on the surface. These are all good indicators that there is too much on the plate or that your layer is too thick.

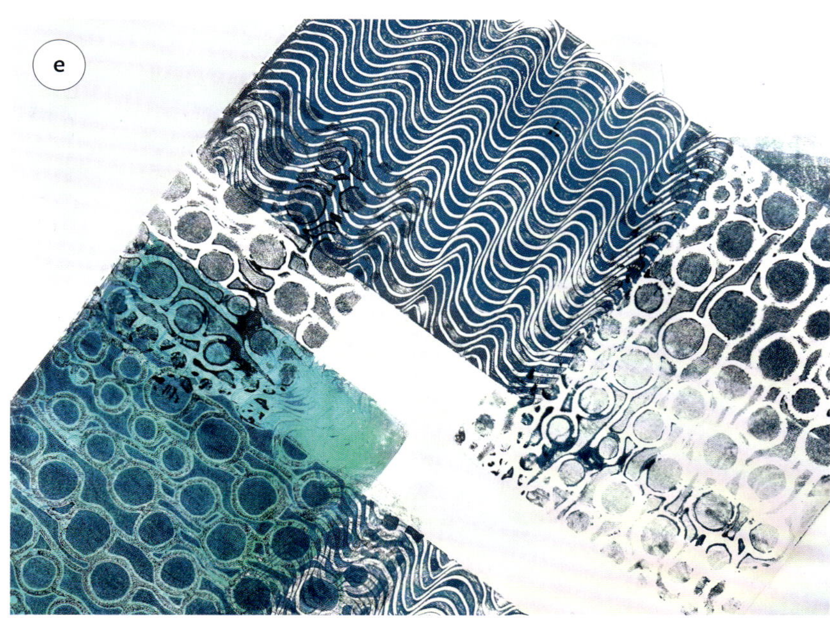

Creating windows of light

Creating windows of light is one of my favourite techniques, and it's so simple to do. Start with a dark or opaque light colour – something that will stand out against your other prints. Apply the paint a little more heavily than usual on this layer (a). I used Indigo here, but White would work well too, depending what colour you will contrast it with.

Using a silicone spatula, scrape away sections of the paint to create shapes (b). I love using organic, circular shapes, but feel free to experiment with any design you like. After each scrape, wipe the excess paint onto a scrap piece of paper to save for use in later prints.

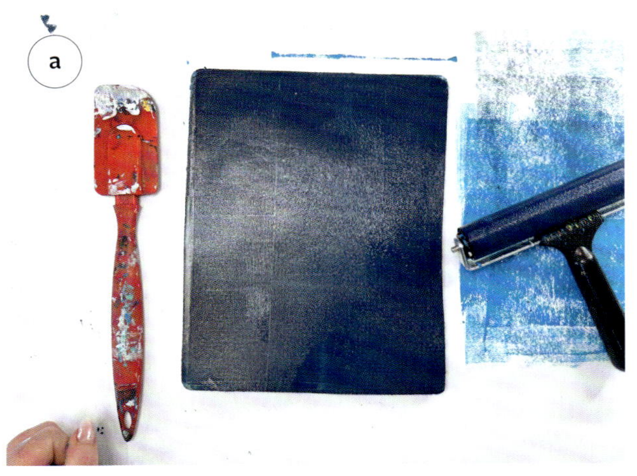

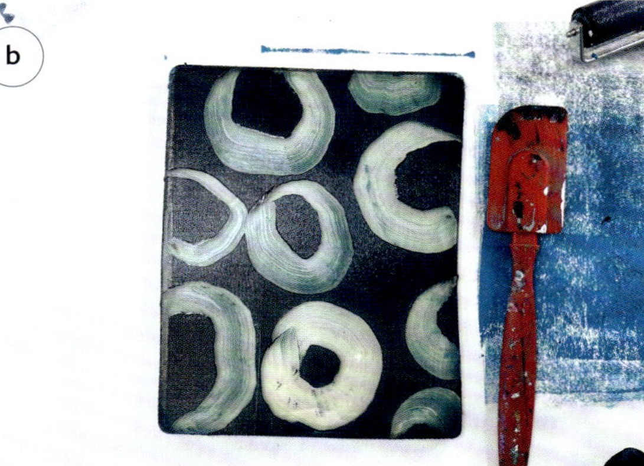

Once your shapes are ready, press your paper onto the plate, either in sections or all at once, and layer on top of your previous prints where possible. Since the paint layer is thicker, you can pull multiple prints from this set-up, creating unique variations with each pull (c).

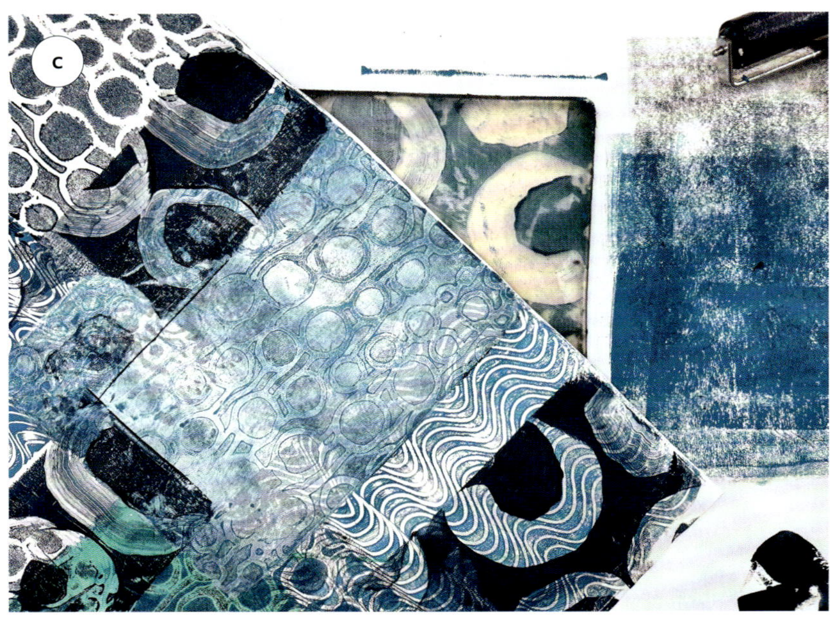

Adding pops of iridescent colour

I love adding pops of Iridescent Orange (a) and Iridescent Gold to my blue-themed colour palettes. Orange accents bring a beautiful contrast to blue, making certain elements stand out and adding visual interest (b), but the Pébéo DYNA iridescent paints come in a wide range of colours.

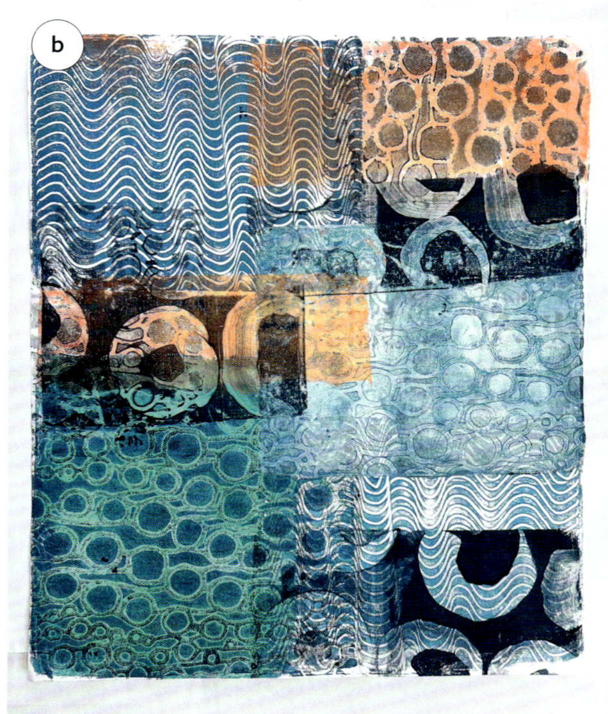

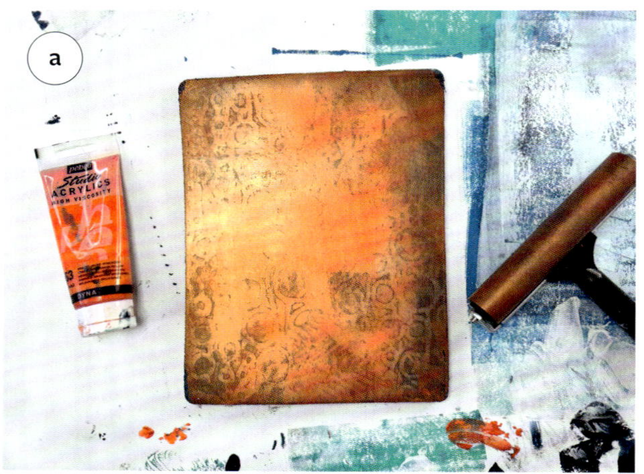

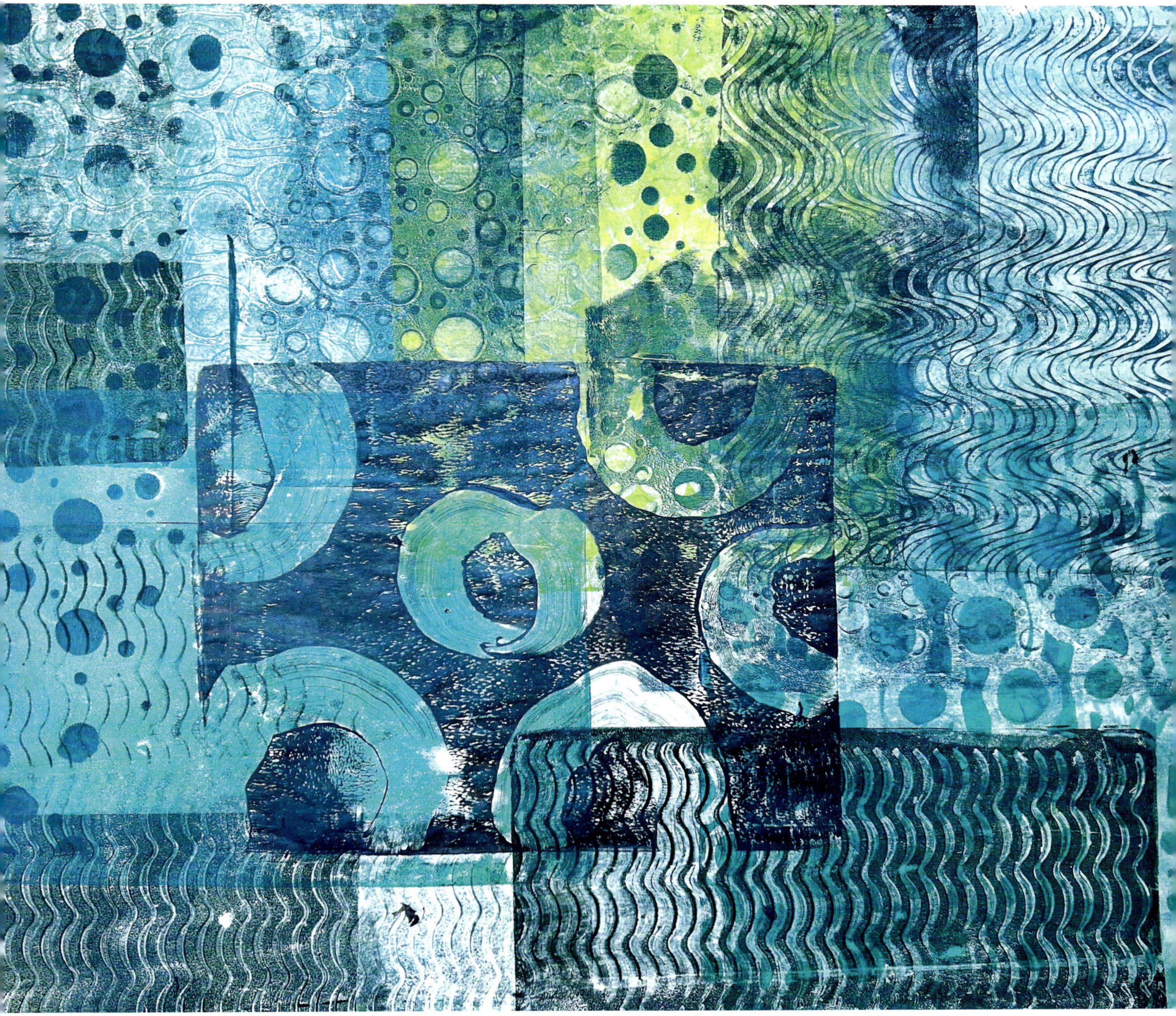

I have used this technique here with a glaze of Iridescent Green paint.

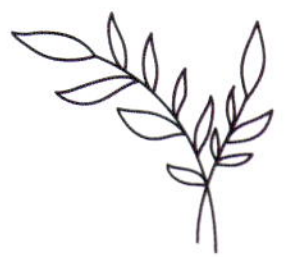

Tip

These colours also work wonderfully as a glaze for your prints. Simply roll a very thin layer of transparent or iridescent paint onto the gel plate, and use it to tone down areas of your print that feel too bright or have too much white. A glaze can help unify your design and create a more harmonious look.

Examples of finished pages.

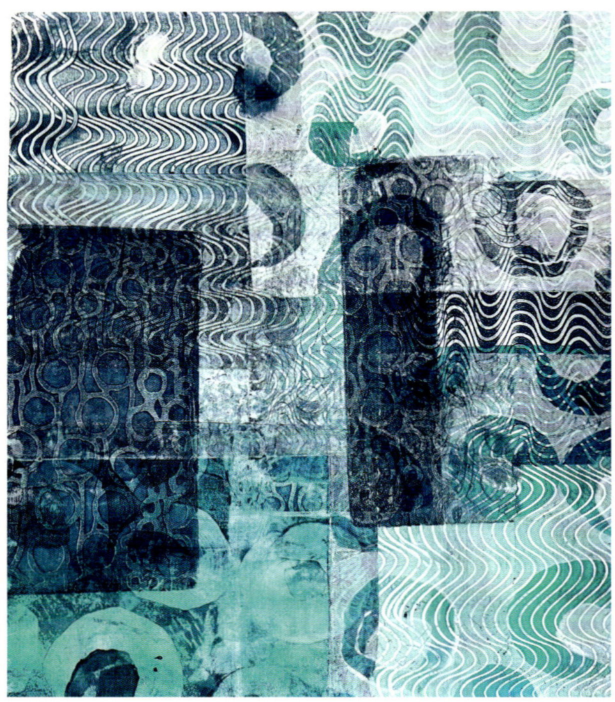

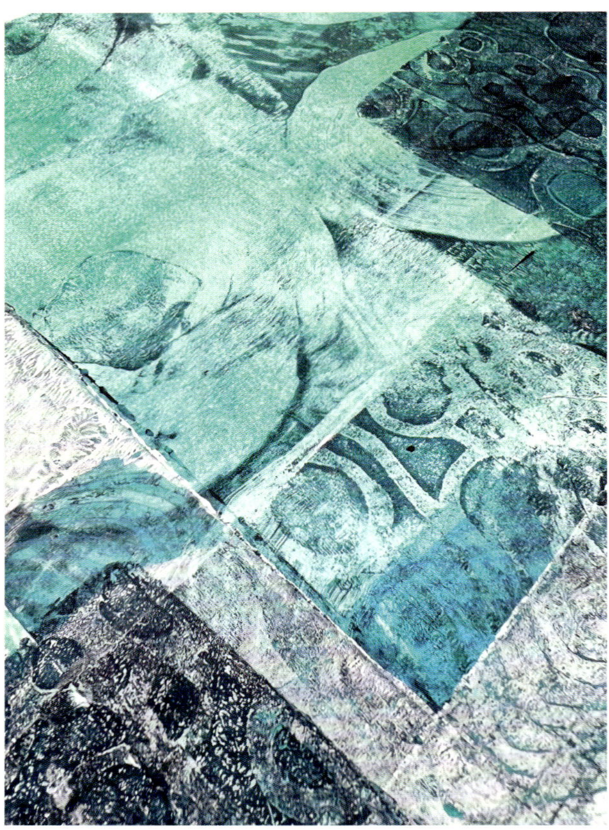

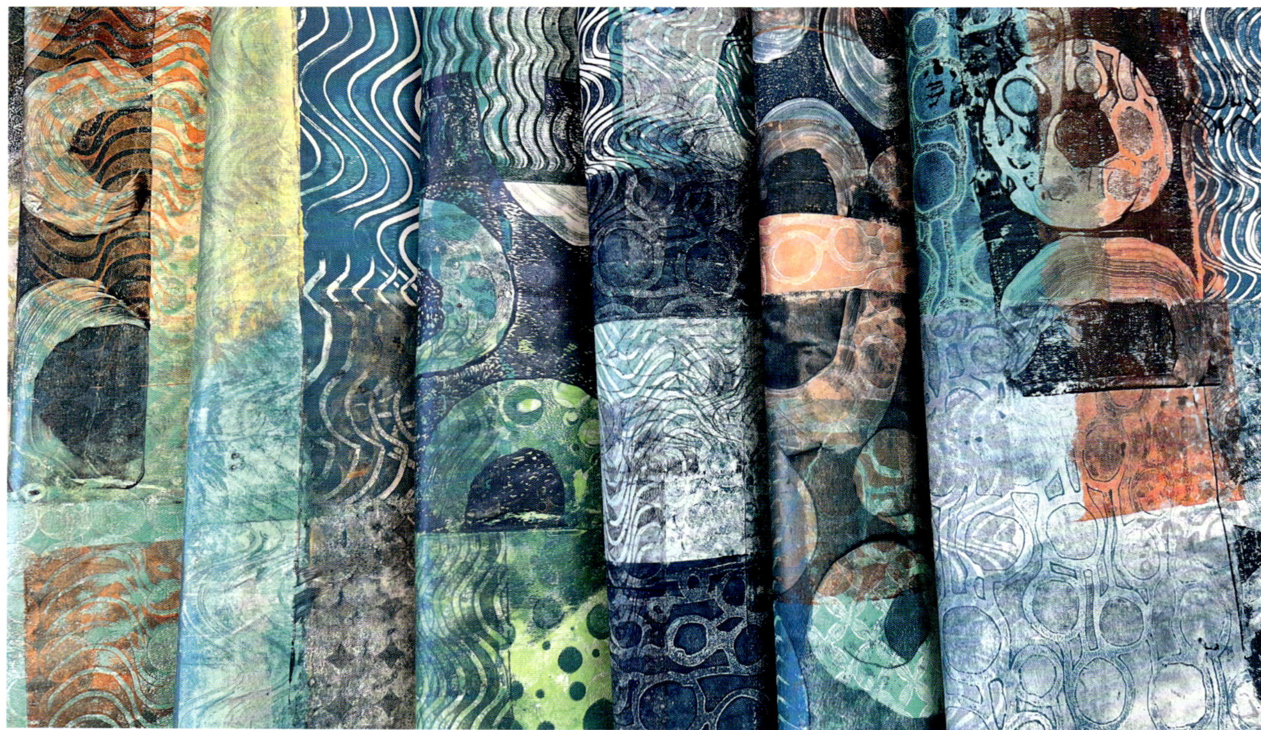

Making a viewfinder

I now cut out two viewfinders (a, b) by measuring and cutting out the shape in mountboard or copy paper. The first is sized to match a small wooden cradleboard, which is 15 x 15cm (6 x 6in) (c), and I go through the process for attaching it on page 165. The second is designed for our bookmark shapes – the size I'm making is 17 x 4cm (6¾ x 1¾in) (d).

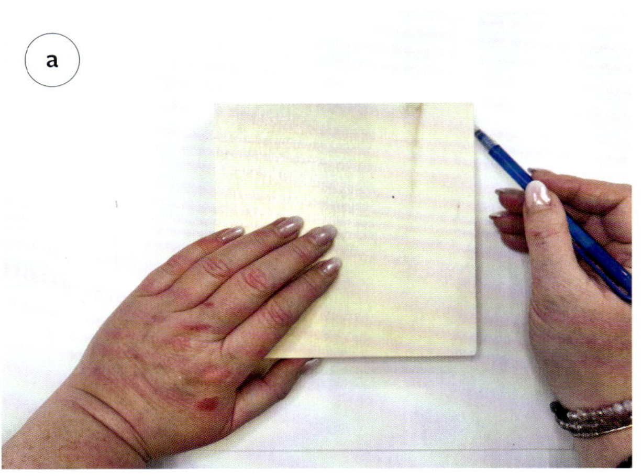

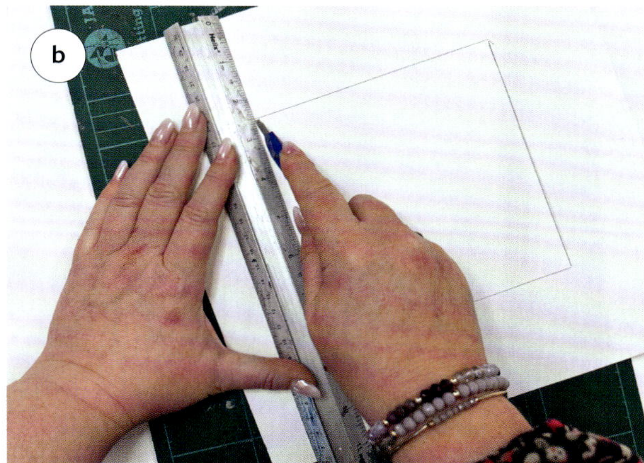

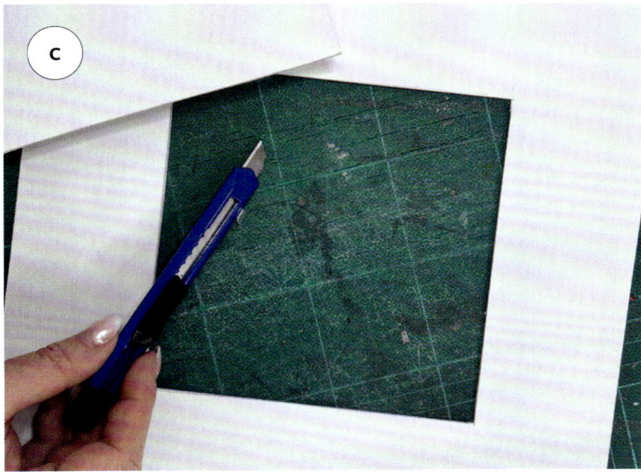

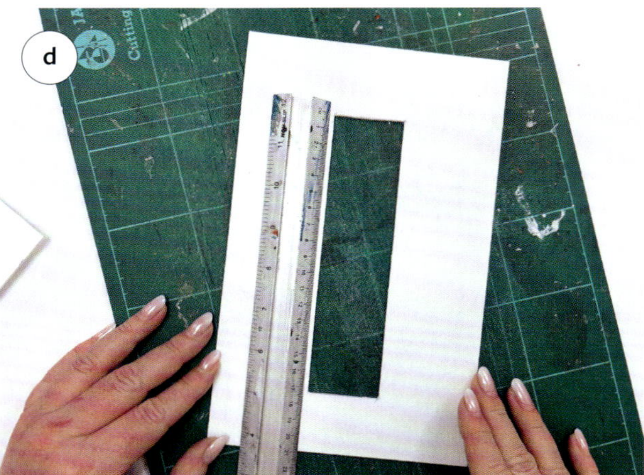

Finding pleasing compositions

Move the viewfinder around on top of your prints until you find a design you like (e, f). Avoid placing key shapes in the centre – shifting them slightly creates a more balanced and visually pleasing composition. This idea, known as the 'rule of thirds', helps your artwork feel more natural and relaxing to the eye.

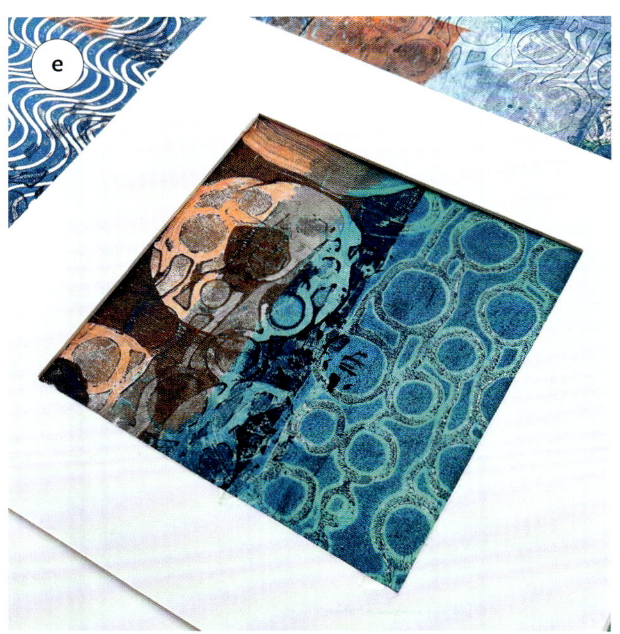

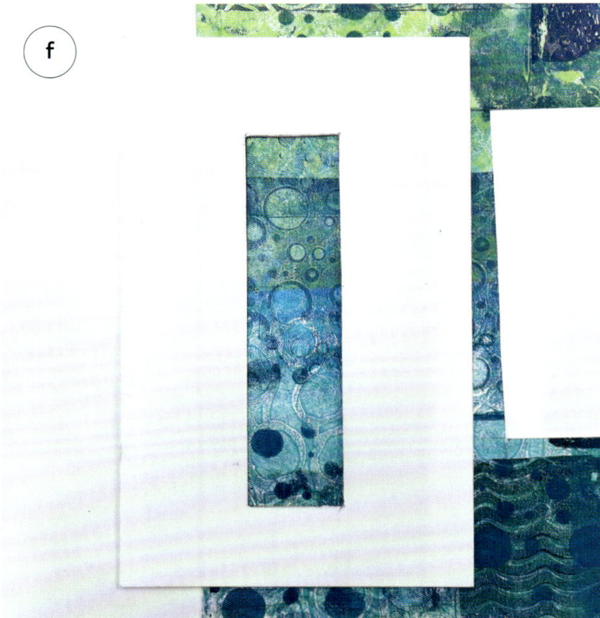

Gluing the bookmarks to the mountboard

Cut the mountboard to match the size of your gel print cut-outs using a sharp craft knife, metal ruler and cutting mat (a). Mine measured 17 x 4cm (6¾ x 1¾in).

Apply matte medium to both the mountboard and the back of the paper (b), then smooth with a catalyst wedge or a credit card (c). If the edges lift, add more glue before setting it aside to dry completely.

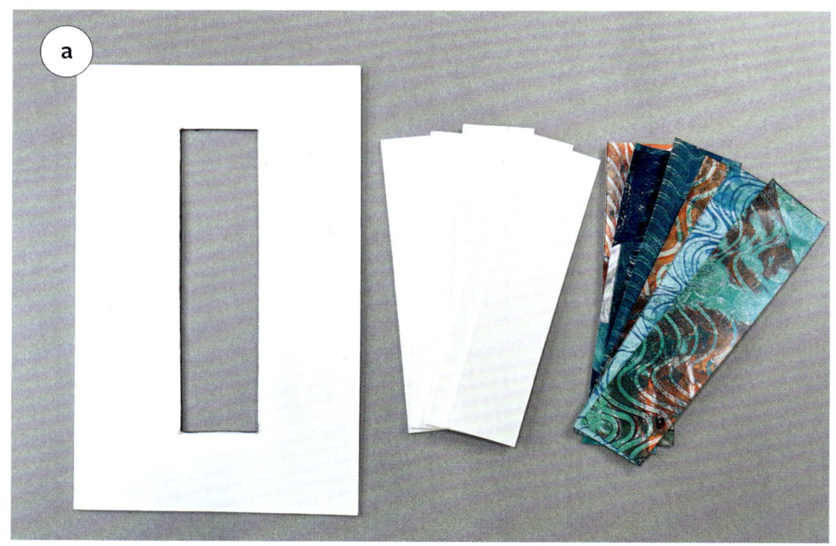

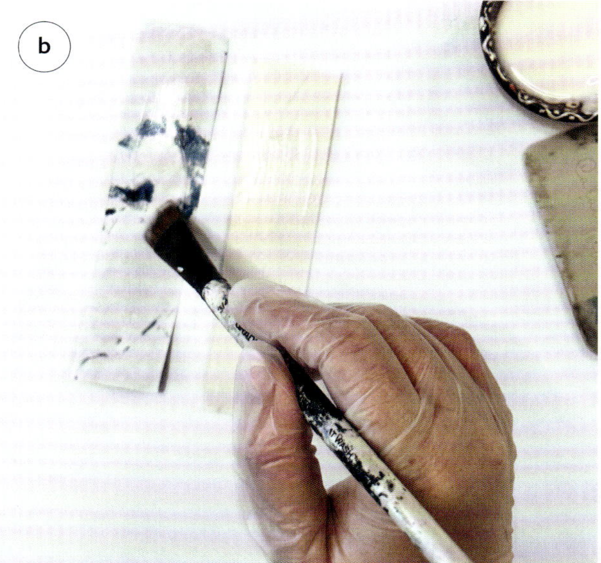

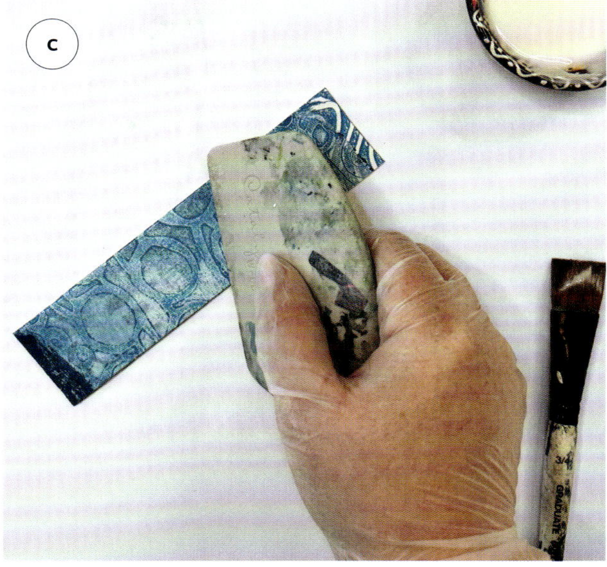

Once dry, file off any excess paper with an emery board (d), or trim any white edges if the paper was cut too small for the mountboard.

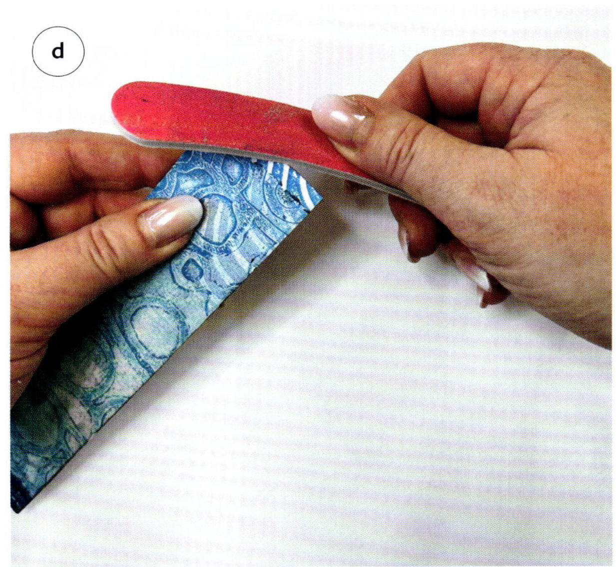

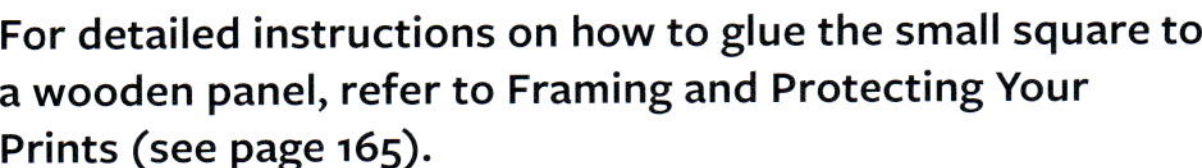

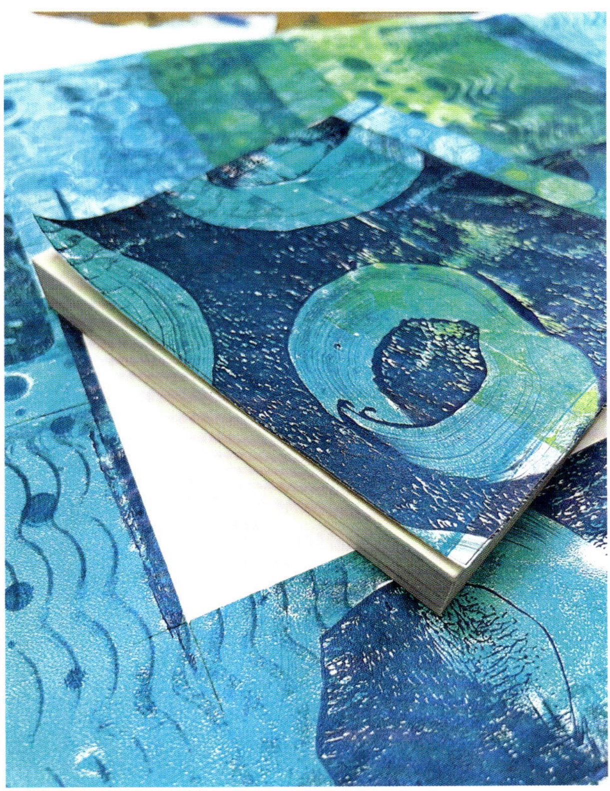

For detailed instructions on how to glue the small square to a wooden panel, refer to Framing and Protecting Your Prints (see page 165).

Adding stencil designs

Begin by laying out a few colours on a paint palette (a). I'm using a piece of mountboard for this, and a mix of contrasting light and dark paints as well as some bright colours to add a bit of pop to the piece. Ensure your sponges are clean and completely dry – this step is crucial for the process to work.

Dab a small amount of paint onto the sponge, then tap it on the mountboard to remove any excess. Using too much paint may cause it to seep under the stencil, while too little won't create a sharp edge.

Place the stencil over your desired area, and pick a colour that contrasts with the base colour of your print.

Tip

It's a good idea to practise on a spare sheet first to get the technique just right.

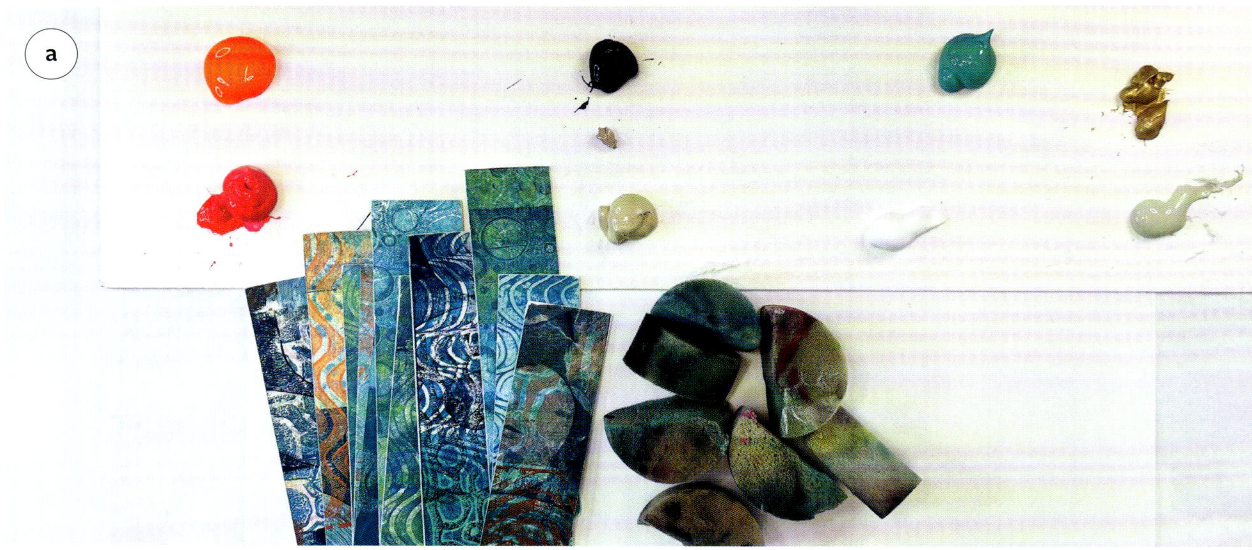

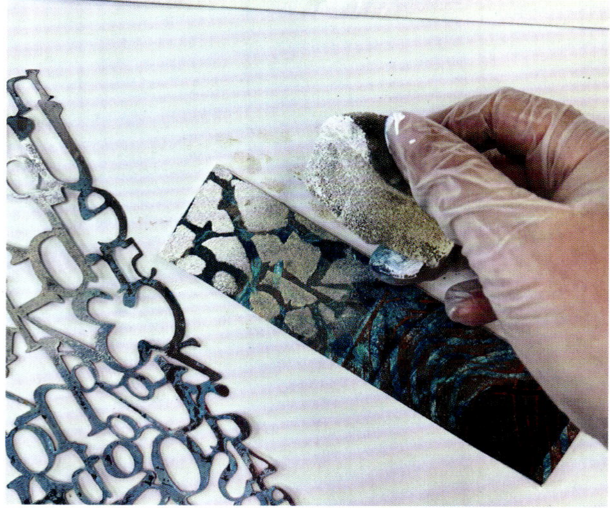

Here, I've blended Titanium White with Titan Buff.

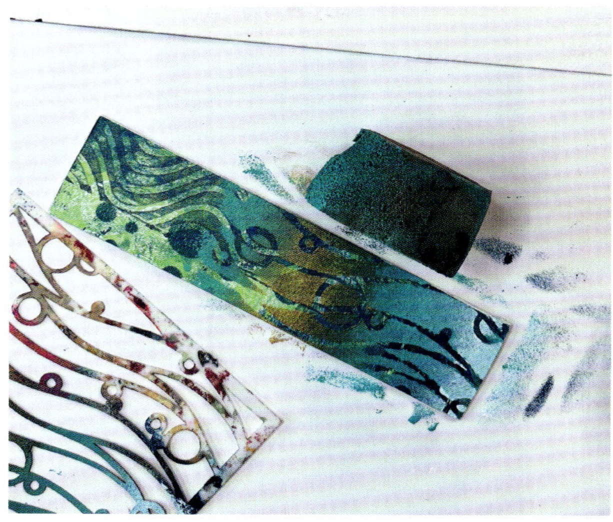

I blended Titanium White, Turquoise and Iridescent Gold.

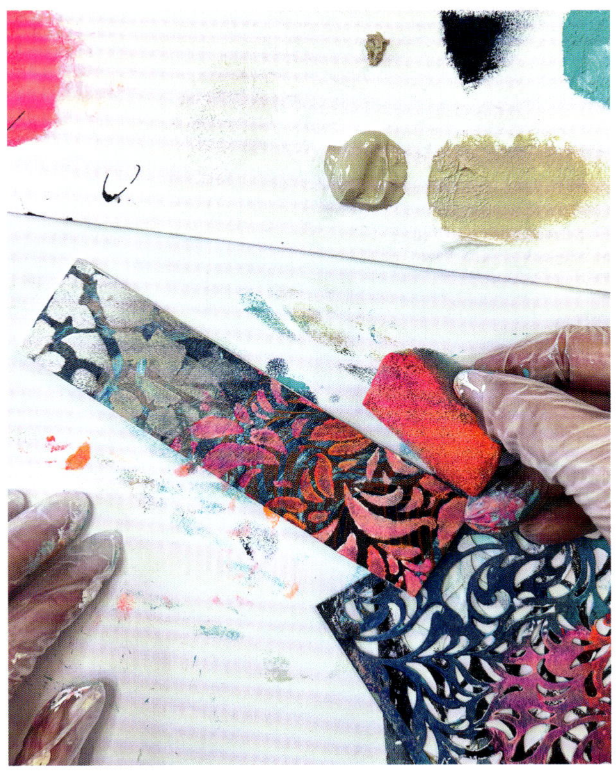

I've added a pop of Iridescent Orange and Fluorescent Pink for contrast.

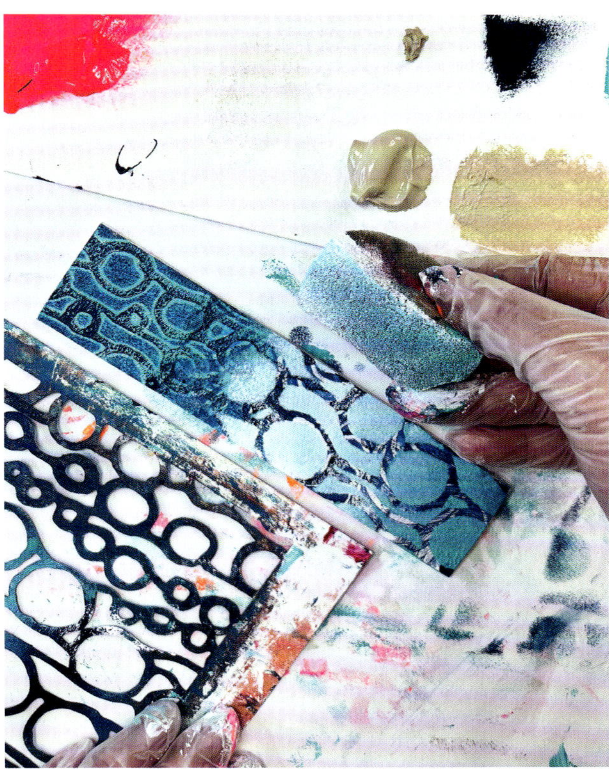

I repeat the same stencil design to complement the print, using Titanium White to create contrast.

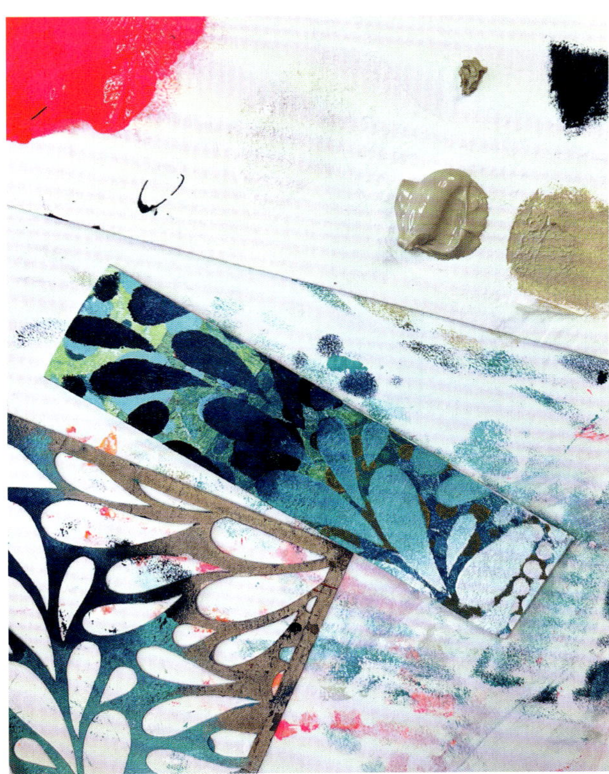

I blend Titanium White, Turquoise and Prussian Blue.

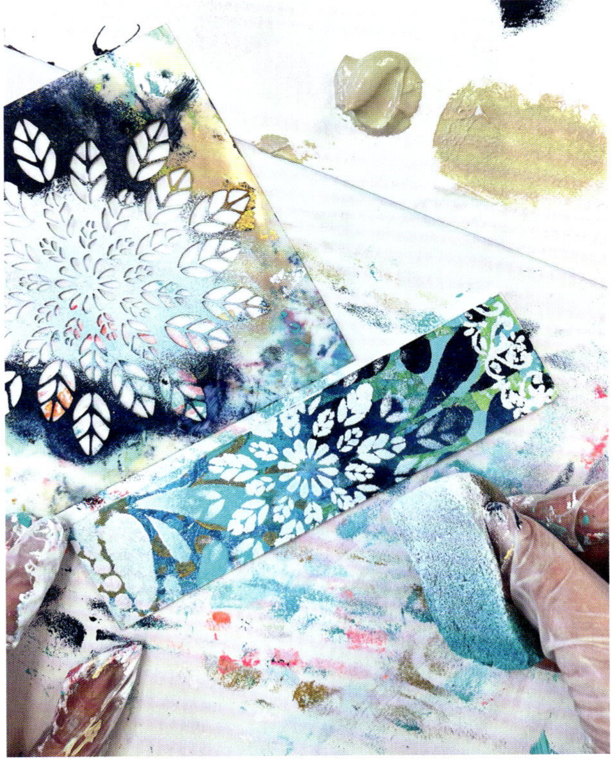

I add a focal point to the centre of the bookmark design with a circular format stencil and Titanium White.

Adding details in pen and coloured pencil

This is my favourite part of the process – adding the details.

I use a white Posca pen to add beautiful lines and dots (a). Since it's filled with opaque white acrylic paint, it stands out well over the stencils. Using pens with different nib widths allows me to vary the size of the dots, creating more interest.

I also use coloured pencils to brighten and blend areas, bringing everything together (b). Another favourite pen of mine is the Uni-ball Signo bronze gel pen, which works beautifully over painted areas (c).

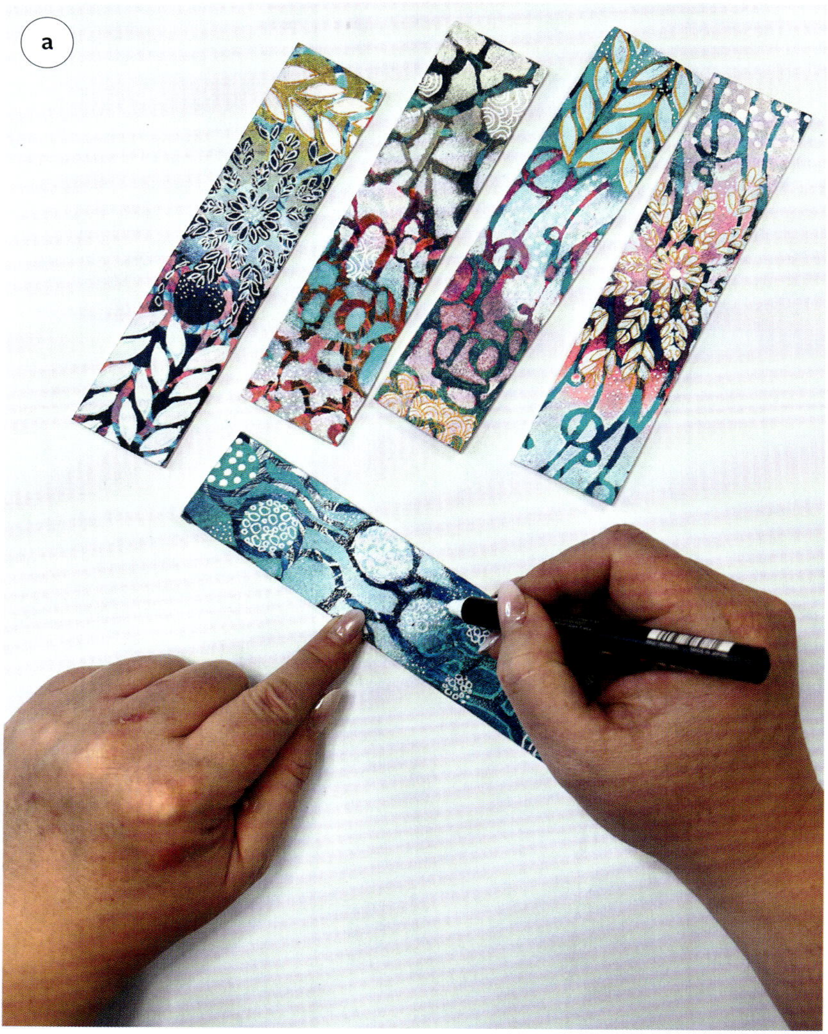

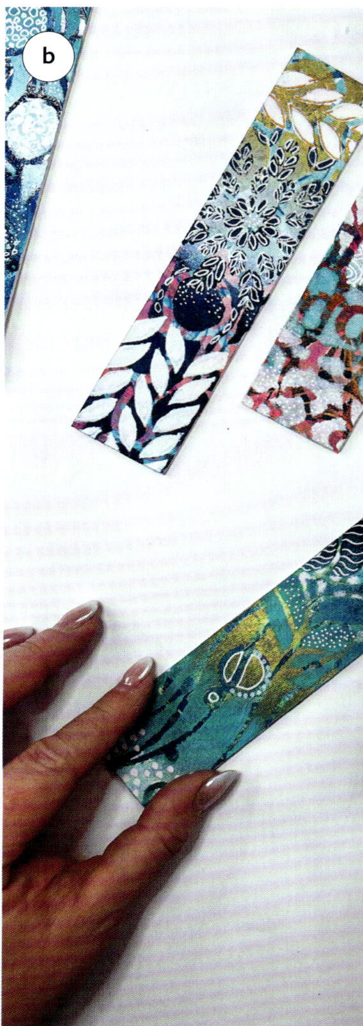

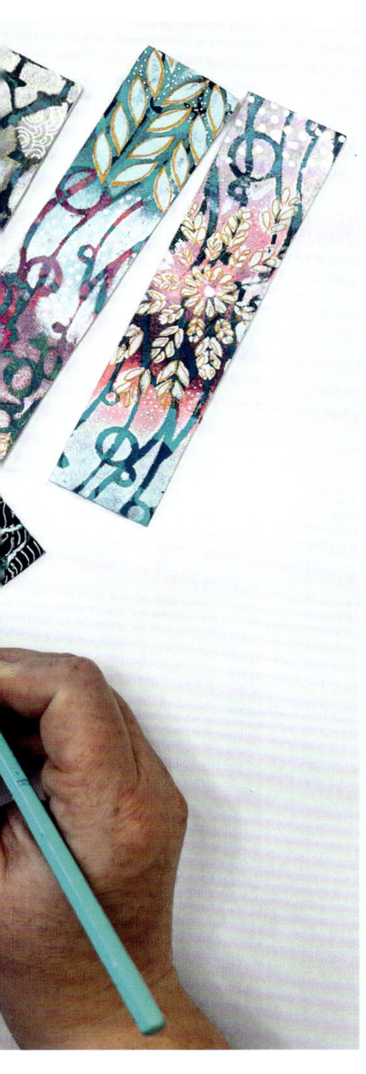

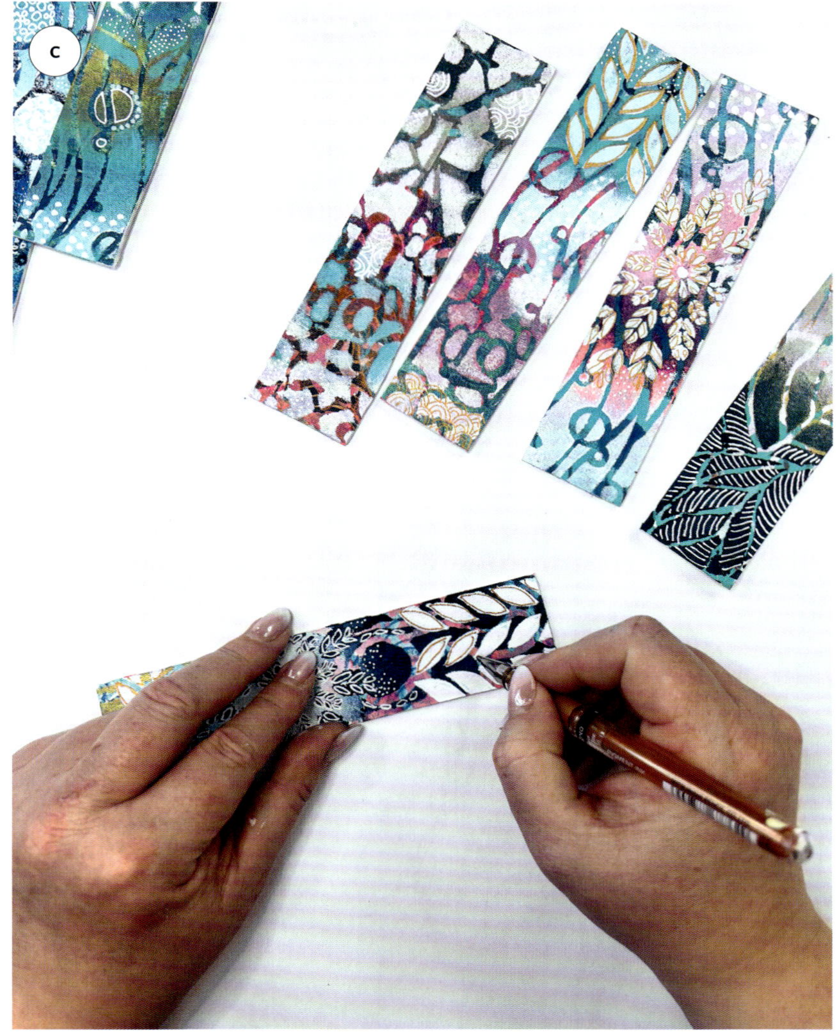

Finishing with finesse

To finish the bookmarks, I want to paint the back of the bookmark with black paint. I place them face down on top of an old margarine tub which helps to keep the paint from getting on the front design. I hold the bookmark over the edge of the tub to paint one half (a), then turn it around to finish the other half. If the paint isn't fully opaque, you may need to apply two coats for an even finish.

For a professional touch, I like to gently rub gold paint along the edges of the bookmark. I use the flat side of the brush (not the tip) to do this (b).

Once the paint is completely dry, I use a hole punch to make a hole at the top of the bookmark. Then, I attach a tassel in a colour that complements the design (c). To store the bookmarks, I use small plastic sleeves. I don't varnish the bookmarks, but if you'd like to protect them I would recommend using a mixed-media spray varnish. Alternatively, you could laminate them if they're glued to a thinner card rather than mountboard.

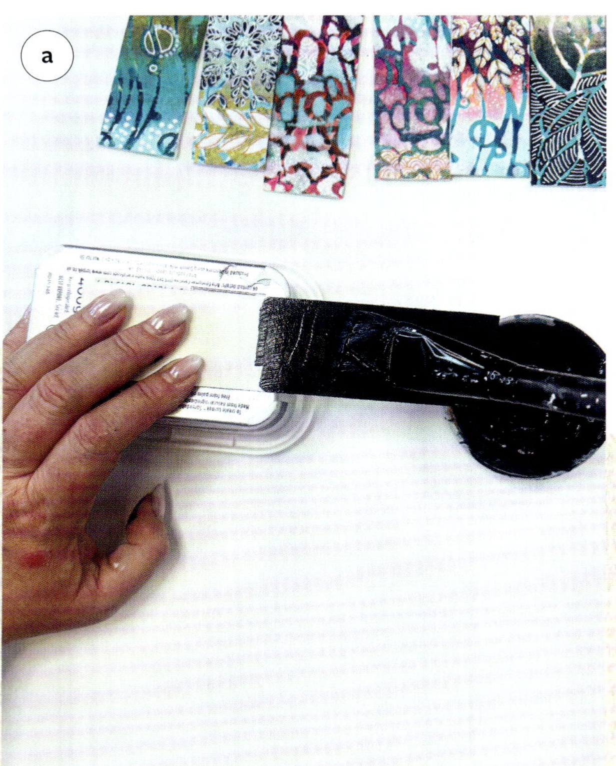

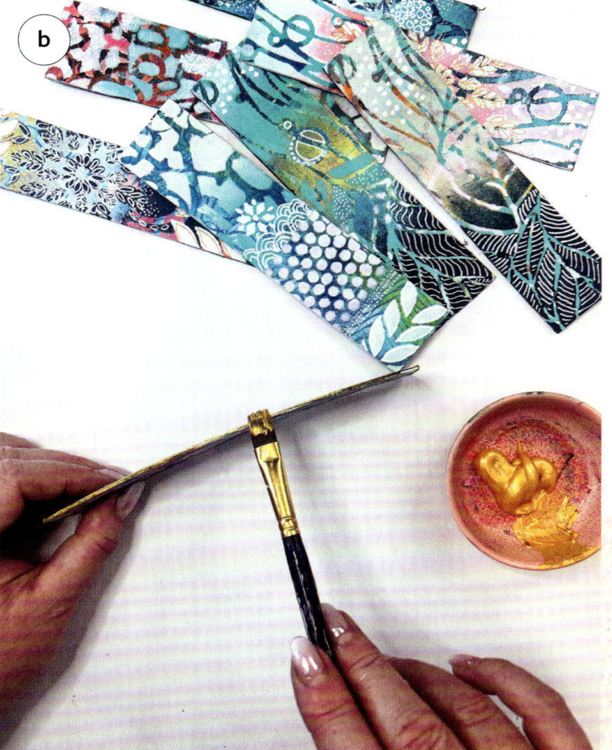

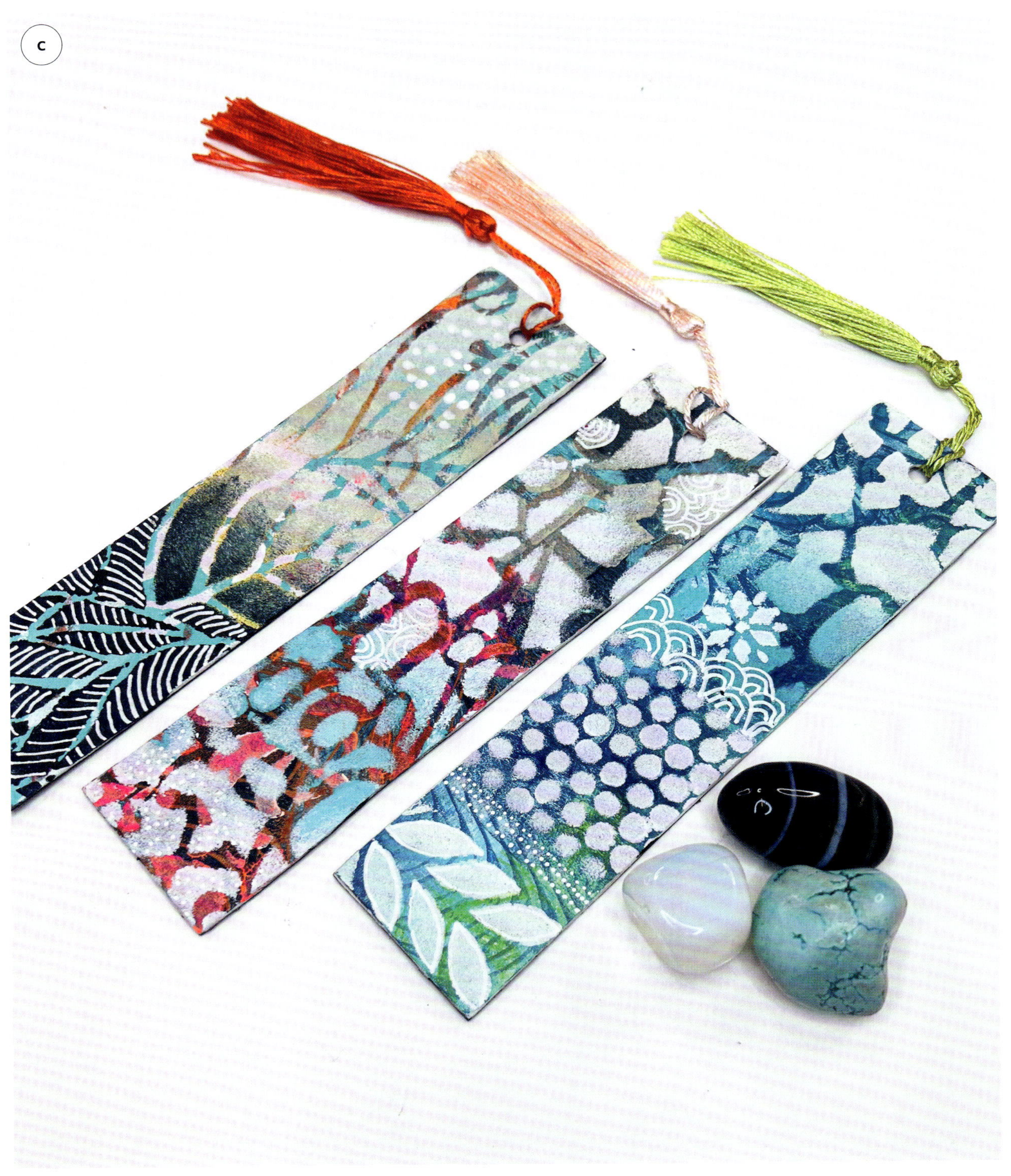
c

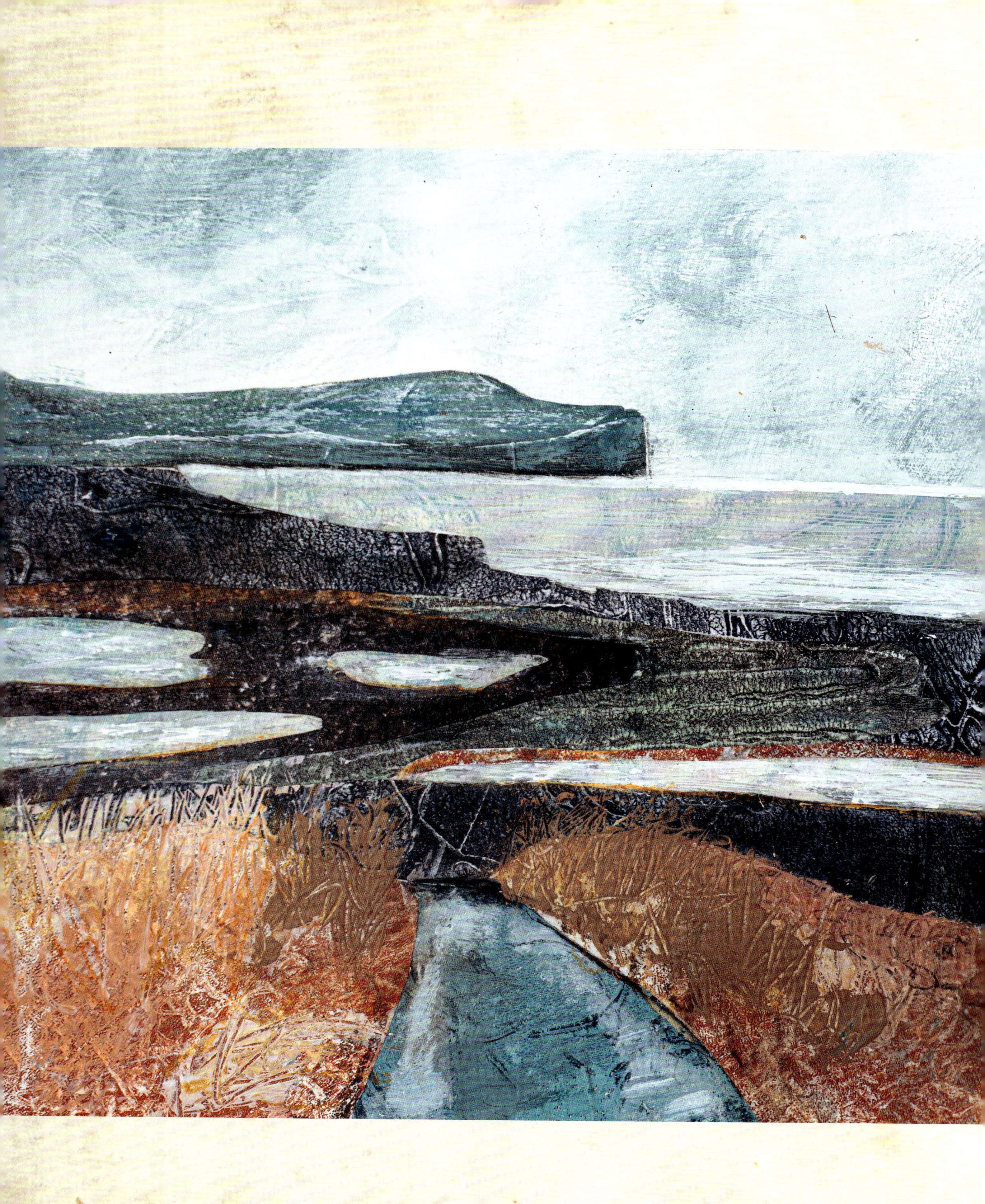

THE ESSENCE OF LANDSCAPE

Let your imagination express the beauty of nature through your amazing artworks. In this project, I will demonstrate how to create gorgeous gel-printed collage papers inspired by beautiful landscapes and interesting textures. I will explore nature's wonders, taking inspiration from rocks and sand bedforms along the shores, to teach you how to print your own papers using fun materials, such as sand and glue. Special prints can be made with the addition of materials like string and cloth for a touchable feel. I'll also share with you some tonal value basics, simplifying the process of analysing photographs to understand light and shadow, and offering easy techniques to manipulate tonal variations. The finished painting will be a combination of collage and paint application.

Opposite is the completed collage of the coastal scene I picked. I have also included a full-sized outline of the shapes – feel free to make copies of this to guide you through the steps. You can alternatively make your own artwork by following these steps using a picture of your choice.

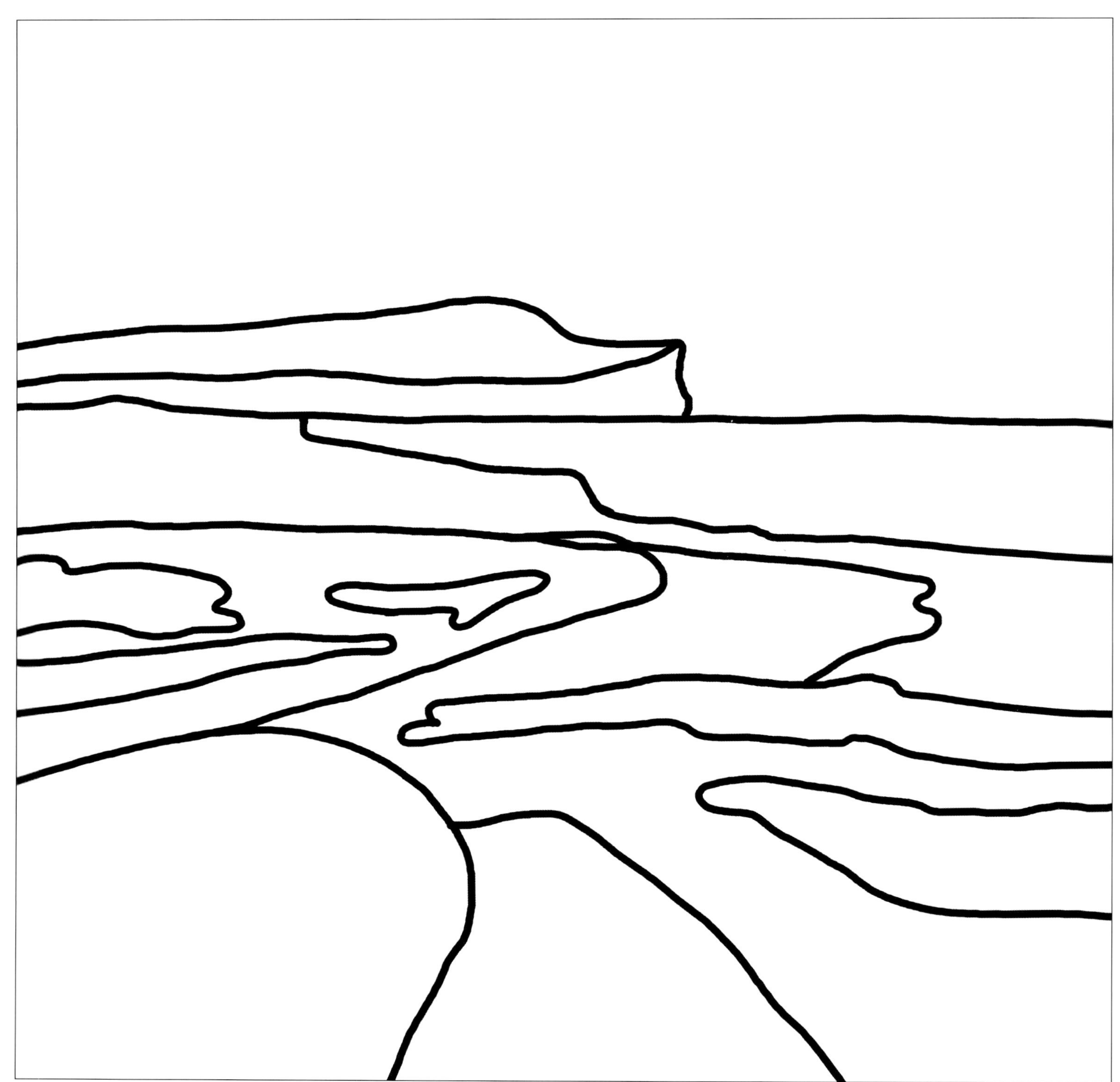

You will need

MATERIALS

Refer back to the master list on page 18 for the essential items.

- Gel plate – 20 x 25cm (8 x 10in)
- Mountboard or stiff card
- 300gsm watercolour or mixed-media A4 paper
- Tracing paper or carbon paper
- Printed images of your landscape in colour and black and white
- Regular copy paper
- Wet-strength tissue paper
- Acrylic paint: Titanium White, Indigo, Quinacridone Scarlet, Burnt Umber, Gold, Yellow Ochre, Turquoise Blue and Black
- Gloss gel medium
- White gesso
- Neocolor® II pastels: Salmon Rose, Turquoise Blue, Golden Ochre and Flesh

OPTIONAL

- String, rubber bands or jute fabric
- Carborundum or fine sand
- Various sizes of paintbrush and decorator's brush
- Silicone spatula
- Old credit card or catalyst wedge
- Metal ball stylus sculpting tool

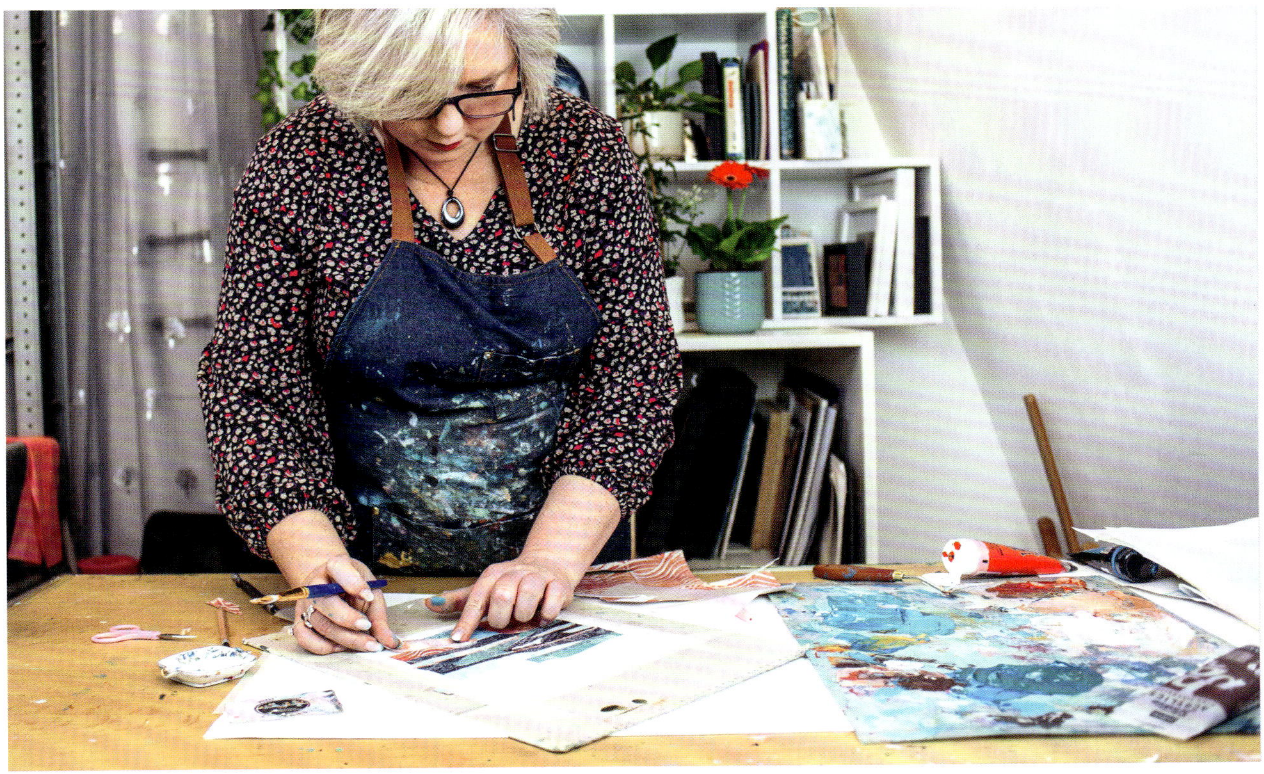

Creating collagraph plates

A collagraph in printmaking is a fun way to make textured and patterned prints. As a printmaker, I used a big printing press for many collagraph prints, but – curious to try something new – I used my gel plate to see if I could achieve a similar effect and was so happy with how it turned out. The gel plate helps to capture interesting textures from the collagraph plate. I get my inspiration from nature, especially the beautiful patterns in rocks and the organic shapes in the sand on beaches.

You start by making a special plate with different textures and materials, such as cardboard or fabric. I use a strong card called mountboard (known as mat board in the USA or passepartout in Europe) as a base, which is also used for cutting mounts in picture framing. You can find this card in A1 sheets at art supply stores. Artists often use carborundum to make collagraph plates, which adds an interesting texture to the prints. Once the plate is dry, ink is applied to it and prints are made using a printing press. Below I will demonstrate how I make my collagraphs and later in this chapter I will show you how I use them with the gel plate.

I use two types of glue for my collagraph prints: runny PVA in a bottle with a small nozzle, which makes it easier to squeeze out the thin lines, and thicker gloss gel medium, which is great for sticking on items such as string or jute fabric.

A collagraph plate made with gloss gel medium and jute fabric.

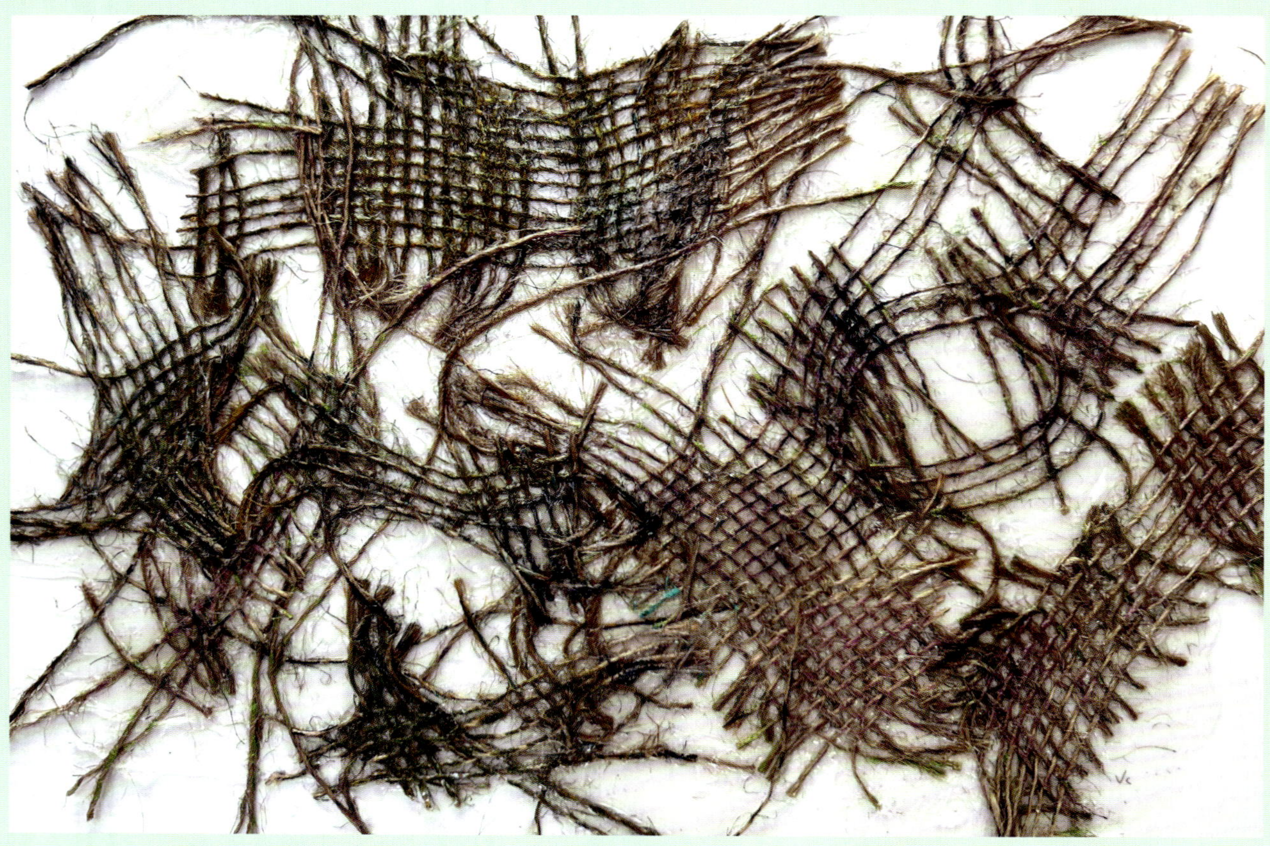

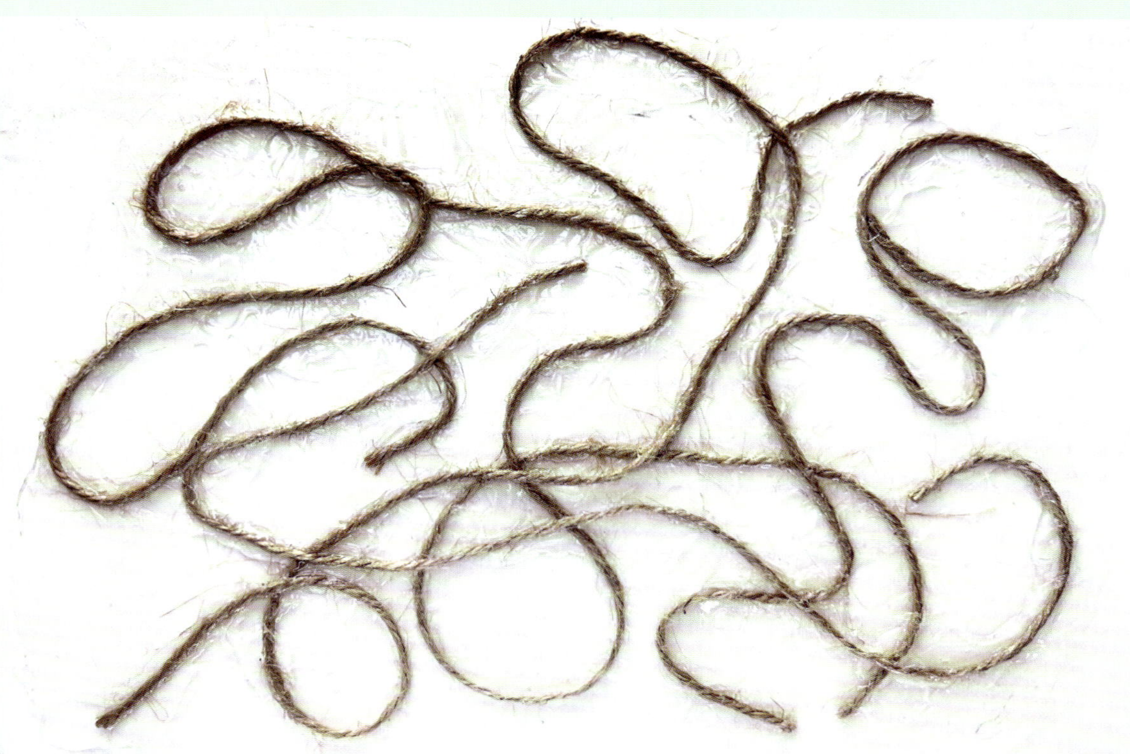

A collagraph plate made with gloss gel medium and string.

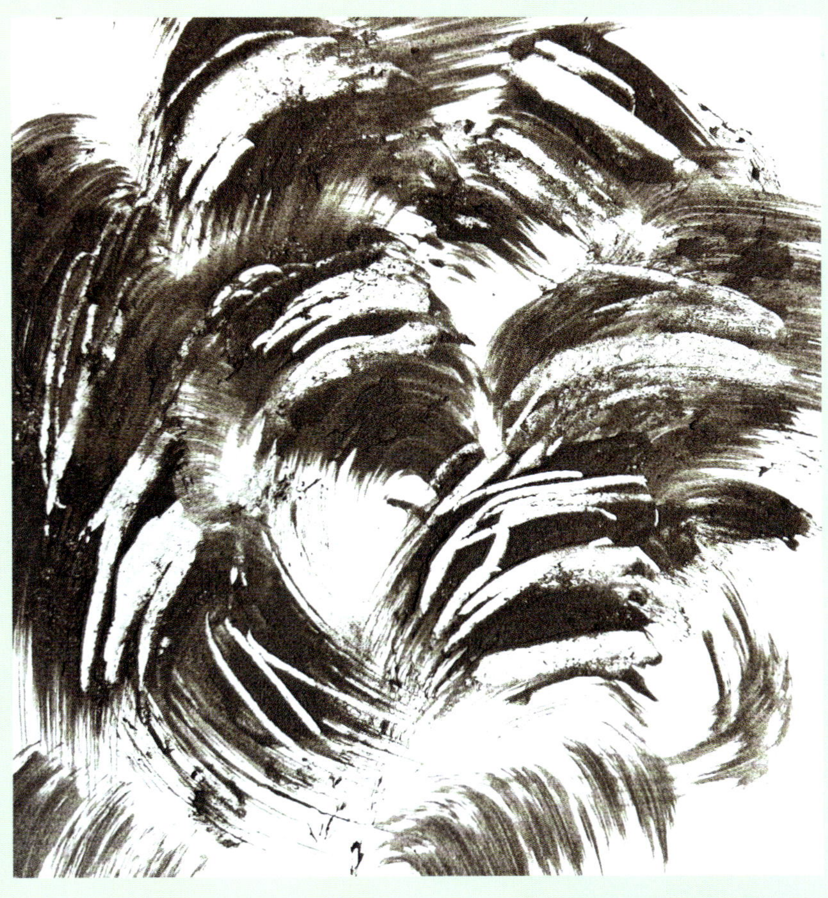

This collagraph was made by spreading PVA glue onto mountboard using a dry decorator's brush, creating a natural, organic texture and then adding carborundum sand.

A simple collagraph plate

I first squeezed PVA glue all over the plate in a squiggly pattern (a). I then sprinkled carborundum into the wet glue (b). Carborundum sand is a tough material made from silicon carbide crystals, which people often use to sand, grind or polish surfaces, especially in metalworking or for sharpening tools. If you can't find carborundum sand, fine sand (also shown in the image) can work instead. I left the collagraph on a flat surface overnight to dry.

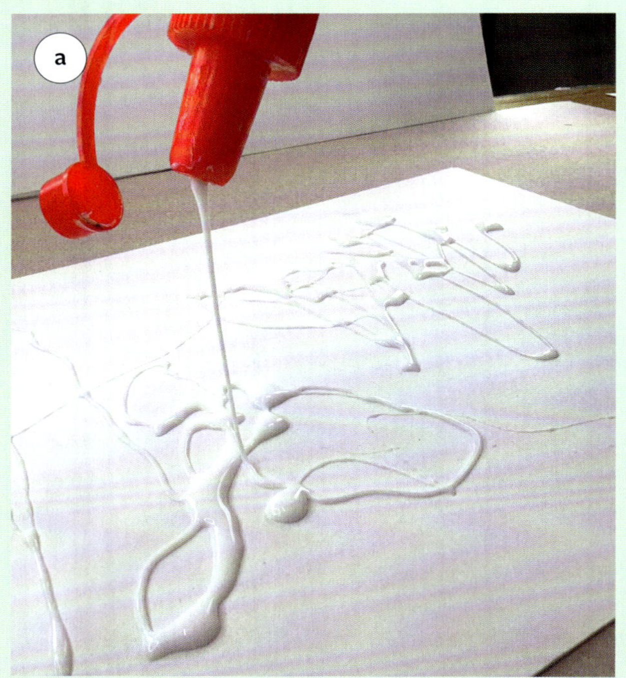

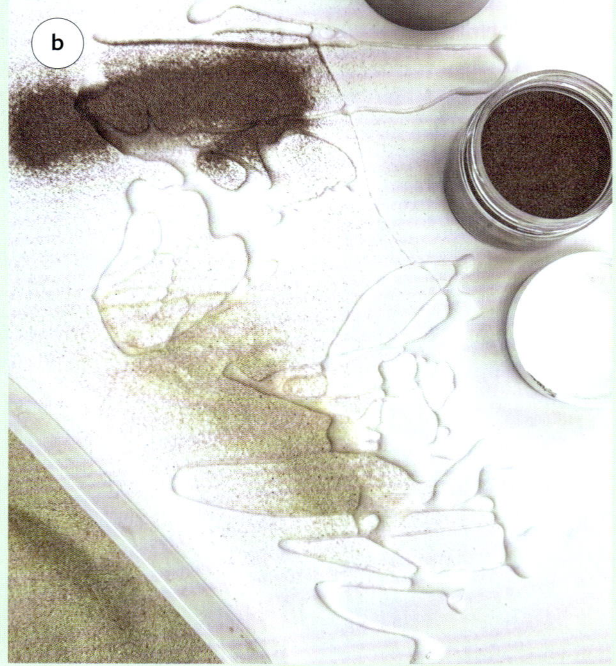

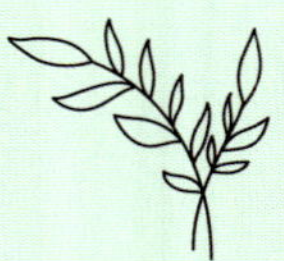

Tip

Save any excess sand by pouring it back into the container for future use. To make it easier to transfer it back into the pot without any wastage, tap the sand onto a piece of paper and fold the paper to create a makeshift spout.

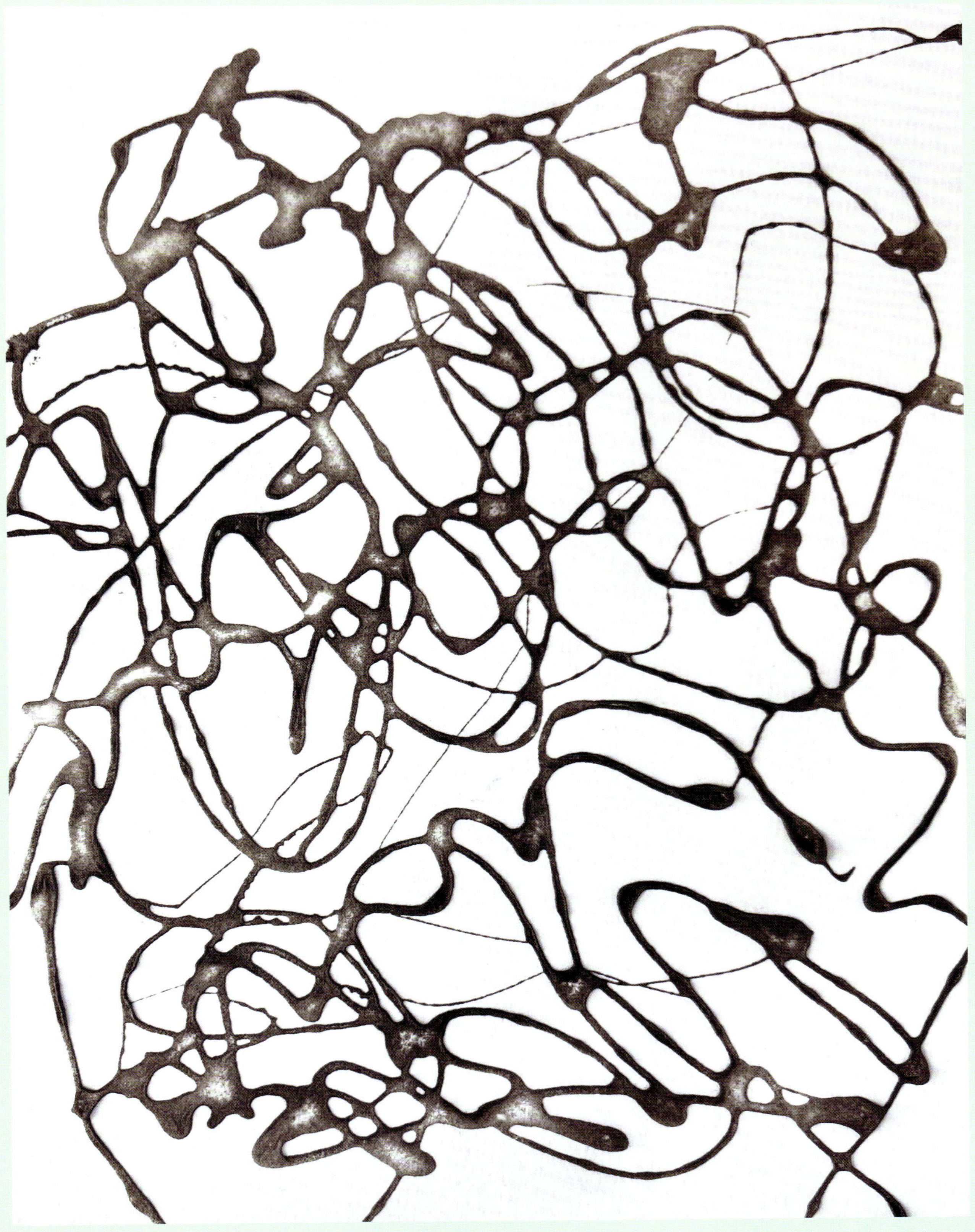

Preparing the paper for collage

In this section, I will walk you through the initial steps to take when preparing the canvas or paper for this collage art project, covering a range of aspects, from choosing the right paper to applying gesso to the substrate.

Selecting the paper

I always stress the importance of paper selection. I prefer using a watercolour or mixed-media paper, such as Fabriano Mixed Media paper, with at least 300gsm – this provides the right weight for my projects. I also like to use a standard size for my paintings, which simplifies framing and cuts down on costs.

We will use a 20cm (8in) square piece of paper for this project. Measure the paper carefully and use a sharp craft knife and metal ruler to cut straight, clean edges (a).

Taping and masking

When it comes to taping, I prefer to use regular DIY masking tapes as I find they work just as well as the more expensive artist tapes. The following simple technique has consistently given me successful results with any masking tape, ensuring clean, crisp lines in the final artwork.

First, I carefully place masking tape around the edges of the paper, ensuring the lines are straight (b). To stop paint from seeping under the tape, I apply a layer of white gesso to it. When removing the tape at the end of the project, I gently heat it to loosen the adhesive and prevent the paper from tearing. You can use a heat gun or the highest setting on a hairdryer to warm the tape for a few seconds before peeling it back.

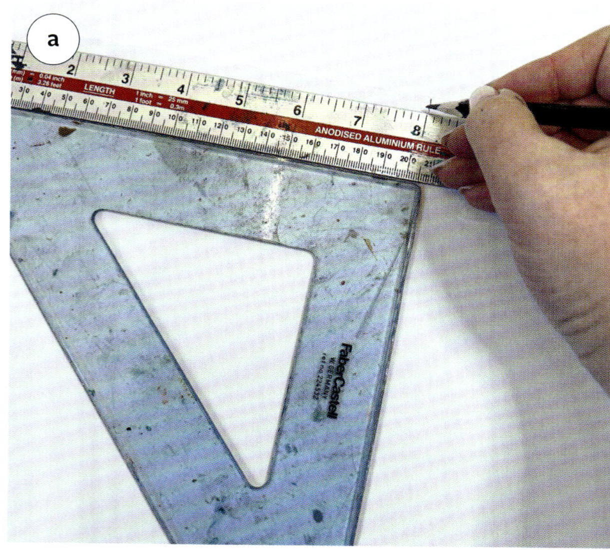

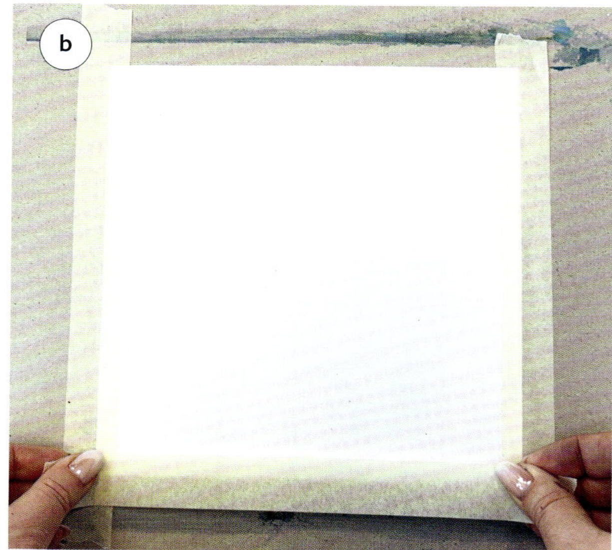

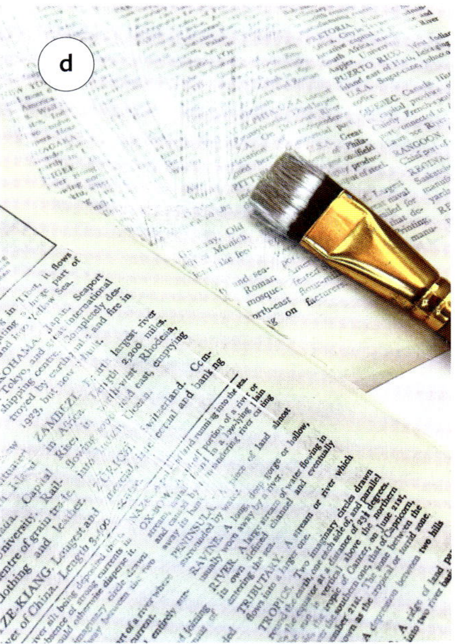

Applying gesso

Gesso is a type of paint used in art projects and is usually found in white, black or clear. It is important in preparing your surface for a collage or painting, as the mixture has a slightly textured, 'toothy' surface which helps layers of paint or collage stick better to the surface you're working on. I use it as a base on wood, canvas and paper.

Using a paintbrush, apply an even layer of acrylic paint over your paper surface (c).

Use old book pages as a surface to paint or print on top of if you have any gesso left over on your palette (d). These will always have uses in collages, background pages in a journal (page 111) or sketchbook.

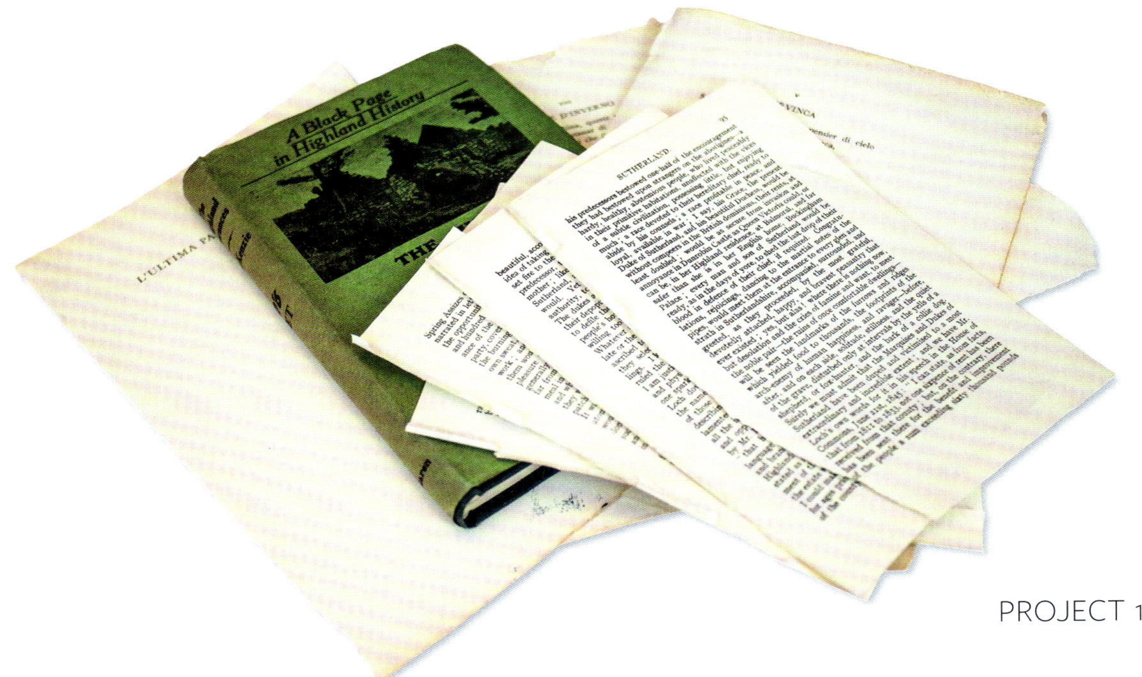

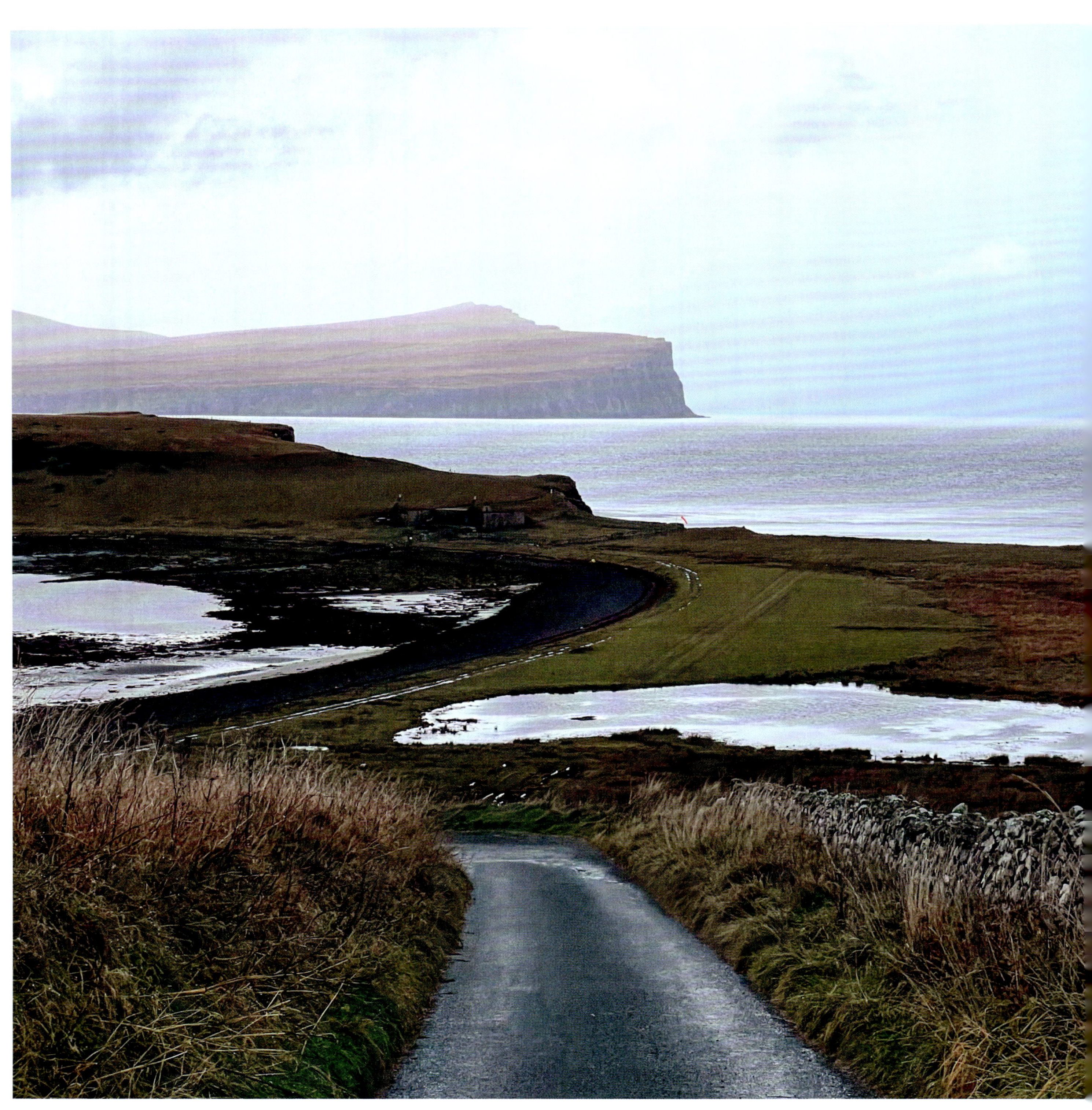

The source of my finished collage is this beautiful photo taken by my friend Anne Bryce from Waternish peninsula in the Isle of Skye, Scotland.

Selecting and tracing your image

You may use the picture I have given as an example (see page 40); however, in time it will be more meaningful if you use one of your own images that evokes a memory for you or the intended recipient of your artwork.

One of my favourite websites to source images from is unsplash.com, which has a great choice of stock photos that you can download and use for any project.

Transferring the image from photo to substrate

Beginners and experienced artists alike can use this simple old-school way of transferring images onto paper.

Place a piece of tracing paper on top of the image, secure it with masking tape and trace the main shapes in your image (a).

If you have carbon paper, that's great – it helps transfer the outlines onto your prepared paper so you can ensure your collage shapes look right. No carbon paper? Not a big deal. Draw on the back of the tracing paper, following the lines (b).

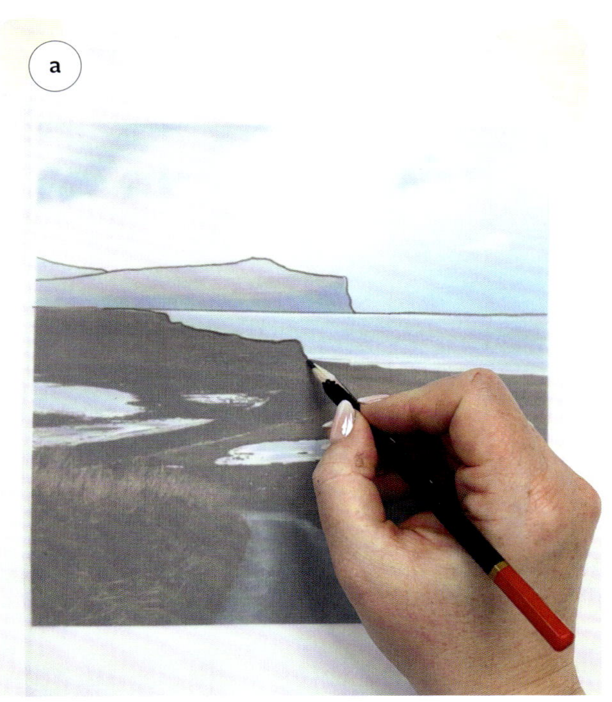

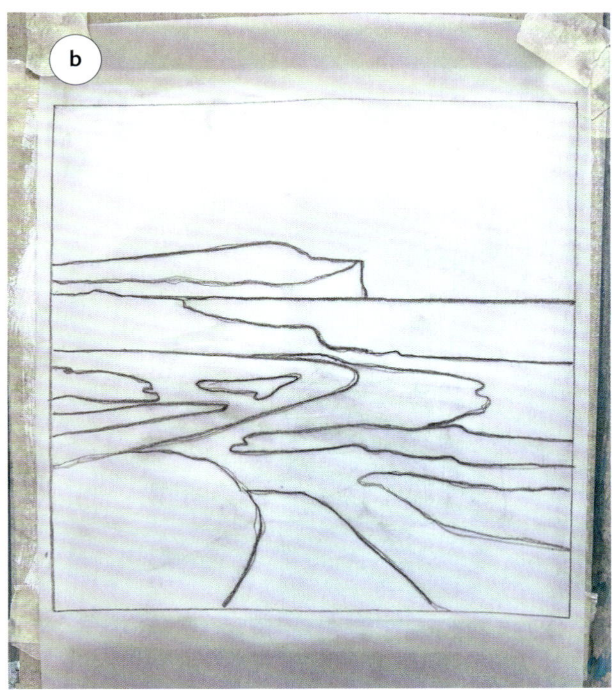

Understanding tonal values

Tonal value refers to the lightness or darkness of a colour or shade in an image. It ranges from the lightest to the darkest areas and is crucial for creating depth and contrast. In black and white, it spans from pure white to pure black; in colour, it's determined by how bright or dark the colours are. Understanding tonal values is key in art and design for creating various visual effects and emphasising specific elements in an image.

When you look at a colour reference image, it can sometimes be hard to see where the light and dark areas are in a painting. I use simple methods to help me see the tonal differences more clearly. This is helpful if you want to create depth in your collage painting or change the colours in your scene, for example, using dark indigo blue for the foreground instead of dark brown. I print the image in black and white so I can focus on the tonal values. I then match the printed papers to the tones, not the colours.

To see the tonal values in your image

Print one colour and two black-and-white copies of your image. Cut up one of the black-and-white copies into small squares from light to mid-tone to dark. Arrange and number the corresponding areas on the second uncut copy to visually understand the tonal range (c).

Or, using your smartphone, you can add a filter to your photo in the edit menu – I'd suggest Mono – and then increase the contrast slightly to see the tones clearly.

Another method is to compare the original image to a black-and-white version on a computer screen.

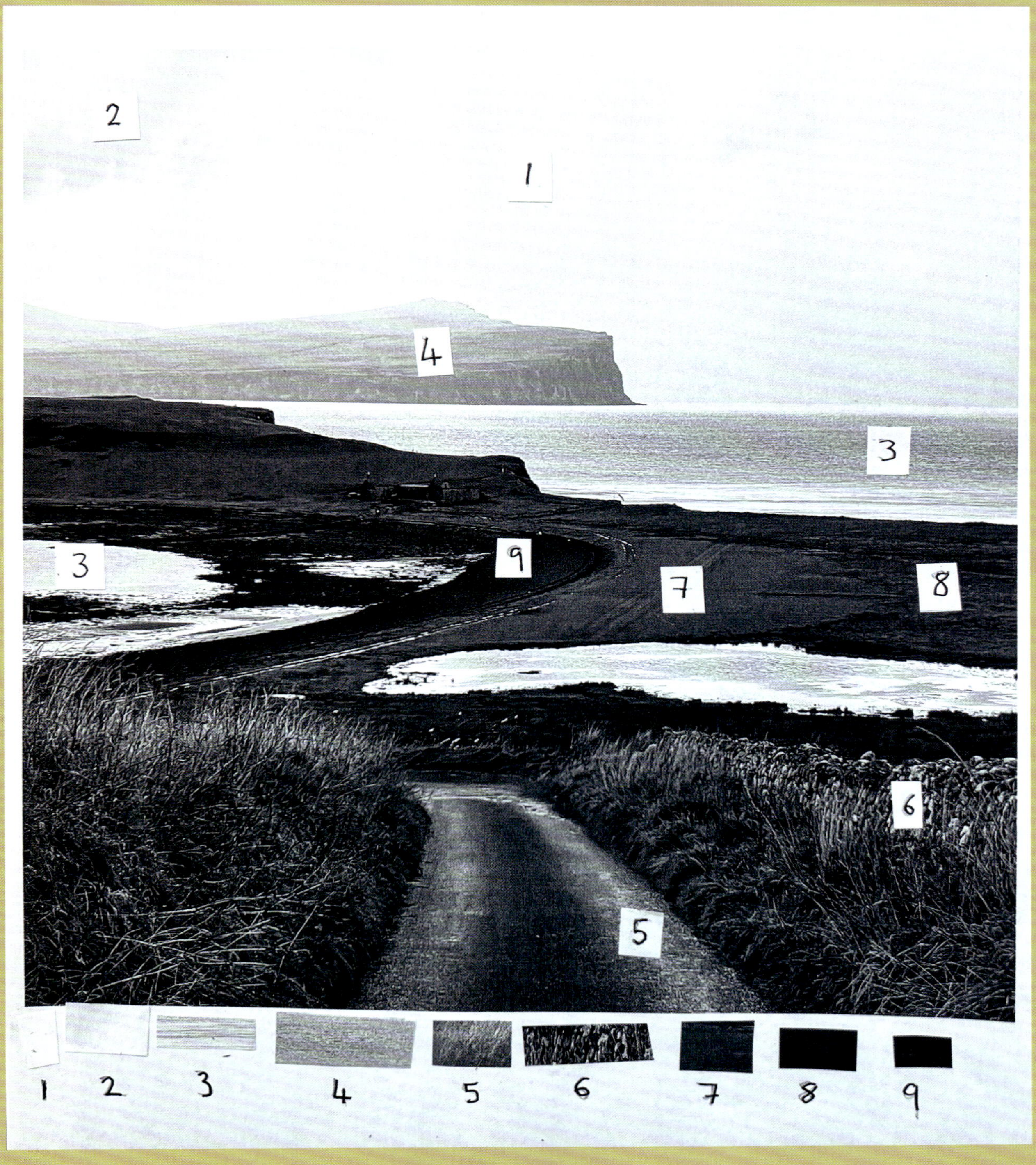
c
2
1
4
3
3
9
7
8
6
5
1 2 3 4 5 6 7 8 9

Creating papers using the gel plate

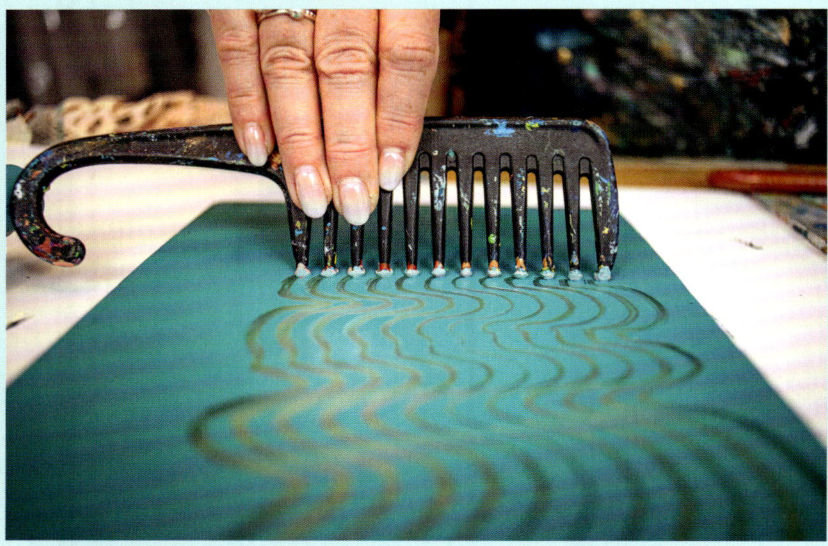

I drag a wide-toothed comb through the paint to create a dynamic, swirly pattern.

Gel printing brings a unique sense of immediacy and takes the pressure off creating art, especially for those who may not feel confident in their drawing skills. It's genuinely enjoyable to experience this medium, where the spontaneity of the process allows for a more relaxed approach to artistic expression.

Monoprinting with a gel plate is a versatile method that lets artists play with textures, layers and colour combinations. One of the fun things I enjoy doing with the gel plate is making unique papers using everyday items to leave impressions in the paint.

Patterns are all around us! You can press almost anything onto a gel plate – just avoid sharp objects. Try using bottle tops, lids, toilet roll tubes, corrugated cardboard, sink drainers, cotton buds or lace fabric. It's a great way to see your everyday items in a different light.

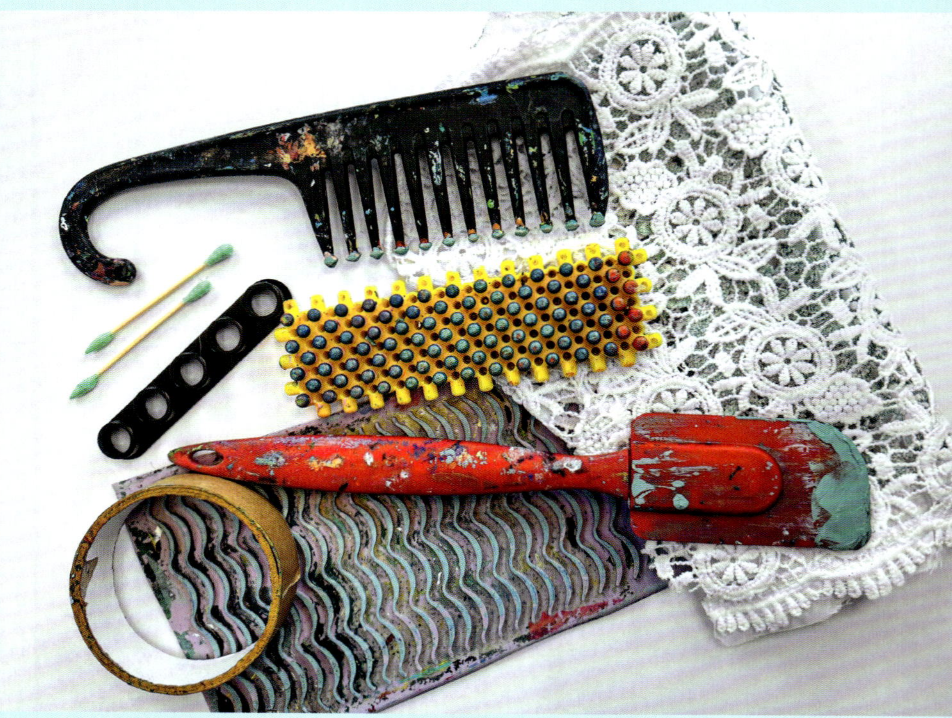

A variety of household items can be pressed onto a gel plate.

Selecting and repurposing papers

Digging through charity or thrift stores for old papers and books to repurpose is one of my absolute favourite activities. If I had to choose an animal to be, I'd probably go with a magpie; just like those crafty birds, I find something thrilling about beachcombing and discovering hidden gems that others might overlook.

I love using thinner papers for collage such as wet-strength tissue paper, regular copy paper, old book pages and music sheets. Printing on old papers feels special – it gives them a second life and can even preserve memories of loved ones by using books, letters, or papers connected to them.

If tearing up old books feels wrong, you can find beautiful, vintage ephemera on Etsy or old magazines and newspapers will also work well. Sometimes, print from these will transfer onto the gel plate, and I love how bits of text or numbers can unexpectedly peek through – it's a little creative surprise every time!

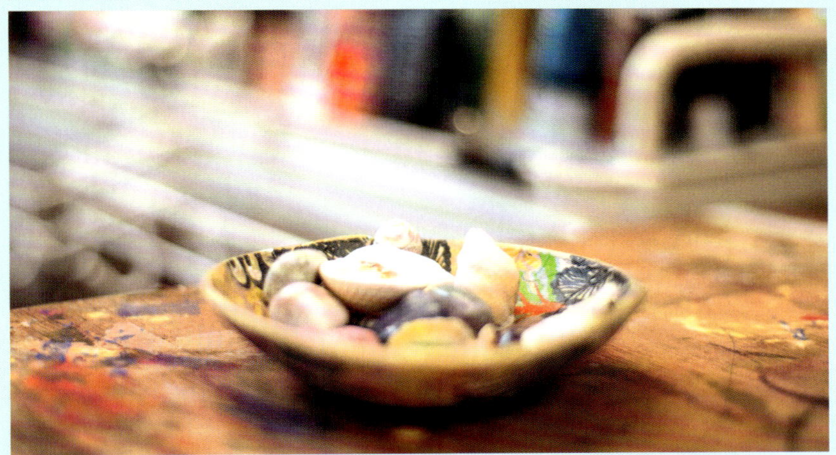

Beach finds.

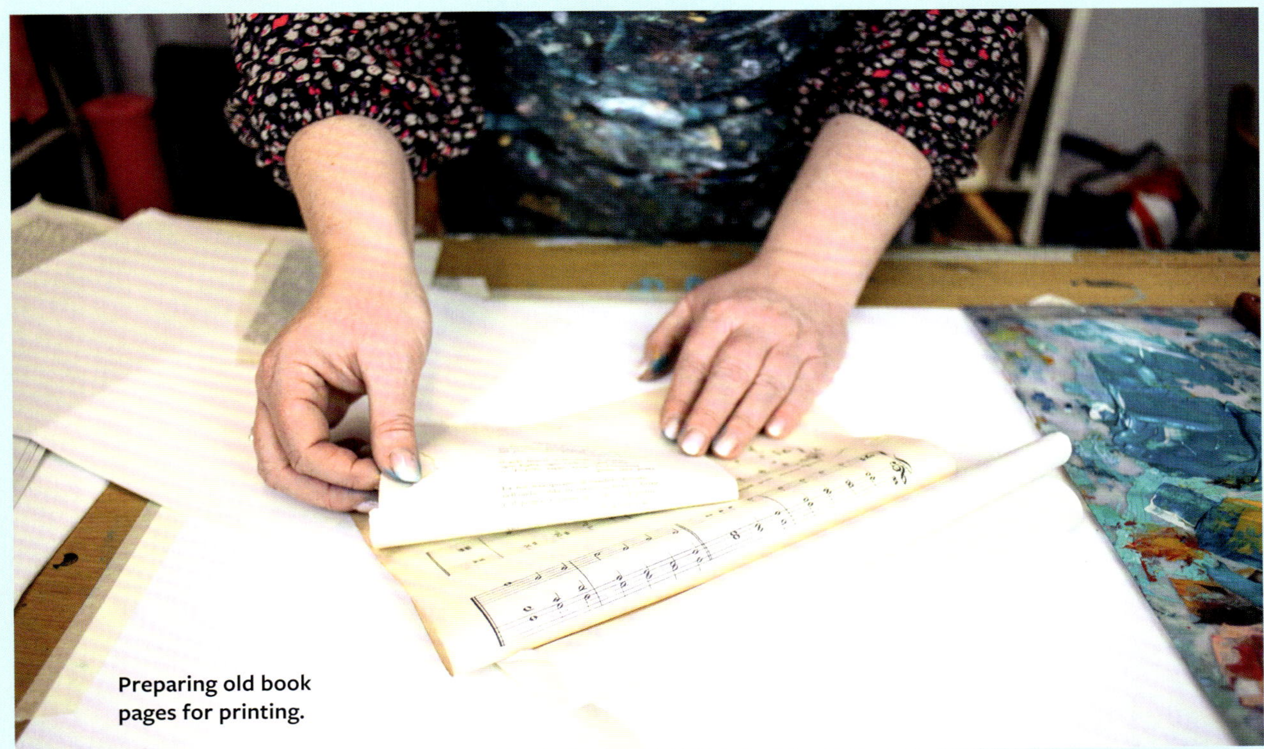

Preparing old book pages for printing.

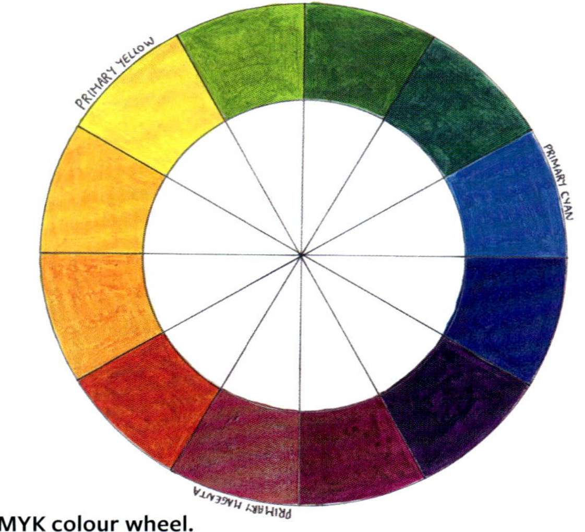

CMYK colour wheel.

Choosing a colour palette

I picked my favourite colours for this project. To keep it easy, if you choose colours next to each other on the colour wheel, they'll match well (we call that analogous or harmonious). I like throwing in a splash of a contrasting colour to make things really pop. So, if you have lots of blues and greens, adding a little orange can make it more exciting.

You can also use online tools, such as Canva and Adobe, to create colour palettes from an image. Once you've uploaded an image, the program instantly generates a palette based on the photo's hues. It is a quick and easy way to find inspiration! Aim to use a range of colours that come in different shades for your printing.

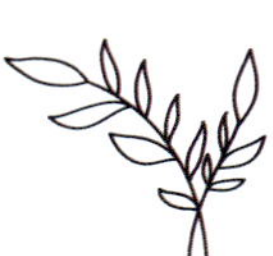

Tip

I recommend buying a book like *The Pocket Complete Color Harmony* by Tina Sutton, which has many examples of colour palettes that work well together.

A range of shades lets you show off light and depth in your collage paintings.

Below are the specific colour swatches I used to create these shades. You might spot that I sometimes used the same four colours – the trick is to adjust the amounts for each shade, starting with roughly a pea-sized amount.

For instance, Mint Green has the whitest paint, while Dark Turquoise has the most turquoise blue paint. It's all about tweaking the mix for each shade!

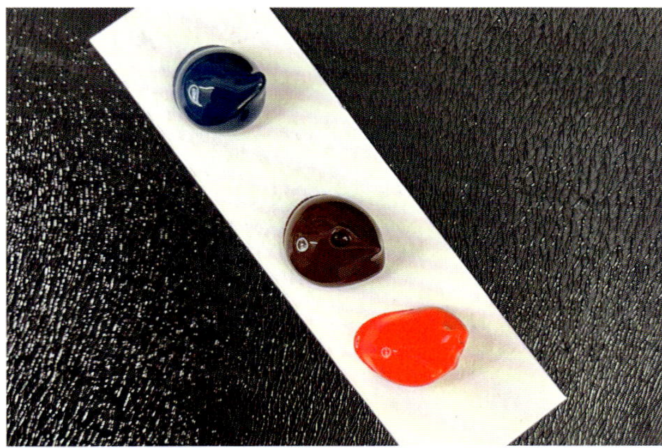

Indigo, Quinacridone Scarlet and Burnt Umber make Midnight Blue.

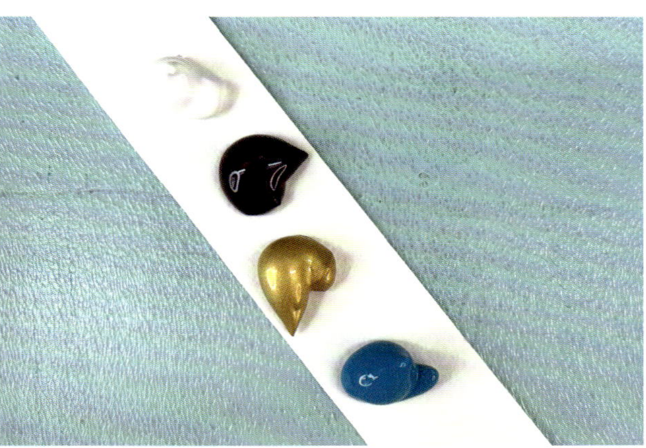

Titanium White, Gold, Burnt Umber and Turquoise Blue make Mint Green.

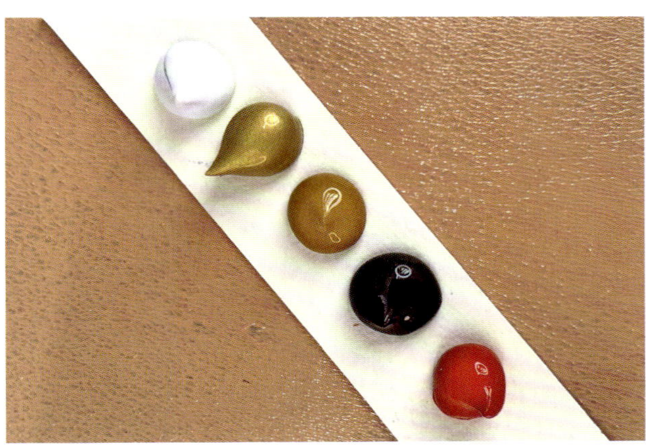

Titanium White, Cadmium Red, Gold and Yellow Ochre make Light Peach.

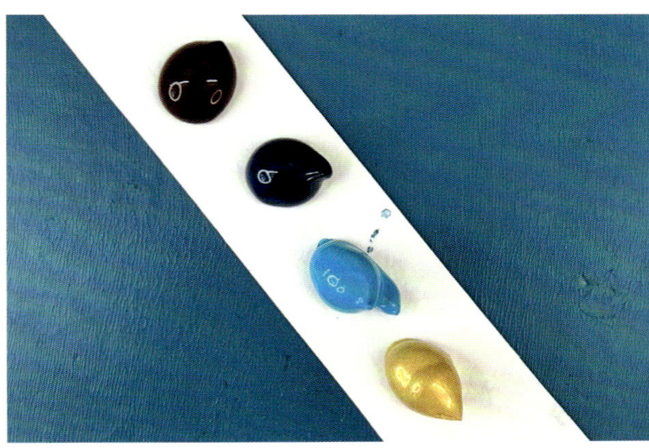

Titanium White, Gold, Burnt Umber and Turquoise Blue make Dark Turquoise.

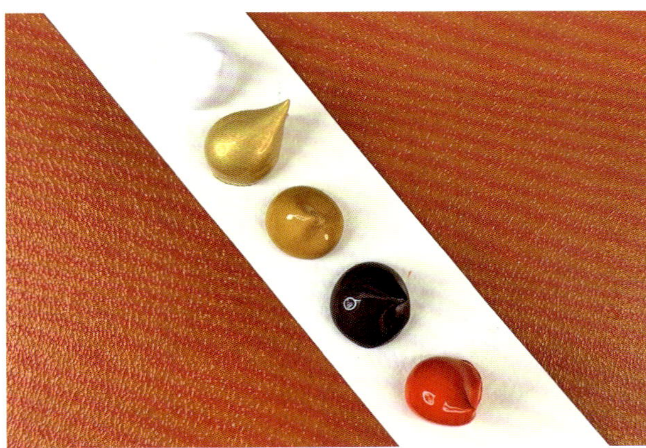

Titanium White, Cadmium Red, Gold and Yellow Ochre make Terracotta.

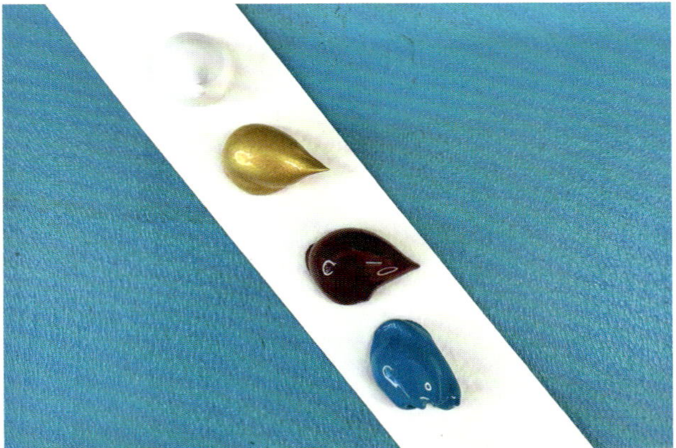

Titanium White, Gold, Burnt Umber and Turquoise Blue make Bright Turquoise.

Making each set of papers

Now, let me walk you through the process of making each set of papers. I recommend premixing some colours on a paint palette to make things quicker, and keeping a variety of your collagraph plates on hand to vary the textures (see page 42 to make these). I like to start off with the blue shades and a neutral light shade to pull the print off the gel plate. Let's give it a try!

For this particular print, I started by rolling a thin layer of the Bright Turquoise shade on to the gel plate using a 15cm (6in) brayer or roller. With the paint still wet, I pressed a jute collagraph plate on to the gel plate. Once the paint had dried on the gel plate, I rolled a thin layer of my neutral light shade straight on top of the print (a).

Immediately, I pressed the wet-strength tissue paper onto the gel plate and smoothed the back. For this, I use either my hand or a tool like a baren or a Pringles lid (b).

I typically wait a few minutes before pulling the paper back (c). Patience is key because if the paint is still wet, it won't lift the first layer along with it.

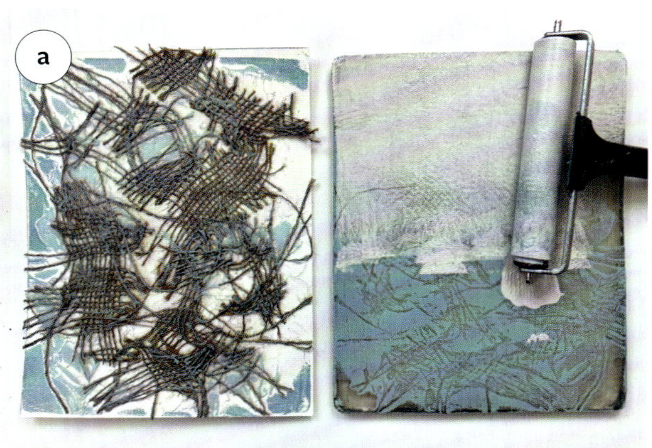

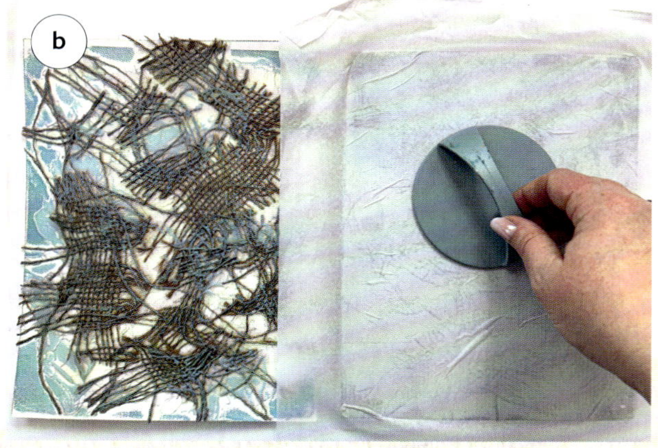

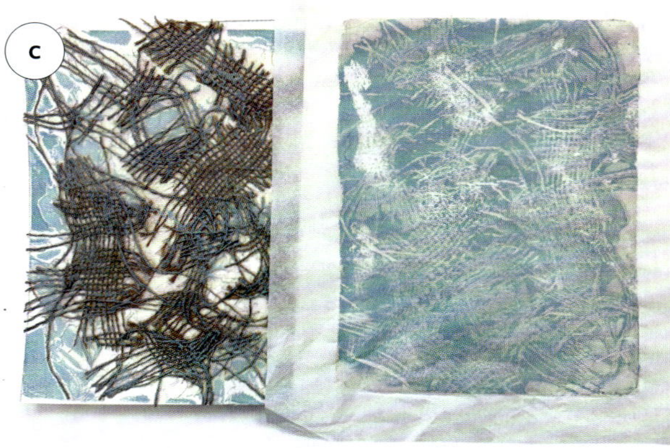

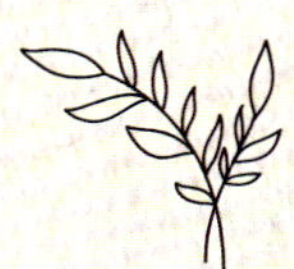

Tip

If you're in a rush, a hairdryer can speed up the drying process. Just be sure to use the cool setting to prevent any damage to the gel plate from the heat.

Notice that the first colour on the completed print, with the texture from the collagraph plate, is on top, and the neutral colour is behind it. This helps to highlight the organic marks printed from the jute cloth. It might take a bit of practice to get used to thinking backward in this process. Just keep in mind that the first colour you roll onto the plate will end up being the one on the front of your print.

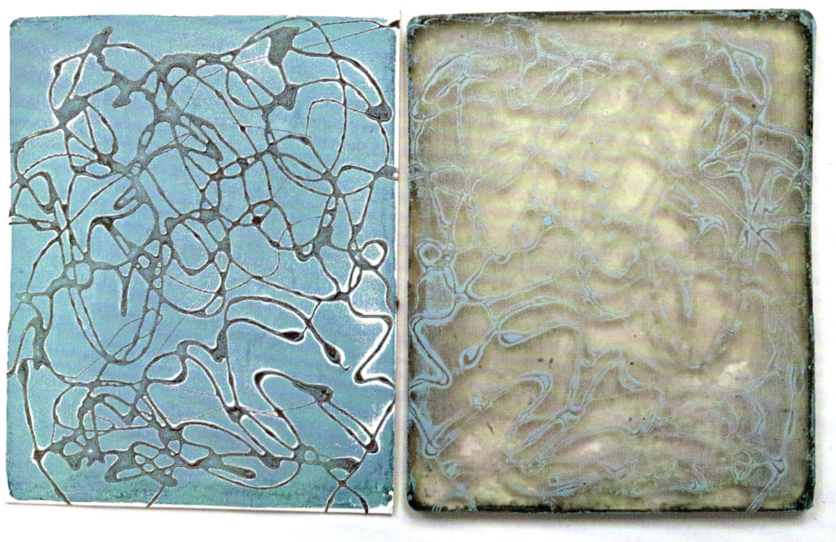

I repeated this with another collagraph print, again using Bright Turquoise for the first layer.

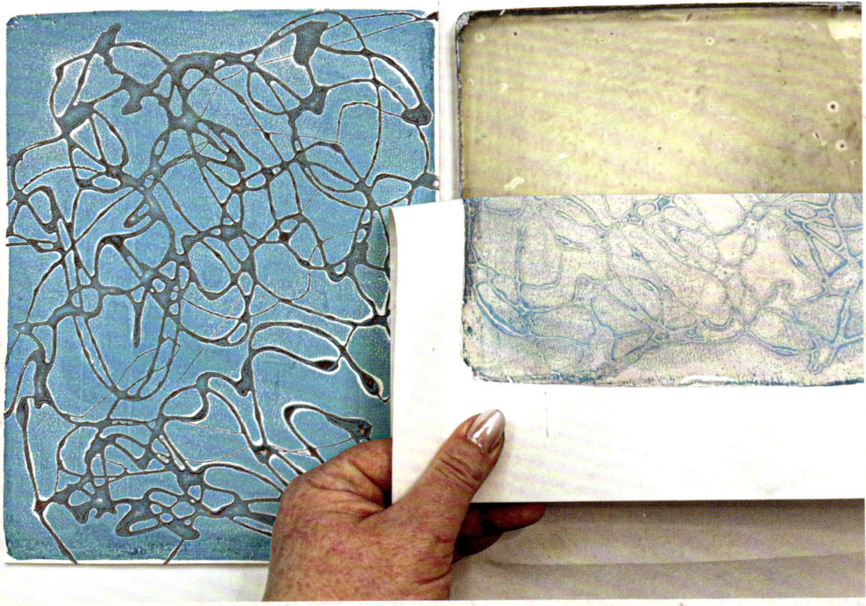

The second layer was the neutral light shade again and I peeled back the regular copy paper after a few minutes to reveal the textured effect.

For the next print I used regular copy paper and a collagraph plate made with rubber bands. I began with my lighter shade of blue, Bright Turquoise, and for the second layer, I rolled a darker blue, Dark Turquoise (a).

For the next print, I switched it up a bit. I started by printing a plain layer of Bright Turquoise (b) onto regular copy paper. Once that dried, I placed it on top of the darker paint, Dark Turquoise (c). This gives the print a slightly different feel compared to the previous one.

In the upcoming examples, I'll be using items you probably have lying around the house or in your fabric stash to make impressions in the paint.

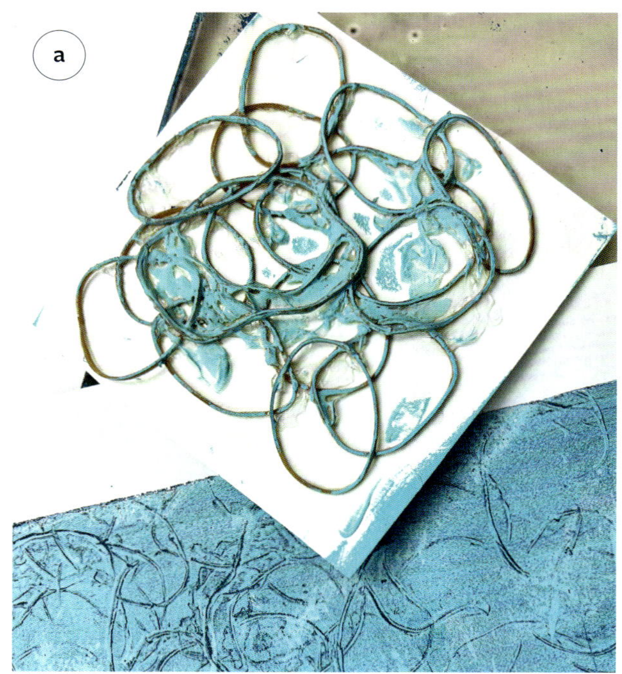

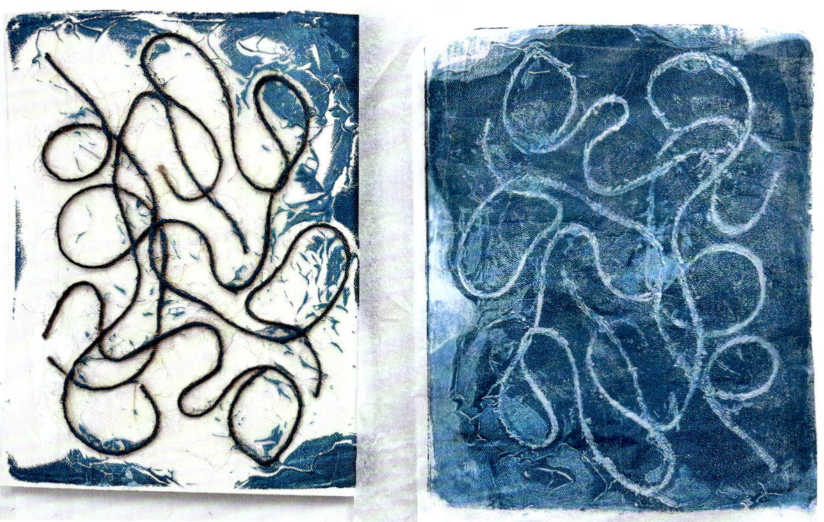

One layer of Dark Turquoise pulled with wet-strength tissue paper, from a collagraph plate with string.

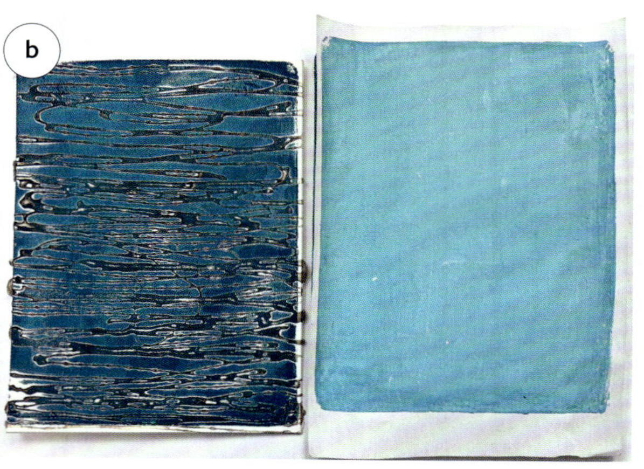

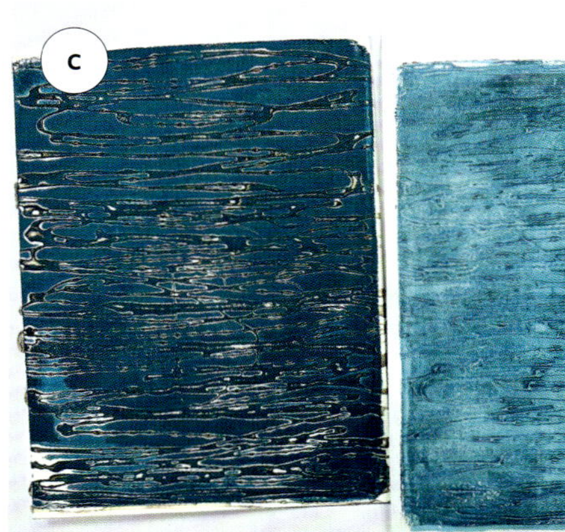

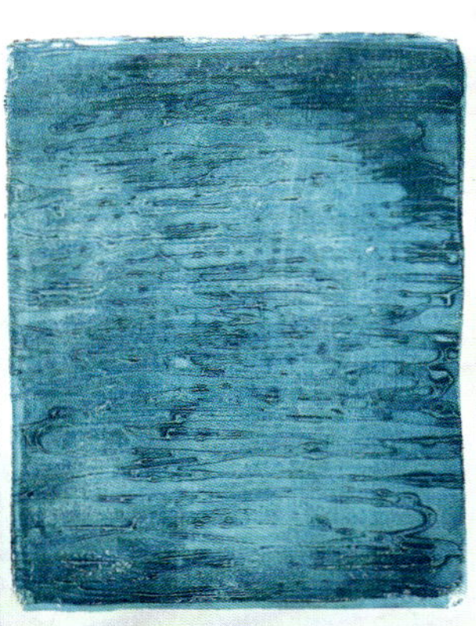

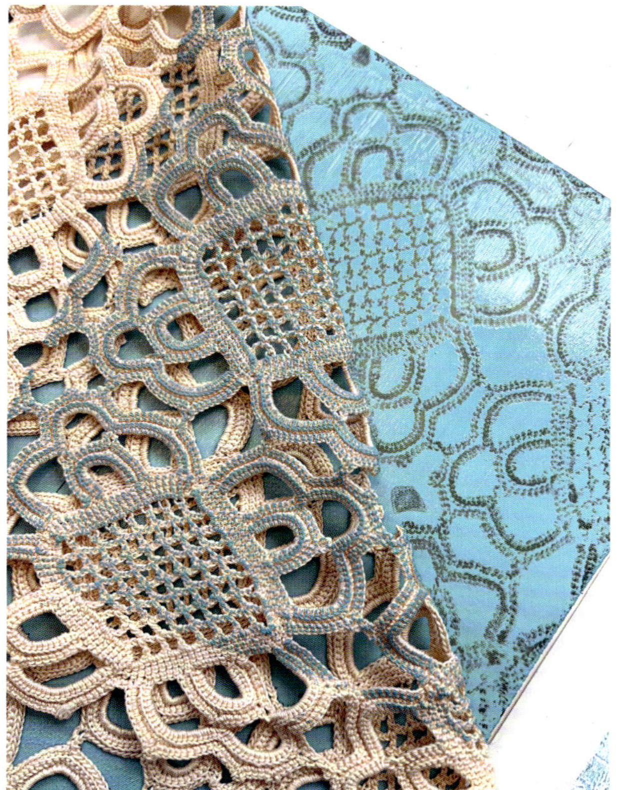

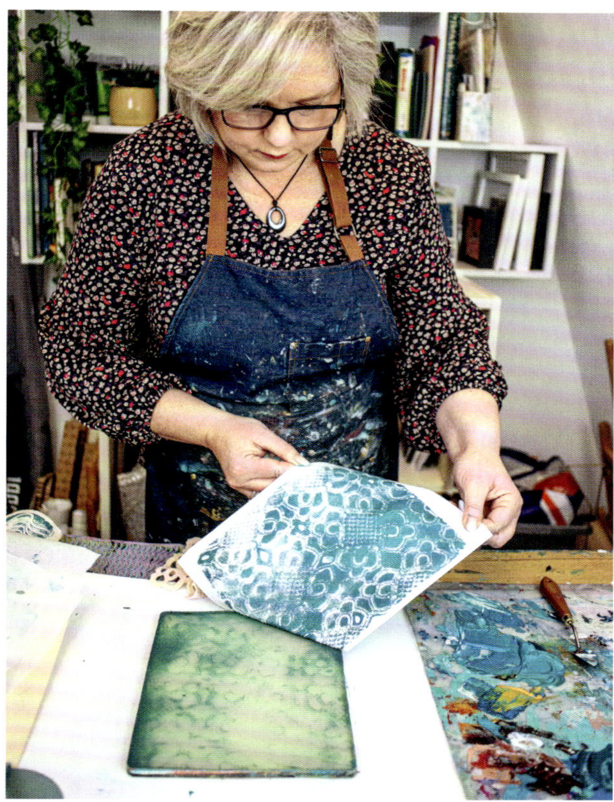

This fabric worked nicely, especially with its open design.

For the next print, I applied a thicker layer of paint because I had a plan to score into it using a comb, creating a wavy design. I chose to use Bright Turquoise.

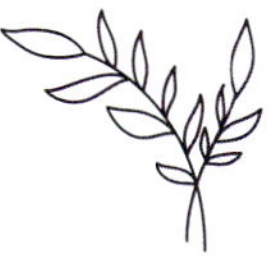

Tip

With a generous amount of paint you can make up to three prints, as there will be leftover paint still on the plate.

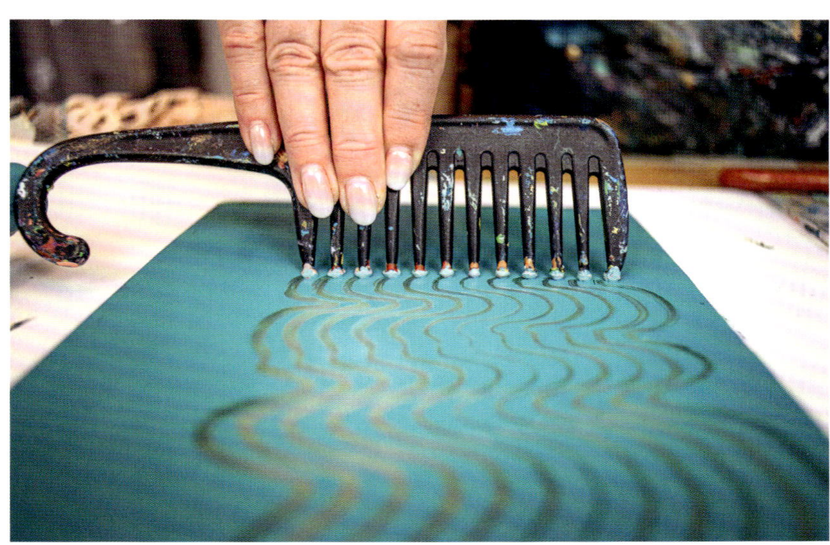

For the second print, I took one of the sheets I had used to clean my brayer on to capture a 'ghost' print, taking advantage of the leftover paint still on the plate (a).

There was quite a lot of paint still remaining on the plate. I let that layer dry then applied a layer of my neutral light shade to pull the print using wet-strength tissue paper (b).

In my final example, I rolled a thick layer of paint again. Using a silicone spatula, I scraped away areas of the paint to create 'windows' on the gel plate, in order to allow the colour beneath to peek through in the final print. I printed my Light Peach onto wet-strength tissue paper and once it had dried, placed it on top of my Mint Green and pulled the print (c).

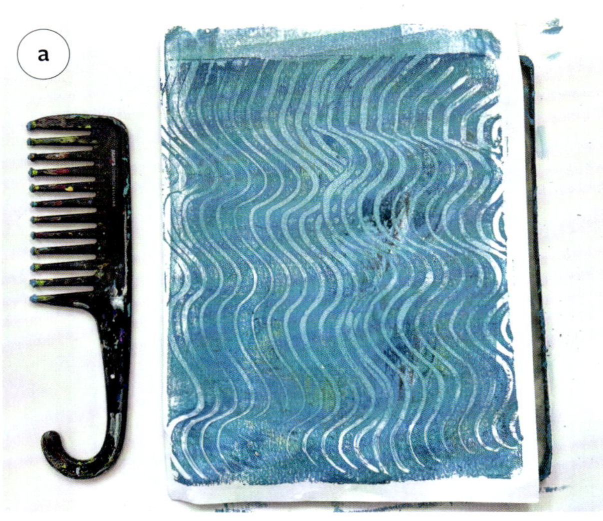

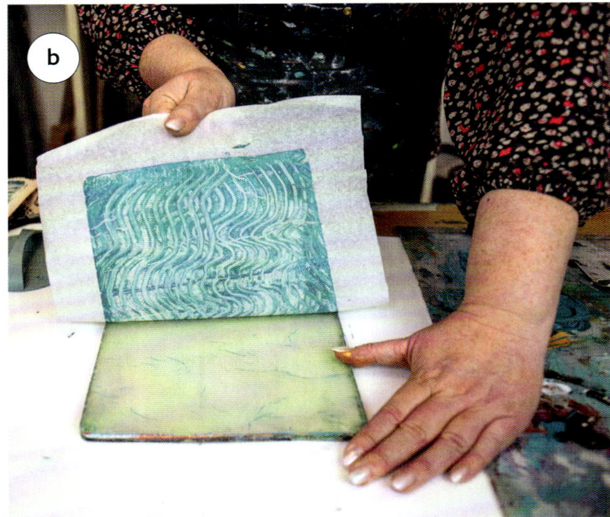

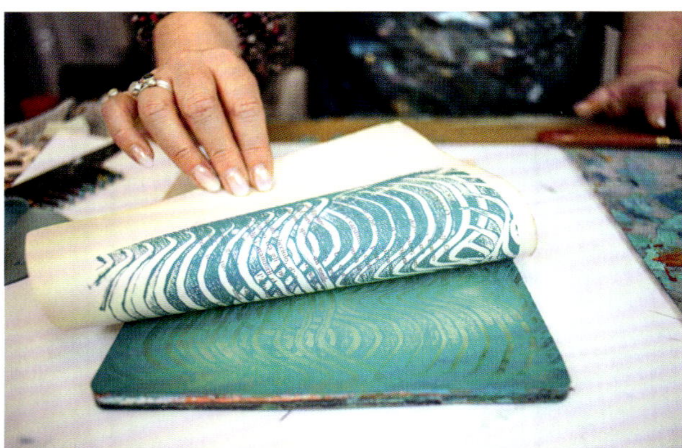

This print was on an old book page, which added an intriguing text element.

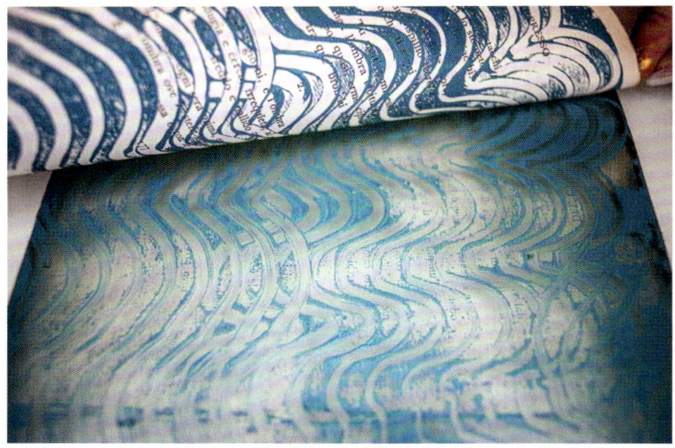

If you look closely, you will see that some of the text from the book was transferred onto the plate, creating more interest.

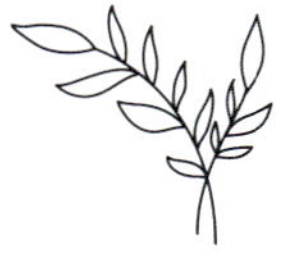

Tip

If the layer of paint is too thin, it won't be easy to scrape it off with the silicone spatula.

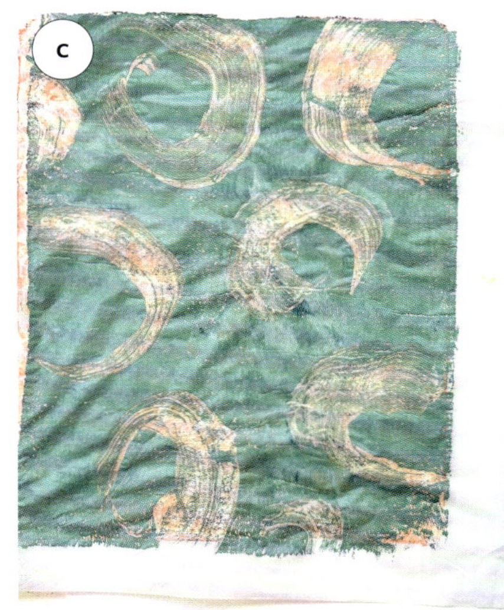

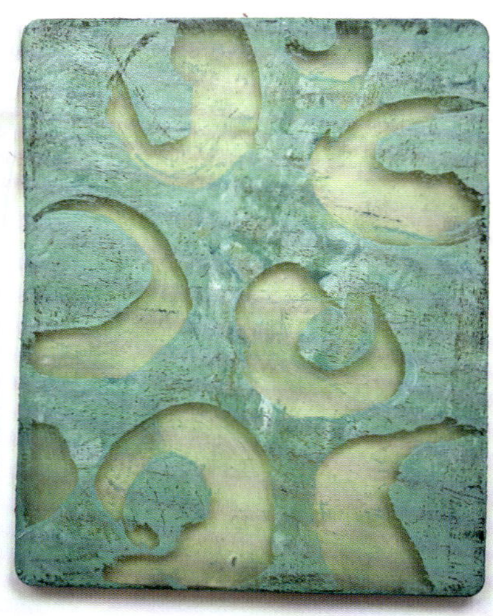

Cleaning up leftover paint from the gel plate

If there's leftover paint on the plate, it is easy to clean it up. A baby wipe works well (d) or simply spray some water and wipe it off with a kitchen towel.

By now, you should have a wonderful assortment of papers with various tonal values and textures (e). These papers are all set for the next phase of your project, where you can begin sorting them, cutting them up and incorporating them into your collage.

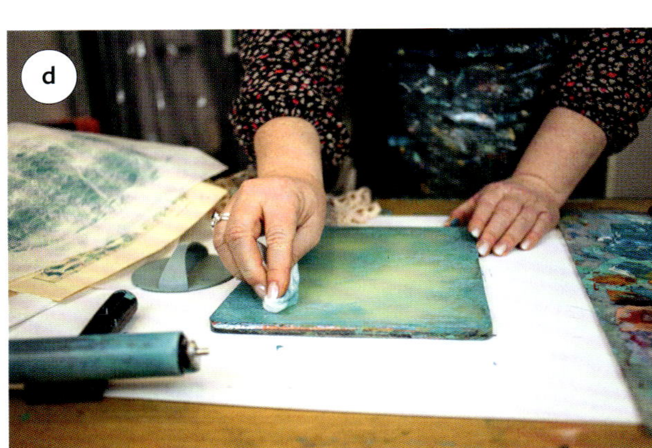

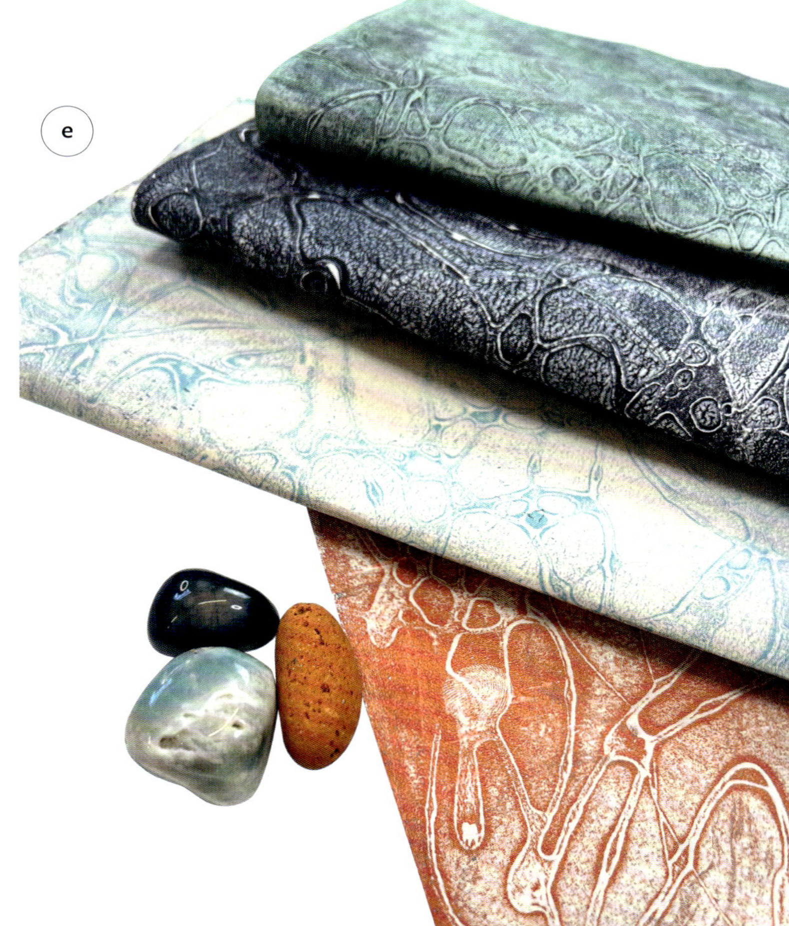

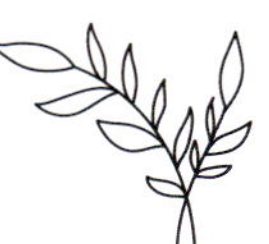

Tip

Dealing with stubborn paint? Try using baby oil; it effortlessly removes any paint stuck to the gel plate. See page 12 for more cleaning tips.

Creating the finished painting

In this section, I'll guide you through cutting the pieces for your collage in a way that makes your painting fit together like a jigsaw puzzle. Begin by sorting through your papers and figuring out where each piece fits. You might need a little trial and error to make your picture look just right; if something doesn't quite work, try a different colour or shade until it clicks. Once the image is glued in place, you can then apply some mixed-media painting techniques on top of the collage to bring the whole composition together.

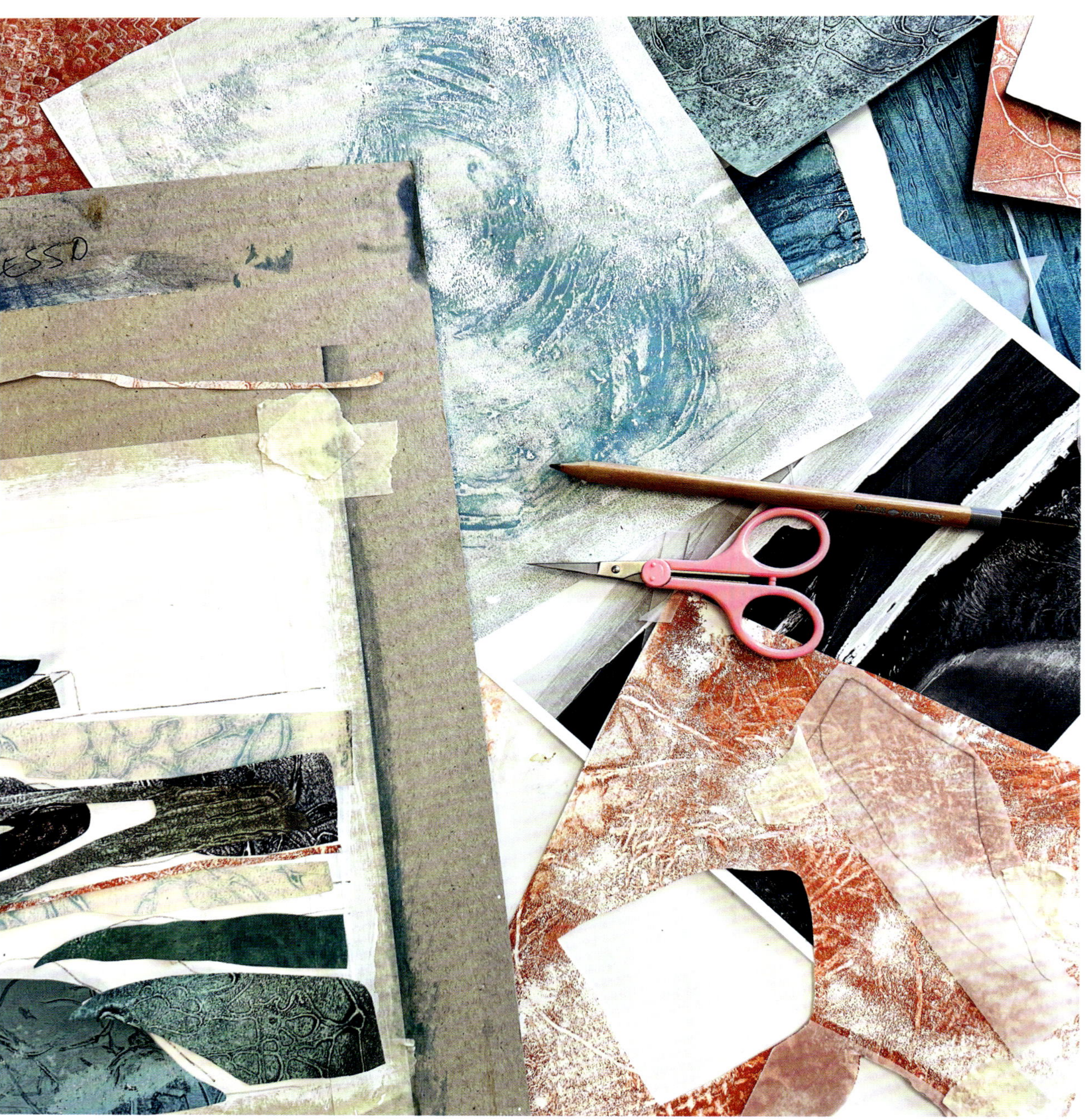

Cutting out the collage pieces

If you're struggling with the tonal values, look back to page 50 and use the small black-and-white squares you cut earlier (a). Placing them next to the paper should give you a better idea of where the tone fits in to the collage. Alternatively, take a photo of your print and convert it to black and white, as you did with the original image at the beginning of this project.

Sketch the outline of the shape you want to cut out onto tracing paper (b) and cut it out. You can also trace along the lines you transferred onto your paper substrate.

Tape it onto the printed paper you've chosen for this section and cut out the shape from the print (c).

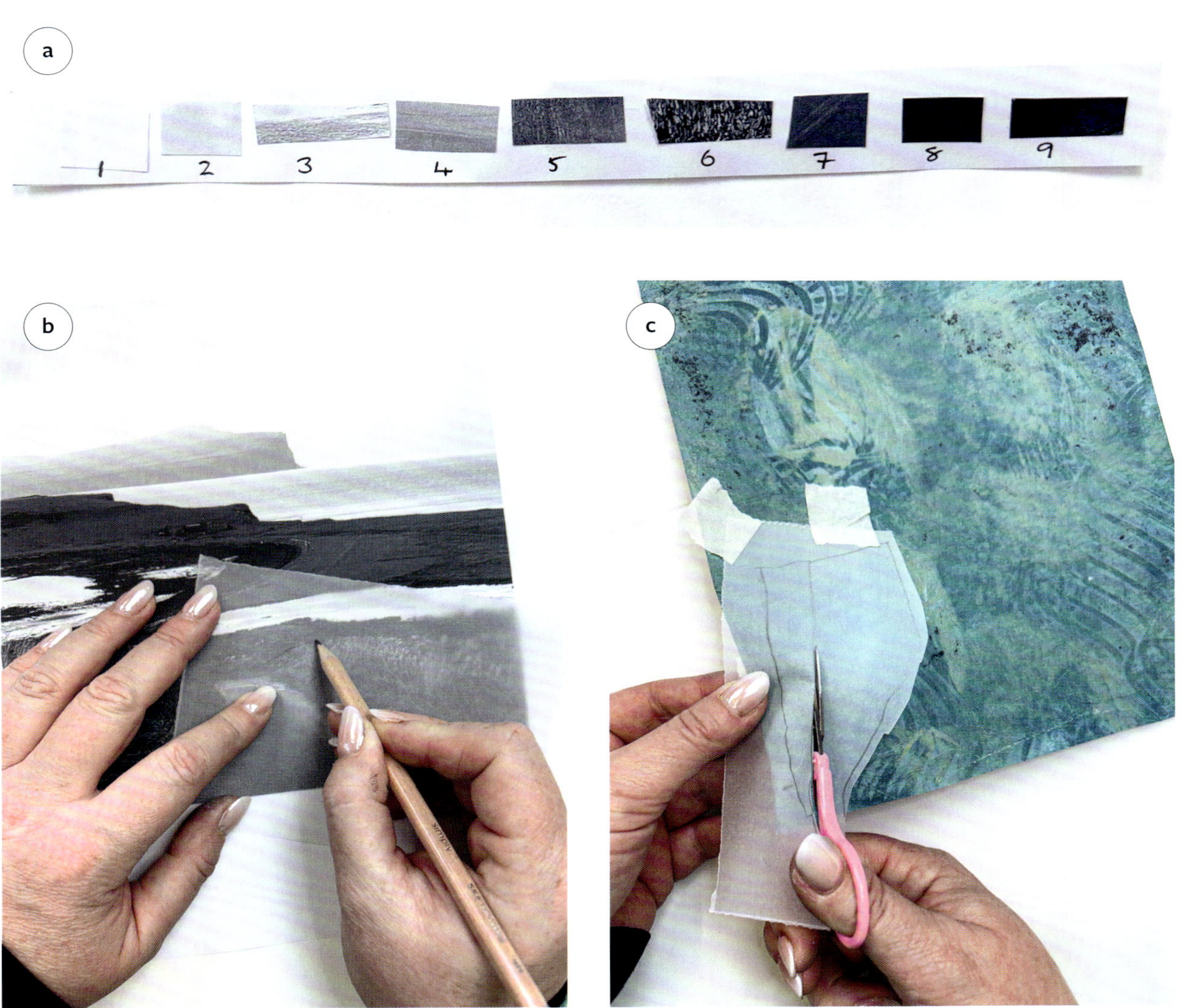

Arrange your cut-out pieces on your paper to form your image (d), then glue the sections down with matte medium glue (e). I apply glue on both the substrate and the back of the paper before sticking them together. Use a wet brush over the top of the paper and an old credit card or a catalyst wedge to smooth out any wrinkles (f). Once your collage is glued down, you can speed up the drying process with a hairdryer or let it sit for an hour or so until it's completely dry. If you can wait overnight, that's even better – patience pays off!

Tip

Don't stress if there are white gaps in your collage – you can fill those in with small collage pieces or paint at the next stage.

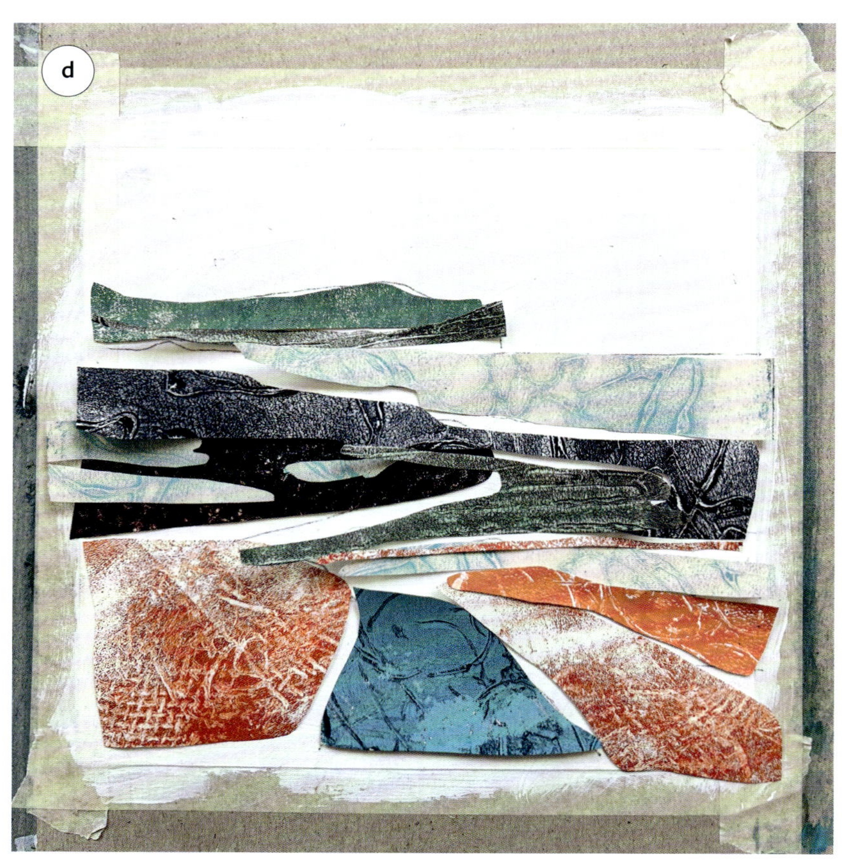

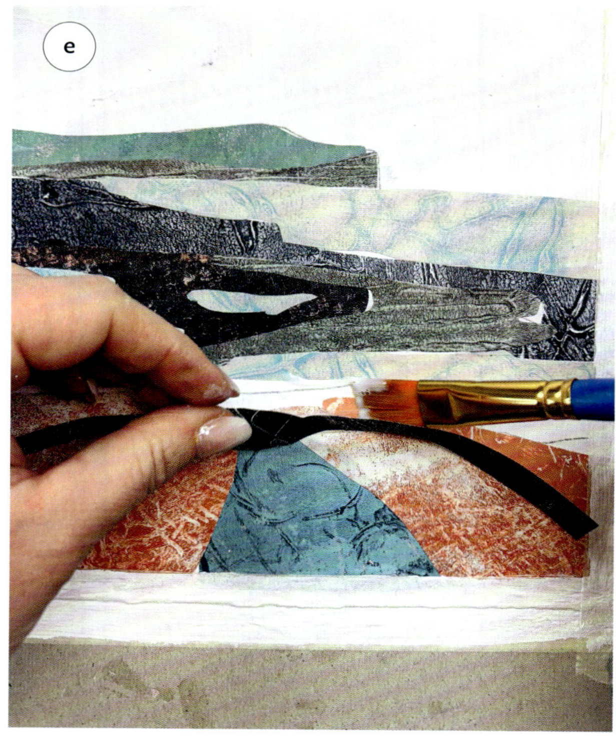

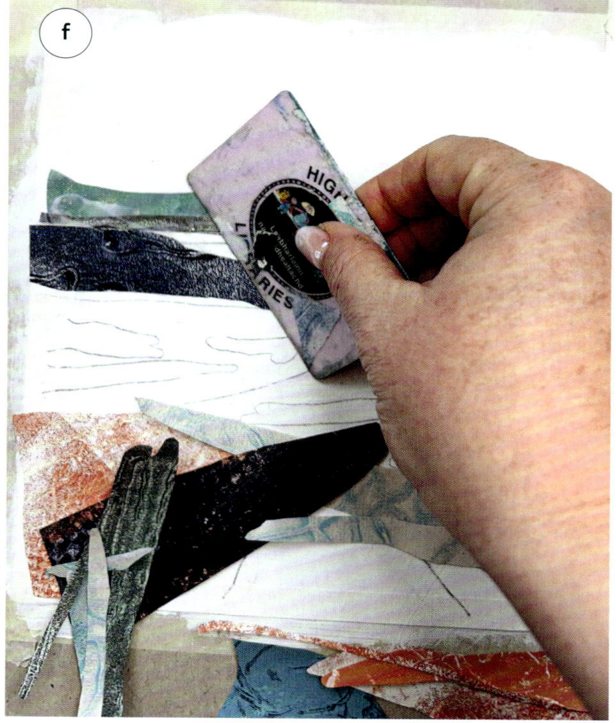

Using mixed-media painting techniques

I mixed Titanium White, Indigo and Black acrylic paint for a painterly sky, using minimal amounts of Indigo and Black, and mainly focusing on white. Applying the paint with a dry brush, I gently scuff or scumble it onto the surface (a).

I then painted a touch of Titanium White paint over the lightest sea areas and, using a metal ball stylus sculpting tool (b), I scratched into the wet paint, revealing lines that expose the collage paper underneath. I repeat this technique to create the illusion of long grasses by the roadside (c). It's all about playing with textures in my art.

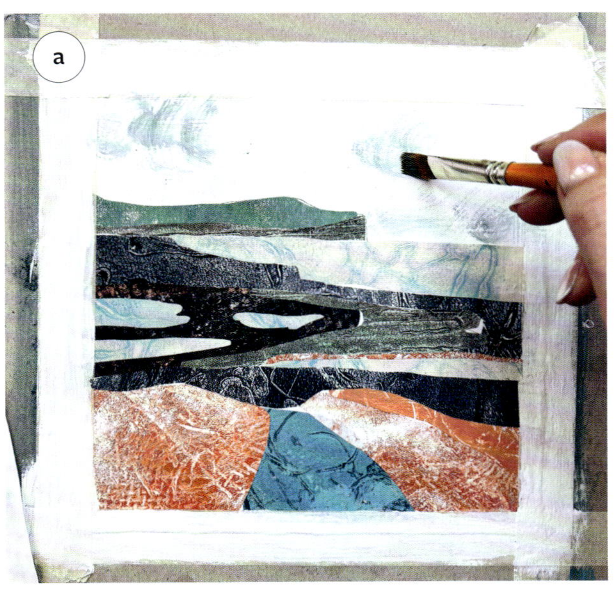
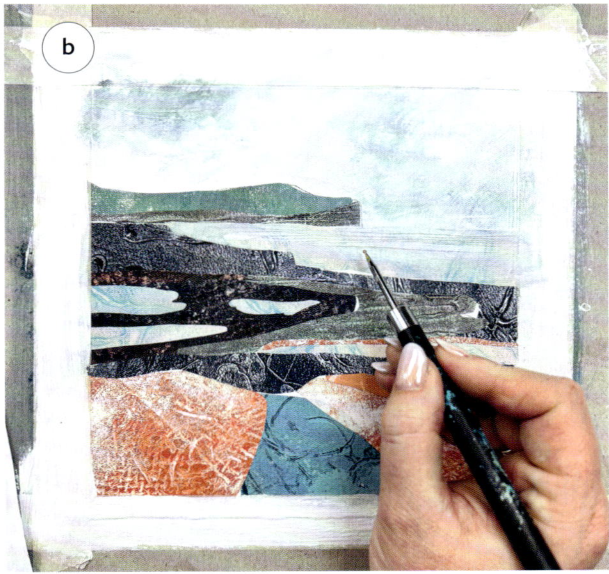
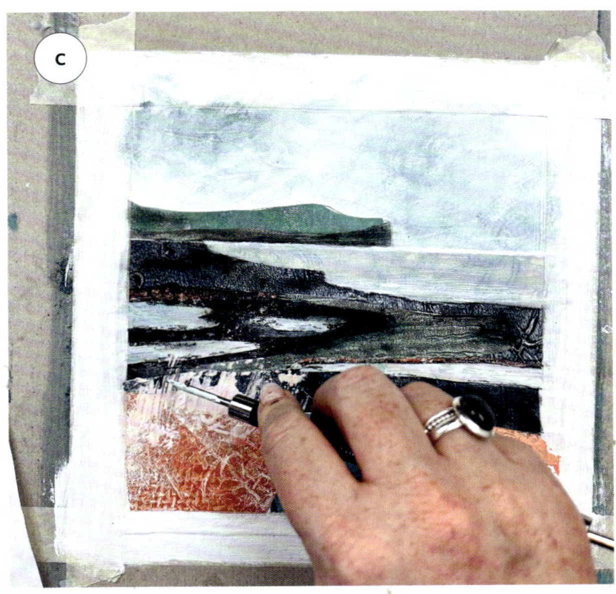

I introduce a Neocolor® II water-soluble pastel (d), which is perfect for adding distinct marks and infusing a sense of untamed grasses into the final artwork. If you make an error at this stage, you can easily remove the paint or pastel with a baby wipe (e).

Removing the tape

Once you are satisfied with the finished painting, it's time to delicately remove the tape. Lightly score the paper around the painting, cutting through any collage pieces that overlap the masking tape. Avoid cutting too deeply; the goal is to release the masking tape for a clean removal but not to remove the paper border. Gently lift the tape while applying heat with a heat gun or hairdryer on its hottest setting (f). This loosens the glue to prevent ripping or tearing. Take your time; it might be a bit fiddly, but the effort pays off for that pristine white edge.

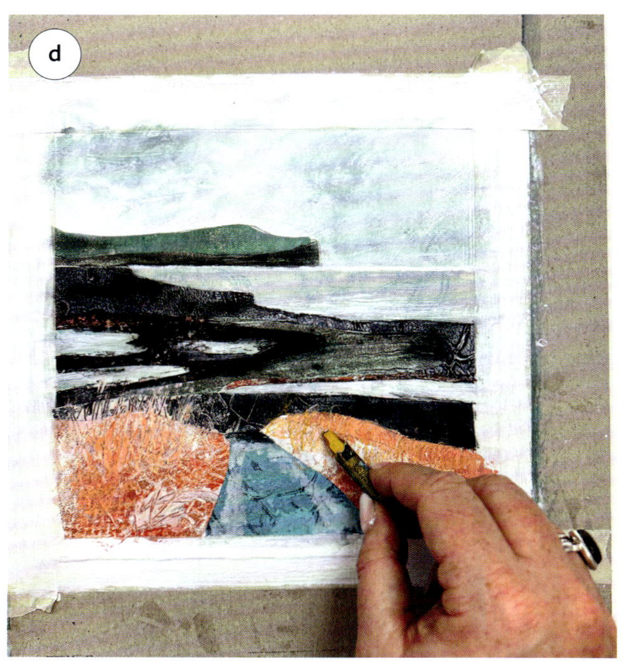

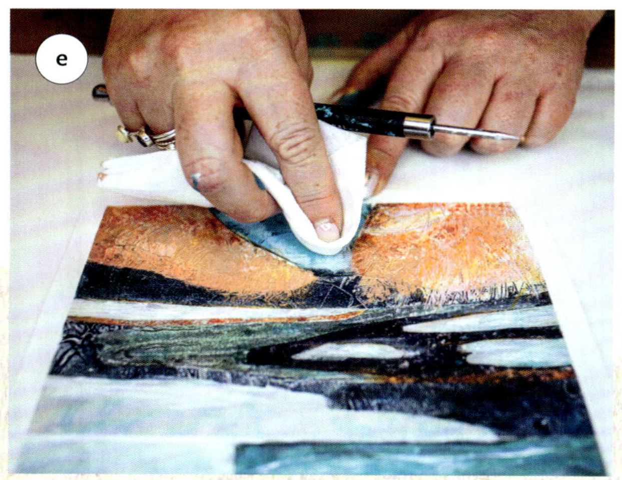

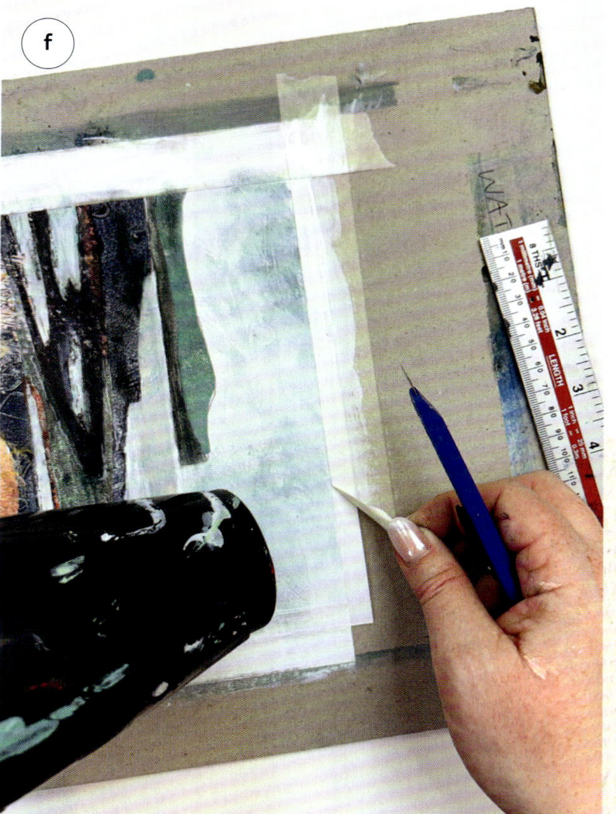

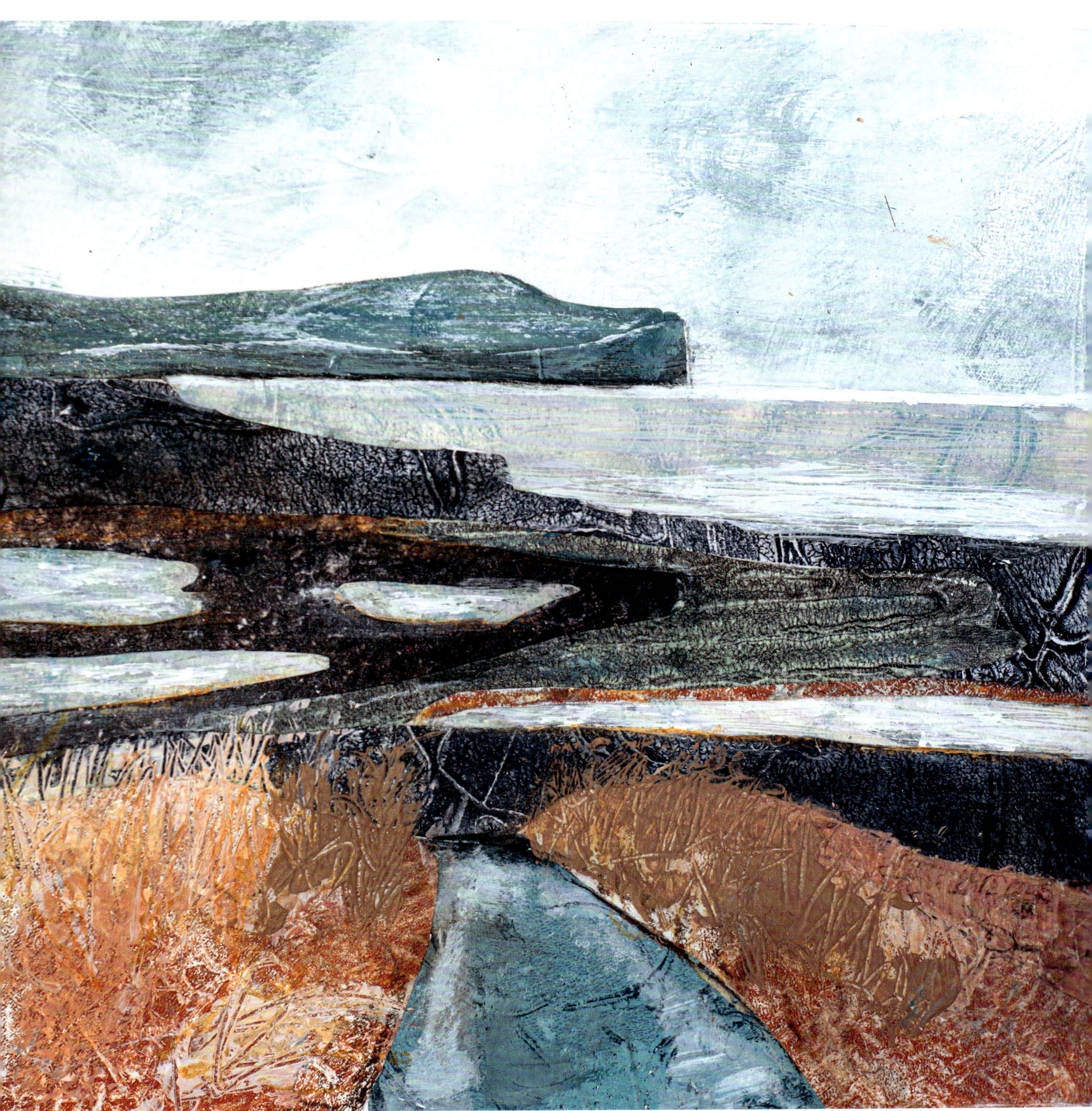

I hope you find joy in this project. Use personal photographs and infuse new life and memories into those special moments.

Examples of other landscapes I've printed using this method.

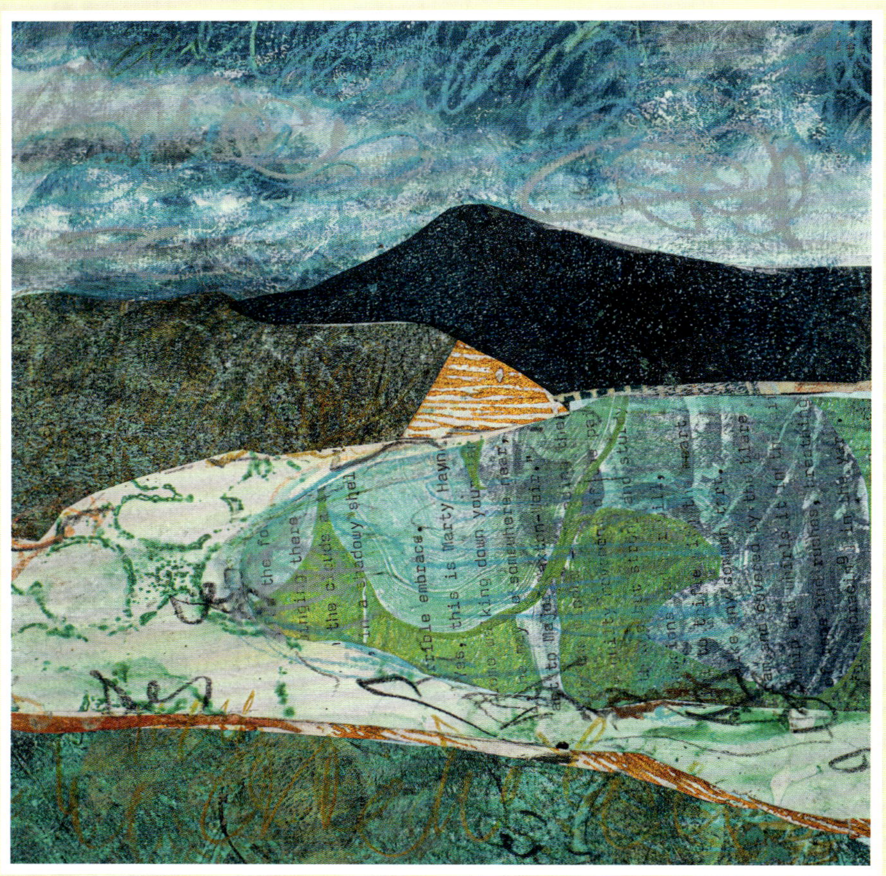

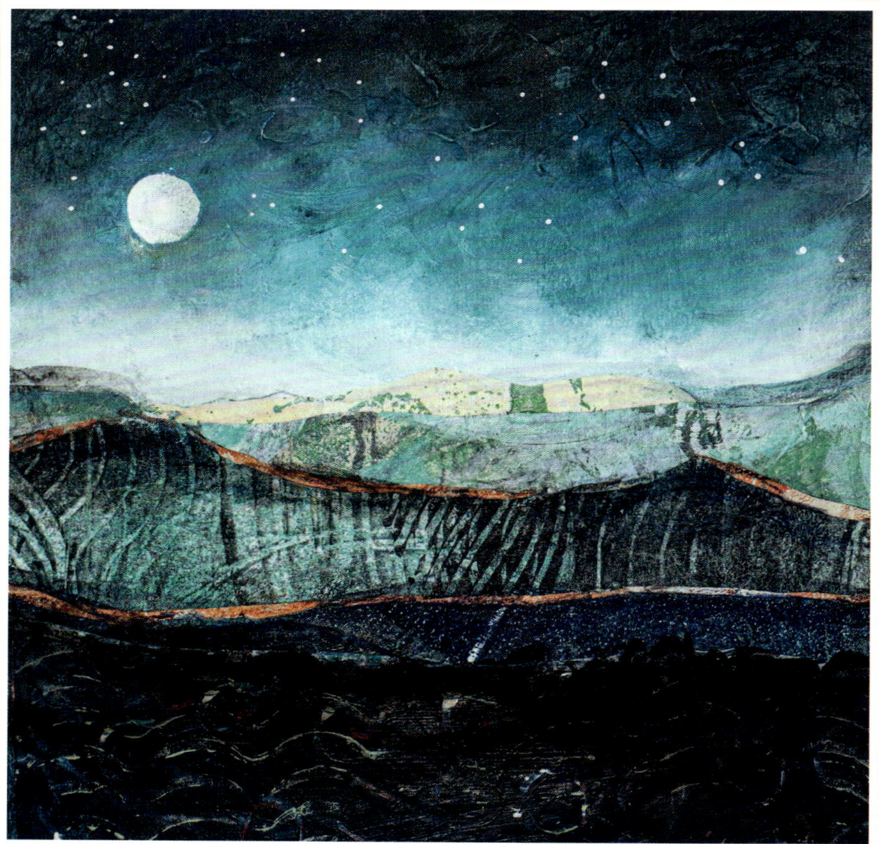

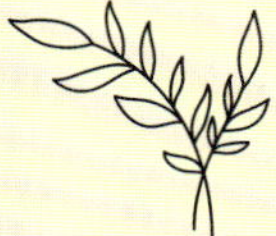

Tip

To create a night sky on your collage, start by cutting out a small circle of paper to create a simple mask for your moon and stick it to your page with masking tape. Use a dark blue paint for a midnight sky, then dot on a 0.7 white Posca pen for bright stars, and a bronze Uni-ball Signo pen for shimmering ones. Stipple paint around the moon's edges, then remove the mask. Add a light layer of yellow for a soft, warm moon glow.

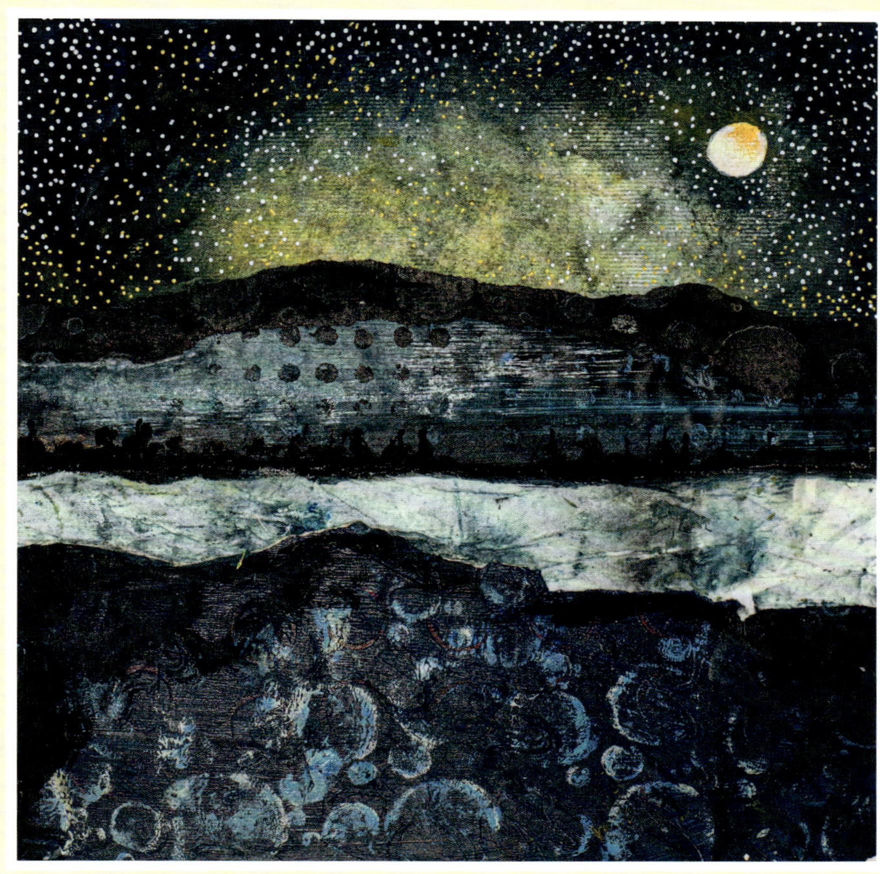

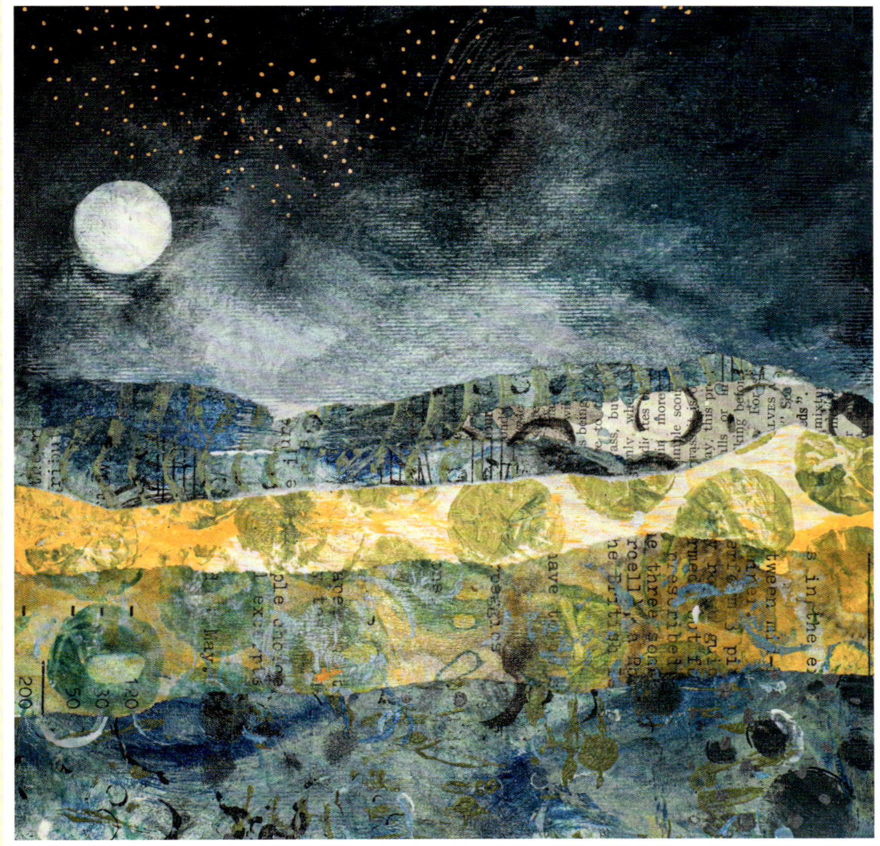

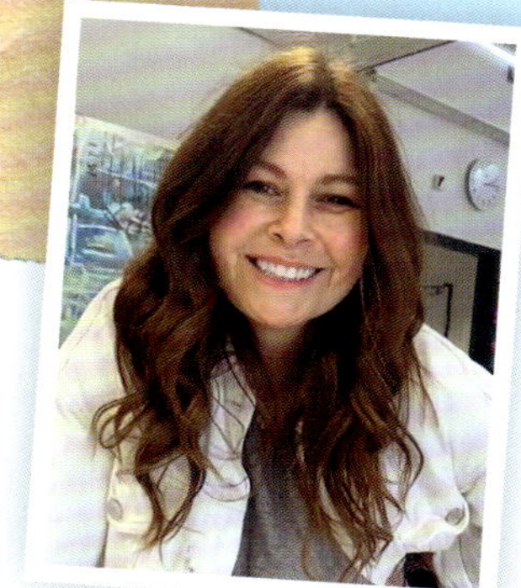

Q **Can you share a little about your background and how you discovered gel printing?**

A A friend sent me a gel printing reel on Instagram and I thought, 'What is this magic?' My initial attempts failed epically as my images didn't transfer and my papers stuck to the plate. One of the reasons it frustrated me so much is that I am a trained artist with several degrees in art, and I even teach printmaking classes. I documented my struggles on social media, and many artists shared their tips and guidance. With lots of trial and error, I started to grasp the process and found my stride.

This determination to master new techniques has been a constant in my development as an artist. I've been fortunate to teach art and exhibit my work internationally. I'm originally from New York, and in 2007 I moved to Europe on a Fulbright grant to teach art in Bratislava, Slovakia. From there, I started teaching at an international school in Florence, Italy. I married my amazing husband and we started a family. After nine years in Italy, we moved to Germany, where I continue to teach, make and exhibit my art.

Q **What drew you to using a gel plate in your artwork?**

A It wasn't just the technical challenge of achieving a good image transfer that drew me in, but also how gel printing allowed me to combine key aspects of my art – mainly painting and photography. Some of my prints focus on architectural details, while others capture more intimate scenes. The immediacy and tactile nature of the gel plate process allows for quick experimentation and the creation of unique prints each time.

Q **Who or what are your main influences in your art practice?**

A My work is influenced by personal experiences, art-historical references and cultural narratives. Living in multiple countries has greatly shaped my work.

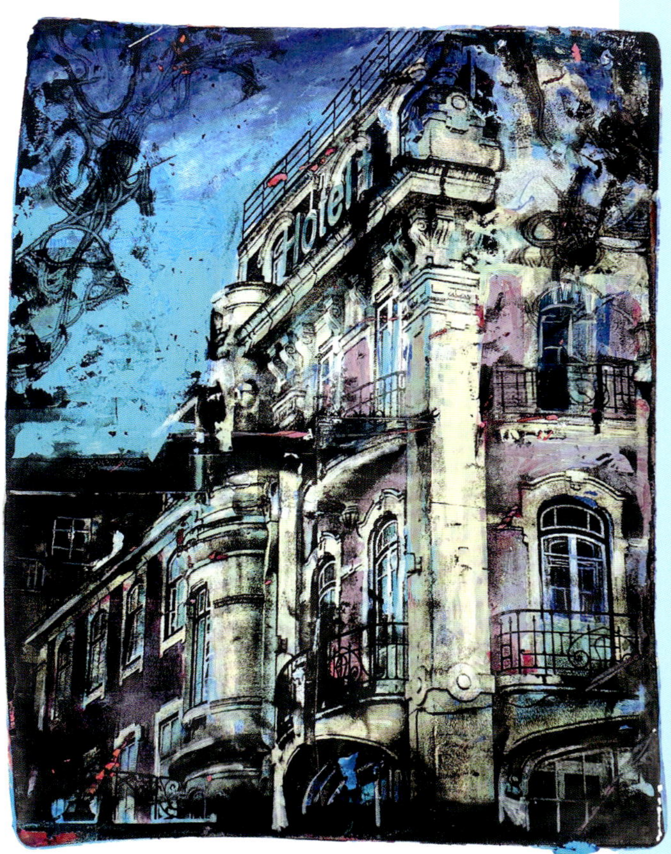

Lisbon Internacional Design Hotel,
monotype, 16 x 20in, 2024

Rather than directly representing places, my travel and life experiences are reflected in the emotions connected to the places I've visited and lived.

Likewise, art history is essential to my career as both an artist and an educator. During my nine years in Italy, the Renaissance had a profound impact on me, which led me to move to Florence. Being near museums like the Uffizi was incredibly inspiring. Contemporary art, with its boundary-pushing nature, also plays a key role in my work. I enjoy combining traditional elements layered with contemporary themes and aesthetics.

Q   How do you see the role of gel printing in the broader context of contemporary art?

A   Gel printing isn't a new technique, but social media has given it a new role by allowing artists, like me, to share their processes. Gel printing's accessibility aids experimentation and innovation, which can help artists push the boundaries of their creativity. Its use with various media makes it great for mixed-media artists. It can be integrated with painting, collage and drawing, making it a versatile medium. Plus the dopamine-driven moments of pulling a gel print, unsure of the results, are incredibly exciting.

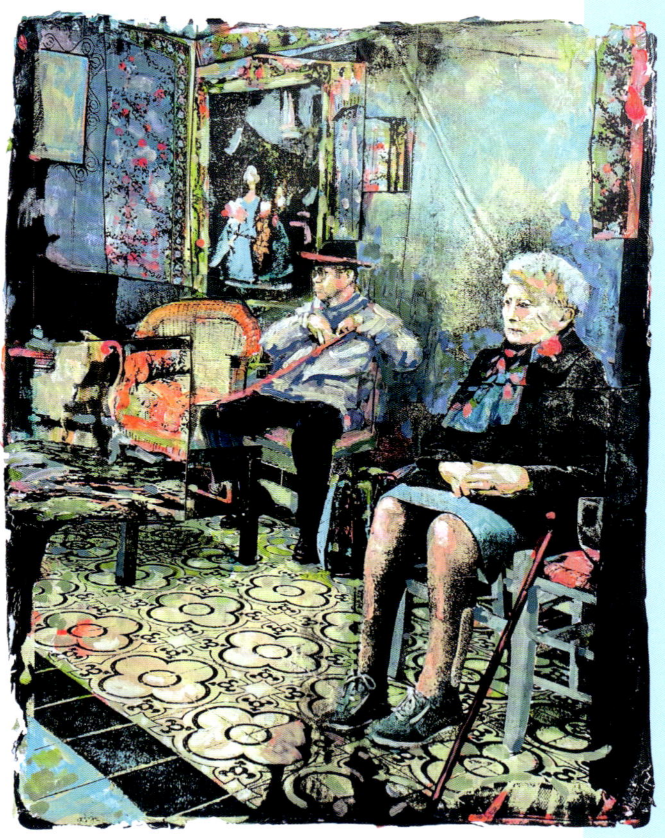

Elles Attendent, monotype, 16 x 20in, 2024

Q   What projects or directions are you excited about exploring in the future?

A   I'm excited about pushing the boundaries of gel printing to create intricate, layered compositions. I'm passionate about expanding themes of memory and culture in my art. I look forward to having more exhibitions where I can share my work. I also love sharing my process through teaching and social media, making art more accessible and inspiring to others.

Q   What advice would you give to beginners who are just starting with gel printing?

A   Embrace the struggles as part of the process. To improve your transfers, build up your photography and editing skills; these can make a significant difference in your results. Image transfers can be frustrating, but when they succeed it feels so great. Repurpose failed gel prints; they can lead to unexpected creativity and new techniques. Most importantly, be resilient and enjoy the journey. Each attempt, whether successful or not, contributes to your growth as an artist. Keep pushing forward, and let your creativity guide you.

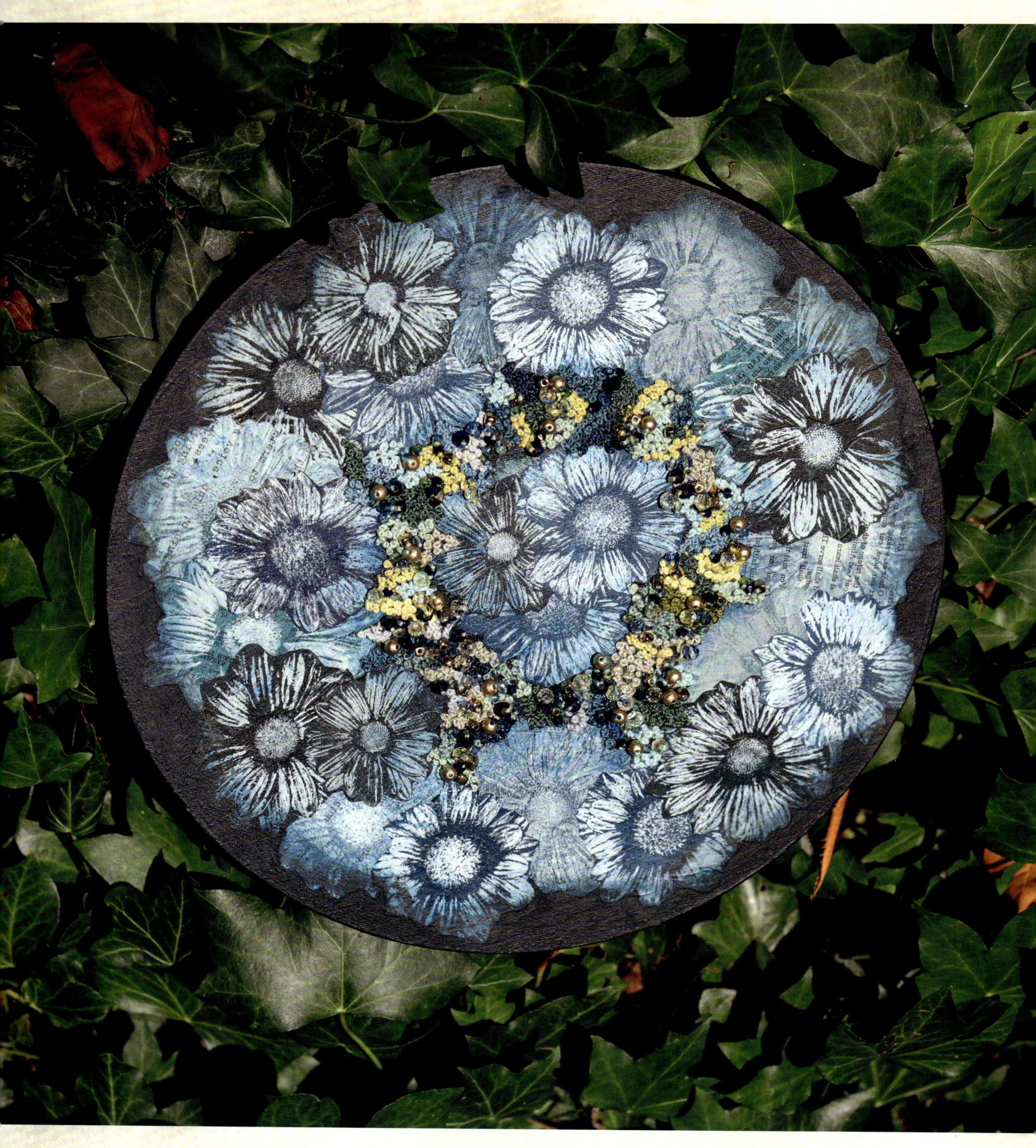

SAPPHIRE BLUE BLOOMS

The idea for this project came to me during a time of unexpected rest. Earlier this year, I was away on a weekend to Paris with some friends from art school when an accident there left me with a broken shoulder. Back home in Inverness, I found I needed to slow down and take a break from my usual busy routine.

During my recovery, I picked up Fleur Woods' *The Untamed Thread,* which inspired me to try slow stitching. It felt like the perfect way to gently ease back into creating since slow stitching is a mindful process which encourages focus without distractions.

As a mixed-media artist, I love the endless possibilities for creativity. I recently designed a flower-themed course for a collaboration with Francisca Nunes on the Flowers Magic Art Fest. The lesson involved making a circular collage painting from flowers printed using a gel plate. This finished piece was in my studio when I decided to experiment and add some stitching and beading to it.

I didn't know too much about embroidery so I bought a beginner's kit to start learning, in particular about how to do French knots because they looked so pretty. I tested stitching through the canvas and found it worked perfectly, except over the wooden frame. To stitch here, you could remove the canvas material, stitch and reattach it.

Combining printmaking with stitching has been a great discovery, and it has opened up exciting new possibilities for my work which I'm looking forward to exploring further. I hope you will enjoy following along with this relaxing project. Take your time and enjoy the process.

MATERIALS

Refer back to the master list on page 18 for the essential items.

- 30cm (12in) circular canvas
- Gel plate – I used a 18 x 13cm (7 x 5in) one
- White gesso
- Various sizes of paintbrush
- Acrylic paint: Indigo, Payne's Grey, Titanium White and Titan Green Pale
- Palette knife
- Brayer or roller (two, if possible)
- Wet-strength tissue paper, Maruishi paper or Chinese rice paper
- Fresh flowers – I used chrysanthemums

- Baren or flat lid
- Copy paper, old book pages, music sheets, dressmaking pattern paper and hand-dyed paper
- Small precision scissors
- Matte medium glue
- Rubber catalyst wedge
- Acrylic ink: Muted Turquoise (I used Liquitex)
- Paper towels and baby wipes
- Matt UV varnish
- Various colours of embroidery thread and an embroidery needle and threader
- Small beads

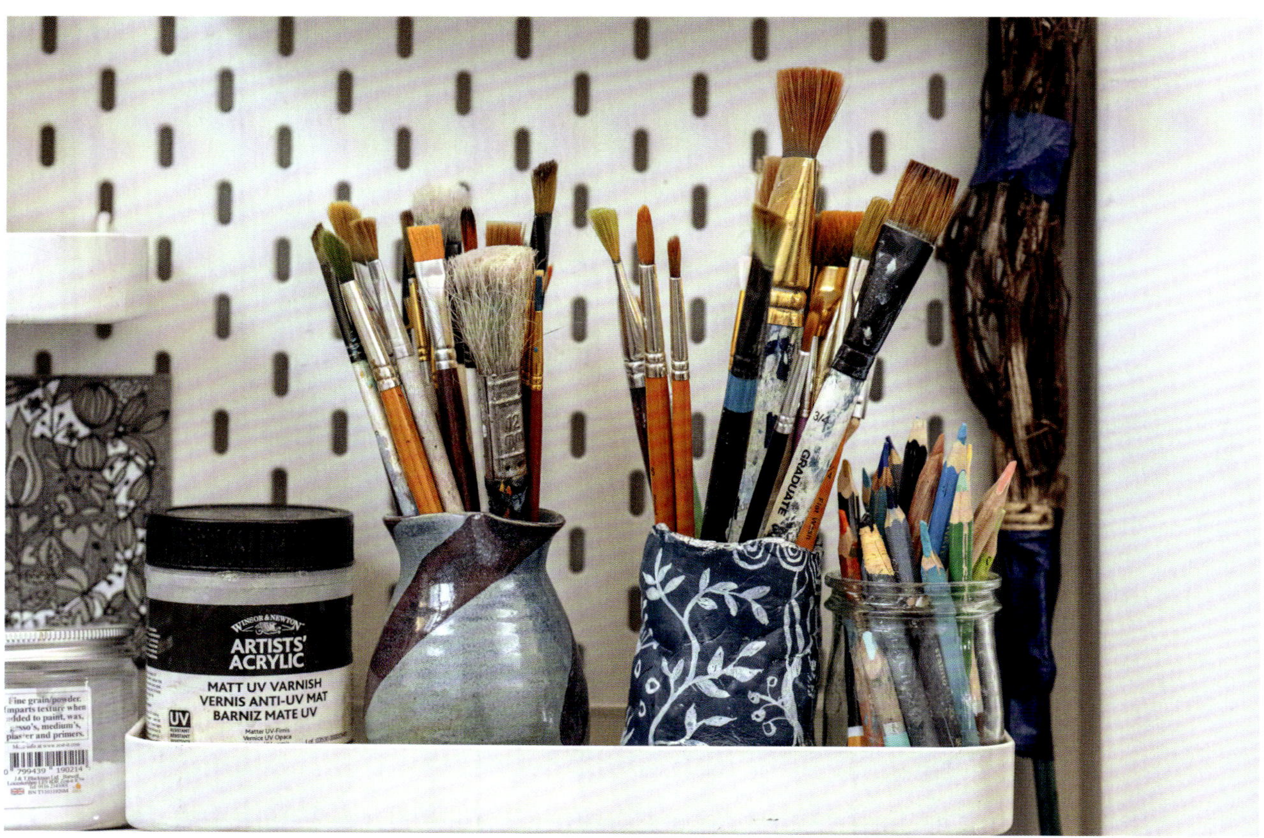

Notes on the equipment and materials used

The canvas

For this project, you'll need a circular canvas. These can be bought individually or in sets of different sizes. Here, I've used a 30cm (12in) frame, but I've also made similar projects using smaller sizes, so don't worry if you can't find this exact size. Since you can only stitch through the open areas of canvas, it's also important to consider the width of the wooden frame when choosing your canvas.

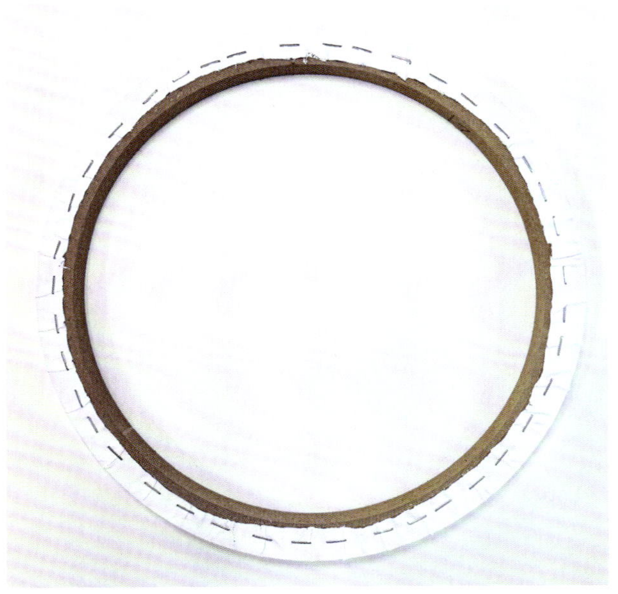

The wood around this frame is quite narrow.

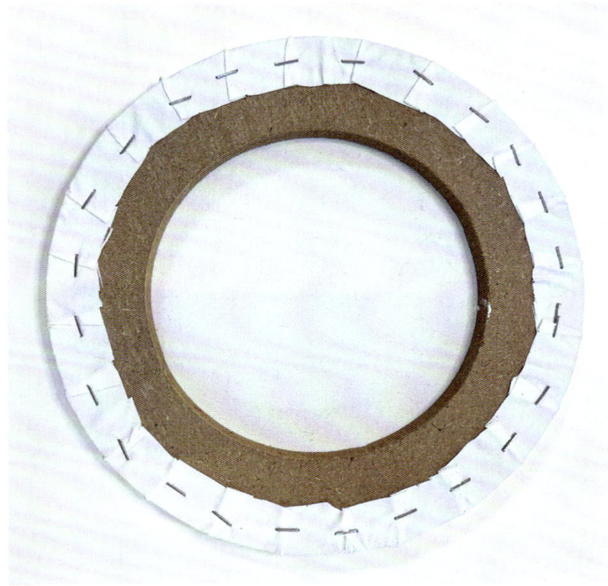

Here, the frame is chunkier.

The gel plate

I've chosen to use a smaller gel plate for this project because I only need to ink up small areas with paint. If you only have a larger plate, simply use a small section of it.

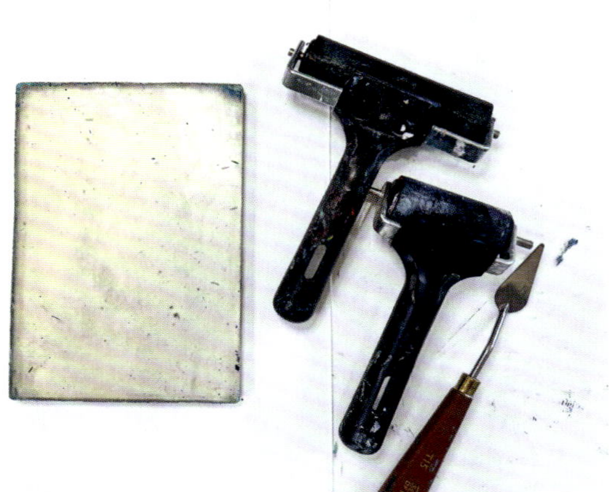

My 18 x 13cm (7 x 5in) plate.

The flowers

This project can be made year-round. The flowers I've used are chrysanthemums, which are available from florists throughout the year.

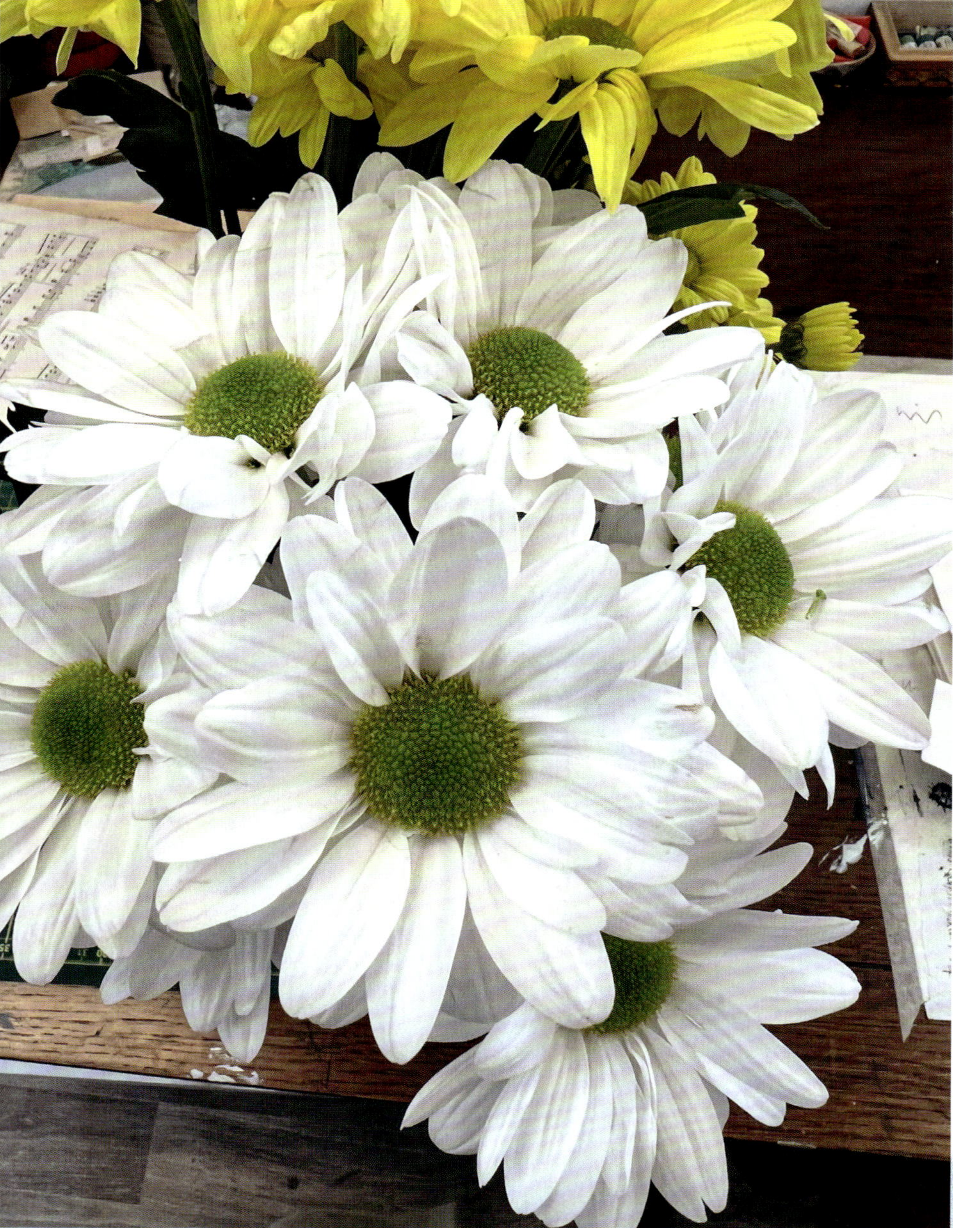

I like chrysanthemums because they lie nice and flat, and the central disc floret doesn't protrude too much.

The paint

The paint I used was a mix of student-grade, professional and open acrylics. I also used acrylic ink as a final step. I always recommend using what you already have instead of rushing out to buy more paints.

The paper

For this project, I primarily used wet-strength tissue paper and Maruishi paper – they're very thin and have a beautiful transparent quality. Chinese rice paper also works well as it doesn't leave raised edges when glued down. Additionally, thin book pages, music sheets, hand-dyed copy paper and dressmaking pattern paper work well for collaging, as they blend seamlessly into the composition.

I use an assortment of thin papers to create the collage.

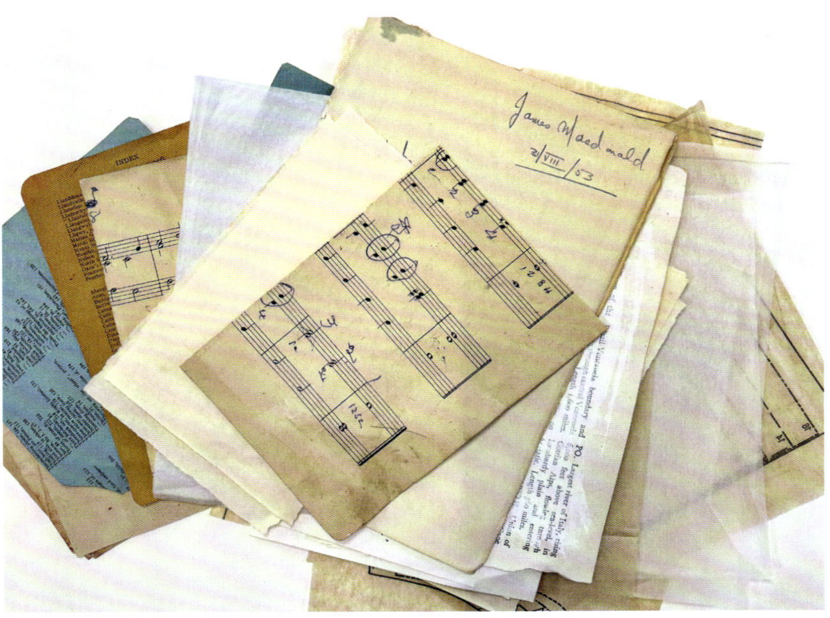

Embellishments

To decorate this project, I used embroidery threads, an embroidery needle, a needle threader and small beads.

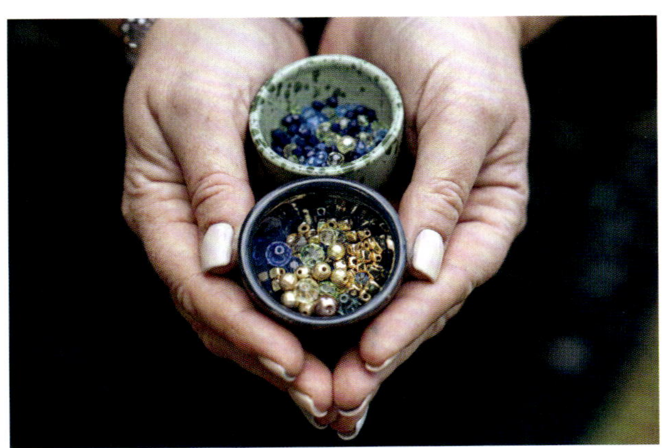

I've chosen beads in cool colours that complement the blue flowers to create a calm, soothing effect. To add contrast, I've included gold beads, as I love how they pair beautifully with blues and turquoises.

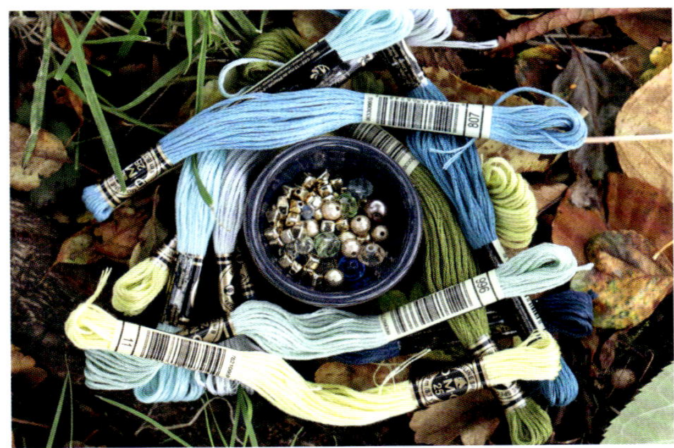

Embroidery thread is made of six strands twisted together. Separating them allows you to choose how many strands to use, depending on whether you want thick or fine stitches.

Printing the flowers

Start by painting the canvas with white gesso (see page 47) to prepare the surface for the paint and collage. Next, paint the background with Indigo (a); two coats will cover the white gesso nicely.

Mix some Indigo and Payne's Grey using a palette knife to create a dark blue colour on your palette (b). Apply a small amount of the paint to the plate and then roll it out using a brayer or roller (c). Next, gently press the flower onto the paint, making sure all areas of the flower are lightly pressed down (d).

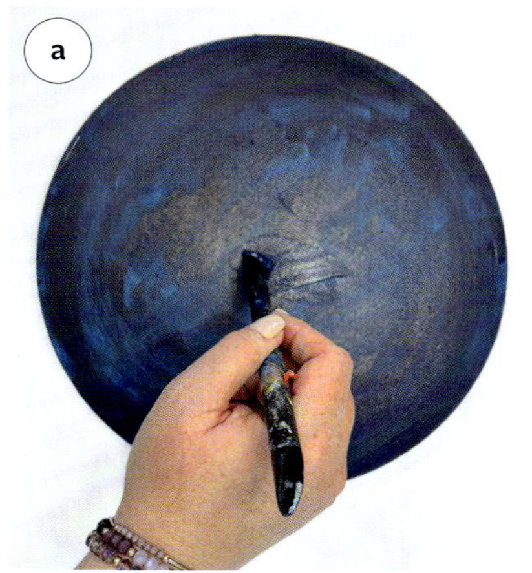

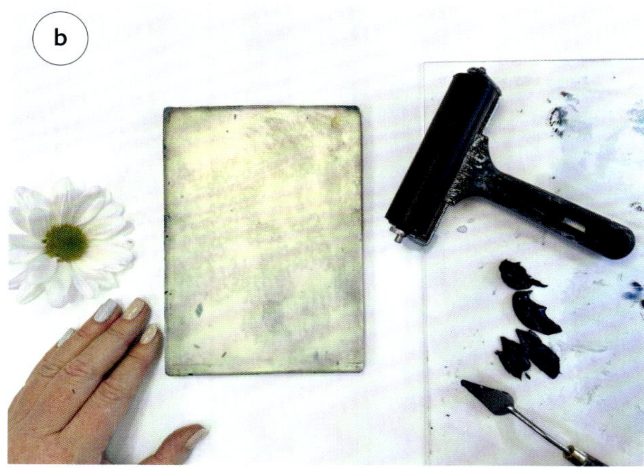

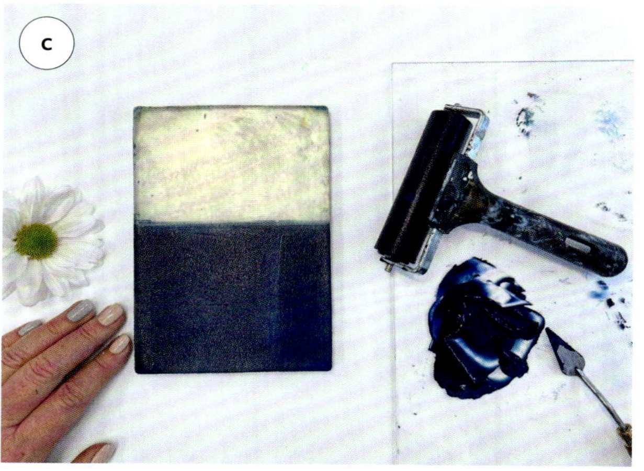

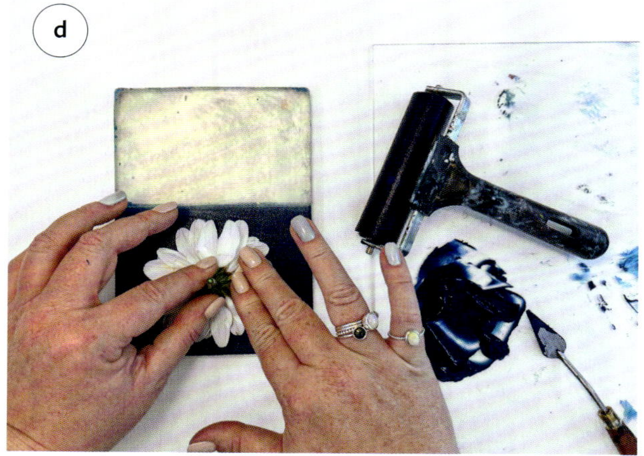

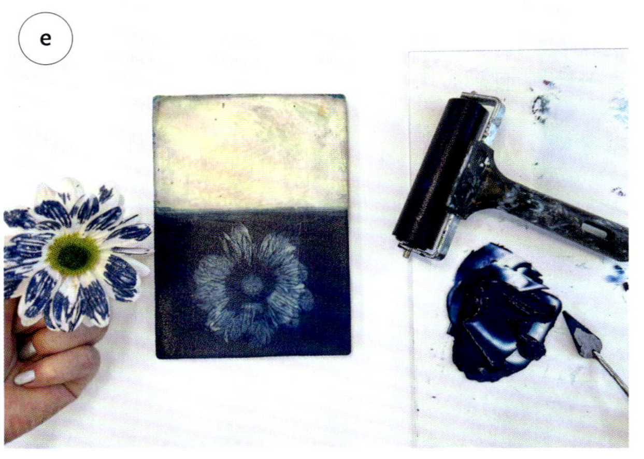

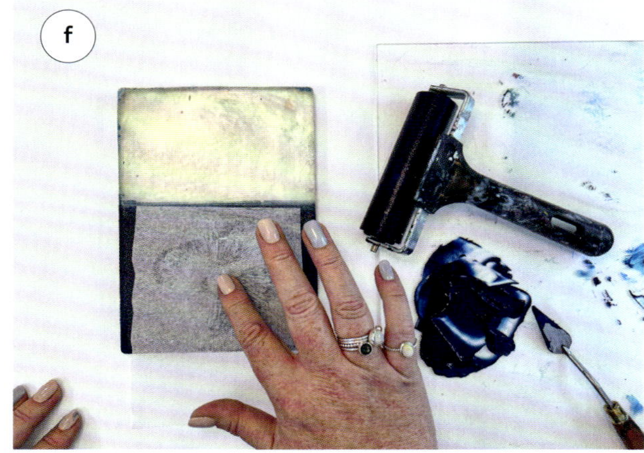

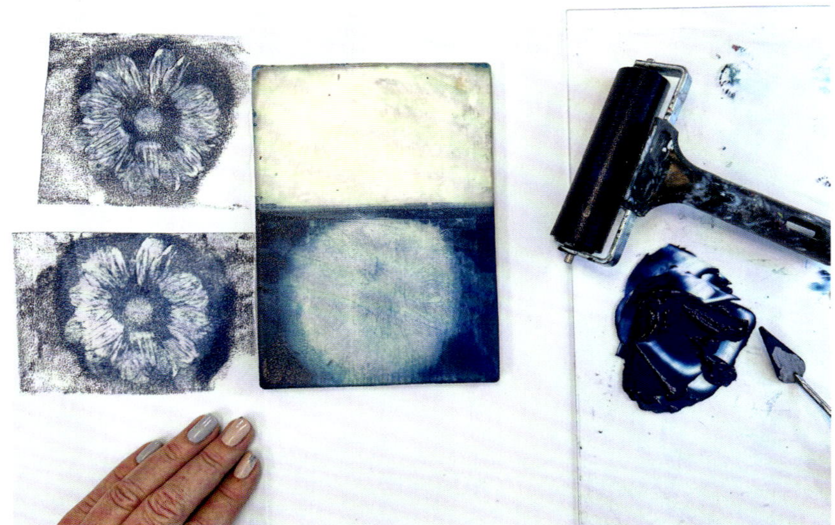

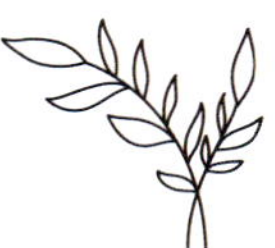

Tip

When I place a print on a dark background, it sometimes disappears. To help the flower stand out more clearly against the dark blue background, I roll some Titanium White or Titan Green Pale paint onto the gel plate and press the back of the print onto it.

Lift the flower to reveal the imprint on the paint (e). You can use the same flower two or three times, but after that the petals will fall off and the impression won't be as detailed. Next, gently lay a piece of tissue or Maruishi paper on top (f); you may be able to get two prints from this impression (g). Continue the process on a variety of papers. As some prints will be more detailed than others, it's a good idea to have a number of prints to choose from.

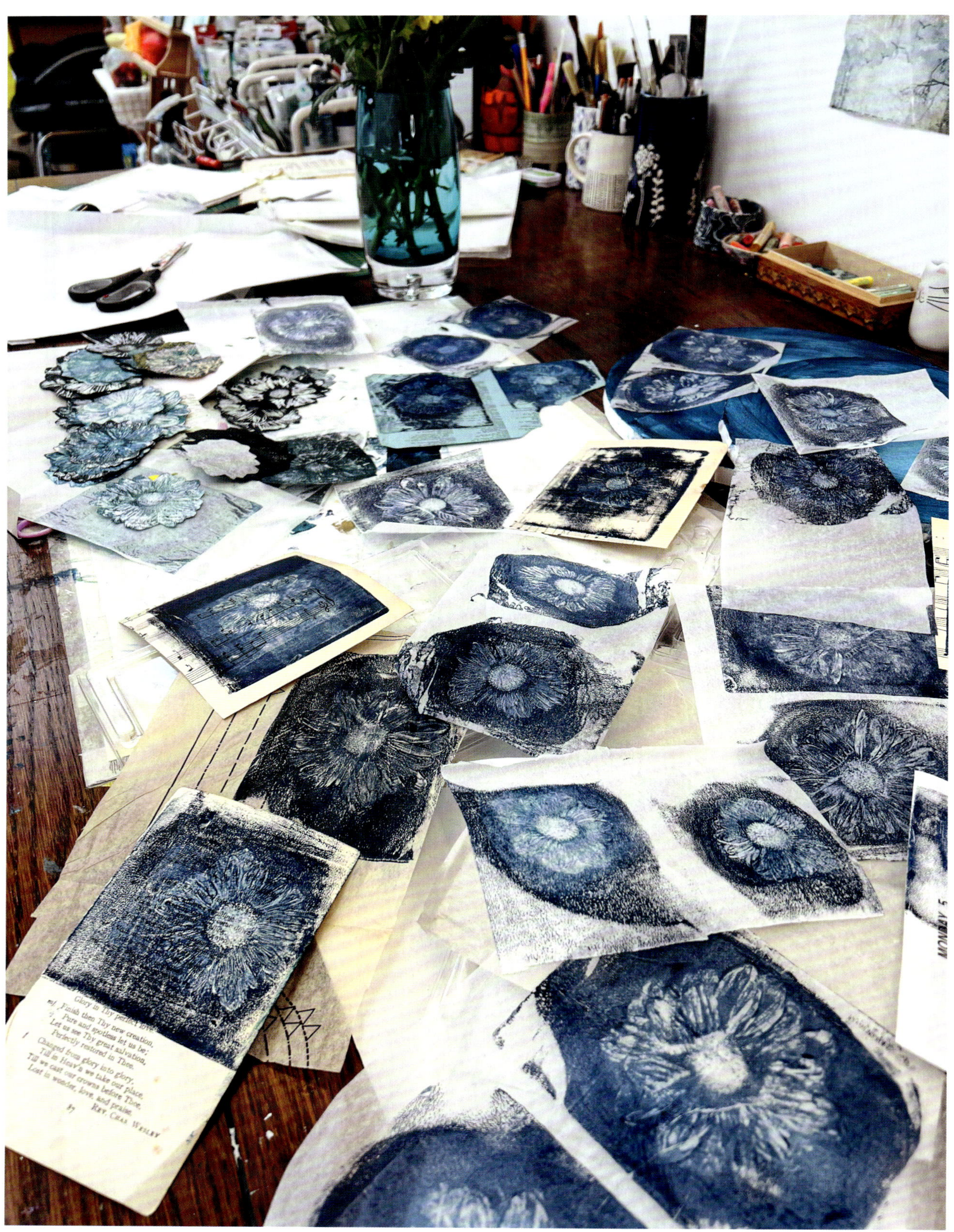

Here you can see how many prints I have made. Not all of them will be used for this project; I like to save extras for future projects.

Creating contrast

I rolled a thin, even layer of dark blue paint onto the gel plate and placed a sheet of wet-strength tissue paper over it to create a dark background. I repeated this process several times to make multiple dark background papers ready for printing. If you have a spare gel plate or a larger one, you can place your paper directly on top of the gel plate and press firmly (a). This adds more pressure and improves the print quality.

Next, I cleaned the gel plate and rolled on a layer of white paint – heavy body Liquitex Titanium White works well for this technique (b). I pressed the flower into the white paint (c) and stamped it onto the dark paper (d), creating a striking contrast.

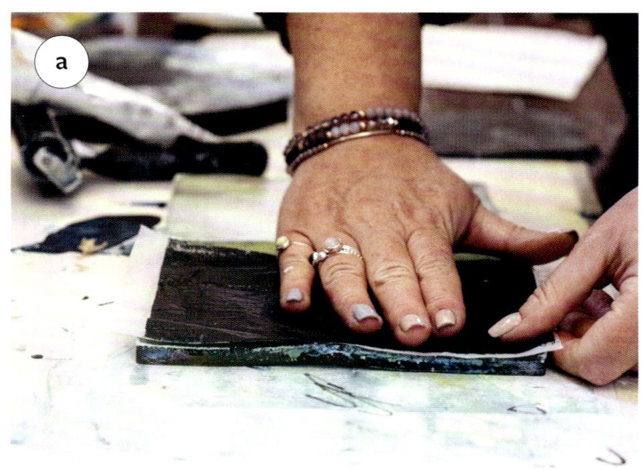

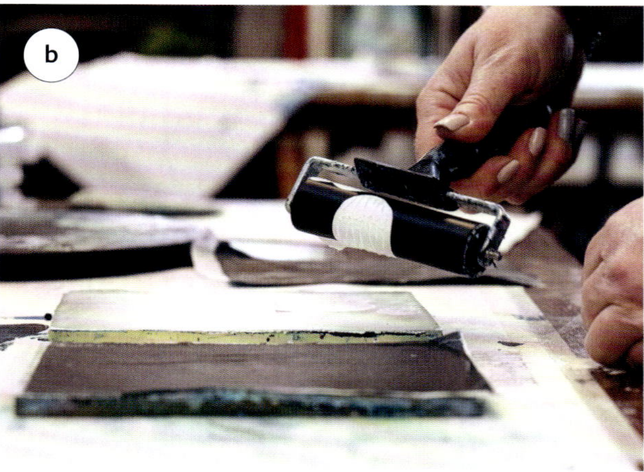

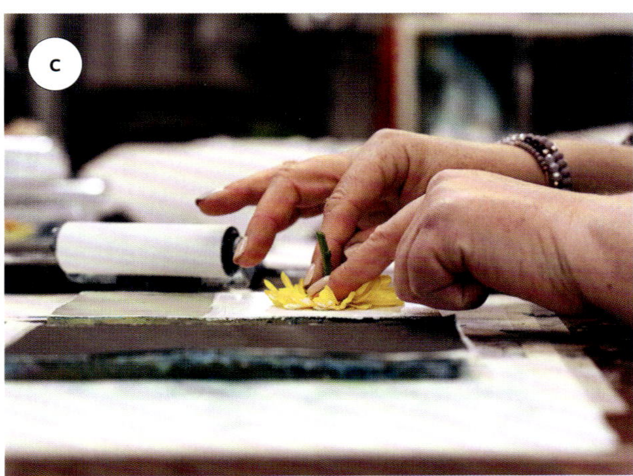

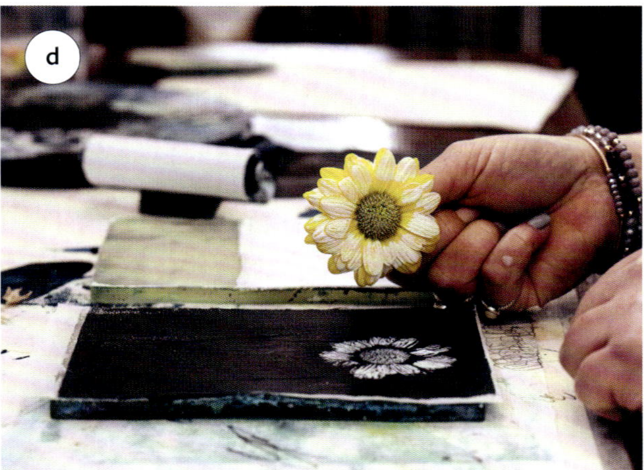

Arranging and gluing the flower shapes to the canvas

I use precision scissors to carefully cut out the flower shapes. If the paper is very thin, I place another sheet behind it to make cutting easier and neater (a).

Next, I place the flowers on the dark blue background, arranging them in a layered circular pattern (b).

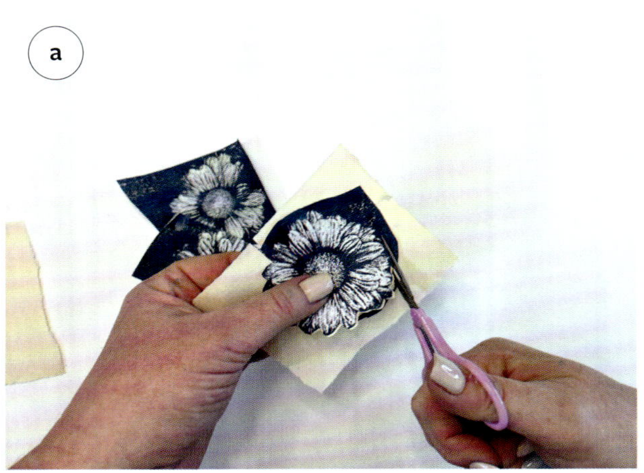

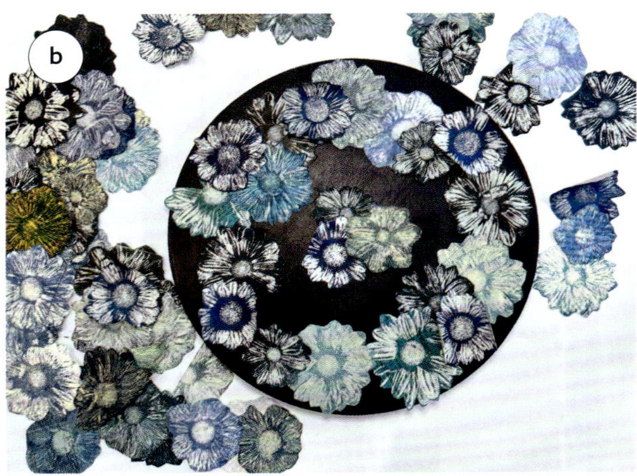

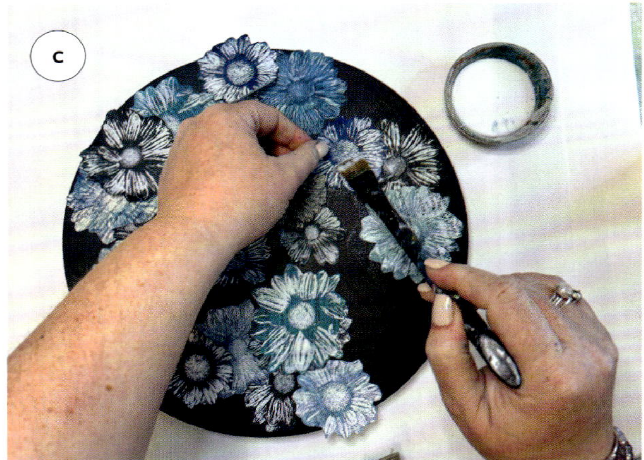

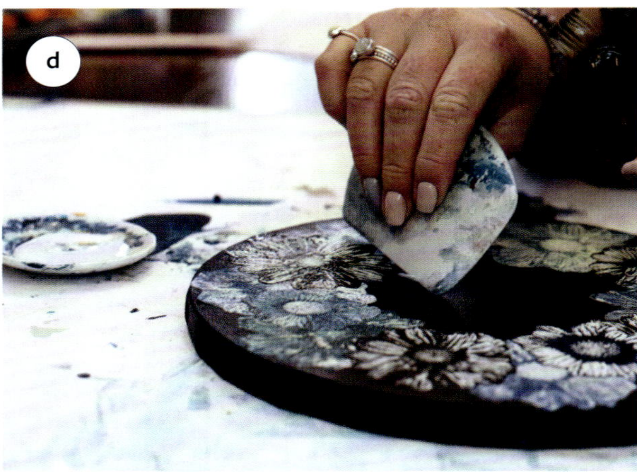

To glue the flowers onto the canvas, I use a brush to paint a layer of matte medium glue on the surface (c). If the paper is thicker, I apply the medium to both the canvas and the paper. For tissue paper, I can place it directly on the canvas.

I then use a brush to smooth out any wrinkles and gently press out any air bubbles or excess glue with a rubber catalyst wedge (d). Once all the papers are glued down, I let that layer dry completely, then I paint the entire surface of the canvas with matte medium glue to make sure everything sticks well.

Tip

Take a photo when you're happy with the arrangement of the flowers, as it's easy to forget once you start gluing them down.

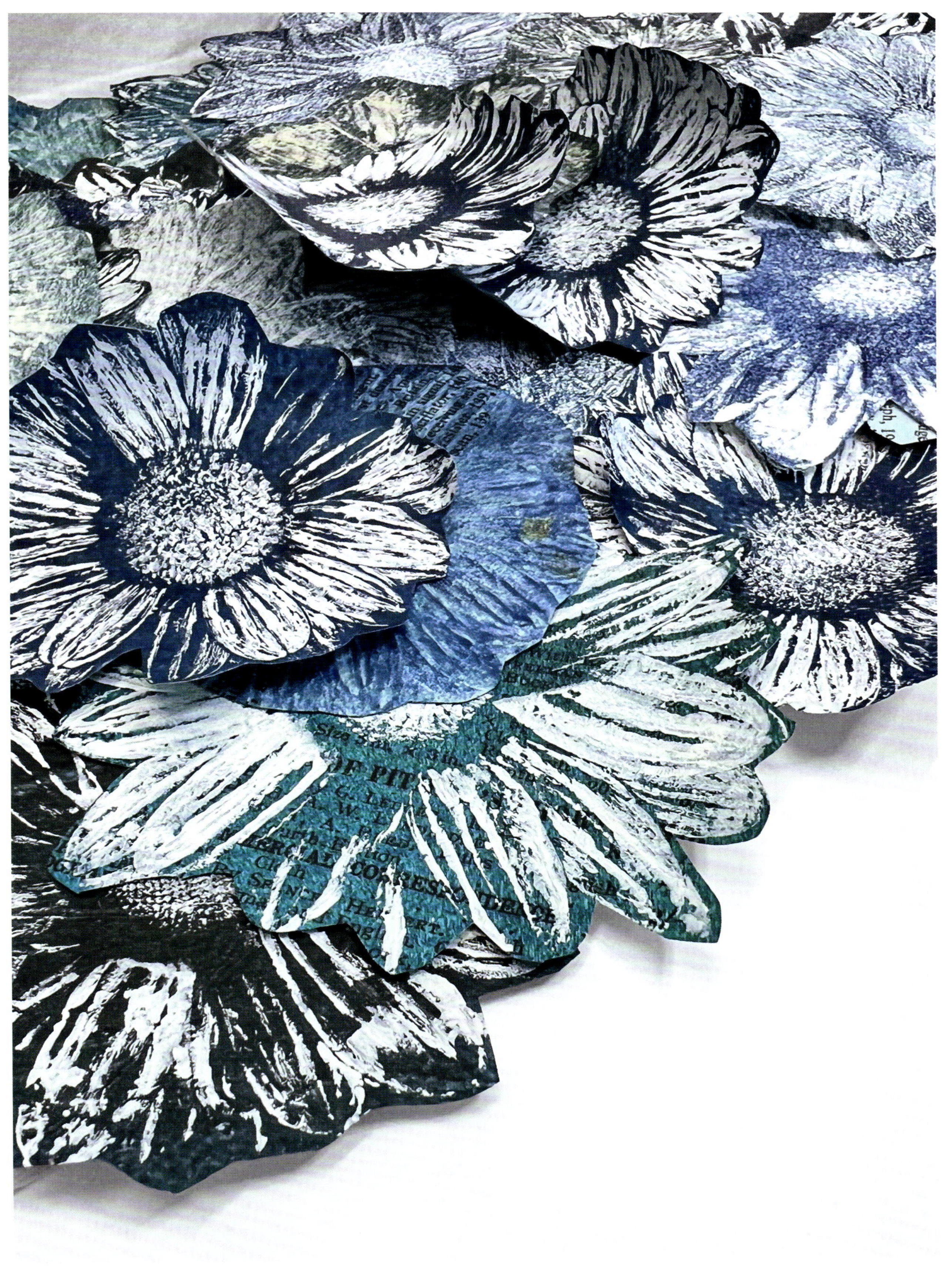

Adding an ink wash glaze

For the final layer, I use Muted Turquoise acrylic ink to create a glaze that brings the piece together. I dilute the ink in a small dish before painting it over the flowers (a). I blot some areas with a dry paper towel and use a baby wipe to lift the ink in certain spots, adding highlights.

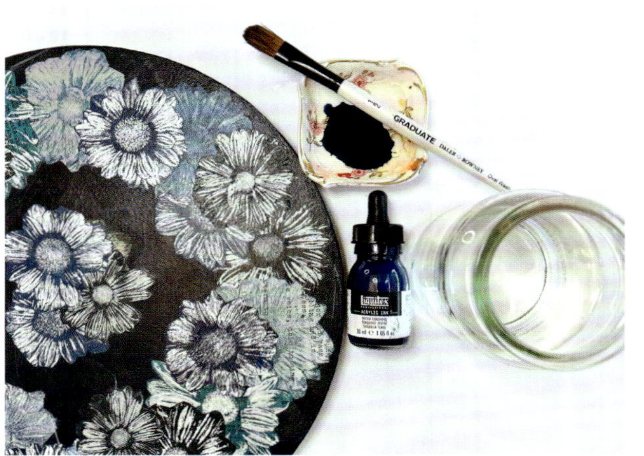
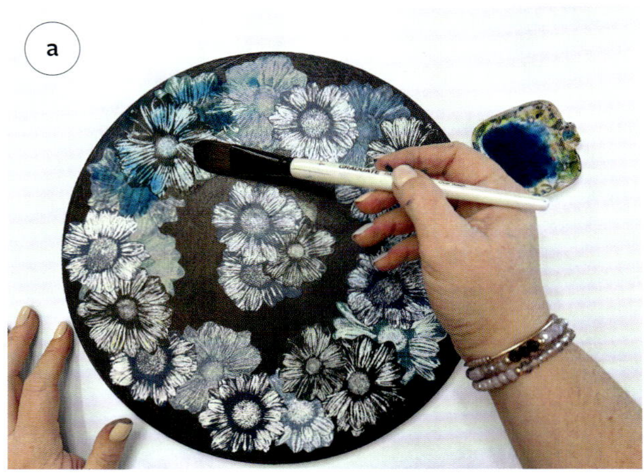

Tip

If you're unsure about the ink's strength, test it on a separate piece of paper before applying it to your finished painting.

If you are selling the artwork, as a final step for protection and to prevent UV damage, you can apply a couple of layers of matt UV varnish to the piece.

Embellishing the project

Begin by cutting a piece of embroidery thread about 65cm (26in) long – any longer, and it becomes harder to handle. Use a needle threader to thread the embroidery needle (a) – I'd recommend using three strands of thread.

Adding beads

Bring the threaded needle up through the back of the canvas at the spot where you want to attach the bead. Slide the bead onto the needle (b) and push it down onto the thread until it rests against the canvas.

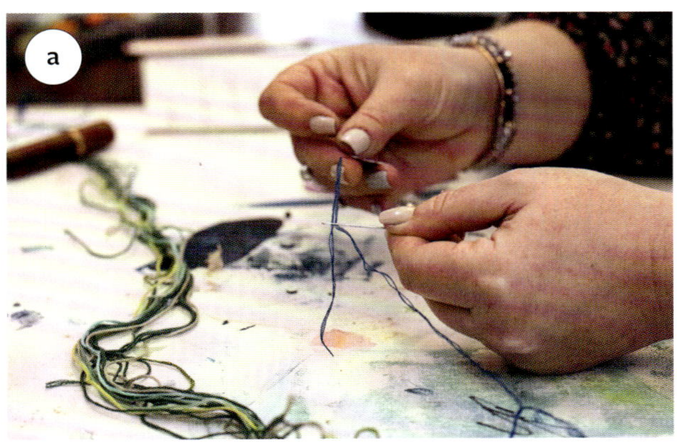

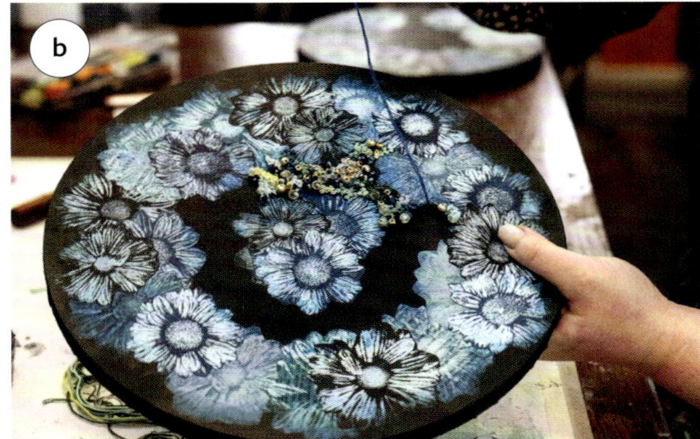

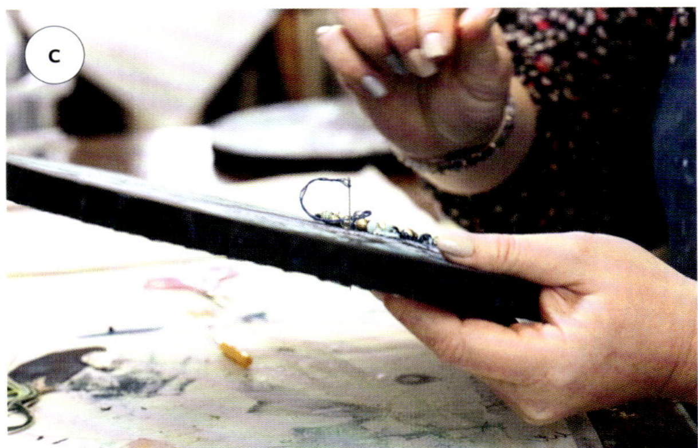

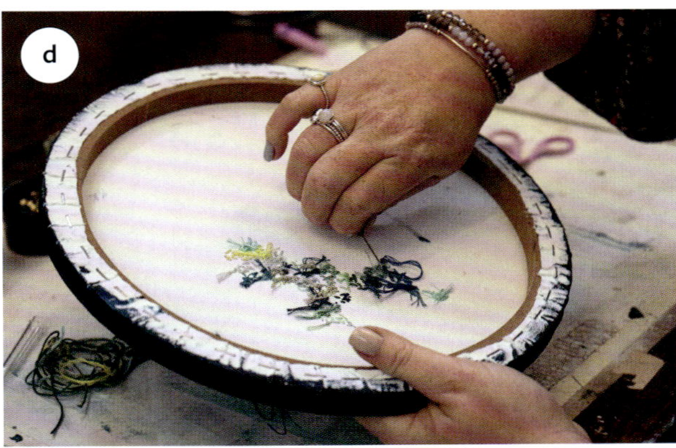

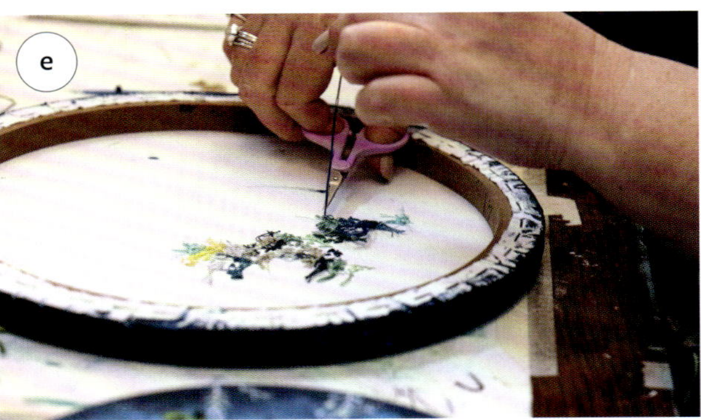

Next, insert the needle back into the canvas very close to where it first came up, pulling the thread snug to secure the bead in place (c). Repeat this process for each bead, spacing them as needed for your design.

When you've finished sewing on the beads, bring your needle through a few stitches at the back of the canvas to secure your thread and prevent it from coming loose (d). Tie and then trim any excess threads to neaten the back (e).

French knots

Thread three strands onto the needle, move it to the middle and tie the ends together in a knot. This will ensure you get a larger, thicker knot. Bring the needle through the fabric from the back to the front at the spot where you want the knot (a). Hold the thread taut with one hand and wrap it around the needle twice (b).

Point the needle back down into the fabric very close to where it first came up, but not in the same hole, to prevent the knot from slipping through (c). While holding the thread tight near the canvas, slowly pull the needle all the way through to the back. This will tighten the wrapped thread into a neat knot (d). To finish, secure the thread on the back with a few small stitches or tie it off.

Tip

To make it easier to see where to start sewing, use your needle to stab a few small holes in the canvas to create a guide.

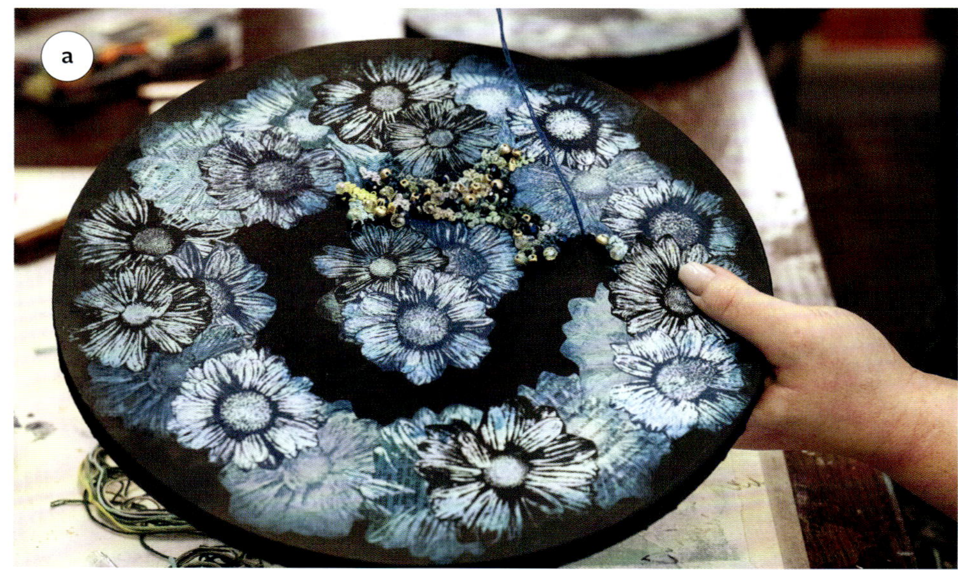

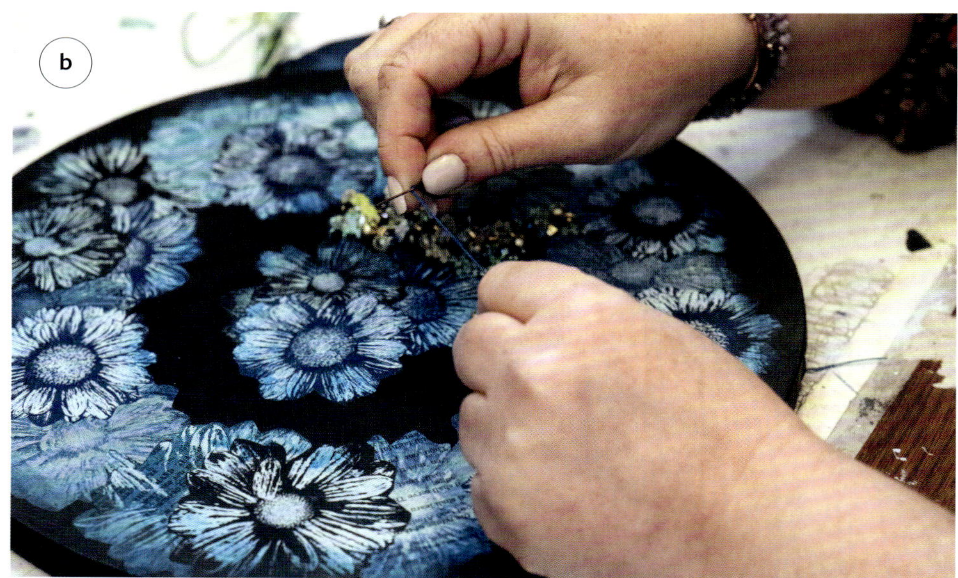

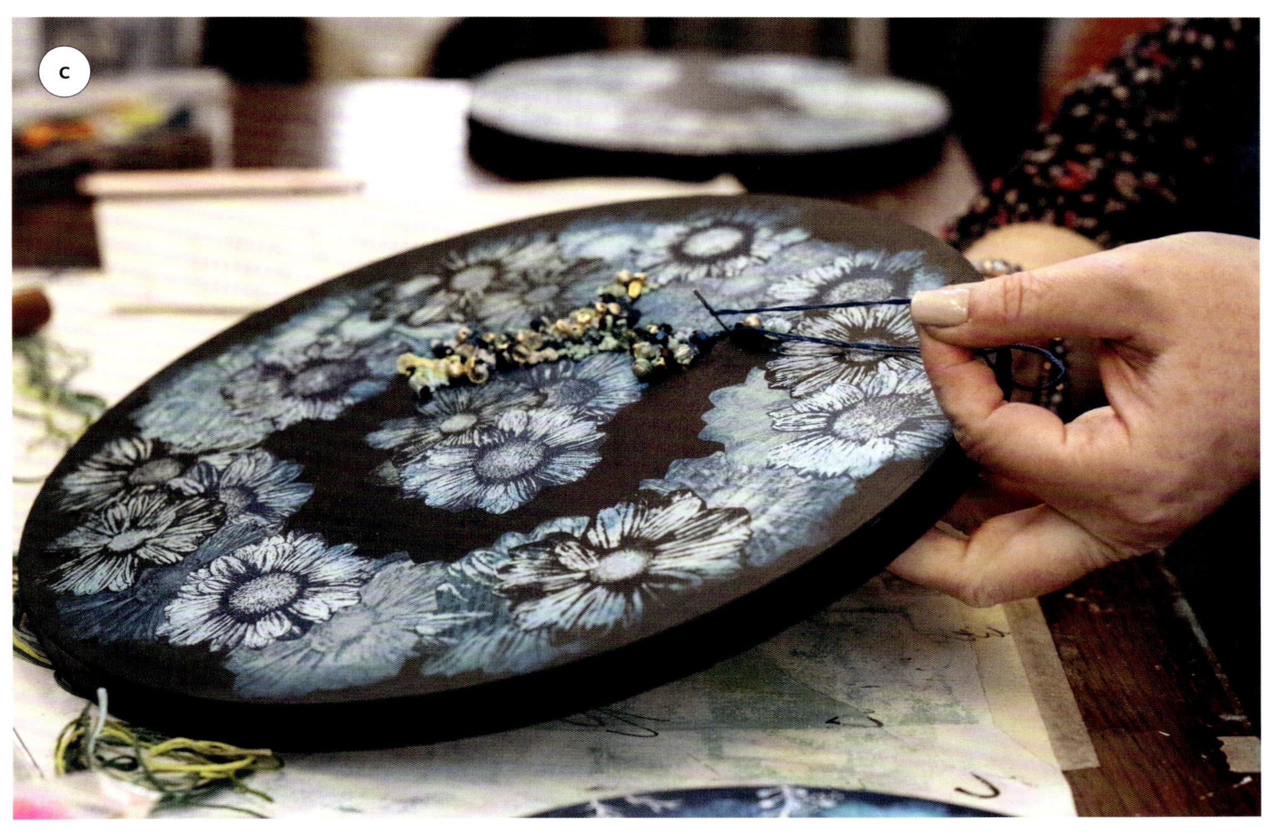

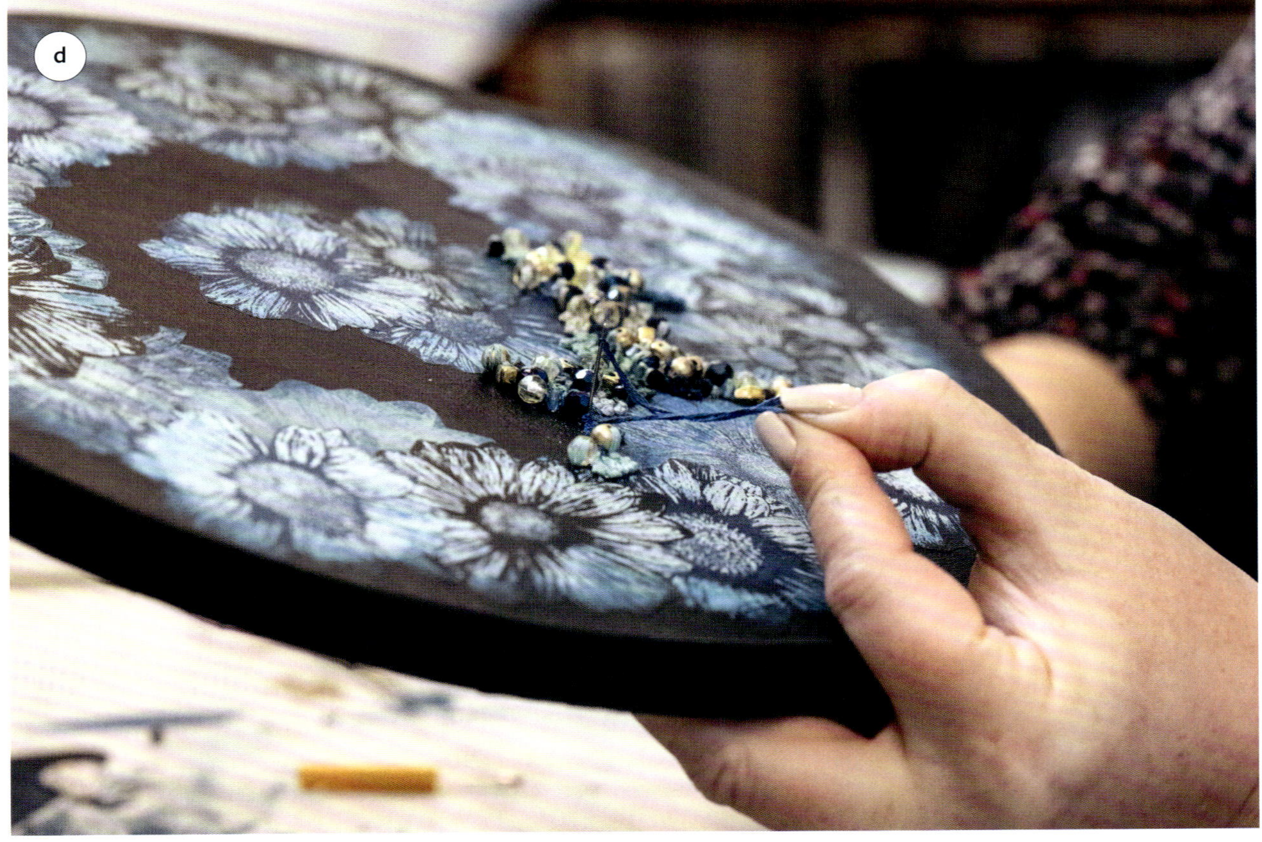

Q **Can you share a little about your background and how you discovered gel printing?**

A I have had an eclectic creative journey. When my firstborn was 8 months old, I began attending an evening college course in calligraphy. This led me to studying graphic design and starting my own wedding stationery business. For years I tutored groups in calligraphy and special-occasion stationery. I also spent several years in the print industry, working as a graphic designer and later as the manager of a print shop. Throughout this time, I developed a passion for photography and completed a diploma in the field. Urban sketching, particularly architecture, is another area of interest. For the past twelve years, I have worked full time as the creative director of a not-for-profit Australian media company.

It was a sketching friend, Anne, who first introduced me to gel printing. Intrigued, I bought my first gel plate that very afternoon, and the incredible world of gel printing opened up to me.

Q **What drew you to using a gel plate in your artwork?**

A In *Refuse to Choose!* Barbara Sher talks about scanners – those people who love too many different things to choose just one. This book gave me permission to accept and embrace what I'd struggled with for years. Gel printing allows me to bring together many loves: photography, paper, lettering, design, printmaking, sketching, classic colours and patterns, to name just a few. With gel printing, I can incorporate all those (and more!) into my art practice.

Q **Who or what are your main influences in your art practice?**

A This is a tough one to answer! When I first discovered gel printing, most of the prints and artwork out there featured bright colours and cutesy designs. I knew that wasn't my style, but I could see the potential to use the medium in a way that reflected my own aesthetic and colour palette. I looked much broader, in galleries and online, seeking inspiration and always asking myself, 'How can that be adapted for the gel plate?'

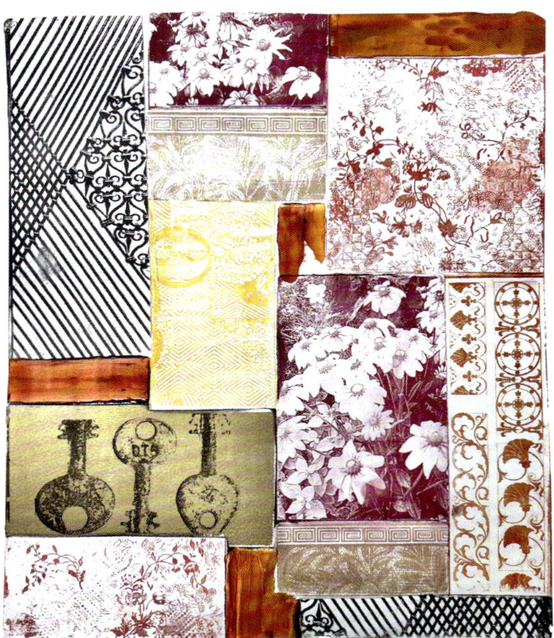

Gel plate patchwork

Q **How do you see the role of gel printing in the broader context of contemporary art?**

A Although gel printing has been around for a while, I think we are currently witnessing significant development in this form of printmaking. I see established artists bringing gel printing into their practice in incredible ways. It's exciting to be part of its growth and evolution.

Q **What projects or directions are you excited about exploring in the future?**

A I am constantly looking for ways to push the boundaries of gel printing, particularly in the area of image transfer. I also love teaching others what I am learning through in-person and online workshops and courses. I am thrilled when I see or hear of those breakthrough 'a-ha' moments! I'm planning to cut back on my day job and delve deeper into my art in the coming years, which is both scary and exciting!

Q **What advice would you give to beginners who are just starting with gel printing?**

A You get what you pay for! Buy a well-known branded gel plate (Gel Press and Gelli Arts are the main ones). You can also make your own gel plate, but I recommend you leave that until you have more experience. Buy a quality brayer or roller; my favourite is the Speedball Soft Rubber Roller.

Start by learning the basic techniques. They will set you up well for your gel printing journey to come. Rolling smoothly, principles of addition and subtraction, using stencils, stamps and botanicals will all give you great results early on. Save the more complicated techniques (such as laser image transfer) until you are more familiar with gel printing.

Be inspired by what you see posted on social media but not limited by it. Do your own research and exploration. Record your results in an art journal. Find your own unique style, colours, patterns and techniques.

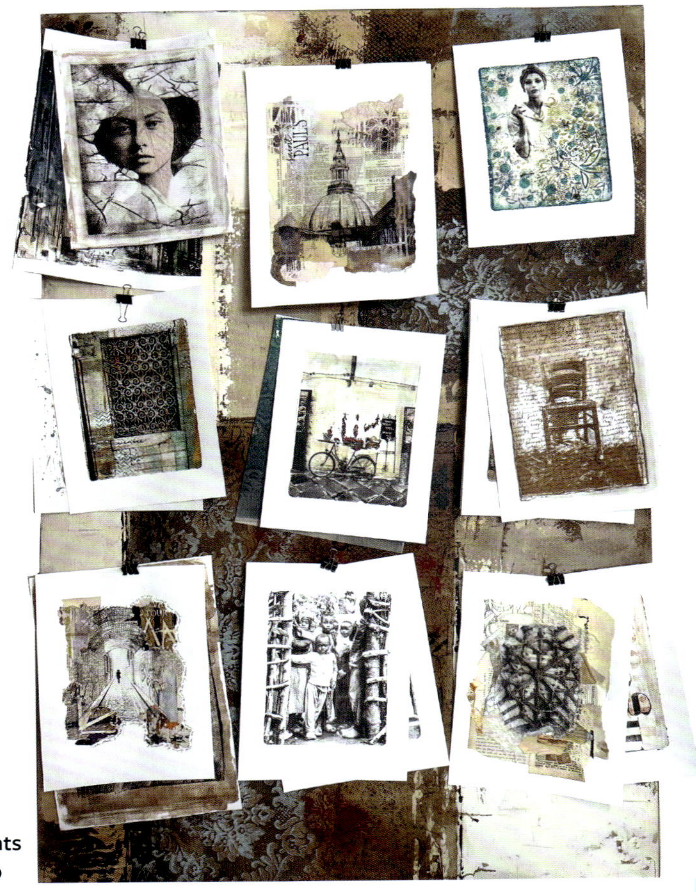

Collection of gel prints hanging in my studio

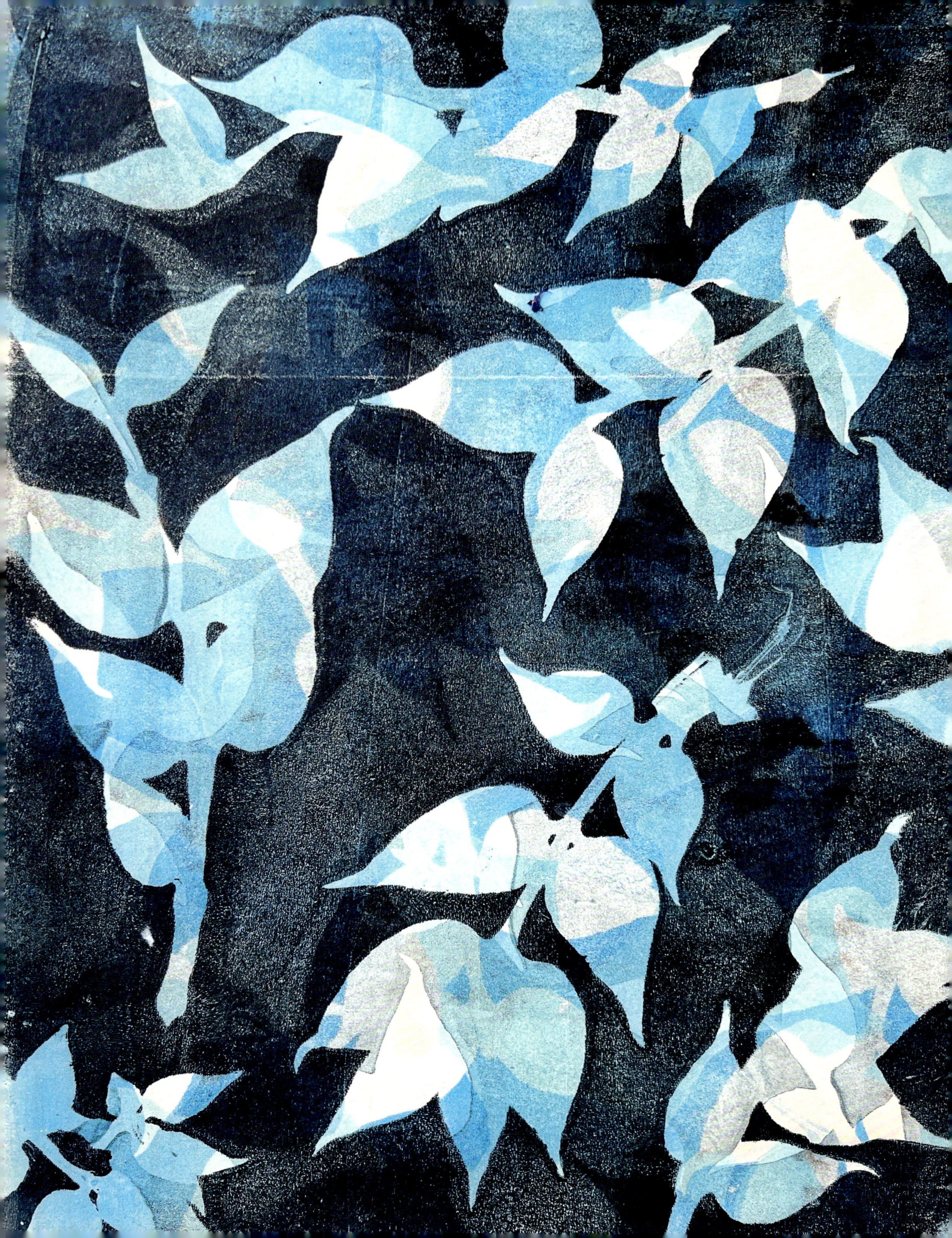

CREATING LAYERS WITH BOTANICAL AND IMAGE TRANSFER

I'd like to show you some of the techniques I use to create layers in my botanical prints. When I talk about layering, I mean building up textures, colours and patterns by adding different elements on top of each other. I usually start with a simple base layer, like a plant silhouette. Once that dries, I continue adding layers. The key is to mix transparent and opaque colours – sometimes I want the lower layers to show through, and other times I cover them completely. I also use transparent papers to reveal parts of the design underneath. By layering this way, I create a rich, multi-dimensional effect, adding both depth and texture as I work.

Now, I'm going to walk you through step by step how I create a series of prints that will be used for a contemporary art journal, which I'll show you in the next chapter. Let's get started!

MATERIALS
Refer back to the master list on page 18 for the essential items.

- 41 x 51cm (16 x 20in) Gelli Arts plate (you can also use a smaller sized plate)
- Papers: Carnival wet-strength tissue paper, old book pages, A3 (11¾ x 16½in) and A4 (8¼ x 11¾in) copy paper, drawing paper, newsprint, recycled sugar paper, black tissue paper, dressmaking pattern paper, thin sketch paper (around 90gsm)
- Acrylics: Titanium White, Titan Buff, Phthalo Blue (Green Shade), Raw Umber, Phthalo Blue (Red Shade), Teal, Titan Green Pale and Manganese Blue Hue. I used Golden Open Acrylics
- Roller
- Plants and leaves, such as Rowan leaves
- Cotton buds/Q-tips
- Baby wipes

To get the variety of shades you see here, I used avocado stones and skins, tea bags, coffee granules and onion skins boiled in water.

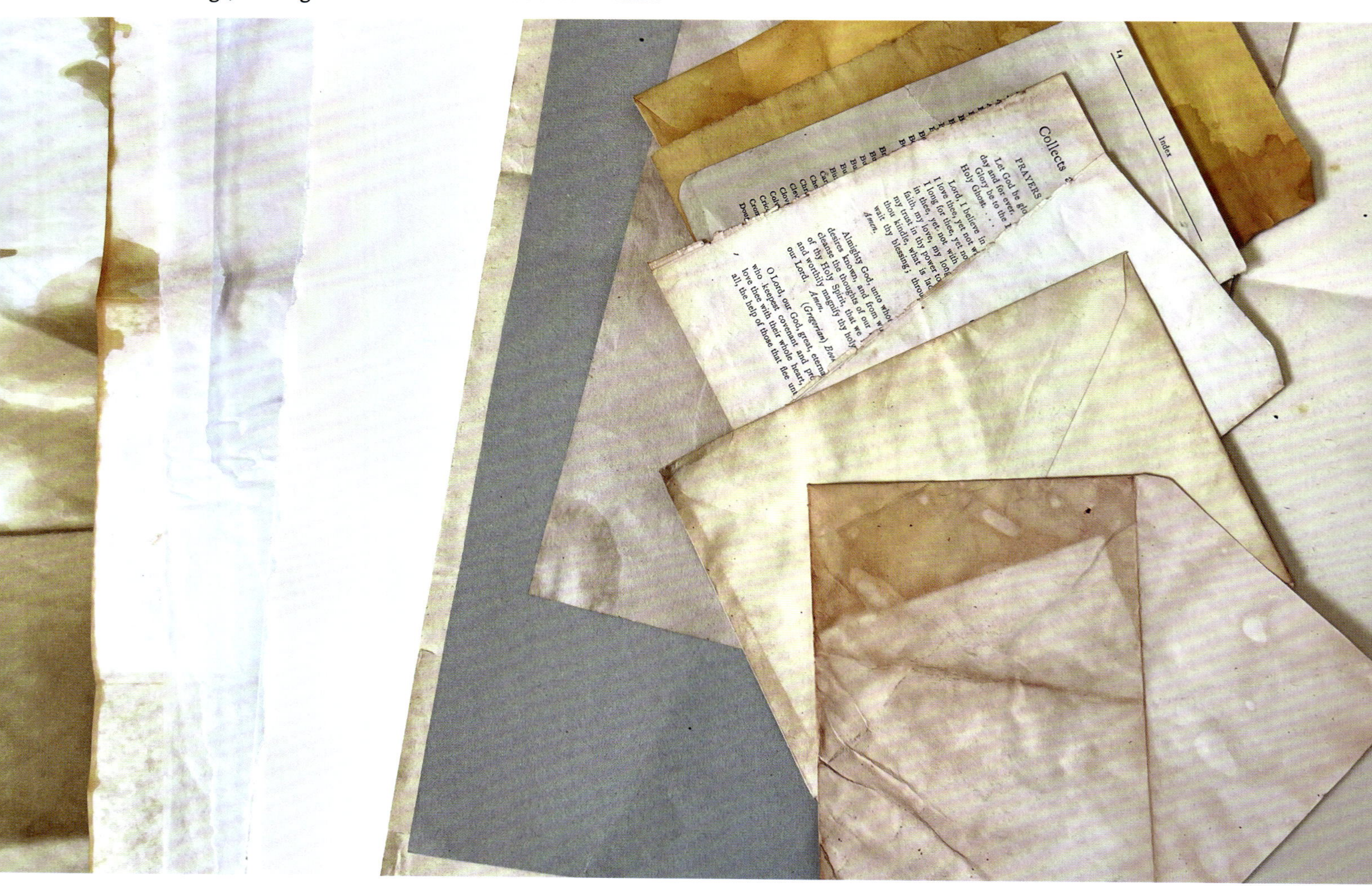

Notes on the equipment and materials used

The papers

For this project, I wanted to give my journal a vintage feel. To create this look, I selected papers with an aged patina. Some of the tones were achieved using natural dyes.

Envelopes, book pages, sketchbook/copy paper can all be dyed easily with items that you will likely have at home already such as tea, coffee, onion skins and avocados. I like to use aluminium foil trays for dye baths.

Simmer onion skins and avocado stones/skins in hot water to release the dye before adding to the tray, or use hot water to make some strong tea or coffee.

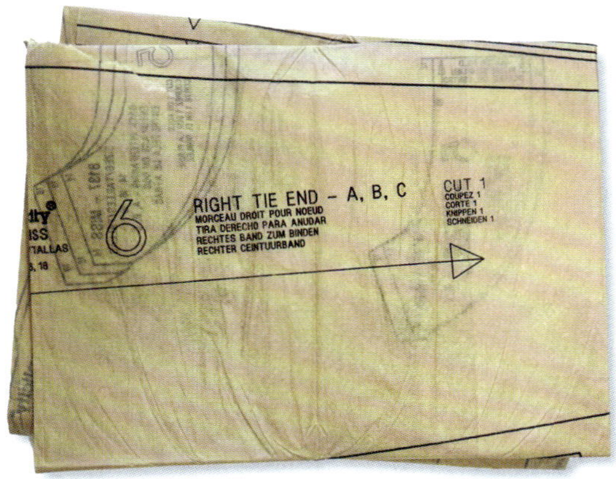

Each ingredient produces its own unique tone, from a ochre yellow to a soft pink, so it is worthwhile experimenting with a few trays to vary your papers.

Submerge your papers one at a time to avoid white patches and leave them to soak overnight. Once dyed, hang the papers to dry and gently iron them to flatten.

Tip

When boiled with a teaspoon of bicarbonate of soda, avocado skins and stones turn the water a surprisingly beautiful pink!

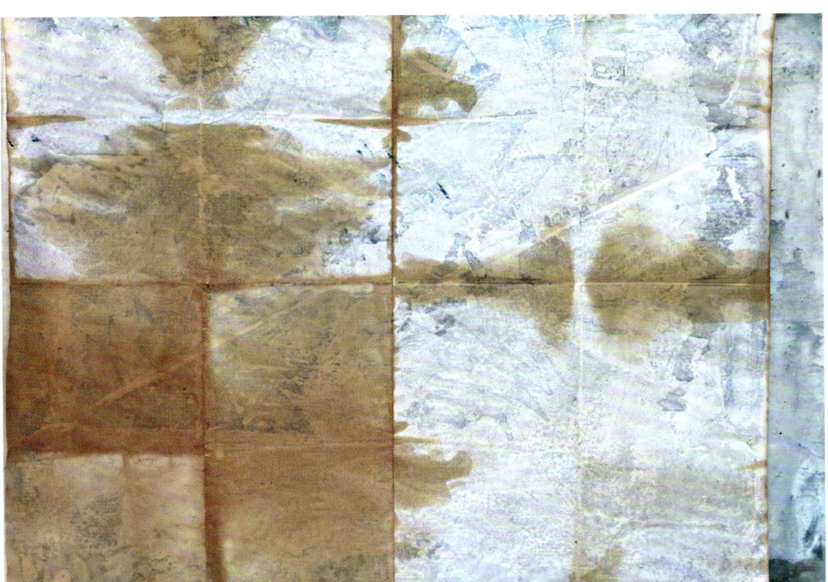

People often ask me, 'Is it archival? Will the paper yellow over time?' Honestly, that's not something I worry about much, because the art style I love has a naturally aged, vintage feel. While it's true that all paper will yellow eventually, there are ways to slow down the process. Using acid-free paper or UV-protected glass and applying UV-resistant varnishes or even encaustic wax can help shield your artwork from the effects of light and keep it looking great for years to come (see page 160 for further useful advice).

One of my studio neighbours at Wasps, Jane Nestor, was having a clear-out and asked if I could find a use for some paper that had been stored away for years. It had belonged to her late father, Austin McCann – an artist himself – and she had salvaged some of his art supplies after he passed. I was delighted to give these papers a new life. I incorporated one of Austin's beautiful botanical sketches that was hidden in the pile of papers into one of my prints (see page 104). Jane was so delighted to see her father's work revived, and even more so when I told her it would be featured in this book. The naturally yellowed pages create a soft, warm background that perfectly complements the shades of blues and teals I love to work with.

For one of the layers I used thin A3 sketchbook paper, folding it before submerging it into tea-infused water to create unique, organic marks on the surface. I also experimented with dyeing old book pages, envelopes and regular copy paper. To add contrast, I incorporated black tissue paper – the opaque silhouettes stand out beautifully against the black paper. Note: this tissue paper is fragile compared to the wet-strength tissue I like to use and tears easily, so you have to handle it carefully when lifting it from the gel plate.

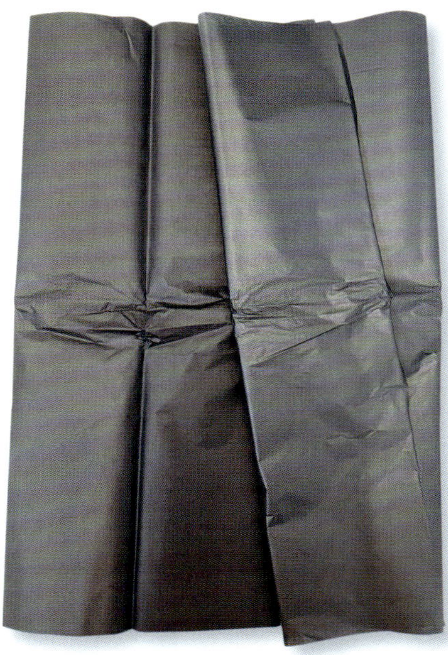

Black tissue paper.

The paints

For this series of prints, I used Golden Open acrylics. These paints are ideal for capturing fine details or working with image transfers because they have a slower drying time compared to other acrylics. They are a bit of an investment, so if you're just starting out I recommend beginning with student-grade acrylics.

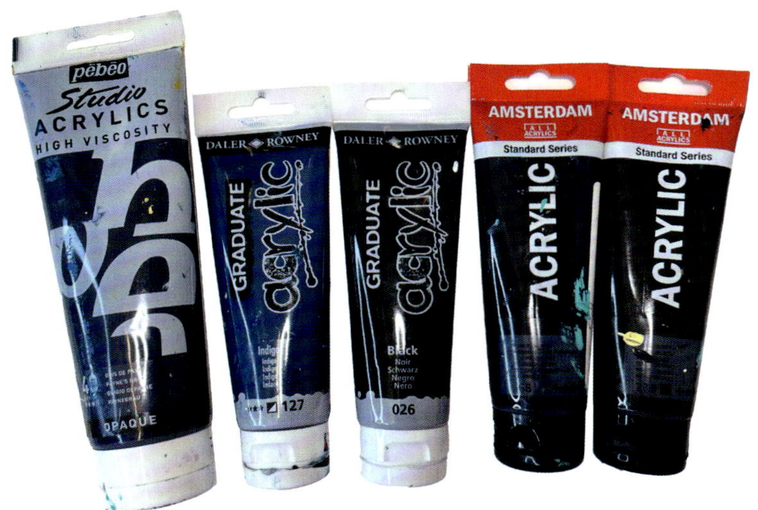

These acrylic paints have worked well for me (left to right): Pébéo Studio Acrylics: Payne's Grey; Daler Rowney Graduate Acrylic: Indigo and Black; Amsterdam Standard Series: Prussian Blue and Oxide Black.

The gel plate

For this exercise, I used my larger 41 x 51cm (16 x 20in) Gelli Arts plate, but you can easily use a smaller plate – your prints will simply be smaller, which works perfectly for this project.

Selecting the leaves and flowers

Below are some examples of leaves and flowers that work well for monoprints. Summer is ideal for gathering these, as fresh leaves lie flat on the plate and produce clean prints. In winter, some trees still hold their leaves, which tend to be waxy and stiff, making them harder to flatten and less effective at creating crisp silhouettes. To work around this during the colder months, it's a good idea to keep a stock of dried leaves and flowers.

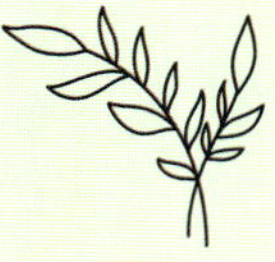

Tip

Sandwich the plants between clean sheets of paper, place a heavy board and weights on top, and leave them for a few months. It's so exciting on a dull January day to open up your plant stash and see which ones have survived. Some might have disintegrated, but others will hold their shape beautifully. Spraying them with hairspray helps keep them intact longer, and once you apply a layer of acrylic paint, the leaf is preserved, as acrylic is similar to plastic when dry.

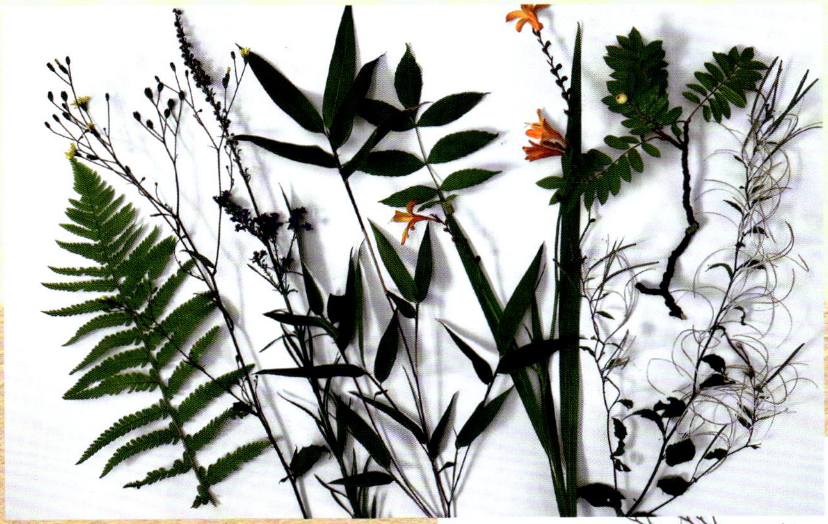

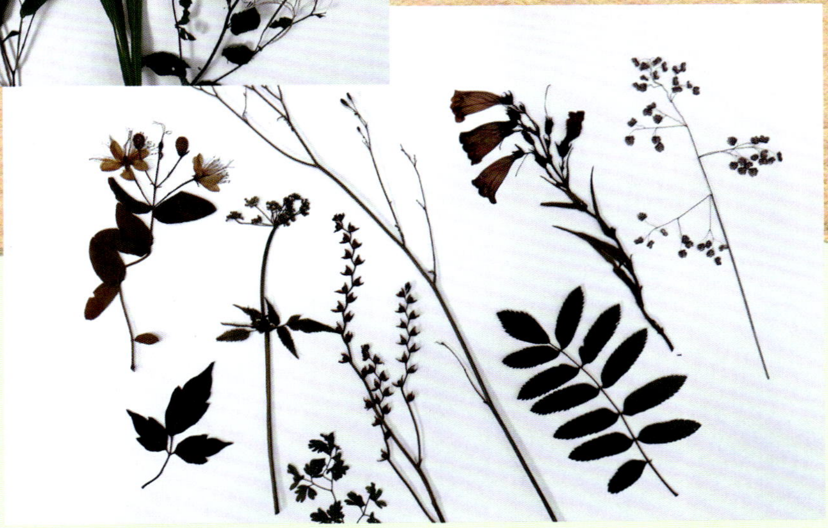

Creating the prints

Start by rolling a thin layer of paint onto the gel plate. For this first print, I used a small amount of Titanium White and Titan Buff (a). Place the plant shape on the plate and then the paper on top (b). Here I chose wet-strength tissue paper – its light colour will layer beautifully over darker areas later on. Press firmly all around to ensure a sharp silhouette before carefully peeling back the paper to reveal the print (c).

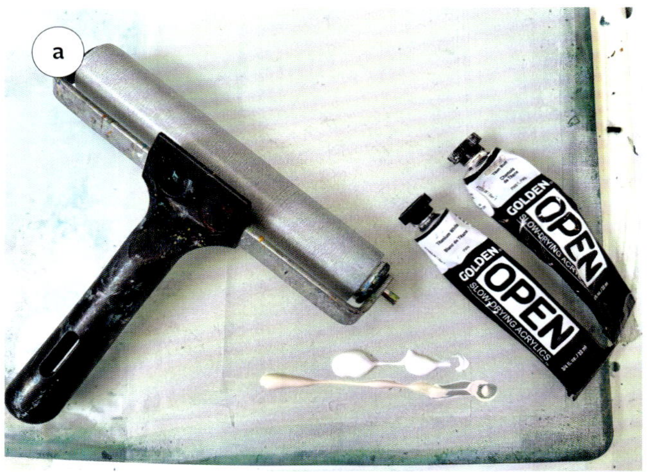

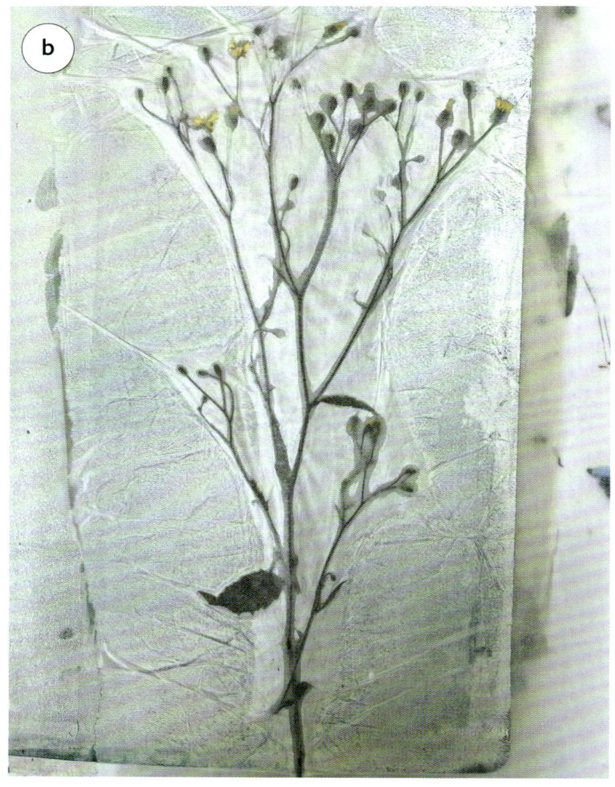

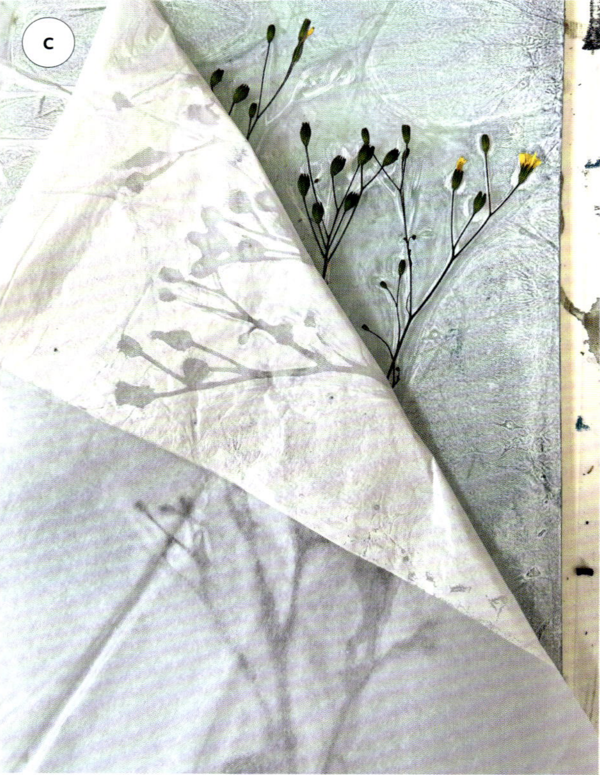

After the plant has been removed, its positive shape remains on the plate in a light colour (d). I pressed black tissue onto the remaining paint, creating a soft print that captures the plant's details (e). This is the second or 'ghost' print – a 'ghost' print refers to the second or third print that can be pulled from the gel plate when enough paint remains on the plate after pulling the first print. The amount of paint on the plate will determine how many prints, or 'pulls', you can take.

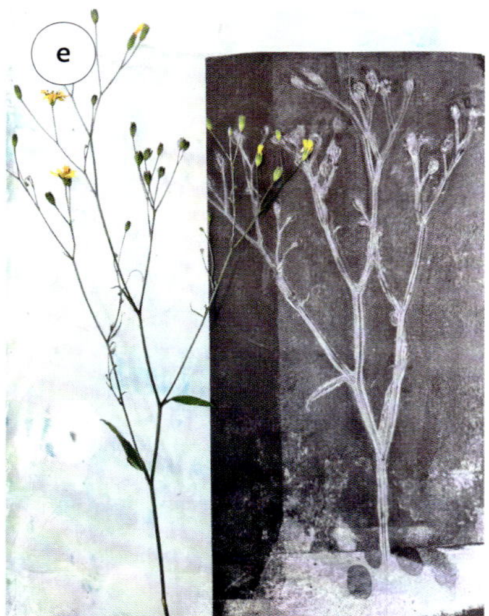

Next, I mixed Titan Buff, Phthalo Blue (Green Shade) and Raw Umber directly on the plate with a roller to achieve a softer blue, rather than using it straight from the tube (f). I arranged Rowan leaves face down in a pattern, alternating their direction and size. Letting some of the leaves hang over the edge softens the borders of the print and creates a more organic feel (g).

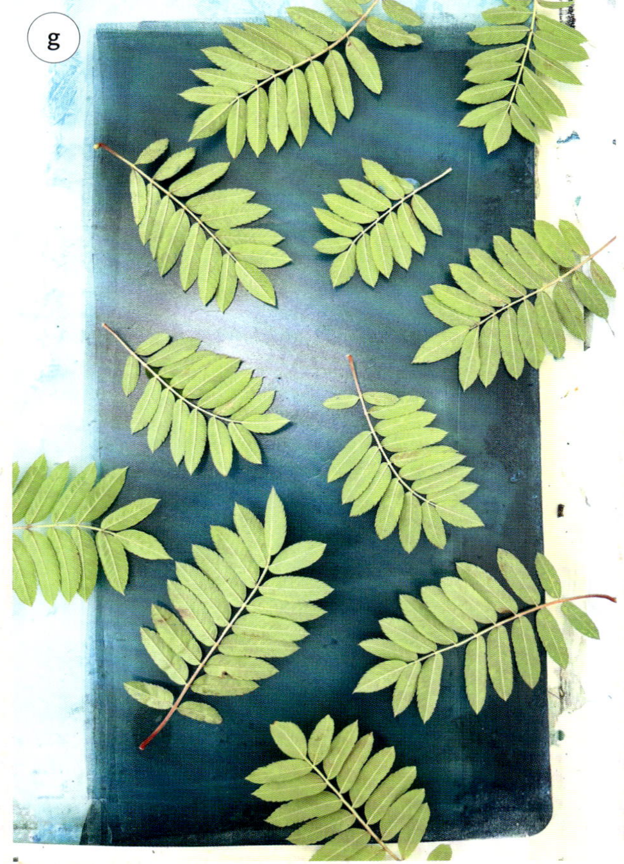

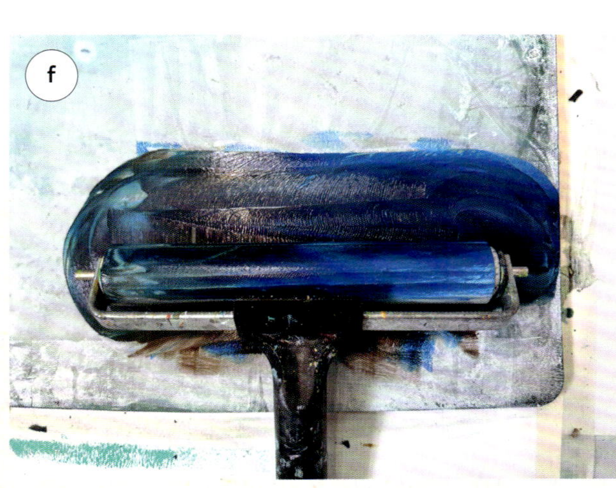

I placed a sheet of wet-strength tissue over the arranged leaves (h) and pressed gently with my hand. Depending on how much paint is applied, you may want to take a second print before lifting the leaves off the plate to ensure all the paint around the leaves is picked up (i). This will give you a cleaner, positive imprint print.

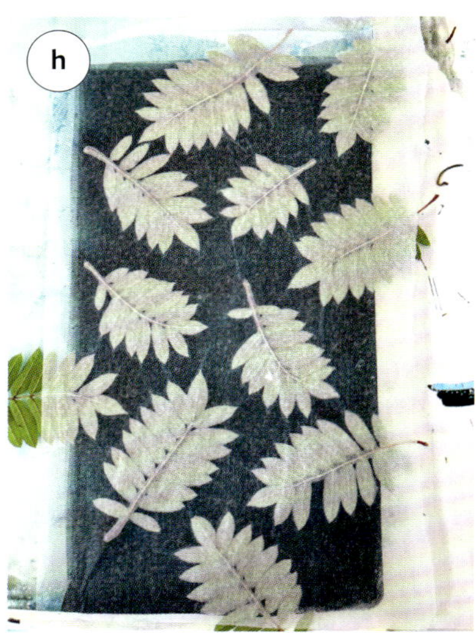

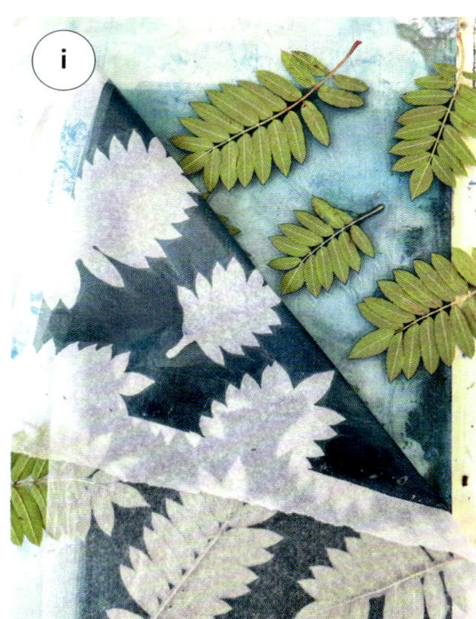

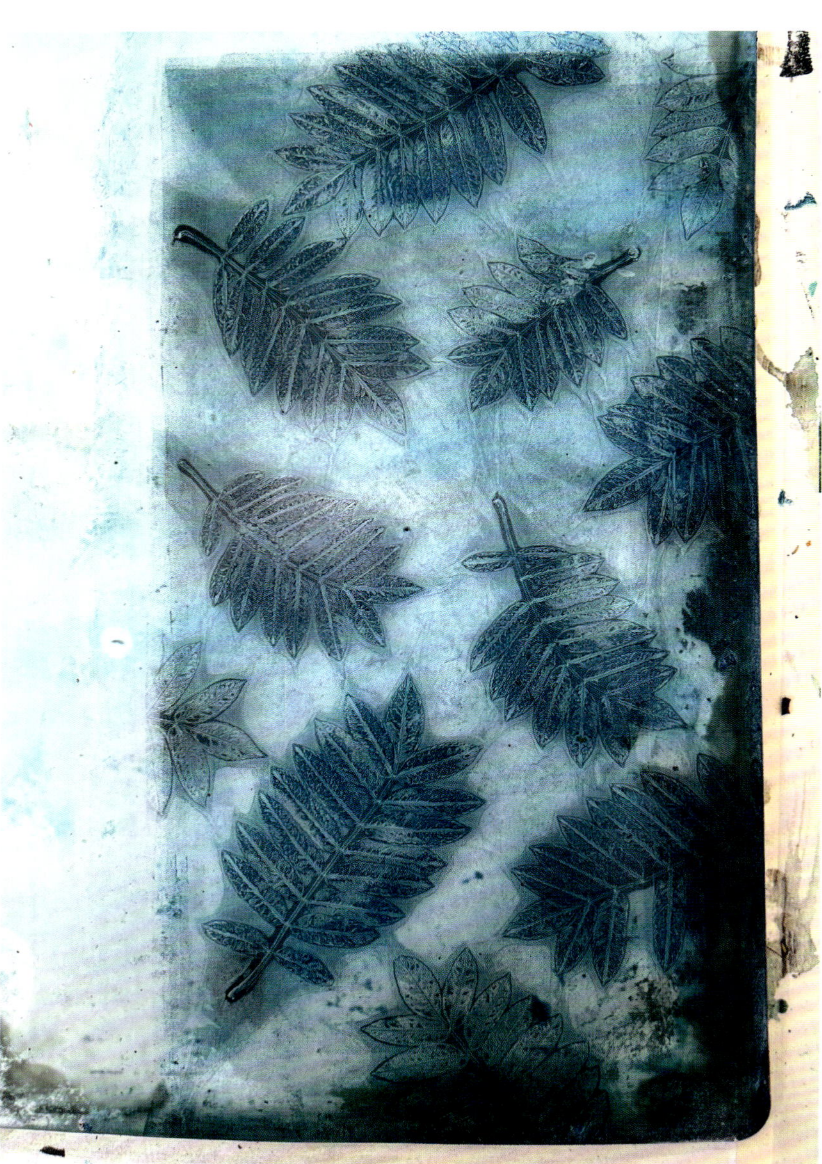

Here is the gel plate with the leaves removed, showing the positive imprint. There is still a lot of colour around the leaves. To make the leaf shapes sharp, lay a clean sheet of tissue paper on top to pull up any remaining paint.

I then placed a page dyed with avocado skins and an old book page over the plate (j). Notice how the text from the book blends with the leaf print, creating a beautifully layered effect, even if the background appears a bit muddy due to excess paint left on the plate.

Tip

To remove unwanted areas of background paint with precision, use a cotton bud (Q-tip) in combination with a baby wipe. If the paint beneath the leaf has dried too much to achieve a clean print, allow it to dry to the touch, then apply a thin layer of clear gel medium or matte medium glue over the paint. Gently place your paper on top, press it down lightly and wait a few minutes for the medium to set. Once dry, carefully peel the paper back to reveal your print.

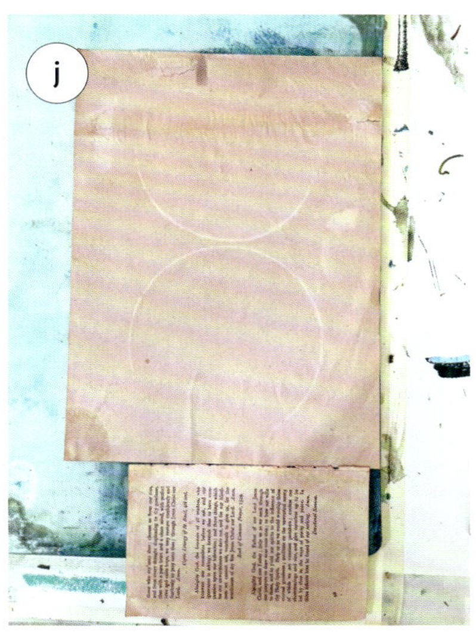

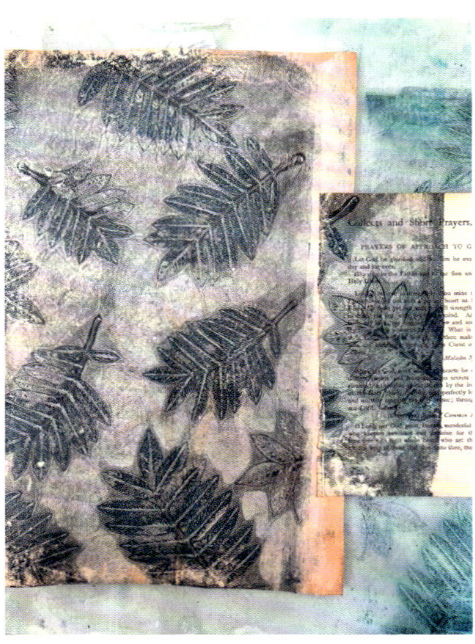

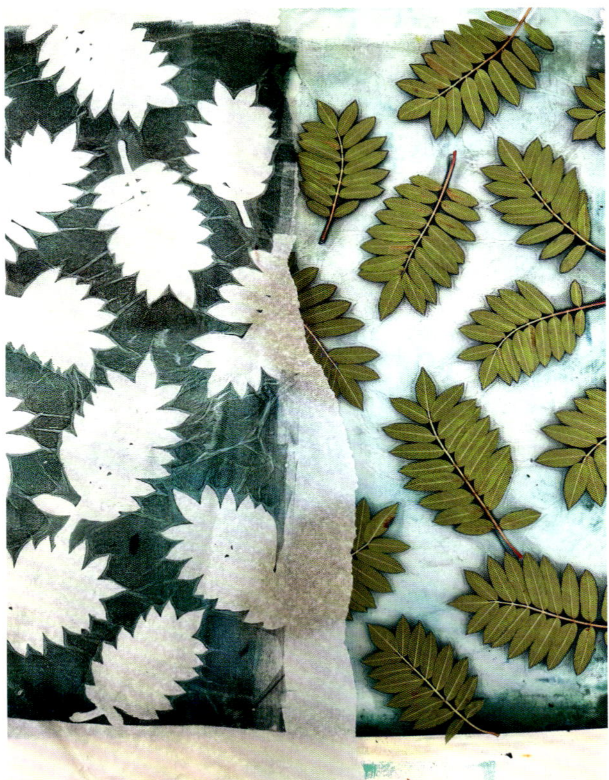

Here is an example of how I 'cleaned' the background more effectively by pulling a second print before lifting the leaves off the plate. You might find this a bit tricky with regular acrylic paint.

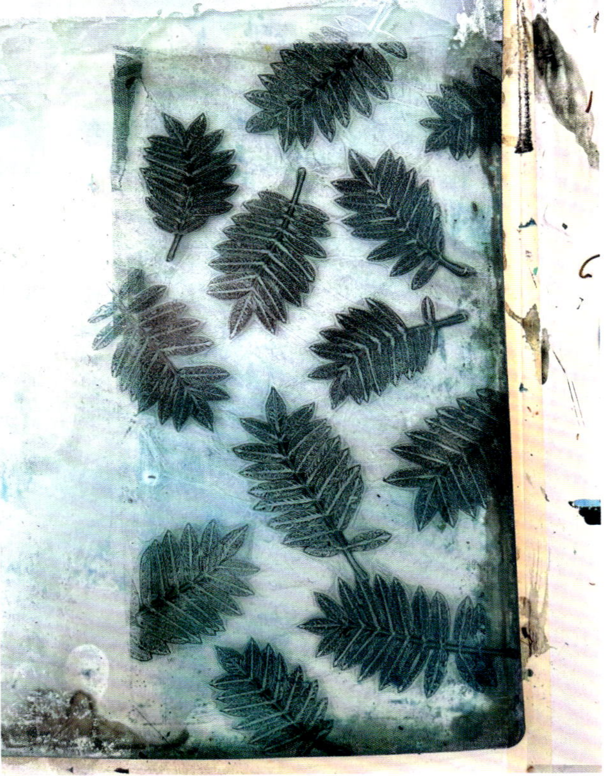

And the print I pulled once the leaves were removed – the positive imprint of the leaves is very clear now.

I arranged the dyed envelopes and book pages over sections of the leaf-printed area (k, l). For the ghost print, I used a larger A3 sheet of onion-dyed paper. I was delighted by the colour variations on the paper and the geometric shapes that appeared in the ghost print.

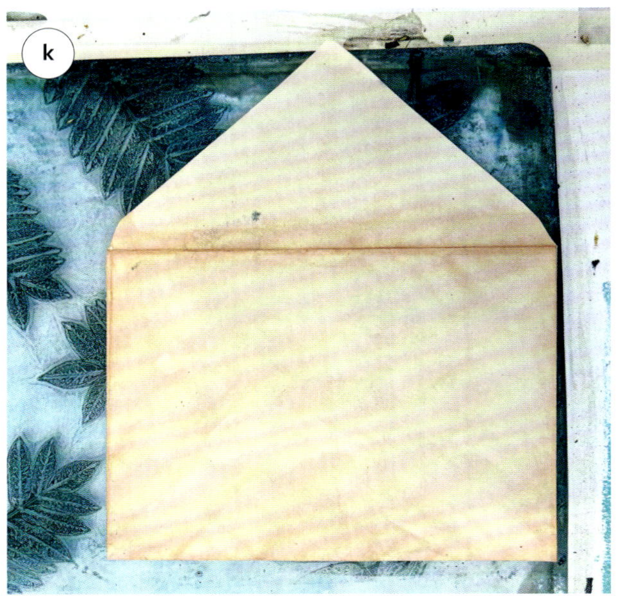

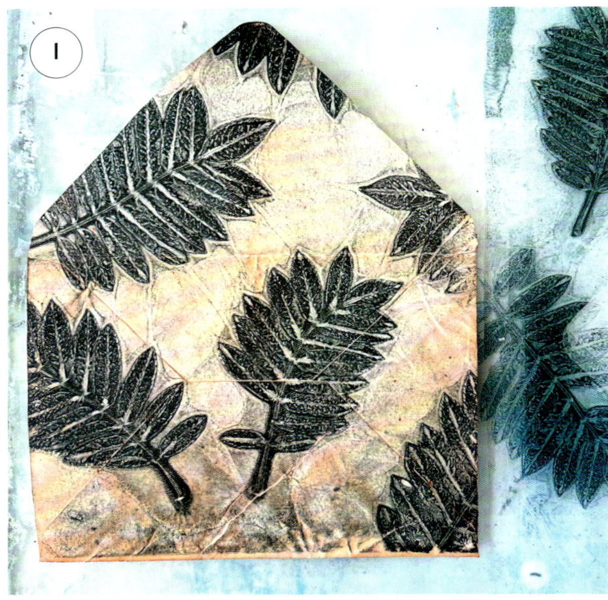

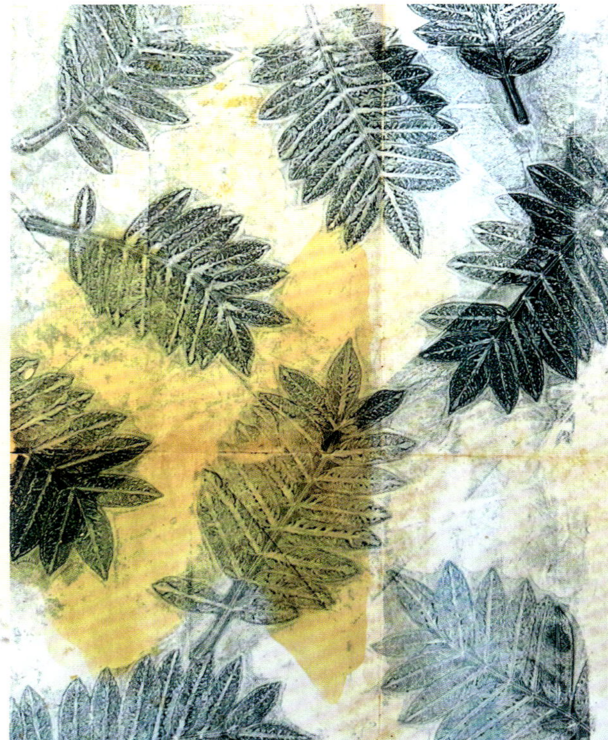

Each time you pull a print, it's a little surprise – you never know exactly how it will turn out, and that's what I love most about this process!

I created another silhouette print in the same way using the same colours but with a more neutral mix, adding a little more Raw Umber into the blend (m, n, o).

Next, I printed with ferns using a combination of Phthalo Blue (Red Shade), Raw Umber and Titanium White on thin sketch paper (around 90gsm, which works well for collage projects) using the 41 x 51cm (16 x 20in) gel plate. The fern's flat shape and the spaces between each leaf create a more defined and detailed print (p). If you use a leaf with tightly packed lobes, the resulting print may lose definition and appear more like a blob than a distinct leaf shape.

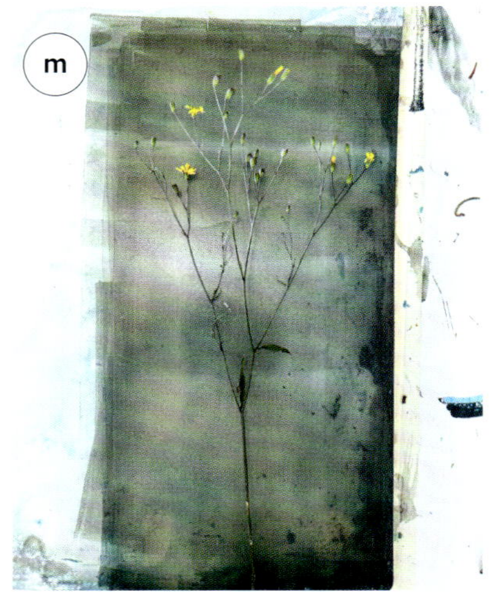

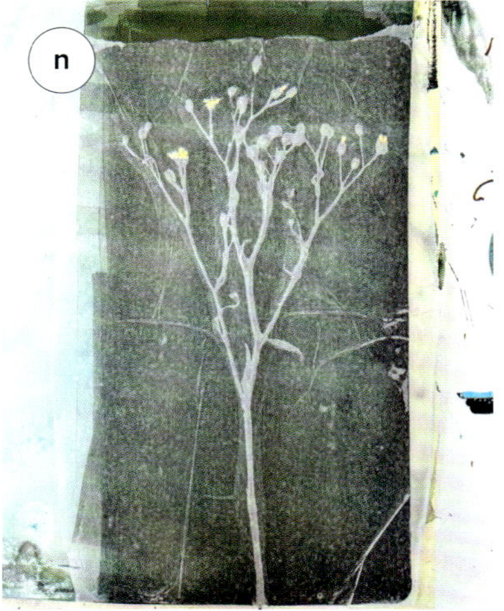

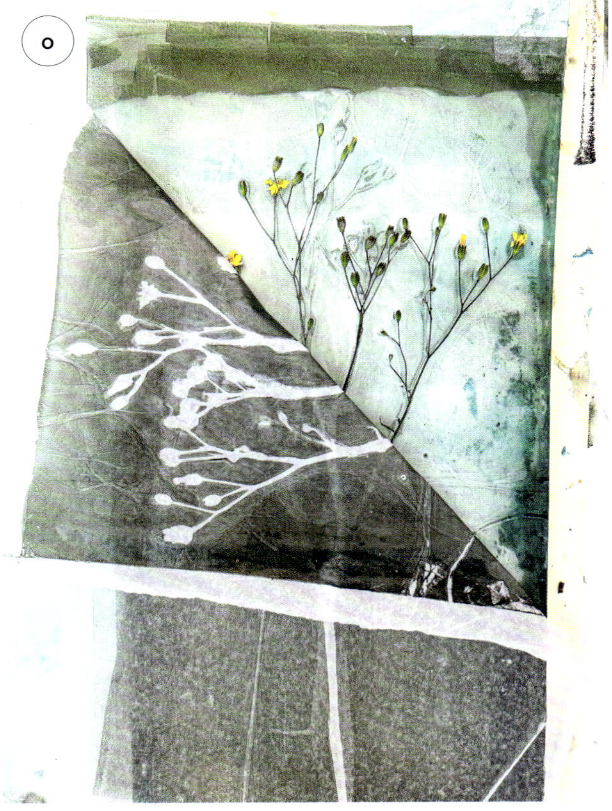

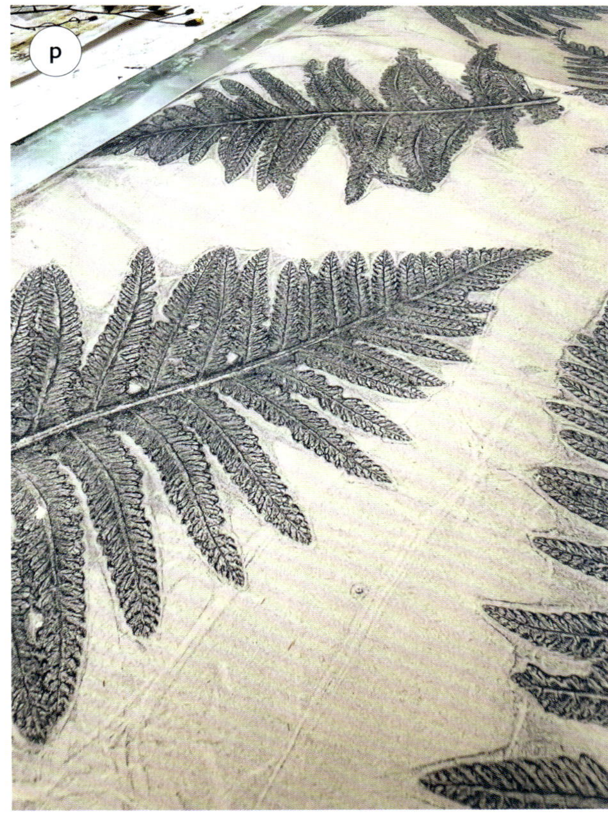

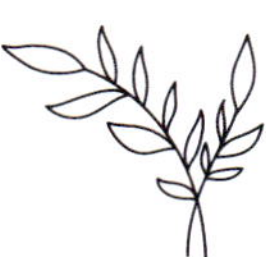

Tip

You can make a Raw Umber shade yourself by mixing a higher proportion of yellow and red and a small amount of blue, and adding a touch of black to deepen the colour.

I also printed some silhouette plant shapes onto black tissue paper using Teal, as here, and others using Titan Green Pale – an absolutely gorgeous shade. For this technique, opaque paints work best.

The first silhouette (q) was printed with the plant still in place on the gel plate. The second print (r) was made after removing the plant to create a contrasting effect. The paper picks up the positive shape of the plant that remains on the plate.

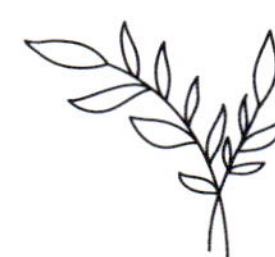

Tip

To make any colour more opaque, simply mix in a bit of Titanium White. This will help the colours stand out beautifully against the dark background.

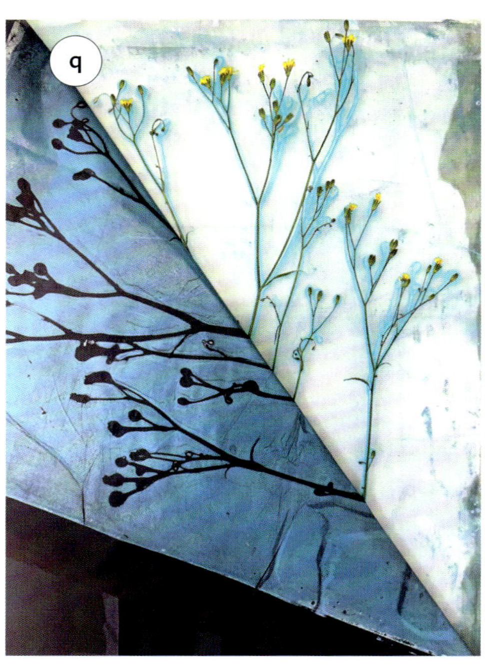

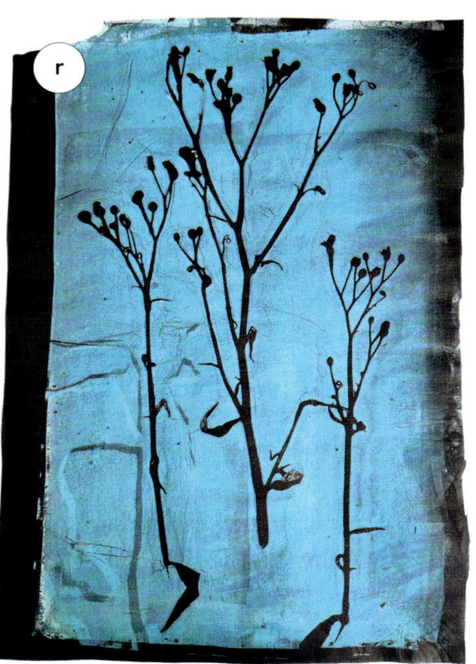

Here's the silhouette print of the Titan Green Pale version, also on black tissue paper.

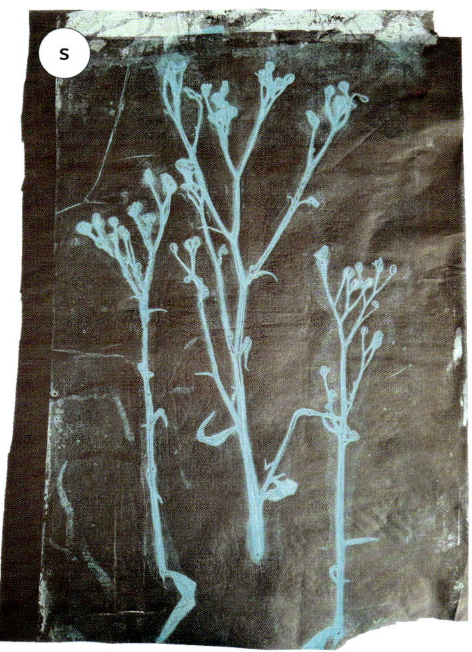

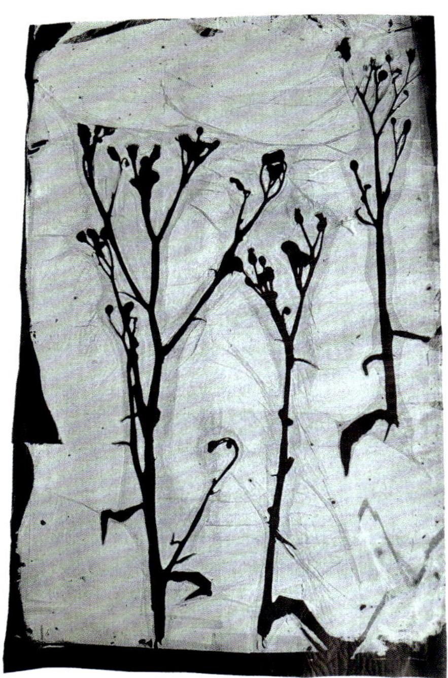

Layering prints on the gel plate

The next step was to start layering designs on top of each other to create a more dynamic effect. This technique adds depth and introduces a whole new feel to the prints.

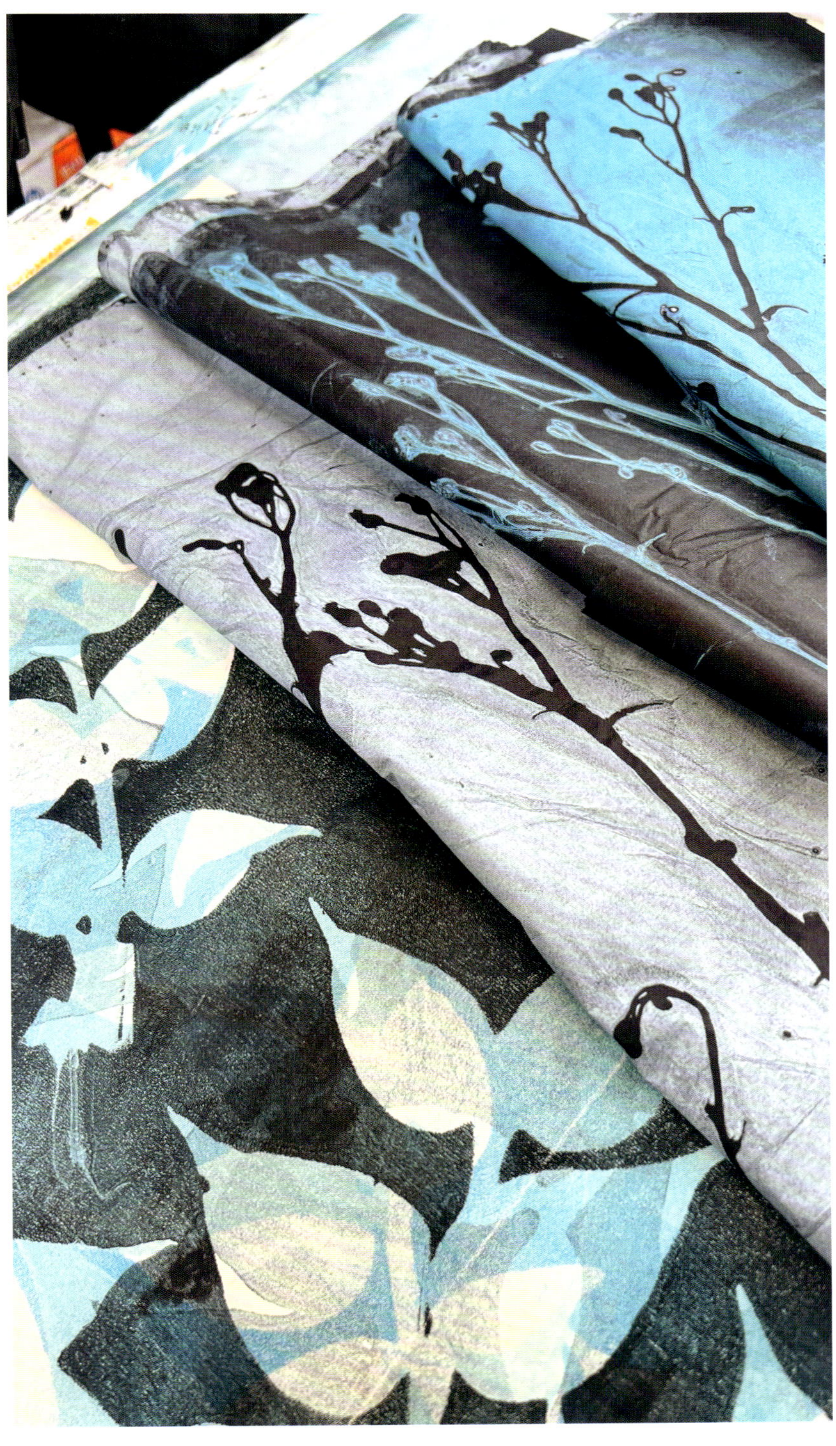

I applied Manganese Blue Hue for the first layer. This paint
has a transparent quality, which you can easily observe by
examining the three black bars at the top of the tube (a).
When the paint is transparent, the black lines remain visible
through the colour. In contrast, if you look at a tube of Teal
paint (b), you'll notice the black lines are nearly obscured
because Teal is an opaque paint, allowing for more coverage.

I positioned a couple of the leaf shapes facing down and
others in the opposite direction. This adds variety to the
lines and creates a lovely flow in the arrangement of the
leaves (c). The paper I've used here has ghost print leaf
shapes on it, which come through beautifully.

I transferred the subsequent ghost prints onto a thin
sketchbook paper I found among the old, yellowed papers
from my studio neighbour. I was delighted to find a beautiful
hand-drawn fuchsia on the paper. I added a dark grey ghost
print and a lighter blue on top, but the ghost print was light
enough that the original drawing still showed through (d).

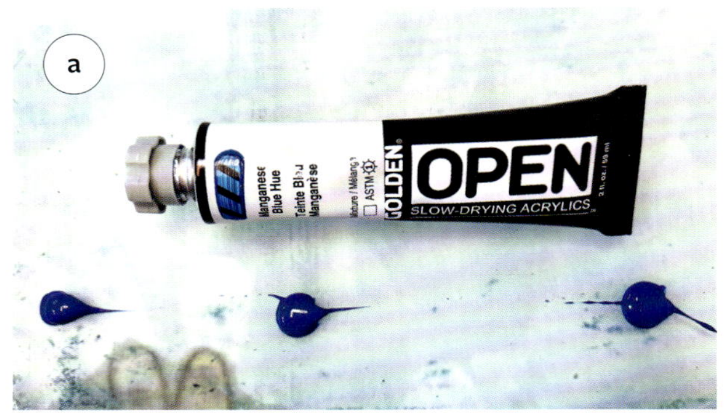

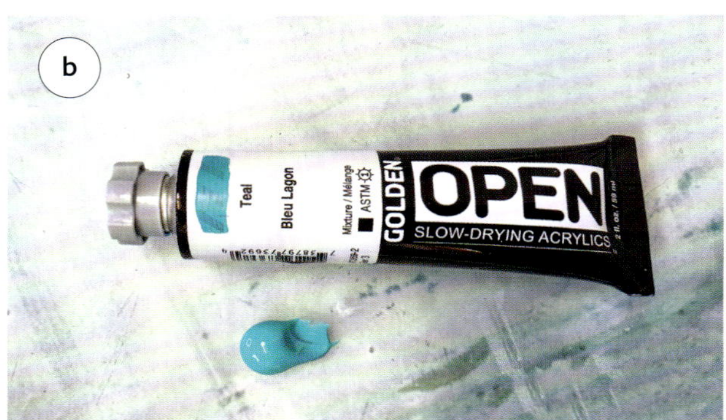

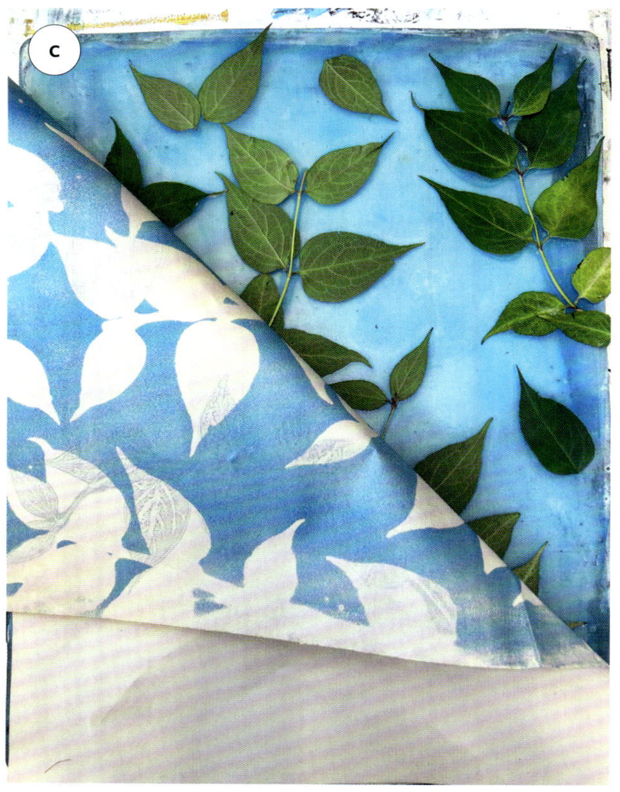

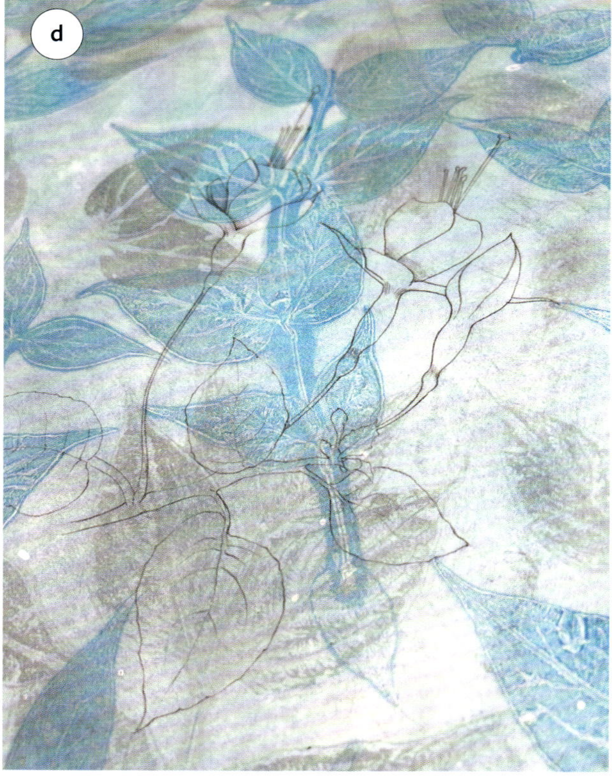

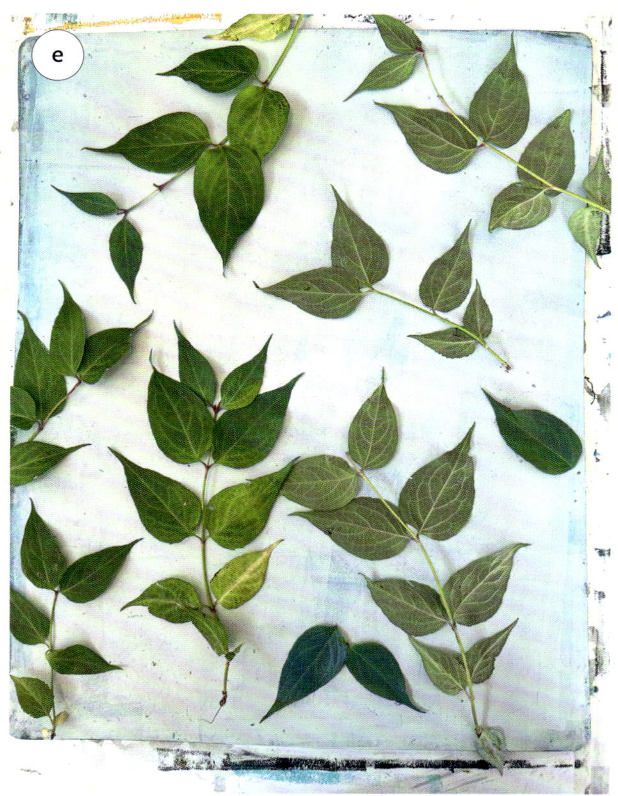

For the next layer, I applied Titan Green Pale to the plate before positioning the leaves on top (e).

I printed straight onto the first silhouette print (f). Interesting windows in the print are continuing to appear and the original black ghost print is still visible underneath. There is no need to line up the papers perfectly since the final print won't be framed. These papers will be used for different collage projects, so exact alignment isn't important.

The ghost print was transferred onto black tissue paper, which printed beautifully, creating a stunning effect that I absolutely loved.

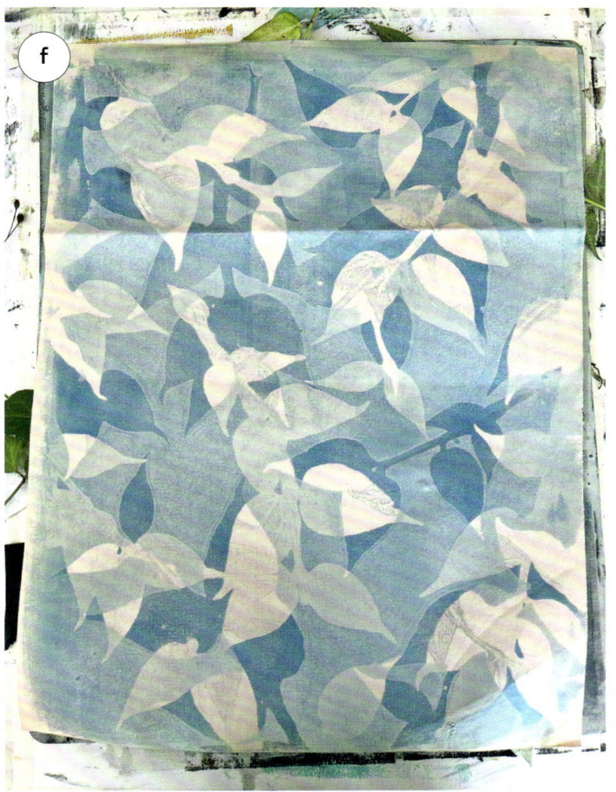

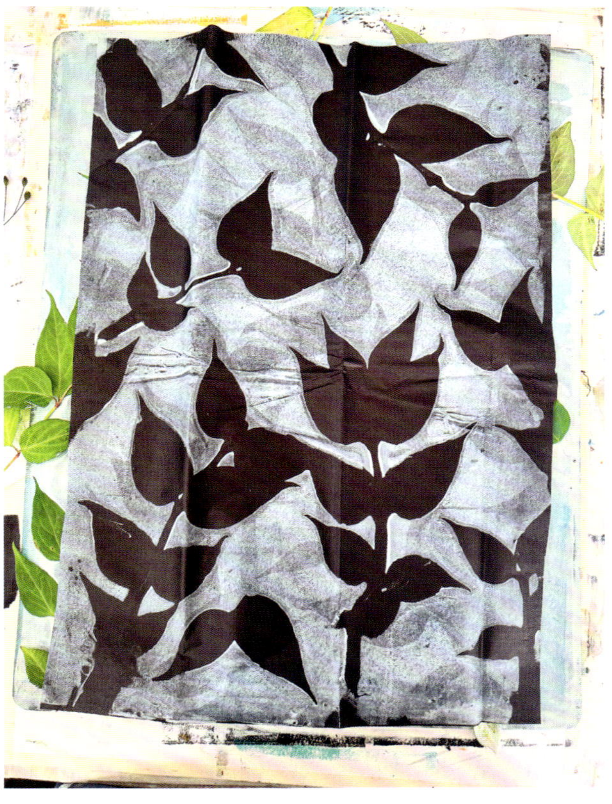

For the third layer I used Phthalo Blue (Green Shade) mixed with a small amount of Raw Umber. There was still a lot of paint left on the plate after my first print, so I was able to pull another before taking off the leaves (g).

After removing the leaves, I printed onto a sheet with layers of mark-making in the background (h).

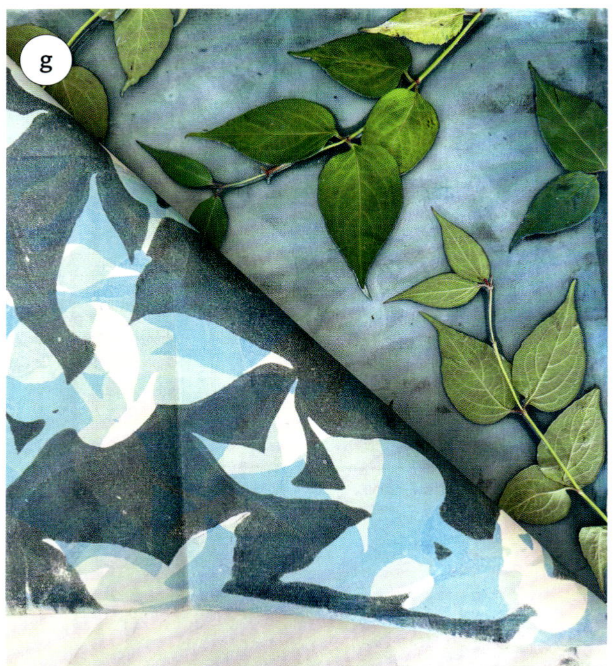

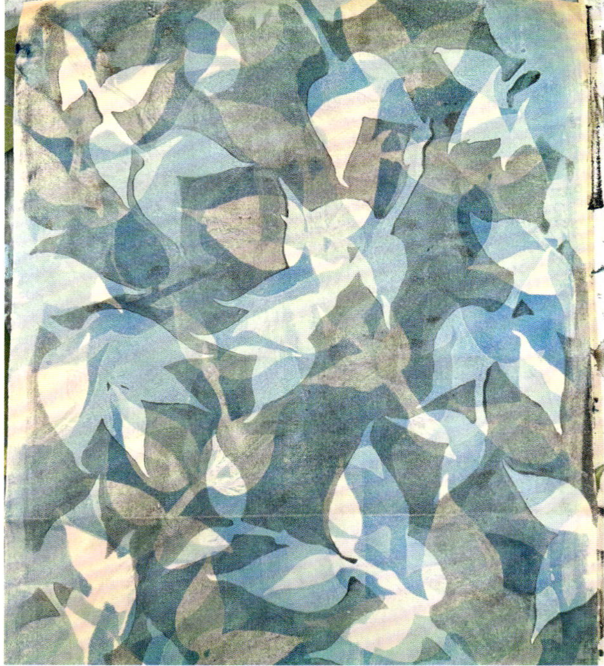

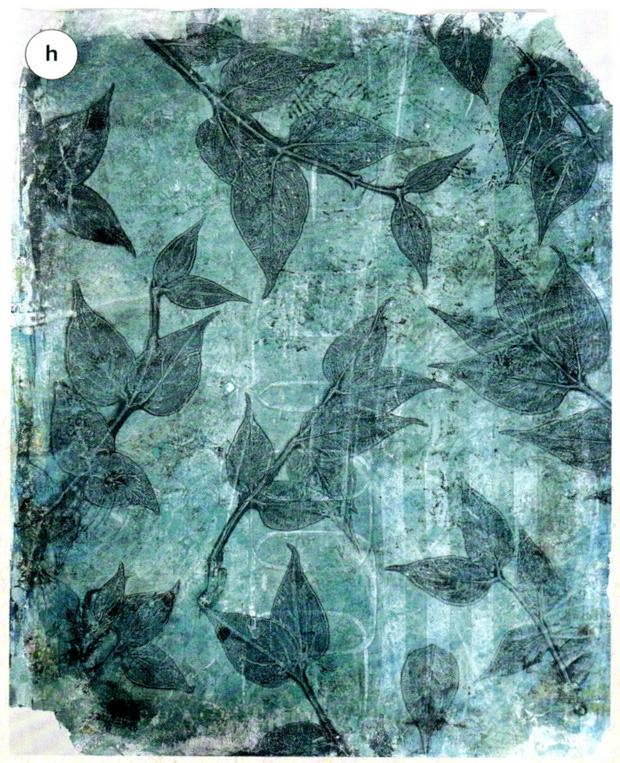

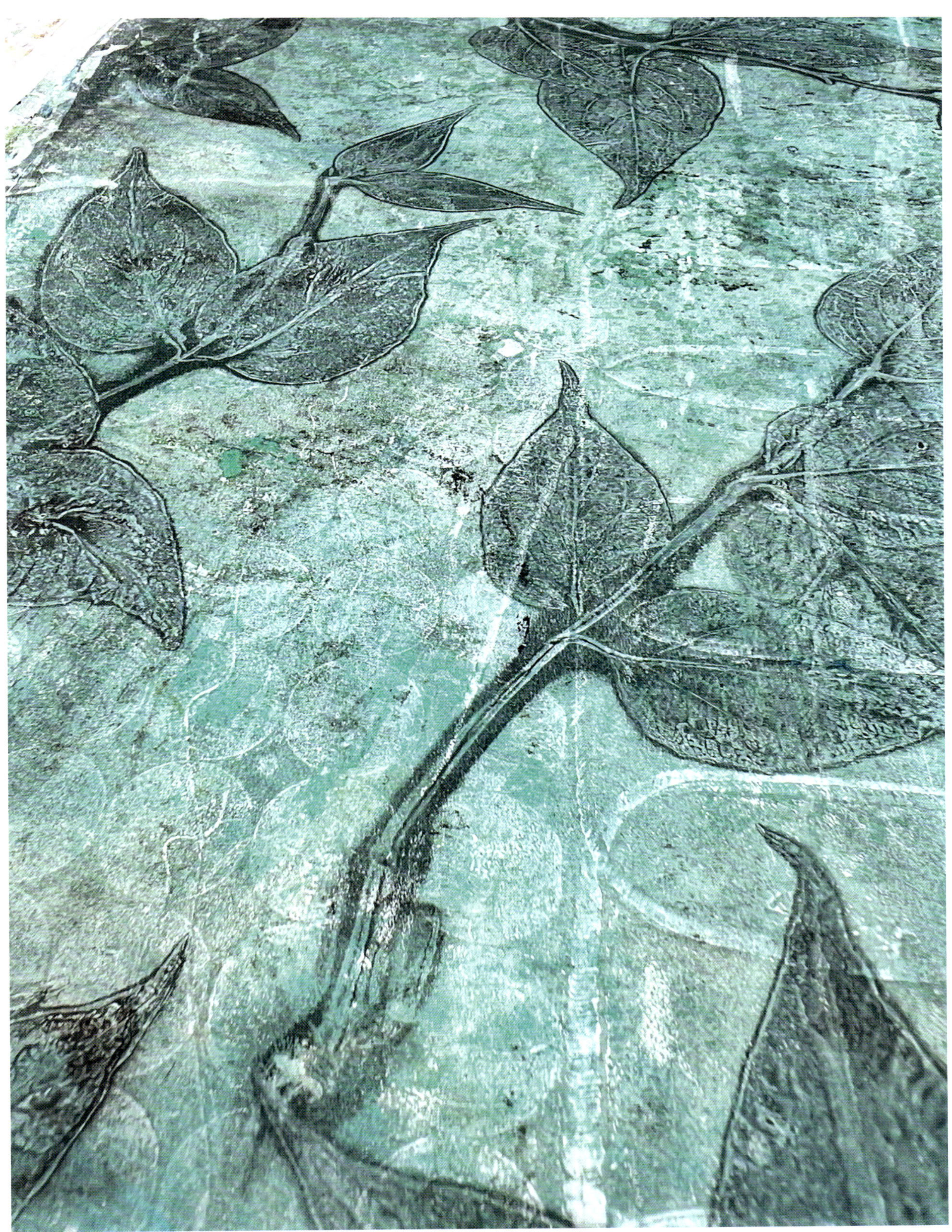

The leaf design really stands out against the texture, creating another nice layered effect.

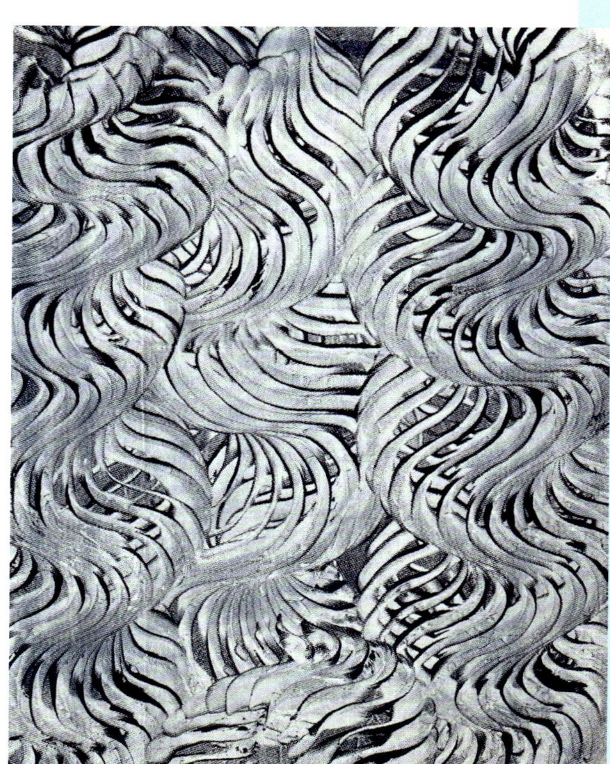

Q Can you share a little about your background and how you discovered gel printing?

A I'm a textile designer, specialising in concepts and innovation. I have been mixing up textile techniques and reimagining reclaimed textiles for the past thirty years, selling my designs to clients ranging from Chanel and Dior to M&S and Boden. In recent years, the gel plate has become an integral part of my practice, allowing me to quickly create textures and prints that I can layer into my patchworks, embroideries and weaves.

My MA from Central Saint Martins is in fashion print; however, my thirst for spontaneity and happy accidents meant that I continued to follow a mixed-media route centred around my vintage Singer sewing machine. Setting up screens to print just took too long!

I dabbled in monoprinting but found the results a little hit and miss. I had almost given up ever finding a print process that suited my way of working. Then I noticed artists on Instagram using gel plates and had to explore this method of printing further.

Q What drew you to using a gel plate in your artwork?

A The gel plate is the ultimate printing tool for impatient creatives! You can be set up and printing in minutes and create the most incredible details and textures.

I was immediately struck by the possibilities of mixing up textile techniques with the gel plate. What if I printed with gathered fabrics, folds, patchwork or lace? I found that I was not only getting incredible textures, marks and patterns on the plate but also on the fabrics.

Q Who or what are your main influences in your art practice?

A I am always drawn to clever technique mix-ups, experimentation and innovation.

I'm inspired by artists who push the boundaries of their mediums, including Anni Albers, Sheila Hicks and the quiltmakers of Gee's Bend.

Vintage glass waves

Q **How do you see the role of gel printing in the broader context of contemporary art?**

A It's the infinite potential, portability and versatility that I find exciting. I love the diverse approaches that are emerging as more and more artists cross-pollinate the gel plate into their practices.

Q **What projects or directions are you excited about exploring in the future?**

A I'm always excited to share my process, igniting ideas via my online courses and membership of the 'No Rules Textile Society'.

Q **What advice would you give to beginners who are just starting with gel printing?**

A Just play! Don't be afraid to experiment. Release your attachment to the end results and let yourself flow from one print to the next. Some will work, some won't – don't worry! Let your intuition kick in, get lost in the process and design through doing.

Print like no one is watching, and enjoy!

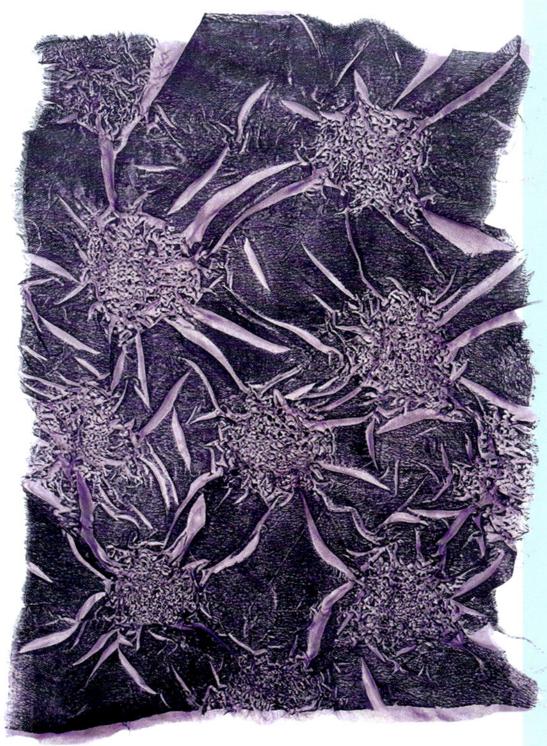

Needle-felted texture

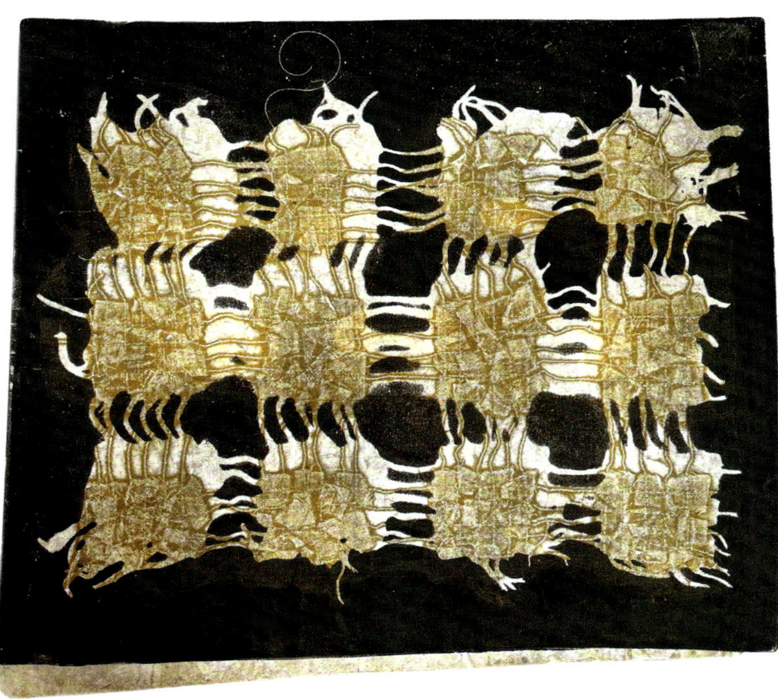

Water-soluble lace grid

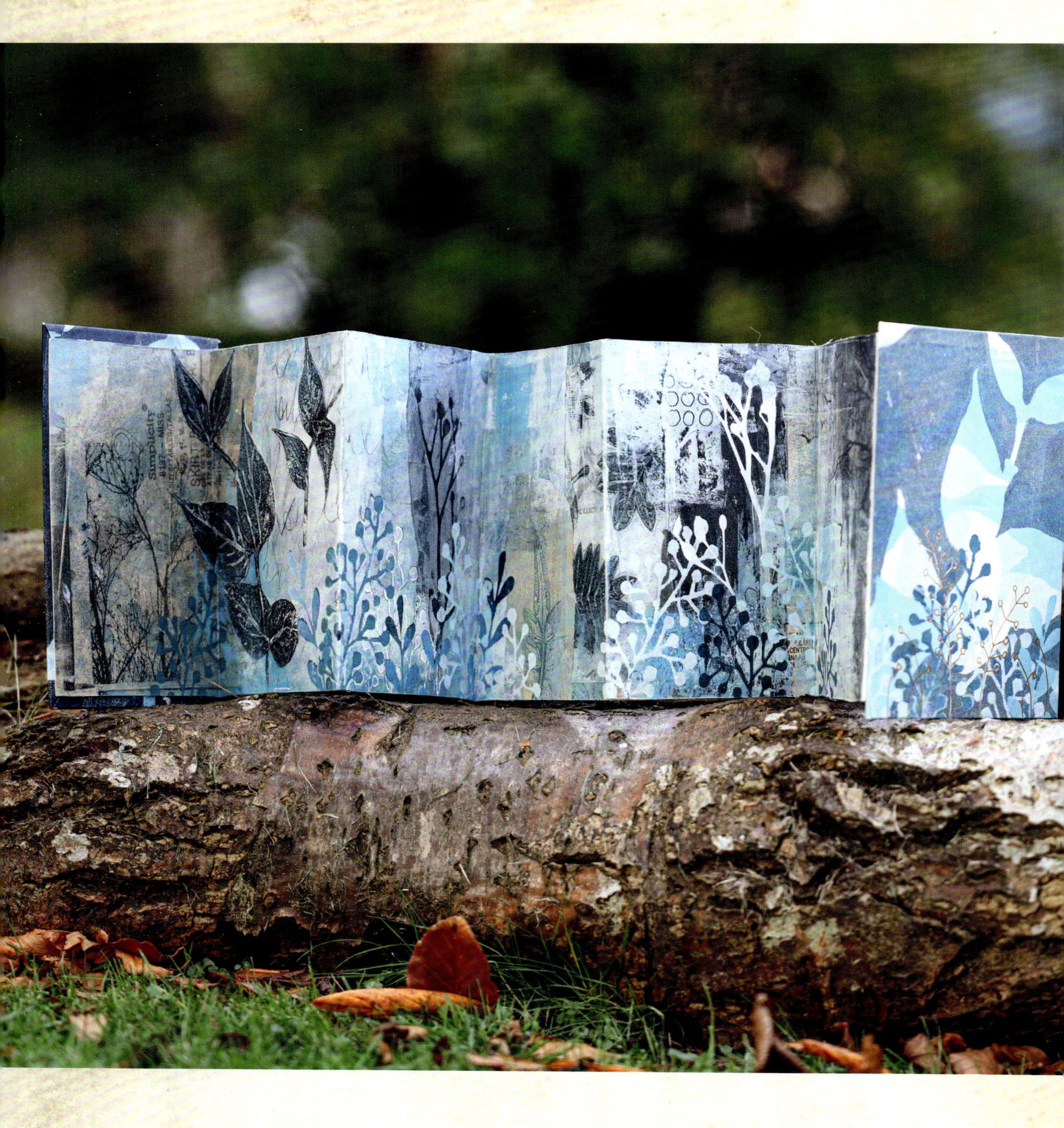

ACCORDION ARTIST BOOK

Now comes the exciting part – turning your prints into something truly unique and beautiful! This stage can feel a little overwhelming at first, especially if you're unsure of how to take your prints and transform them into a finished piece. But, don't worry! By following these steps, it will start to come together and you'll see just how rewarding the process can be.

I wanted this project to feel approachable and enjoyable, but to also encourage you to grow creatively. Large canvases can sometimes feel intimidating when you're used to the comfort of a smaller sketchbook. This project is a stepping stone to help build your confidence as it combines the relaxed feeling of an art journal with the satisfaction of taking on a slightly more ambitious challenge. Hopefully you will enjoy the process, and end up with a piece of art that you love to display in your home.

The possibilities are endless as the 3D concertina format is so versatile. It is perfect for storytelling – you could weave in images, poetry, letters or even layered textures that tell a story or evoke a memory.

Whether you want to keep it decorative or include personal treasures, this project is all about exploring, experimenting and creating something truly your own.

MATERIALS
Refer back to the master list on page 18 for the essential items.

- Papers: cartridge paper, cardstock, mixed-media or watercolour paper (approx. 170gsm) – I used A4 cartridge paper cut to size
- Mountboard (mat board) or stiff card
- Gel-printed collage papers (see pages 56–62)
- Matte medium glue, or glue stick
- Acrylics: I used Titan Green Pale, Teal, Phthalo Blue, Titanium White, Indigo, Raw Umber and Titan Buff

- Catalyst wedge or old credit card
- Small roller/brayer 6cm (2½in) wide
- Metal ball stylus sculpting tool
- Transparent papers
- Glass or Perspex surface and a sponge
- Botanical stencils
- White candle
- Greaseproof paper
- Coloured pencil (optional)

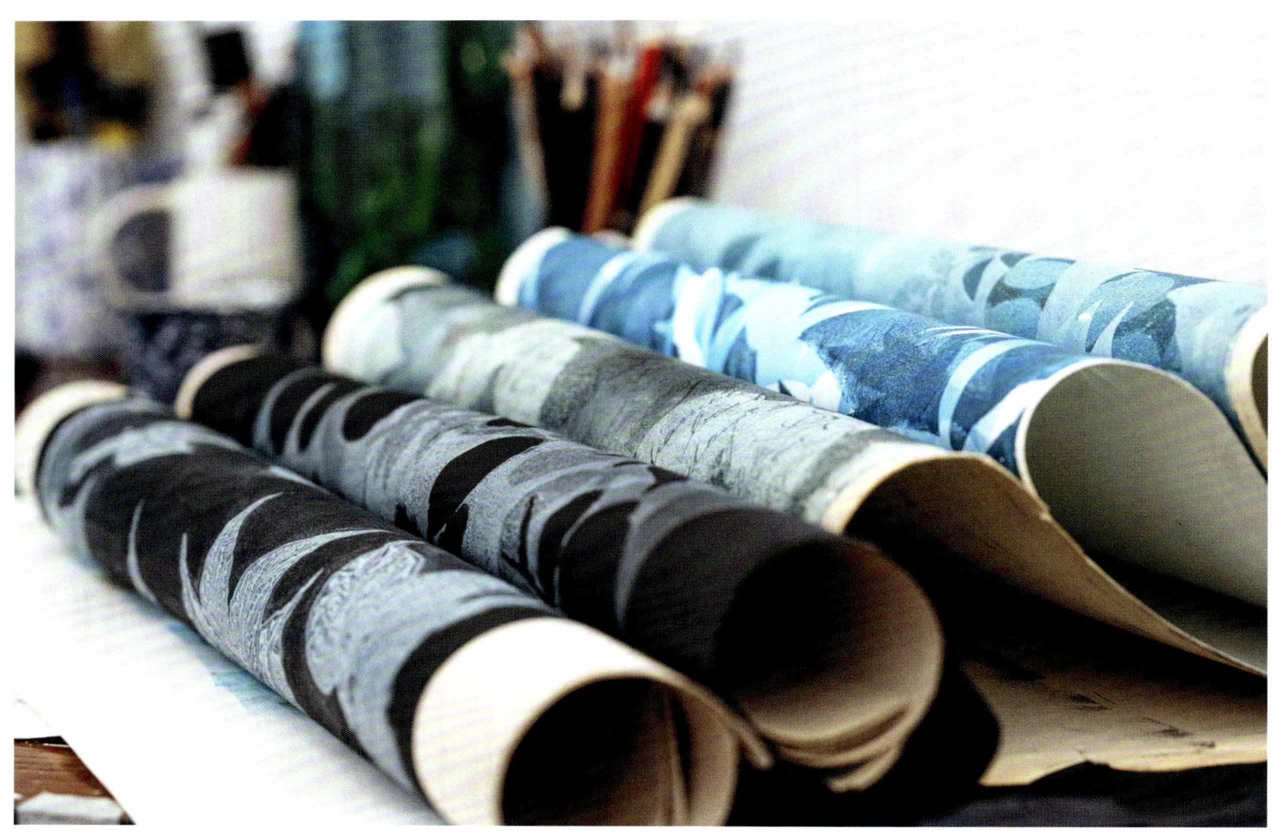

Creating the base for the artist book

Preparing the pages

Using a ruler or a set square for precision, mark seven rectangles on your paper. For my book the inside pages are 19 x 13cm (7½ x 5¼in), so I cut my paper to this size (a). This will ensure that all your pages are even and neatly aligned. Carefully draw the lines with a pencil to guide your cuts. Using a craft knife and a cutting mat, carefully cut out the seven marked pages (b).

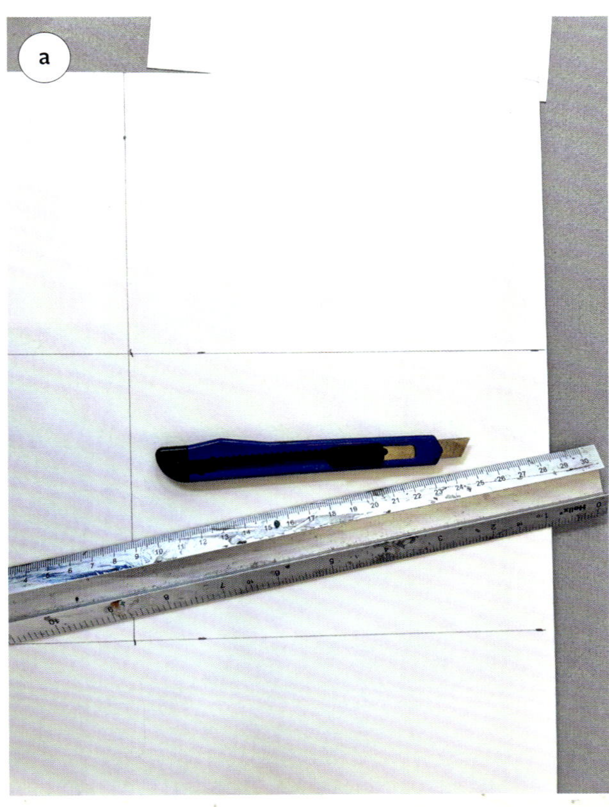

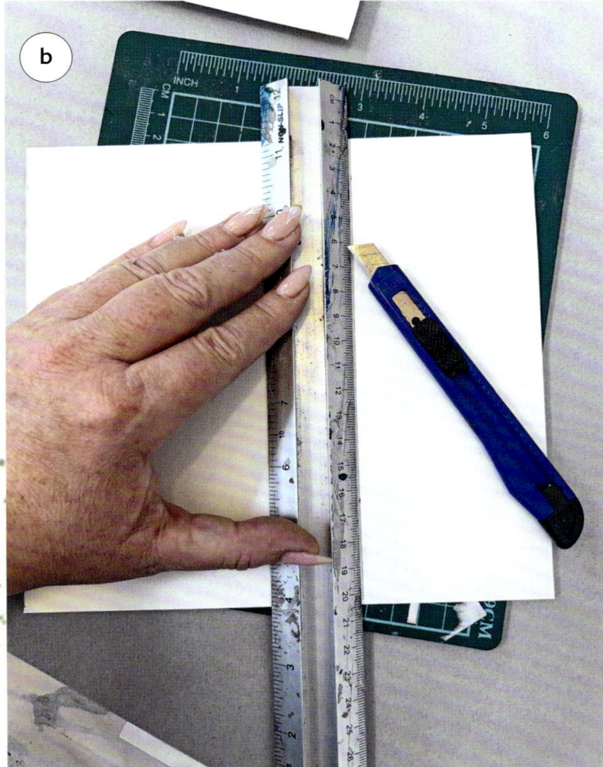

Binding the pages

To bind the pages together, I used masking tape, which works well for flexibility. Lay the pages side by side, leaving a small gap between each one (about 2–3mm/ ⅛in) to allow for easy folding (c). Place the masking tape along the seams between the pages, ensuring it is evenly applied and smooth. Press the tape down firmly to secure the pages, but be careful not to tighten it too much – a slight gap will allow the pages to open and close smoothly (d).

Once you've placed the masking tape between the pages, secure both sides of the paper. Apply masking tape along the front and back of each seam for extra strength. After taping, trim any excess tape from the edges using scissors or a craft knife (e). Continue this process until all six pages are bound together, forming the base of your artist book.

Before you start collaging, mark each of the two end pages with an 'X' on both sides (f). This will remind you not to collage these pages, as they will later be glued to the inside of the covers.

The covers will be attached to opposite ends of the accordion book, on opposite sides.

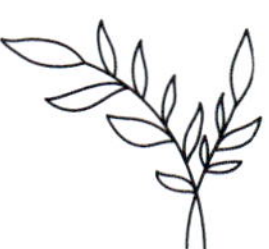

Tip

Check with your local framers to see if they have any offcuts they're willing to give away. These can often be perfect for projects like this and it is a great way to reuse materials. Alternatively, you can repurpose the backing boards from old sketchpads – these are ideal for this artist book.

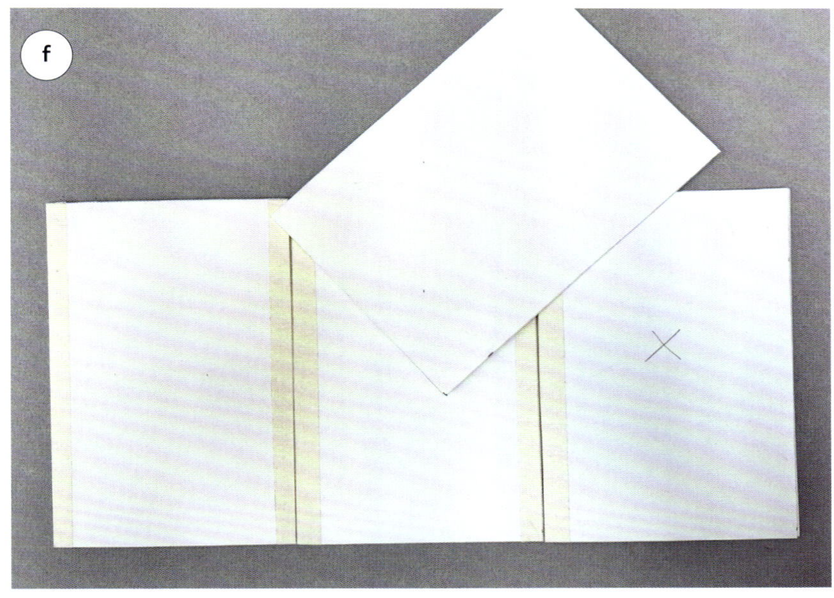

Creating the covers

To make the covers, start by measuring and cutting two pieces of stiff card. I used mountboard for my book and cut it to 20 x 14cm (8 x 5½in) for the covers. To ensure precision while cutting, use a craft knife, a metal ruler and a cutting mat.

Preparing the collage papers

Selecting the papers

Sort through your collection of gel-printed papers and choose a few that will work well together.

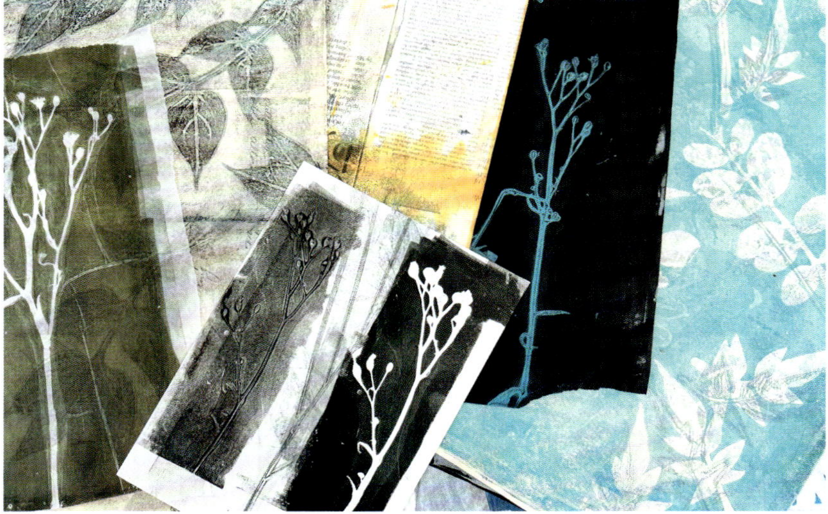

Aim for a balance between light and dark images to create contrast in your design.

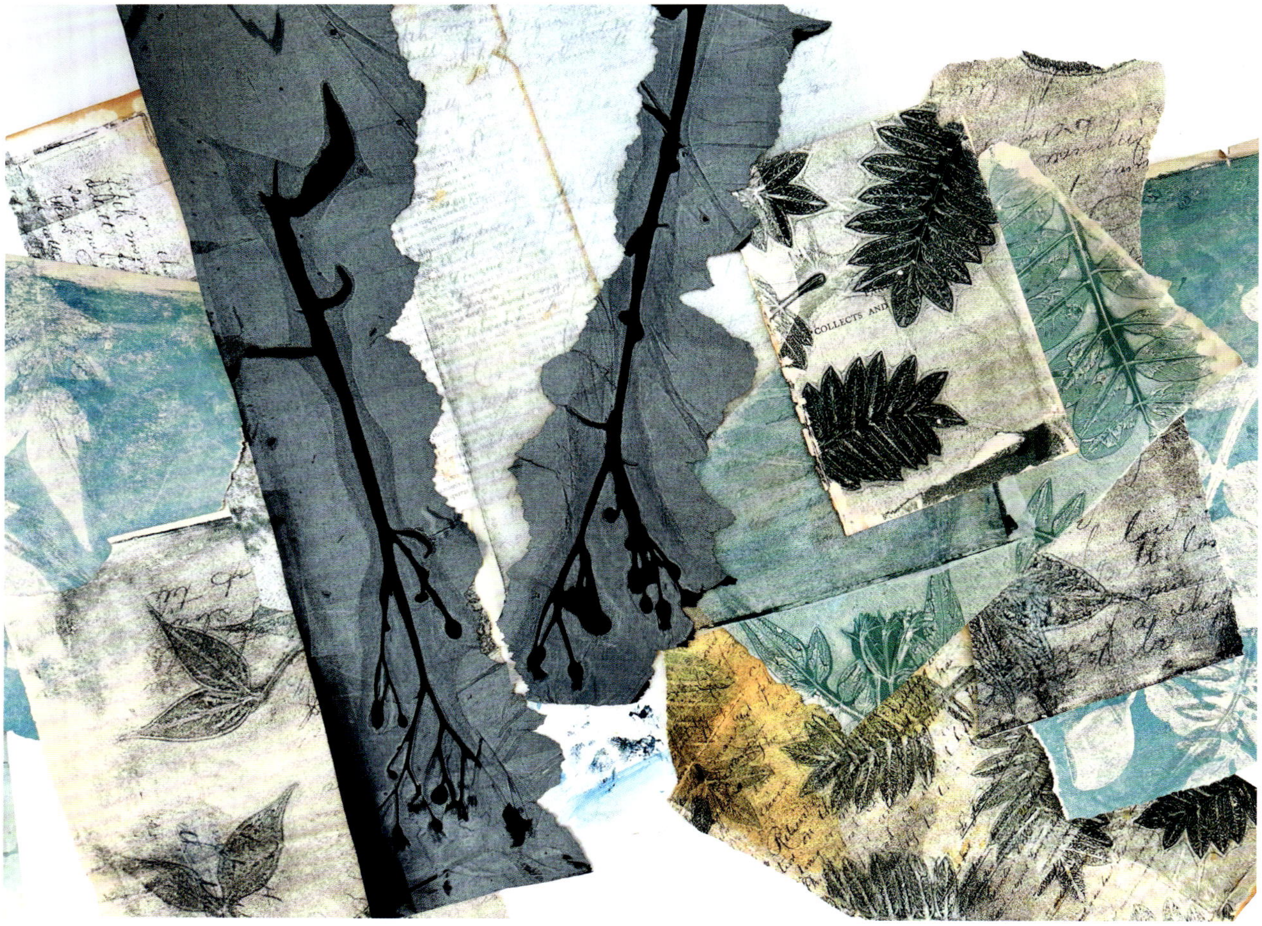

Consider mixing opaque and transparent papers for added depth and texture in your artist book.

Tearing the collage papers

Use a ruler to tear pieces of your selected collage papers to fit the size of your book (a). For a more organic look, try tearing some pages by hand, allowing for natural edges that enhance the visual interest of your design.

Tip

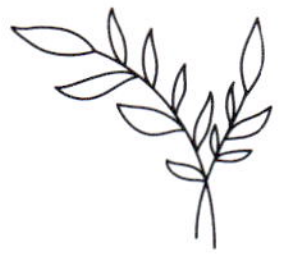

When tearing paper, direction matters. Tearing one way can leave a rough white edge, while the other way results in a clean edge. It's trial and error, much like ripping fabric – one direction is usually easier.

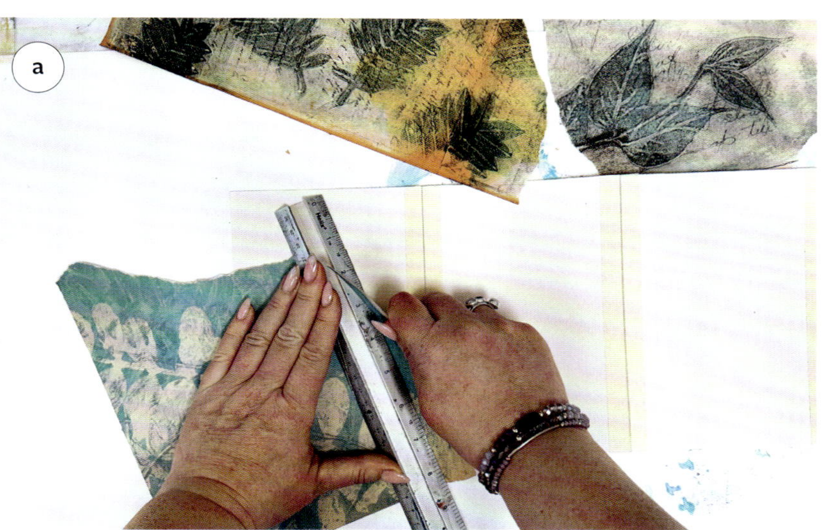

Arranging the collage papers

Lay out the torn pieces of collage paper along the length of the book to visualise the design (b). This will help you see how everything looks before you commit to gluing them down.

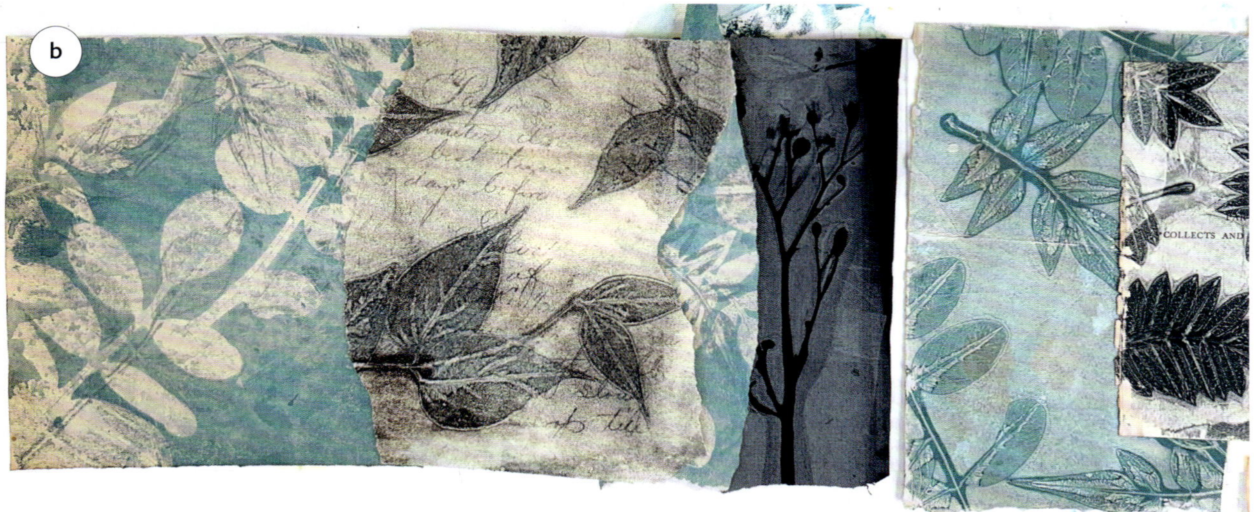

Tip

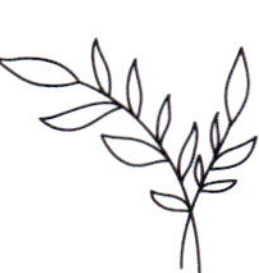

Work quickly during this step, as the initial layers will change as the project evolves. Collage is forgiving; if something isn't working, you can easily cover it with another piece. Don't overthink at this stage or become too 'thinky thinky', as I like to call it!

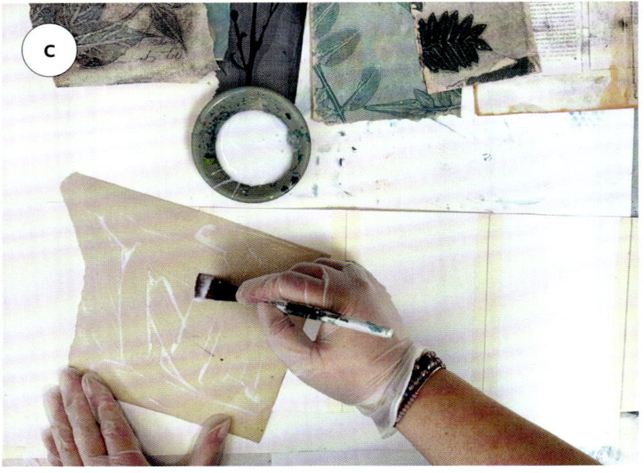

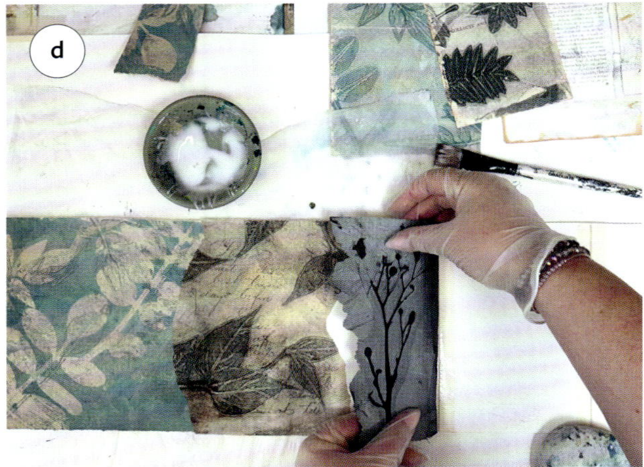

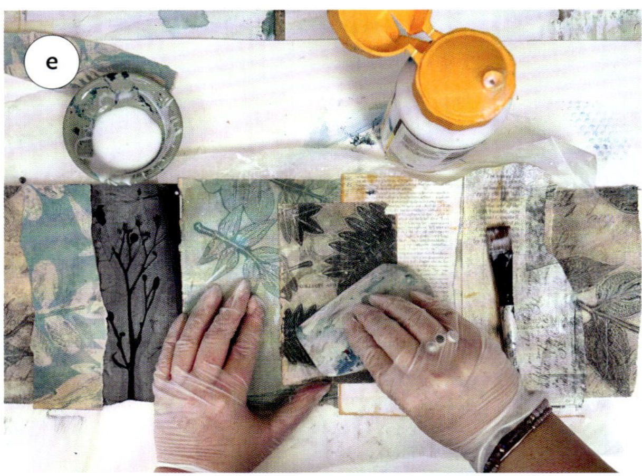

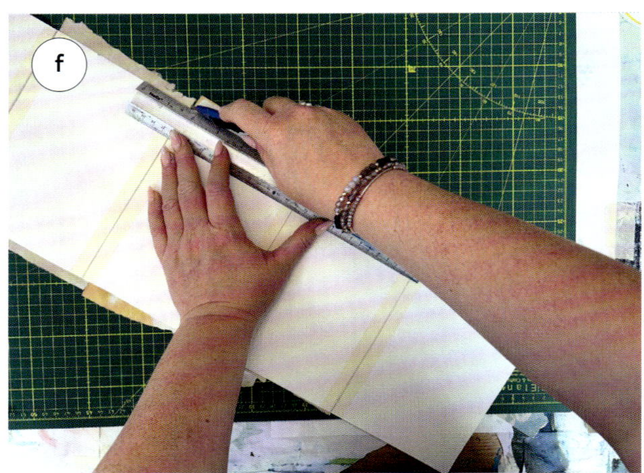

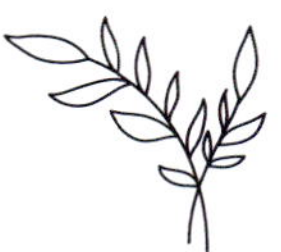

Tip

Place greaseproof paper under the area you're gluing to protect your workspace and keep the underside of the book clean.

Gluing the papers down

I used matte medium glue to stick down the collage papers, which works well for thinner materials. However, I had an issue with the black tissue paper as the wet medium caused the colour to bleed – a glue stick worked much better.

When applying the glue, cover both the back of the paper (c) and the surface of the book. For very thin papers, like tissue, you only need to apply glue to the book surface first. Stick your papers down one at a time and slightly overlap them as you go to create the collage (d); don't worry about the external edges for the moment. To smooth out any bubbles, I used a catalyst wedge (e), but an old credit card will work just as effectively.

Once all the pages are fully covered, allow them to dry completely before flipping them over to trim any overlapping edges (f). Cutting while the paper is still damp makes it difficult to achieve a sharp edge.

Finishing touches to the first layer

Testing the design in folded format

Check how the design looks when the book is folded (a). If you notice areas where the paper is lifting due to the folds, you can resolve this by gluing thinner papers over the spine (b). This technique not only secures these sections but also adds more layers and depth to your piece.

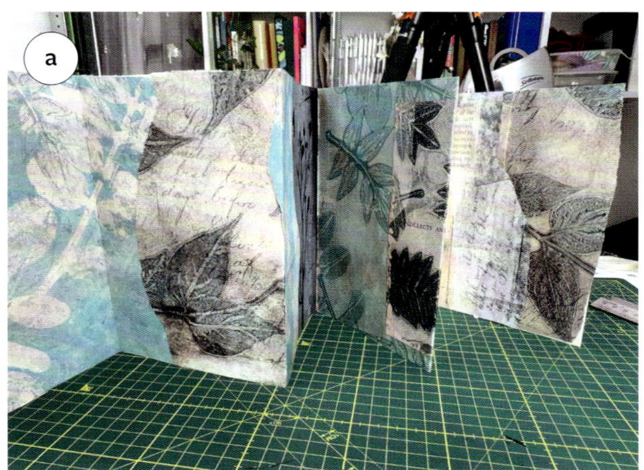

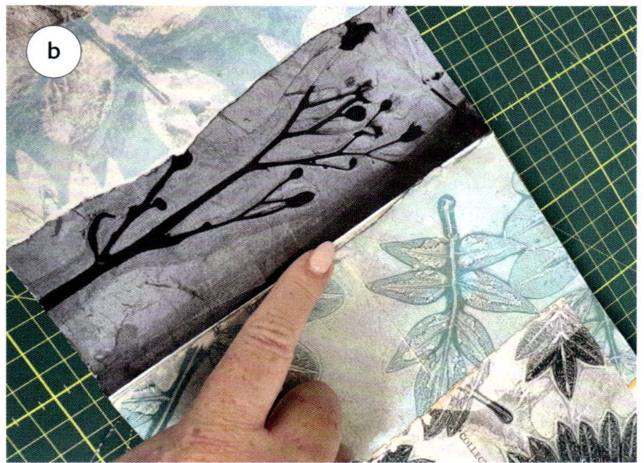

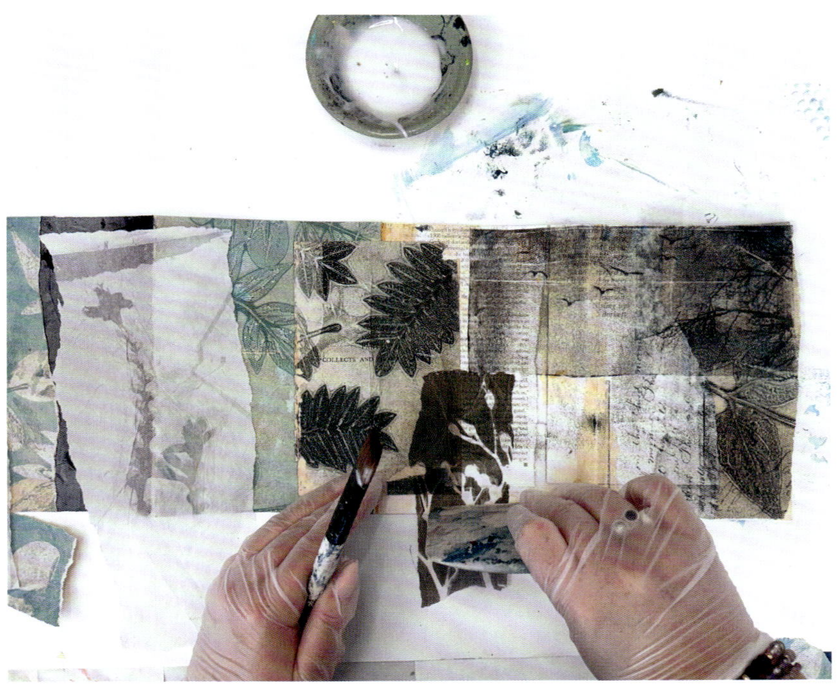

When the matte medium glue is applied to this thin tissue paper, the unpainted areas of the paper become transparent, revealing the text underneath.

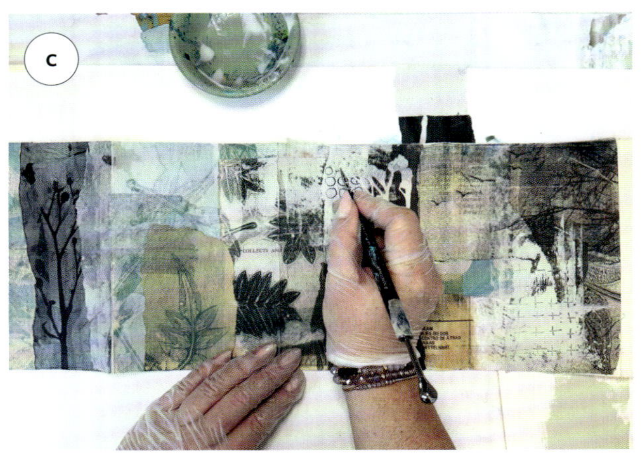

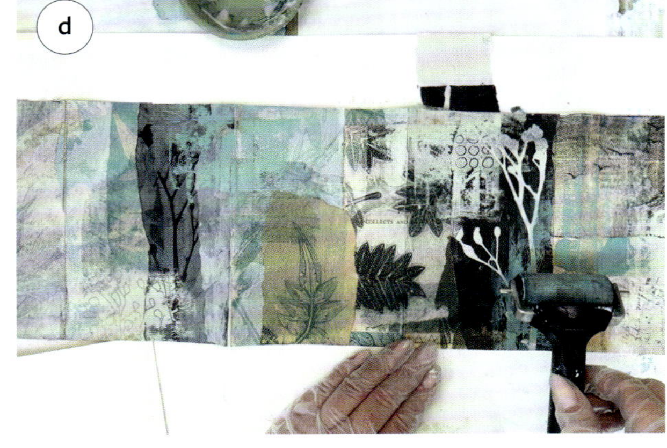

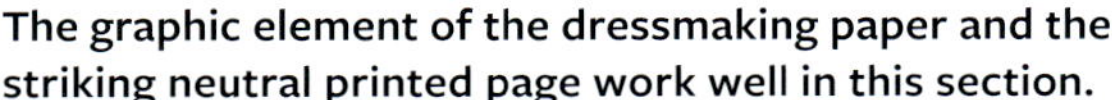
The graphic element of the dressmaking paper and the striking neutral printed page work well in this section.

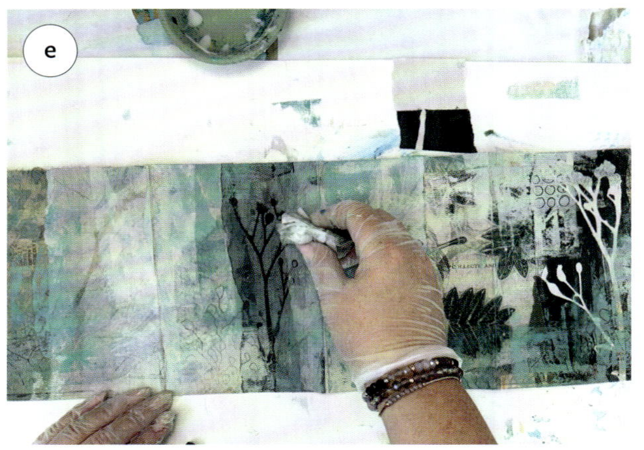

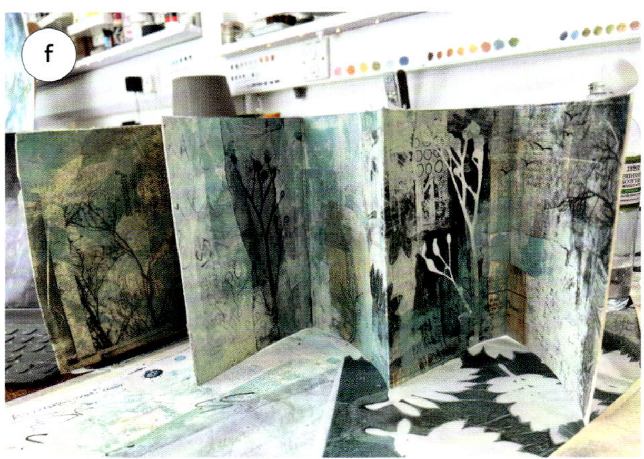

Blending edges with a roller/brayer

For this technique, I used a small roller to apply a small amount of Titan Green Pale to a scrap piece of mountboard. While the paint is still wet, use a tool like a ball stylus to draw into it (c), revealing the darker colour underneath the lighter layer.

Paint over the edges of some joins (d) and stick to the colours in the collage papers to ensure that the design feels cohesive. If you apply too much paint or don't like its placement, you can easily remove it with a baby wipe while it's still wet (e). Once it is dry you can also draw onto the paint to bring in new shapes.

Reviewing the design

Fold the book and stand it up to review the design in its 3D format again, checking how it looks from different angles (f).

After reviewing, I felt that one area (g) needed something extra, so I cut out a positive leaf shape to fill the space (h, i). You can use either a craft knife or sharp scissors.

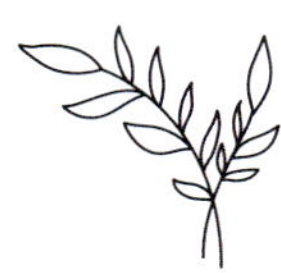

Tip

If the paper is very thin, place another sheet of paper behind it to make cutting easier and more stable.

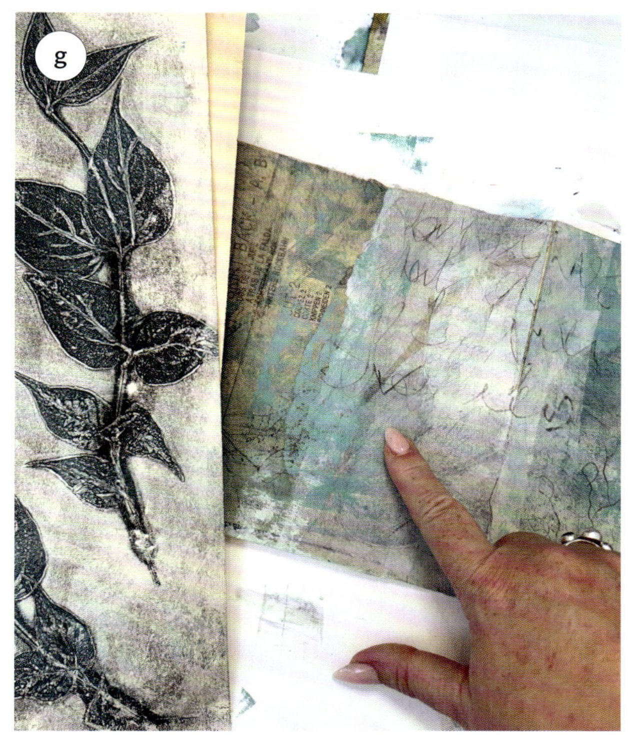

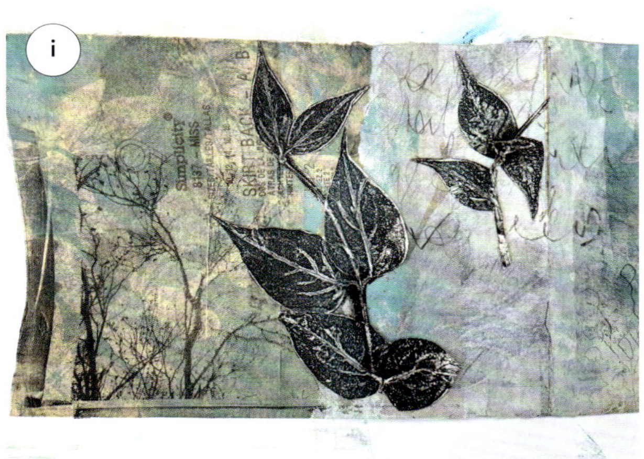

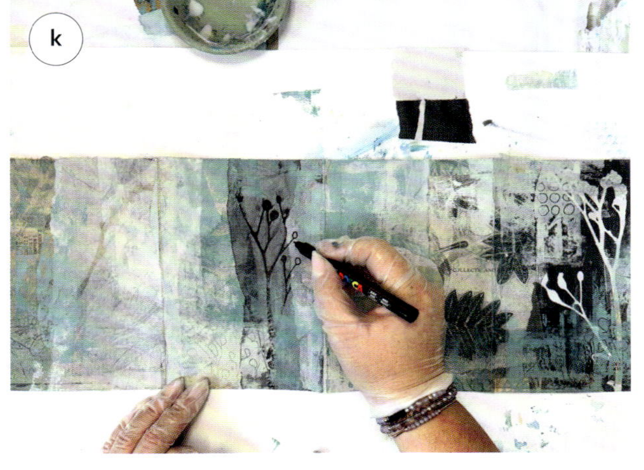

Defining shapes

I used acrylic paint and a small clean, dry brush to define and softly blend certain areas such as the edges (j). Allow this side to dry completely – preferably overnight – before starting on the second side.

Here, the black silhouette of the plant and buds has been hidden by the collage layers. To bring these shapes back, I use a black Posca pen with a fine 0.7mm (⅛in) nib to carefully redraw and outline them (k).

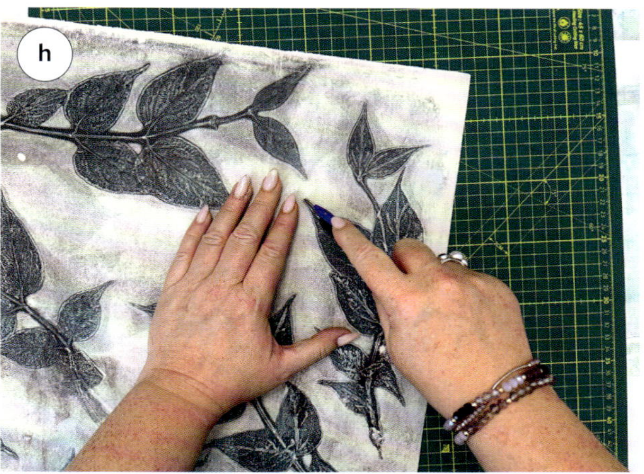

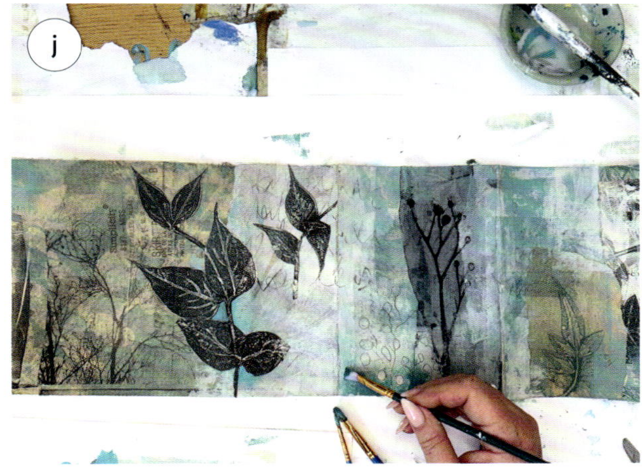

Blending paint

To soften any harsh lines in your collage, lightly apply a matching colour of paint with a dry brush over the edges, then use a clean, dry brush to blend it. This helps to create a more natural transition.

Starting the second side

Preparing the printed pages

I decided to cut out neat rectangles of collage to start the design for the second side. I use a viewfinder cut to the same size as the book pages to identify appealing areas within the larger printed papers (a). Once I select a section, I mark the outline of the rectangle with a pencil before cutting it out (b). I then glue the pieces to the book surface with glue as before (c) (see page 118), using a glue stick for the black tissue.

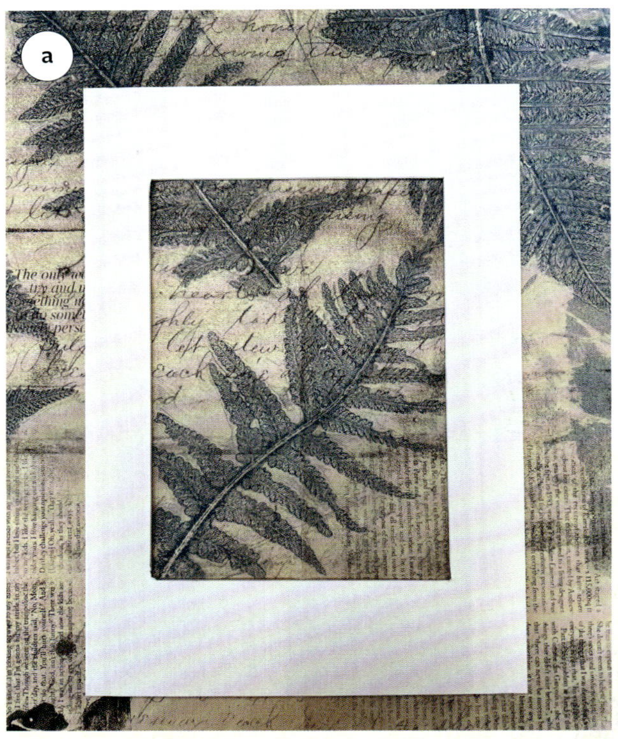

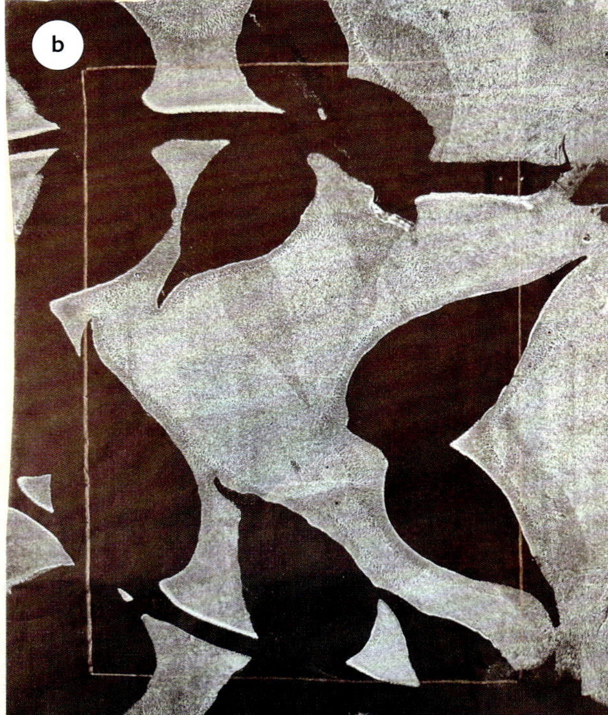

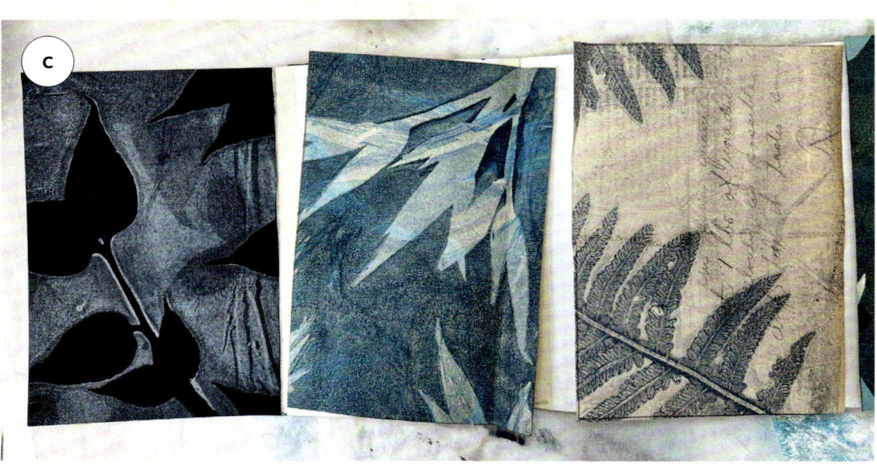

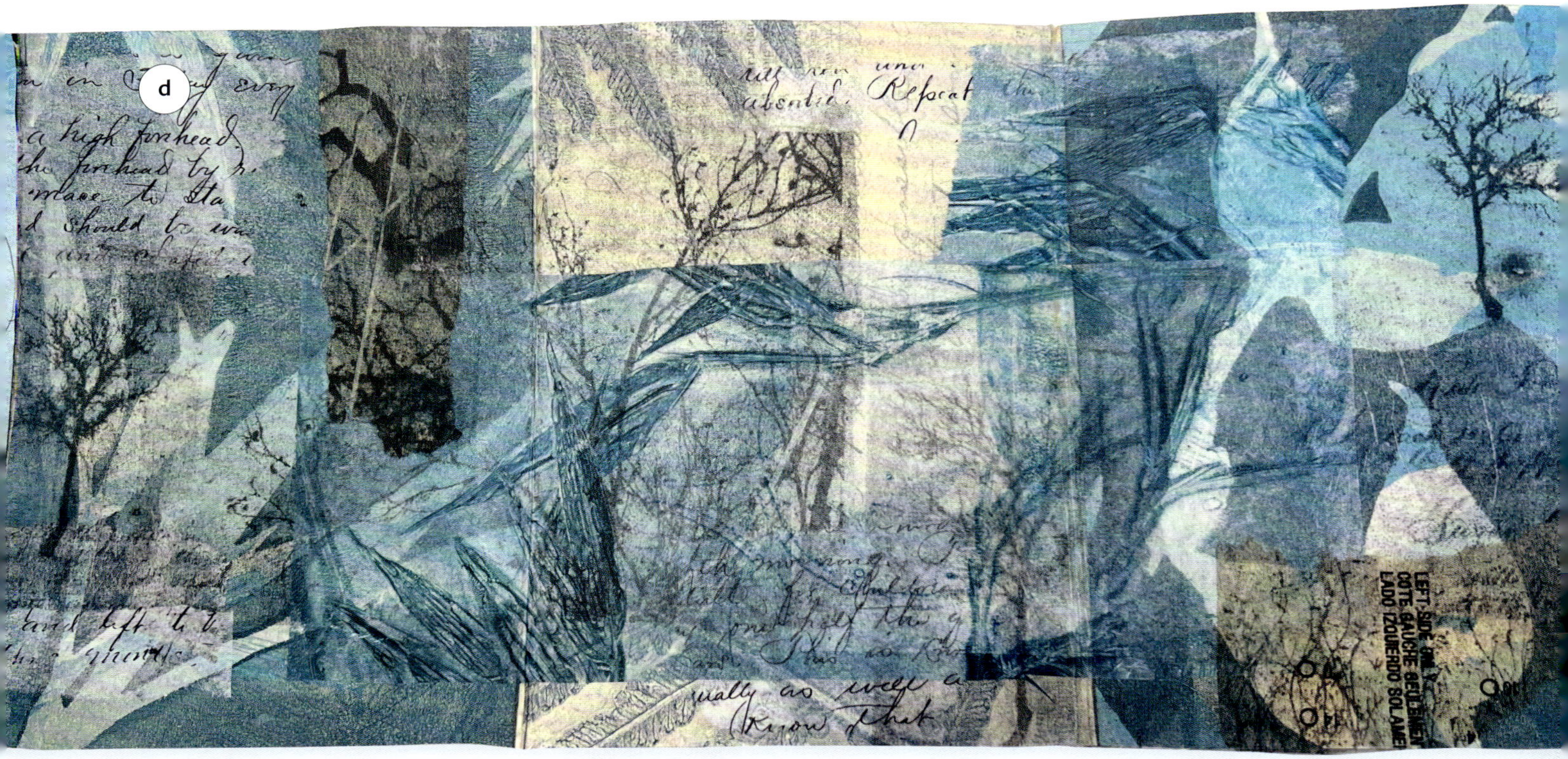

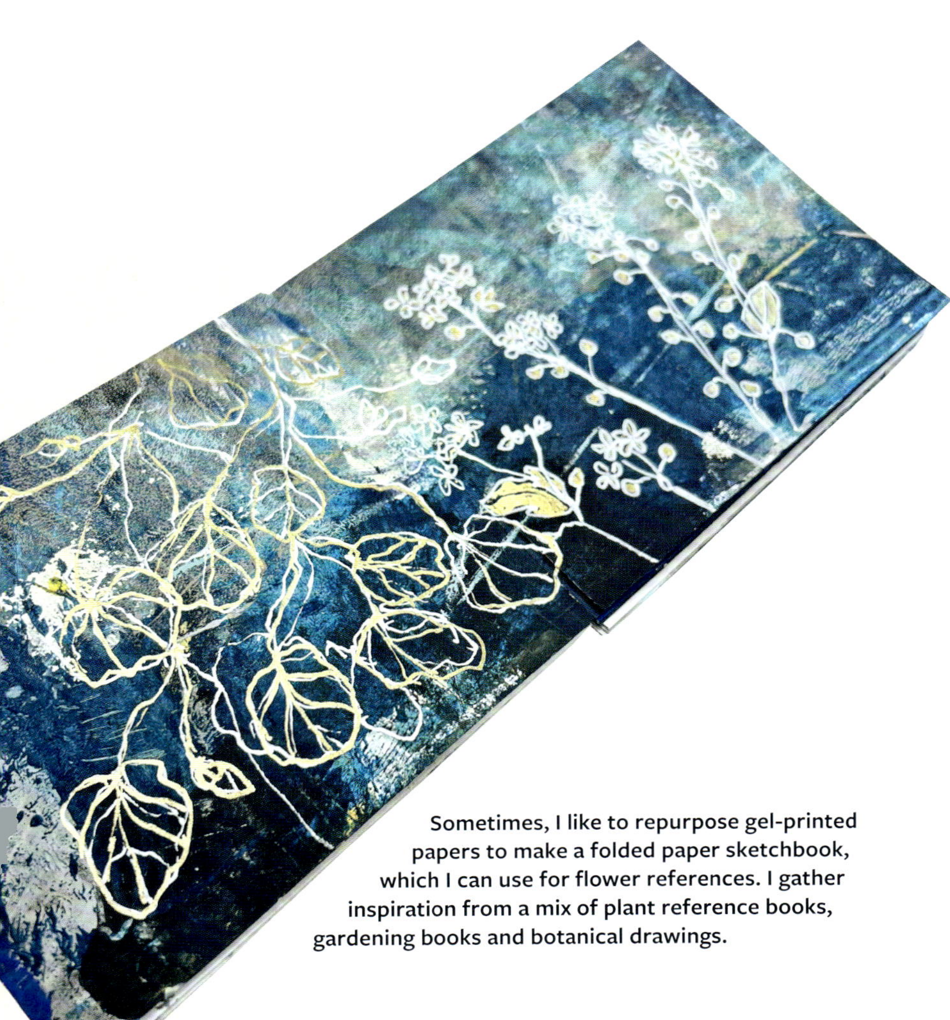

Selecting papers

Next, I choose transparent papers to create a second layer over the first, placing them over the folds to prevent creasing when the book is folded (d). This stage can look somewhat messy and overwhelming, but trust the process – it will all come together in the end!

Sometimes, I like to repurpose gel-printed papers to make a folded paper sketchbook, which I can use for flower references. I gather inspiration from a mix of plant reference books, gardening books and botanical drawings.

Adding text and leaves

I add some text from my ephemera collection (a) (see page 53) and cut out leaf shapes from our gel-printed papers. I held spare paper behind them (see page 82) to make cutting easier (b); this paper can also be used as stencil templates in later prints.

Use the same method as before (see page 118) to glue the leaves (c), applying adhesive to both the paper and the surface to ensure strong adhesion.

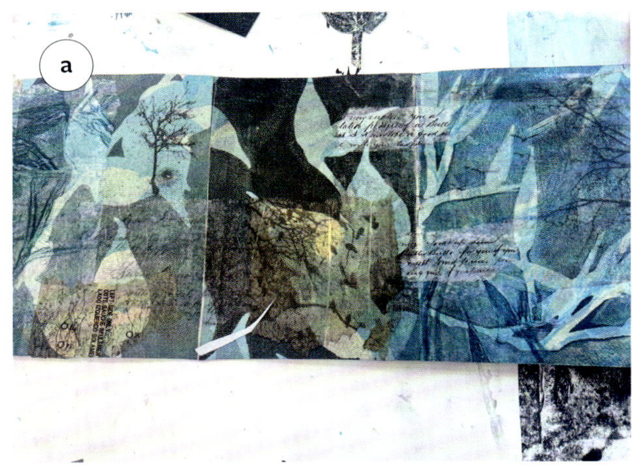

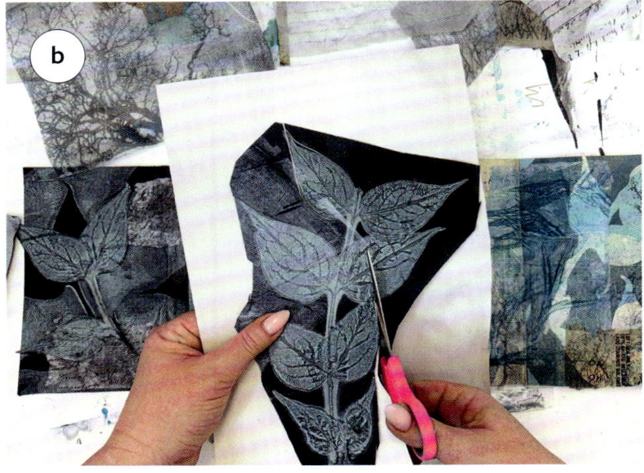

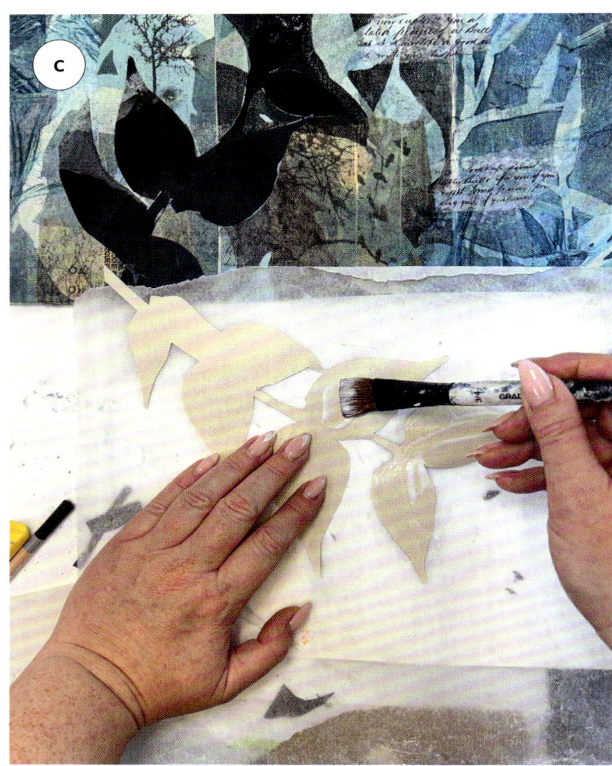

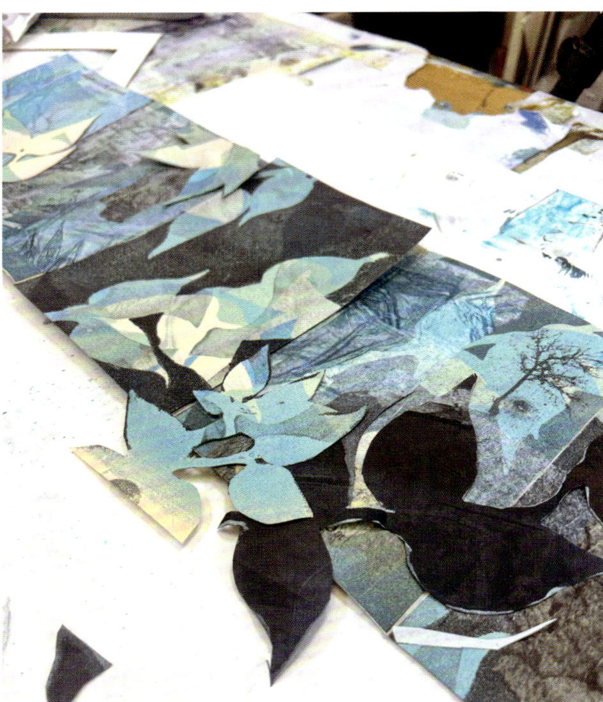

Here, I covered up a whole section that I felt wasn't working well.

Adding definition to the leaves and hand-drawn element

Now that all the leaf shapes are glued down, it's time to define them. I use acrylic paint to outline the edges, then blend areas using a dry brush (d) and add contrast. This helps make the shapes stand out and gives the artwork more depth.

I found a few drawings in the stack of papers gifted by my studio neighbour, and used this in my gel prints on page 104. The drawing felt a bit lost, so I used a slightly darker shade of blue to paint the negative space around the flower shapes (e).

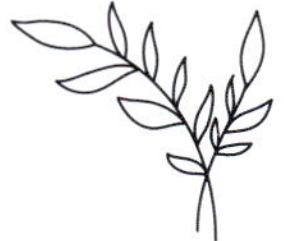

Tip

It's important to include white space – empty or plain areas – in your painting. This doesn't have to be white; it can be any background colour or unpainted area. It gives the eye a place to rest, preventing the artwork from looking too busy. It also adds harmony, helping to balance the composition and make the main elements stand out.

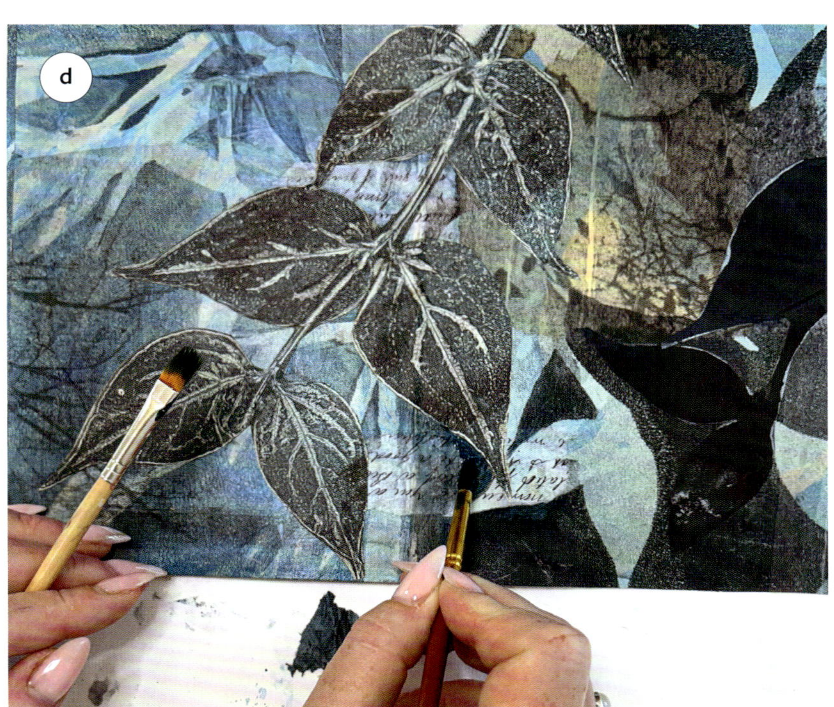

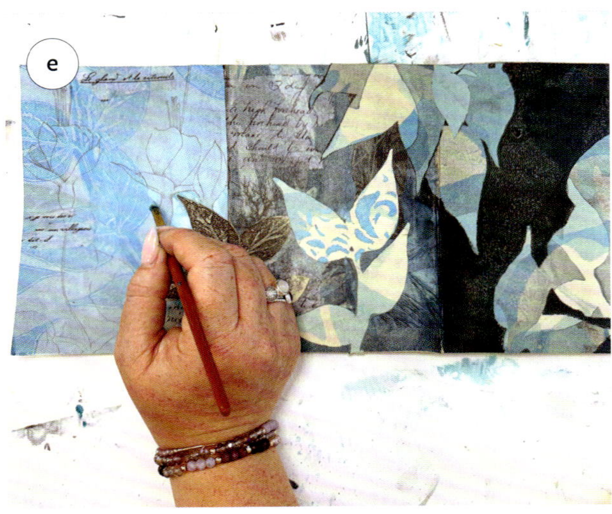

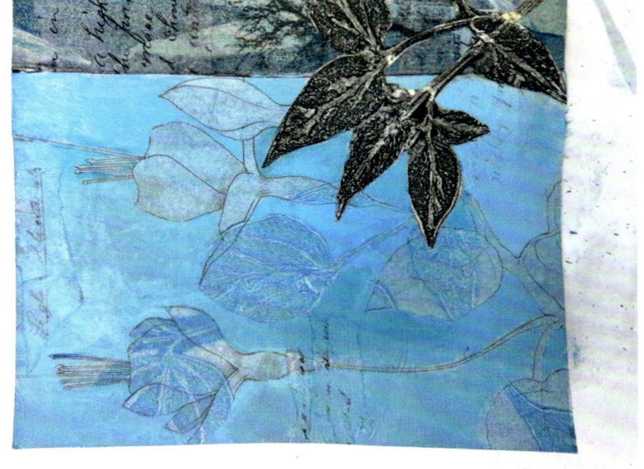

The paint helped to define and highlight the drawings while preserving the delicate feel of the page.

Using stencils

Stencils are a great way to add shapes to your design, whether in the background or as finishing touches. For my artist book, I use stencils to bring the design together. I stick with the same colour palette used for the original papers to maintain harmony.

When selecting stencils to enhance your artwork, make sure they fit the overall theme of your piece. For example, in this project I've chosen botanical shapes to complement the natural elements of the design. Different themes can evoke different moods, but be mindful – bold geometric shapes, for instance, wouldn't suit this composition. Choose stencils that harmonise with the style and subject of your painting.

To use the stencil, I squeeze a small amount of paint onto a flat surface such as glass or Perspex and blend the colour using a face painting sponge cut in half (a). (I've found that Snazaroo sponges work better than make-up sponges.) Practise using the stencil on scrap paper, applying paint with the sponge until you achieve a clean, sharp outline, then position the stencil where desired on your print and apply paint using the sponge (b), being careful not to overload it with paint – this takes some trial and error.

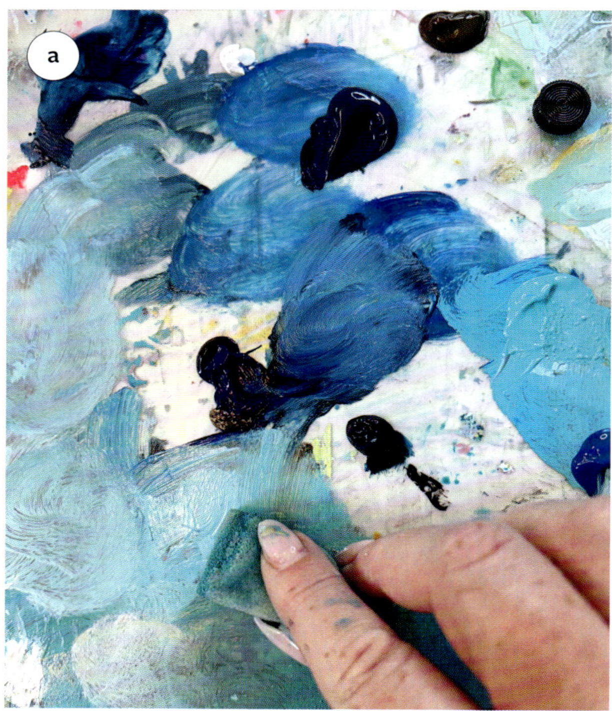

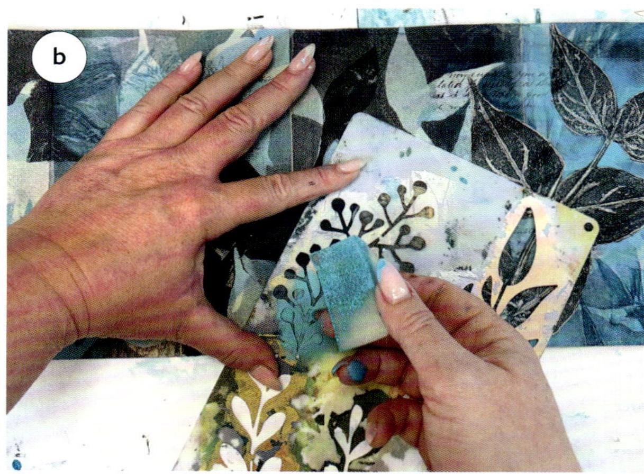

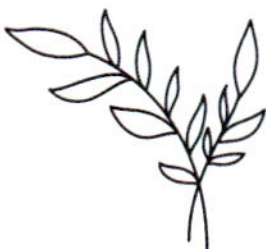

Tip

Be sure not to move the stencil while applying paint, as this can blur the shape.

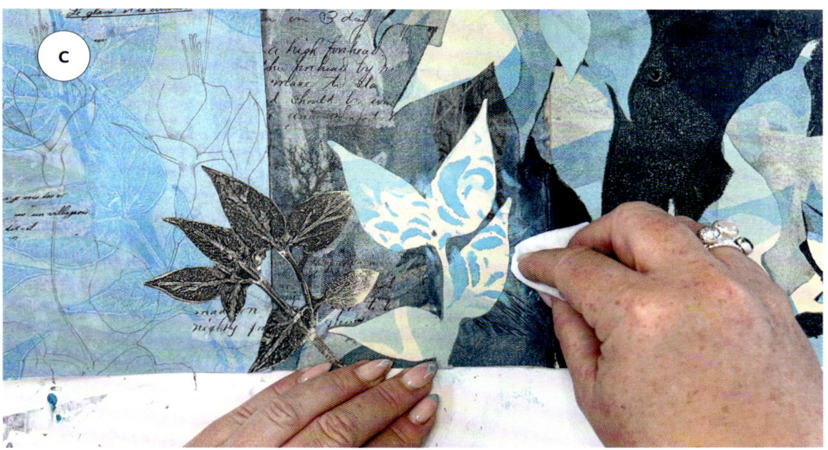

Cleaning up areas

Here I used a larger stencil and wanted the textured design to stay within the leaf shape, but it can be tricky to see the exact shape under the stencil. To fix this, you can either mask the surrounding area with paper or, if any paint goes outside the lines, wipe it off with a baby wipe while it's still wet (c).

Adding pen drawings

The final step in the design is to add the pen drawings (a). Make sure the paper is completely dry for this part, otherwise the pens won't perform as desired.

If you have leftover paint, use it to create a colourful background in your sketchbook. If you want a white edge, tape the page with masking tape before painting. This way, when you're ready to practise your drawing skills, you'll have a prepared page that feels less intimidating than a blank white page.

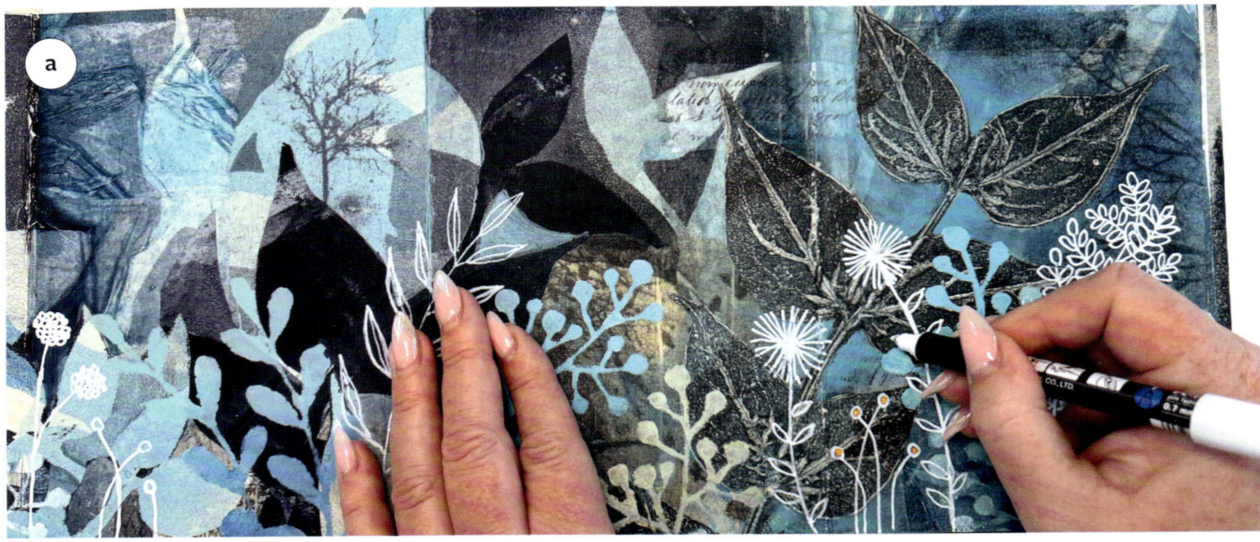

Using Posca pens

If the ink isn't flowing smoothly, shake the pen with the cap on and press the tip down on some scrap paper a few times. If you're getting uneven or streaky lines, press down steadily while drawing and keep the tip clean.

If the colour isn't showing well, try the pen on different surfaces and go over your pen lines until you are happy with the opacity. Absorbent surfaces like sugar paper can soak up too much ink, so I found that the Uni-ball Signo bronze pen worked better on that type of paper.

If you make a mistake, wipe it off quickly with a damp cloth or baby wipe before it dries. Clean the tips after each use to avoid clogs, and if the tips are very dry, soak them nib down in warm, soapy water overnight.

Practising flower and leaf shapes in a sketchbook can help improve your skills and give you references for your finished paintings. You can also draw through stencils rather than freehand, if you prefer. Using paint pens, such as Posca, can also be a little fiddly to use, so be patient and try out pressing down and squeezing the pen as you use it. Sometimes they might need a soak in water to get started!

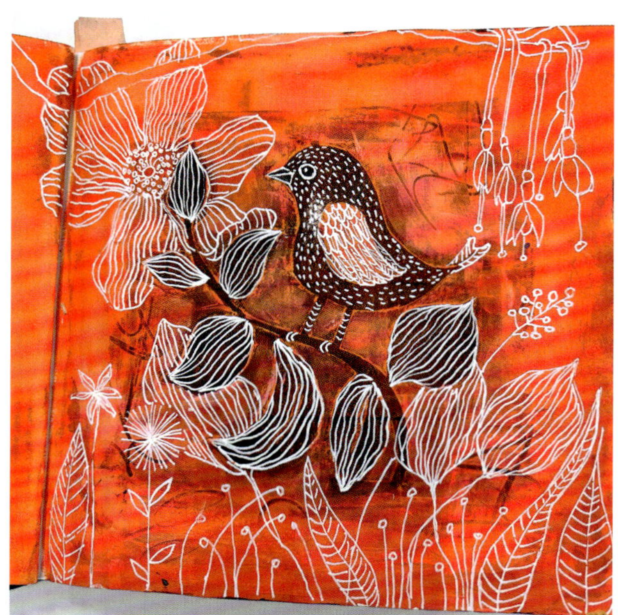

I've tried many pens over the years, but I always return to Posca pens because I love their opaqueness and smooth flow.

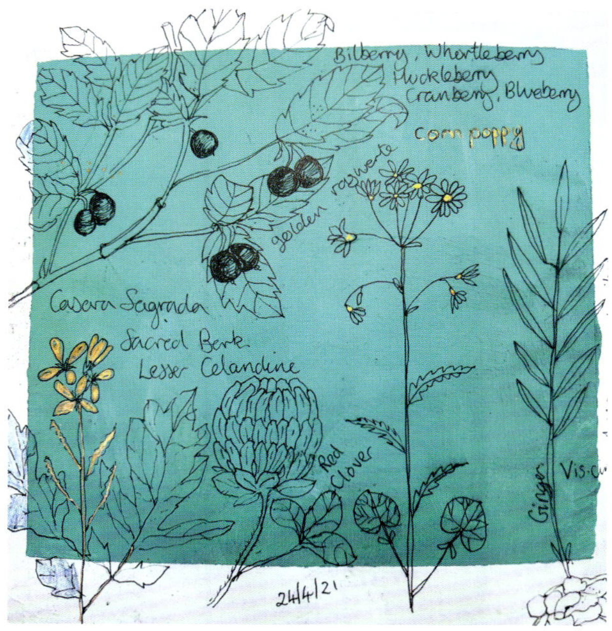

Posca pens are filled with acrylic paint, which gives great coverage and vibrancy.

Making the covers

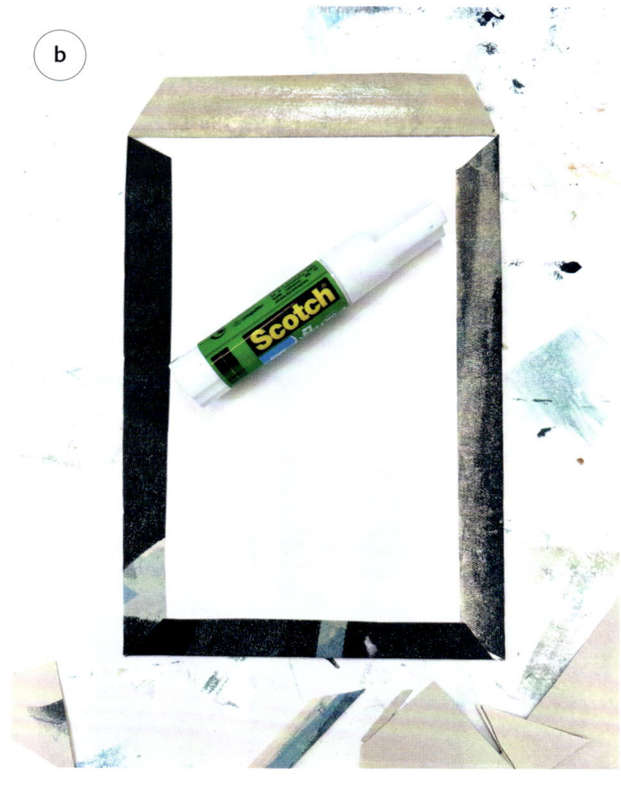

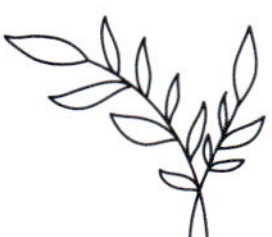

Tip

Rub a white candle over the finished pages to prevent them from sticking together and tearing when closed. This adds a protective layer that saves your artwork from damage.

To create the covers, I used a viewfinder tool to select two areas of artwork that I liked, choosing prints in two contrasting colour schemes. The covers I used measure 20 x 14cm (8 x 5½in), so I cut pieces of paper to 24 x 18cm (9½ x 7in), allowing extra paper for wrapping around the mountboard to give a neat, clean finish to the covers (a).

For gluing, you can use either matte medium or a glue stick. Since the paper I printed on was very absorbent, I chose a glue stick to avoid the risk of ripping the paper with wet glue (b).

Ensure the painted pages in the book are completely dry before gluing the covers on; ideally, wait 48 hours. If they're not dry, there's a chance the pages will stick together, ruining all your hard work. Patience is key!

Adding pen and stencil details

Follow the instructions on pages 126–128 to add details to the covers in the same way as before (c). Draw through a stencil if you prefer this to freehand shapes.

Gluing the covers to the book

Apply a glue stick to the last page of the book and the back of the cover (d), securing both the front and back covers. Place heavy weights on top of the folded book to ensure good adhesion – place sheets of greaseproof paper in between the folded pages to protect them during the drying process.

If you notice that the paper has lifted slightly when the book was folded, use a sharp craft knife to carefully trim any loose paper. Once trimmed, fill in the white area with paint or a coloured pencil that matches the colour (e). This will help repair the spine and give your book a clean, finished look.

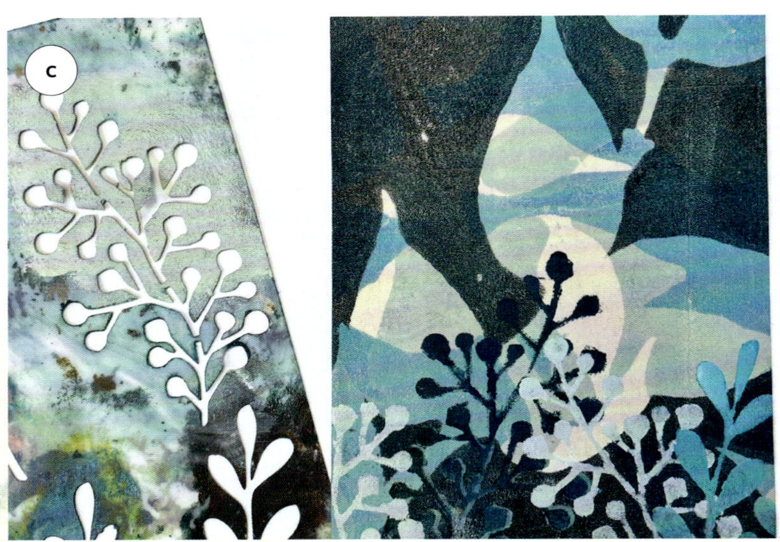

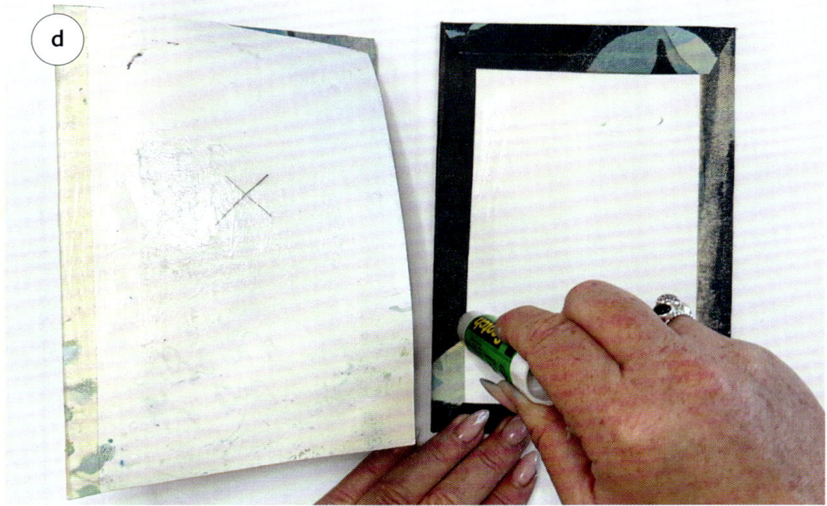

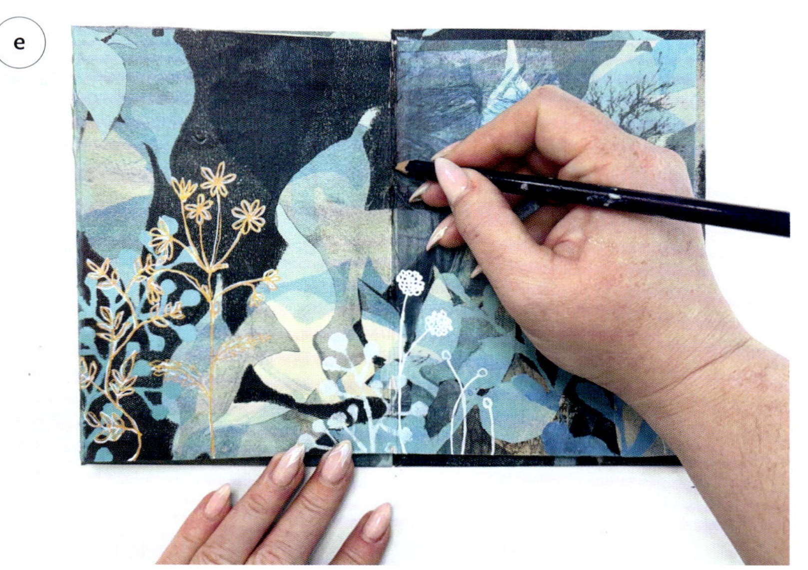

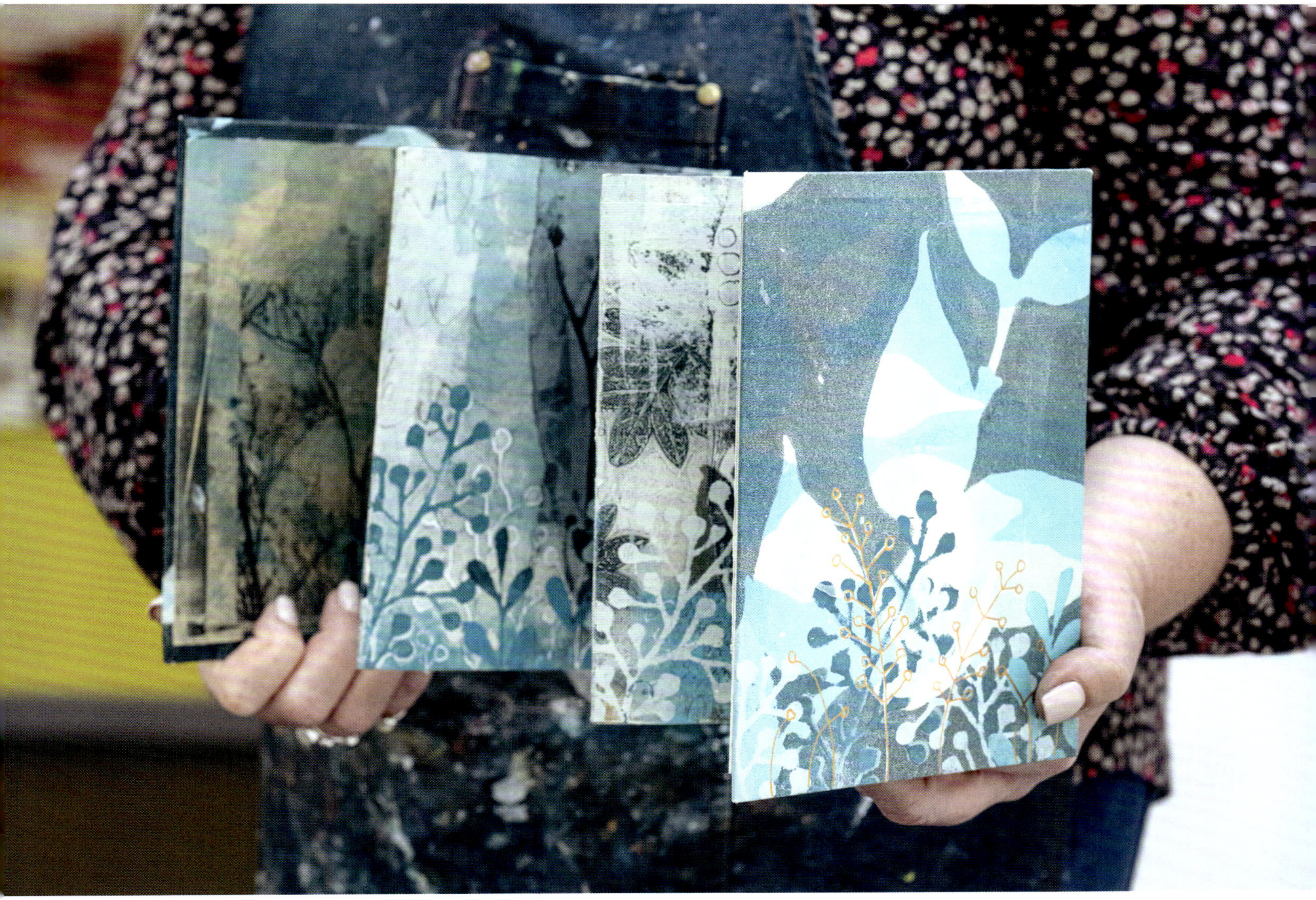

Q **Can you share a little about your background and how you discovered gel printing?**

A

I am a full-time artist currently working in fibre, collage and printmaking, often digitally combining all three. I have always enjoyed working with my hands and being creative from a young age. It was not a surprise that I studied graphic design at university.

Art is something I came to later after teaching myself to knit, then discovering modern quilting. Digging around on the internet, I saw people using gel plates and was interested in its ability to create grungy prints, which is something that I've always been drawn to. I ordered a gel plate and never looked back.

Q **What drew you to using a gel plate in your artwork?**

A

I had discovered the modern quilt movement and was making large art quilts, which can take months to construct. I was looking for a way to work faster; I had always enjoyed collage so I started collaging. The gel plate gave me a way to make my own collage papers, which allowed my collage work to take on a clear voice. This coincidentally also positively affected my quilt work.

Q **Who or what are your main influences in your art practice?**

A

My work is inspired by the controlled chaos and iconography of urban environments.

I have always felt more at home in the hustle, bustle and crowds of cities, even though I would call myself an introvert. Cities are controlled and regulated, yet they can be very chaotic and organic. Most cities in the United States are organised into 'blocks', yet within these containers there are chaotic and contrasting urban elements, such as power lines, graffiti, nature, crumbling concrete, walls with torn posters, billboards, wealth, poverty... these dichotomies inspire my art.

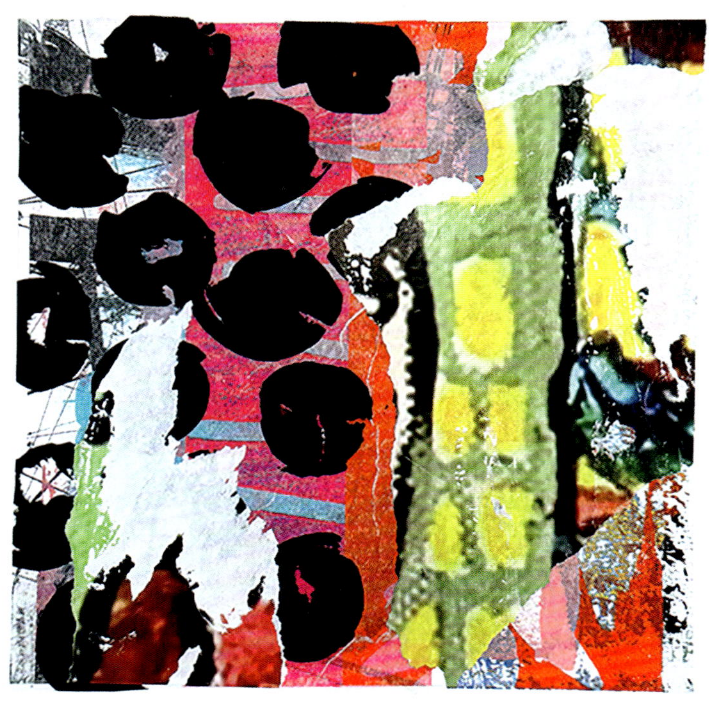

A collage from my sketchbook made with gel plate printed tissue papers and torn posters from NYC

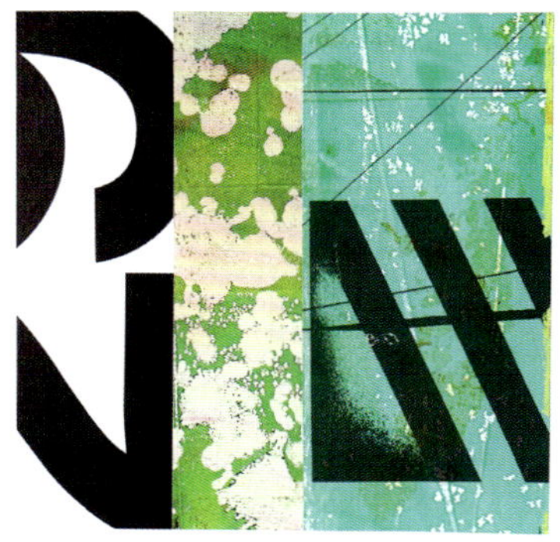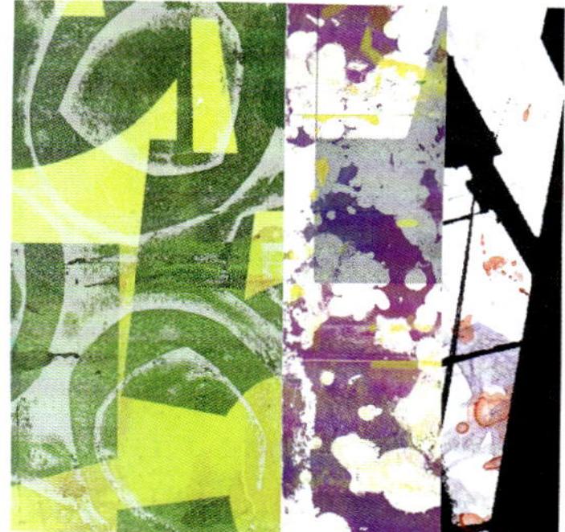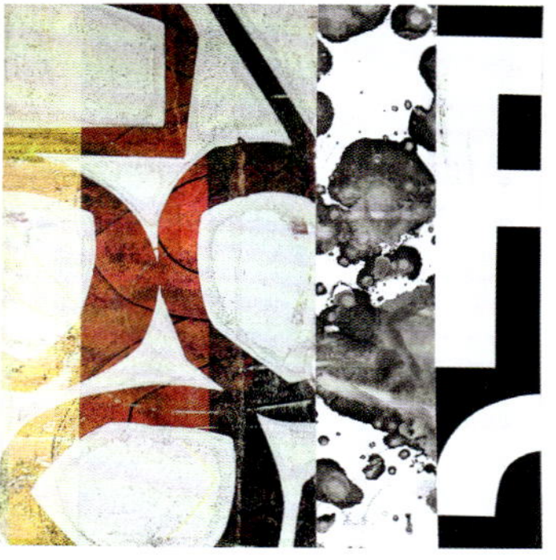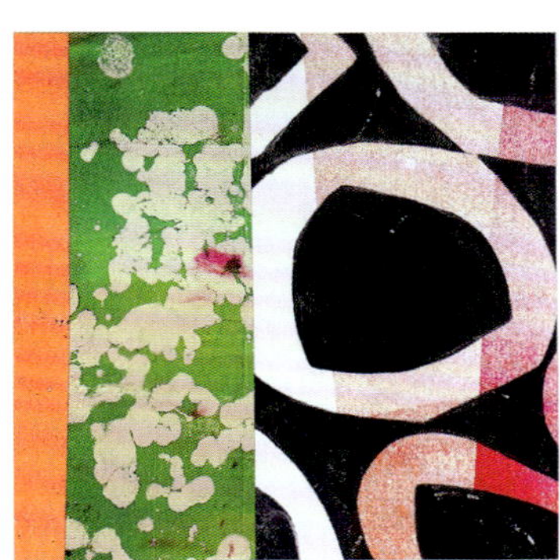

Collage studies. I challenged myself to use only three collage pieces per work. Most papers were printed using gel plate techniques

Q How do you see the role of gel printing in the broader context of contemporary art?

A Right now, a gel plate is seen as a craft tool and exists mostly in the craft world. I do see artists starting to use gel-printed papers in mixed-media and collage work. And I've noticed the traditional printmaking world starting to discover gel plates, especially the larger plates made by Gelli Arts.

As far as the capital 'A' Art world goes, I think gel plate printing has a way to go before it's taken seriously.

Q What projects or directions are you excited about exploring in the future?

A My quilt work has recently changed from solid cotton fabrics intricately cut and pieced to digitally printed fabrics with very few pieces. A gel plate plays a role in these quilt pieces... my monoprints, layered collages and photography are digitally composed and manipulated, then printed onto fabric and finally machine pieced and quilted.

Q What advice would you give to beginners who are just starting with gel printing?

A Give yourself time to experiment with different techniques and learn everything you can about gel plate printing. Be patient and kind to yourself as you are learning and troubleshooting new techniques.

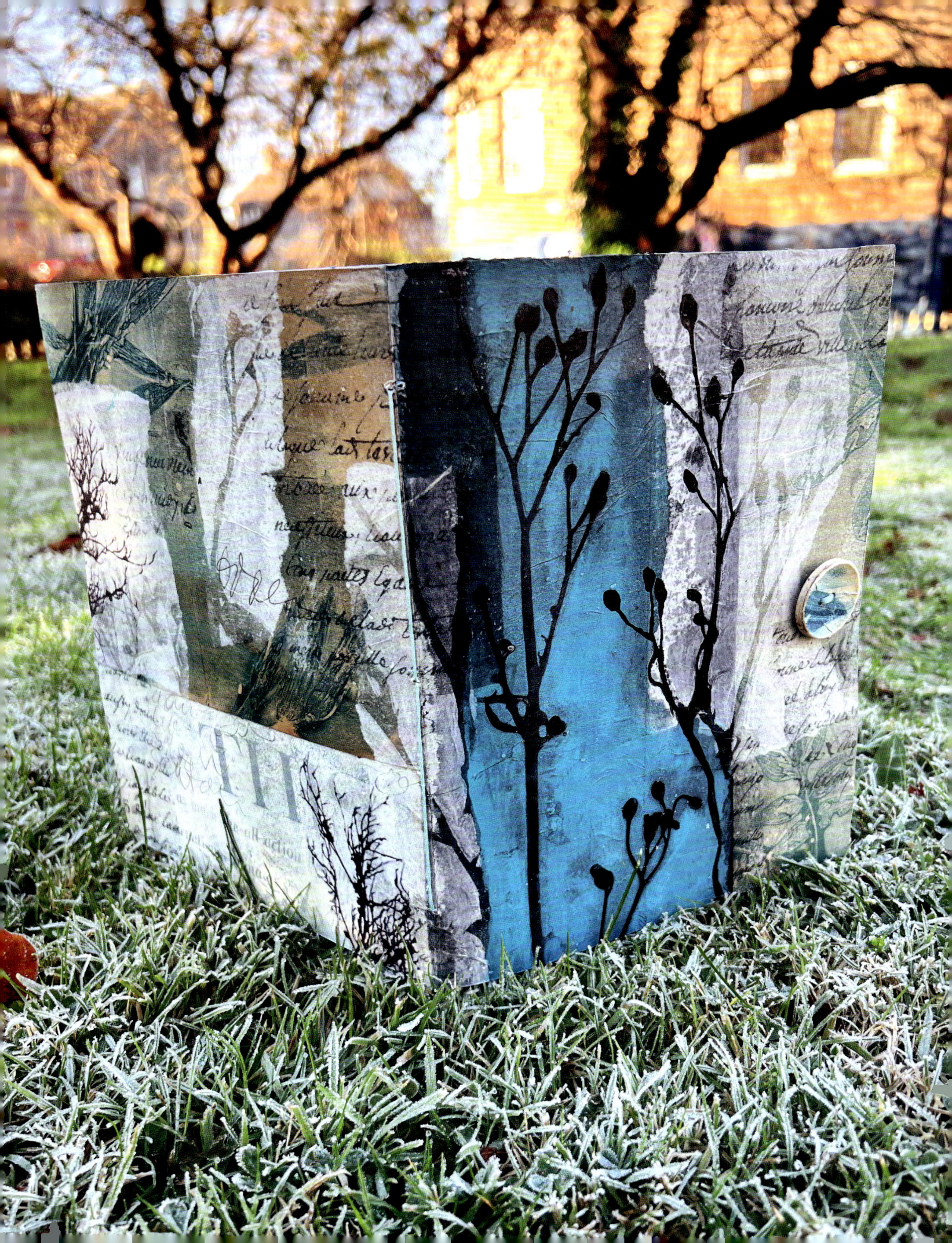

HANDMADE ART JOURNAL

Handmade journals are such beautiful, tactile treasures. I especially love the chunky ones, packed with inspiration – collage papers, magazine snippets, stitched details and ideas bursting from every page. Whenever I see photos of them, I can't help but wish I could flip through those amazing creations, all made with so much love. Honestly, if I could only do one creative thing for the rest of my life, I'd spend it making books like this. Now, I'm excited to show you how to make one too!

In this project, I'll show you how to create a journal cover with a leathery feel, secure the pages with a simple bookbinding stitch and share a few ideas to help you start filling those pages with creativity.

MATERIALS
Refer back to the master list on page 18 for the essential items.

- Cartridge paper or mixed-media paper, 300gsm. I used A2 pages cut to size
- Masking tape and double-sided tape
- Printed collage papers, hand-dyed papers, thin drawing paper, tissue paper
- Heavy gel medium
- Metal ball stylus sculpting tool
- Disposable gloves
- Cold wax, such as Zest-it Cold Wax Painting Medium
- Soft cloth
- Awl
- Embroidery thread and needle and threader
- Wooden button blanks or vintage button
- Glue dots or glue stick
- Curved emery board
- Sari or lace fabric

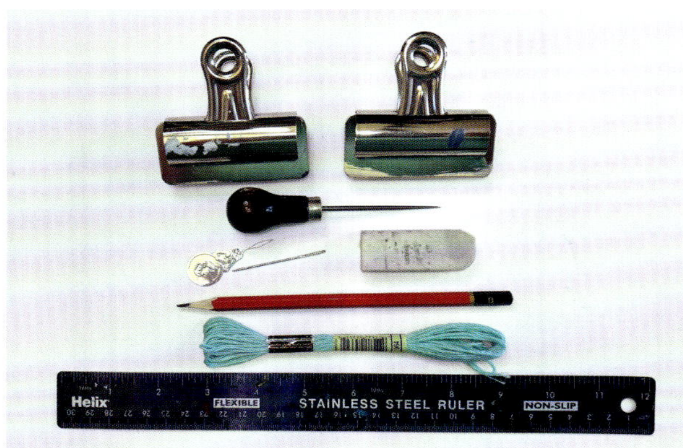

Equipment used to bind the pages.

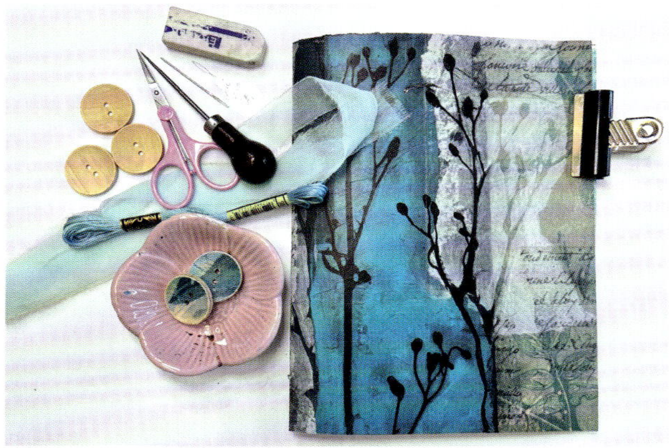

Equipment and materials for attaching the button and fabric to the journal.

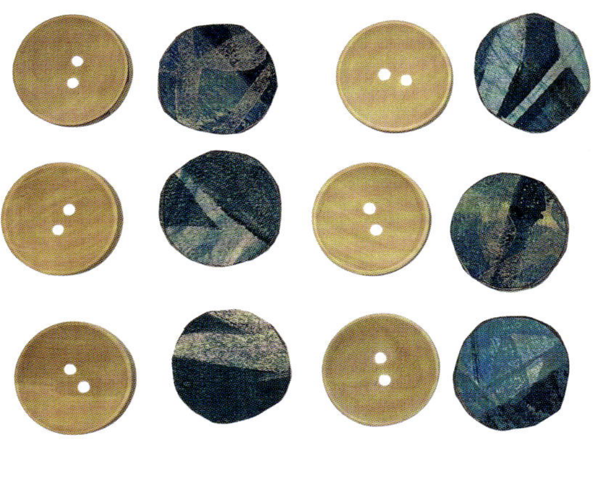

You will need these items to secure your button to the paper.

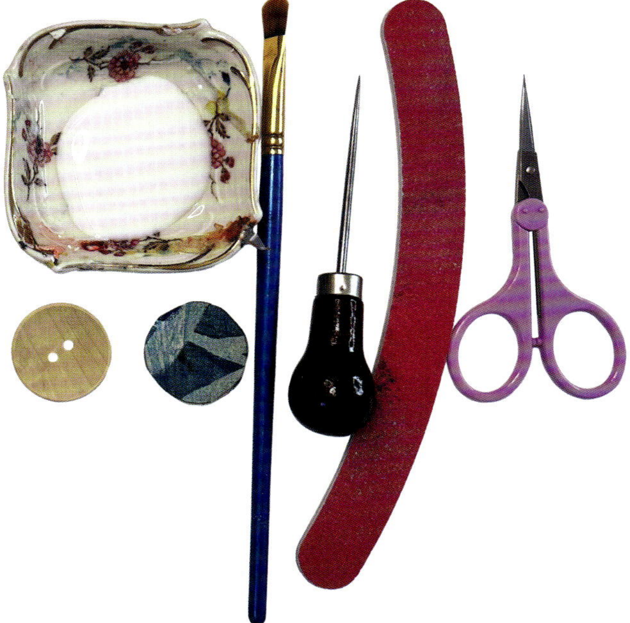

Making the cover

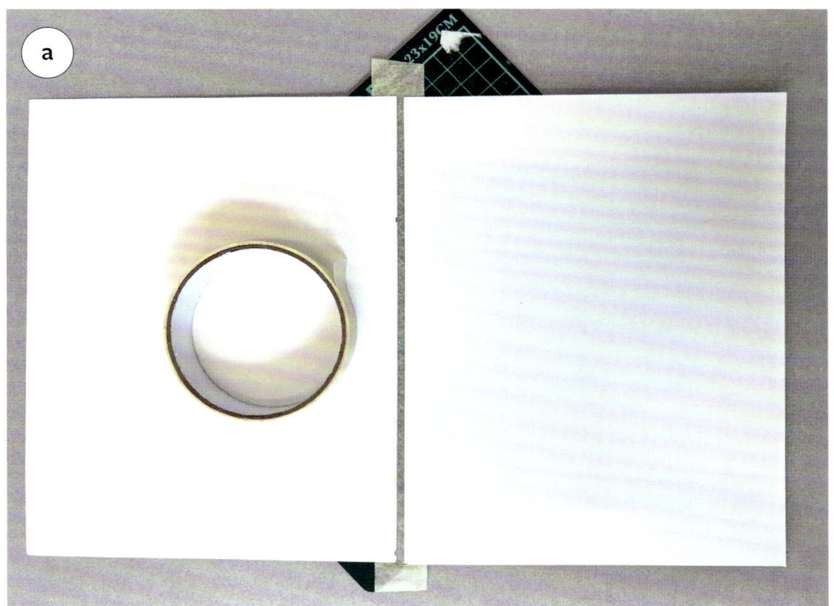

Begin by cutting two rectangles of 300gsm cartridge paper or mixed-media paper. You can make the book any size you like; the one I'm making here will have 23.5 x 18cm (9¼ x 7in) covers. Tape them together on both sides with masking tape, leaving a small gap of a few millimetres between them – this helps the book to fold easily (a).

Collage the cover

Cover the book with your printed collage papers, just like in the Accordion Artist Book project (see page 111) (b). For the inside cover, you can collage too or try something different. I used a roller to create a textured painted surface and, while the paint was still wet, added asemic writing with a ball stylus for a unique, scribed effect (c).

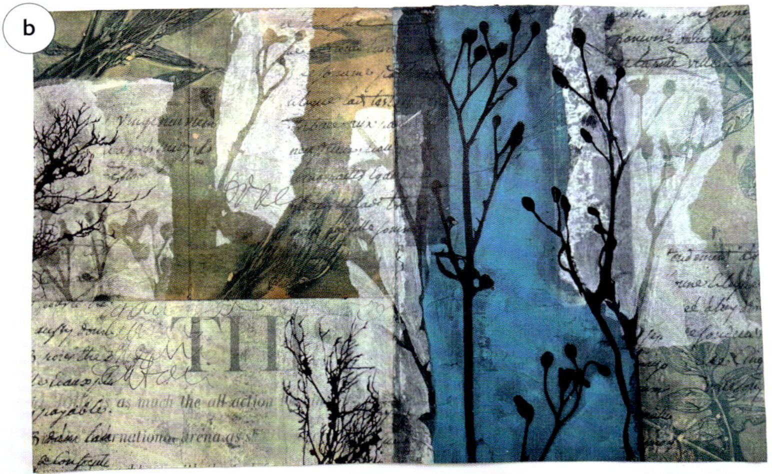

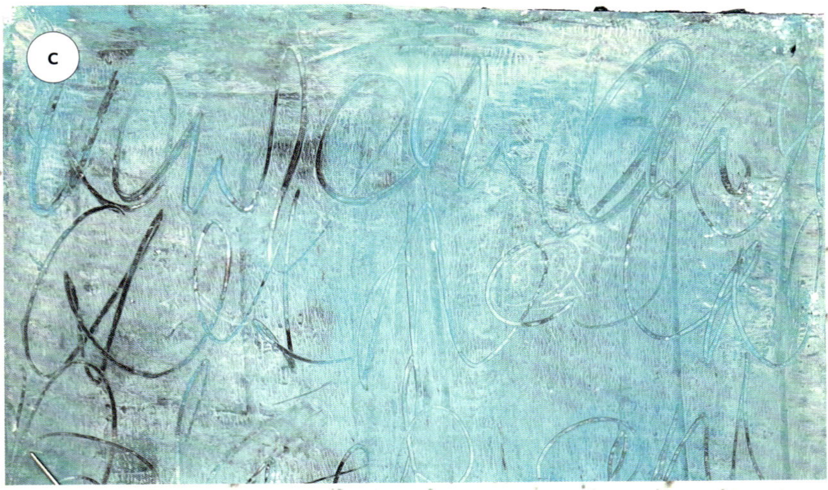

Seal the cover

Next, seal the cover with cold wax to create a smooth, leathery texture. This not only enhances the tactile feel but also protects the cover.

Wear disposable gloves to protect your skin and use a small piece of soft cloth – I like to cut up old T-shirts for this (d). Rub a small amount of wax onto the collage paper using small circular motions until the entire surface is covered (e). Let it dry for around an hour; once it's dry, it won't feel sticky. Then, take a clean cloth and buff the cover until it has a smooth, satin finish.

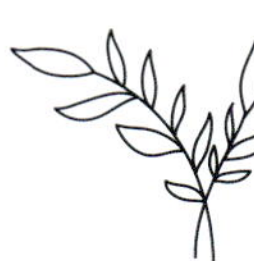

Tip

Make sure to work in a well-ventilated space, as cold wax can have a strong smell. I use Zest-it Cold Wax Painting Medium, which has a lovely citrus scent, but it can still give me a headache if I forget to open the windows first!

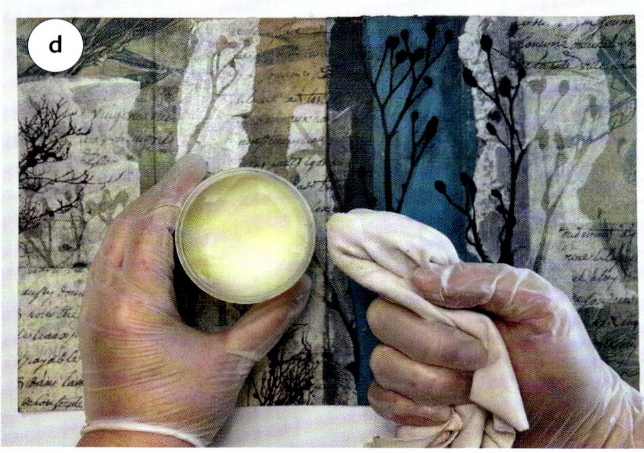

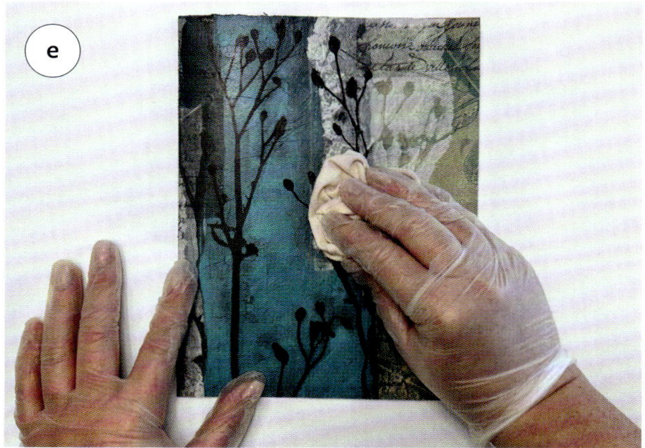

Preparing the pages

Tearing the papers to size

I carefully selected papers for inside the journal, thinking about colour, texture and contrast (a). I settled on using twelve pages, but do not feel limited by this if you wish to add more. Adding pages can be done easily by adding gumstrip (or double-sided tape) to the centre fold and sticking more pages to it.

I prefer tearing the edges with a metal ruler rather than cutting with a craft knife because it gives the paper a more handmade feel. Cut the papers slightly smaller than the cover – my pages were 30 x 21cm (12 x 8¼in). Keep the paper in one single piece for the inside as this helps it stay together better. Don't worry if the papers are not the same size; it just adds to the charm!

Some of my pages are plain, while others are printed or dyed with ink or natural dyes. Thin hand-dyed tissue makes lovely separator pages.

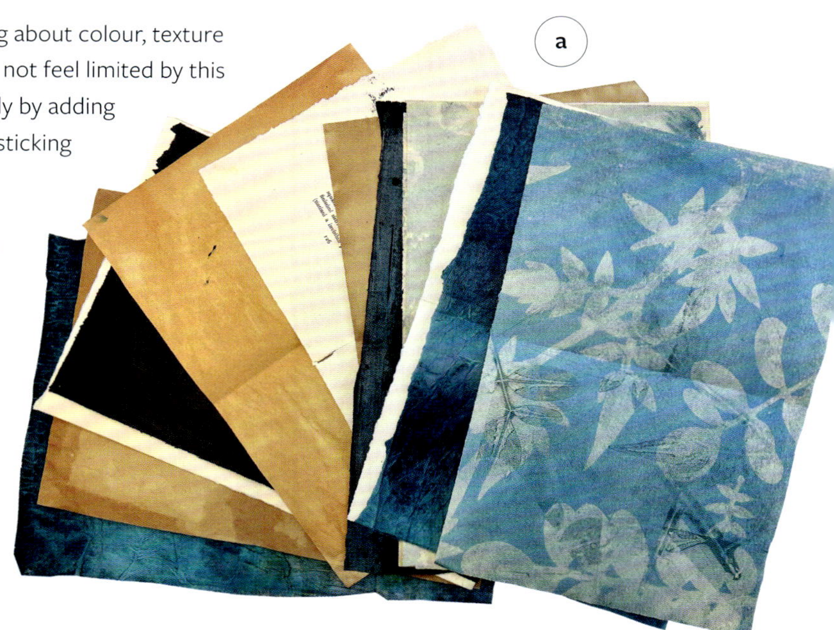

Making hand-dyed paper

1. Prepare your surface

Use a flexible plastic sheet, like a garden waste bag or a plastic floor covering. Avoid glass or rigid Perspex, as the paper may stick to it when wet.

2. Choose your paper

Wet-strength tissue paper works best, as it can handle a good amount of water and glue without tearing. Cut or tear it into the sizes you need. I like to make them A3 size, as this works well for handmade journals – folded in half, it creates two pages.

3. Pick your colours

For these papers, I use various shades of blue: Daler Rowney Turquoise, Indigo and Marine Blue. My favourite Liquitex inks are Muted Turquoise and Turquoise. I also add a touch of Windsor & Newton gold ink for a beautiful shimmer.

4. Apply the inks

Place your tissue paper on the plastic sheet. Drop a small amount of ink into a bowl, wet your brush and paint a line of ink in one colour. I like to work light to dark, blending the colours with water. Add more layers of ink if you want the papers to be darker.

5. Dry and use

Let the papers dry overnight, or speed up drying with a hairdryer. Once dry, iron flat between two sheets of clean paper and use them for collage, journal pages or other creative projects.

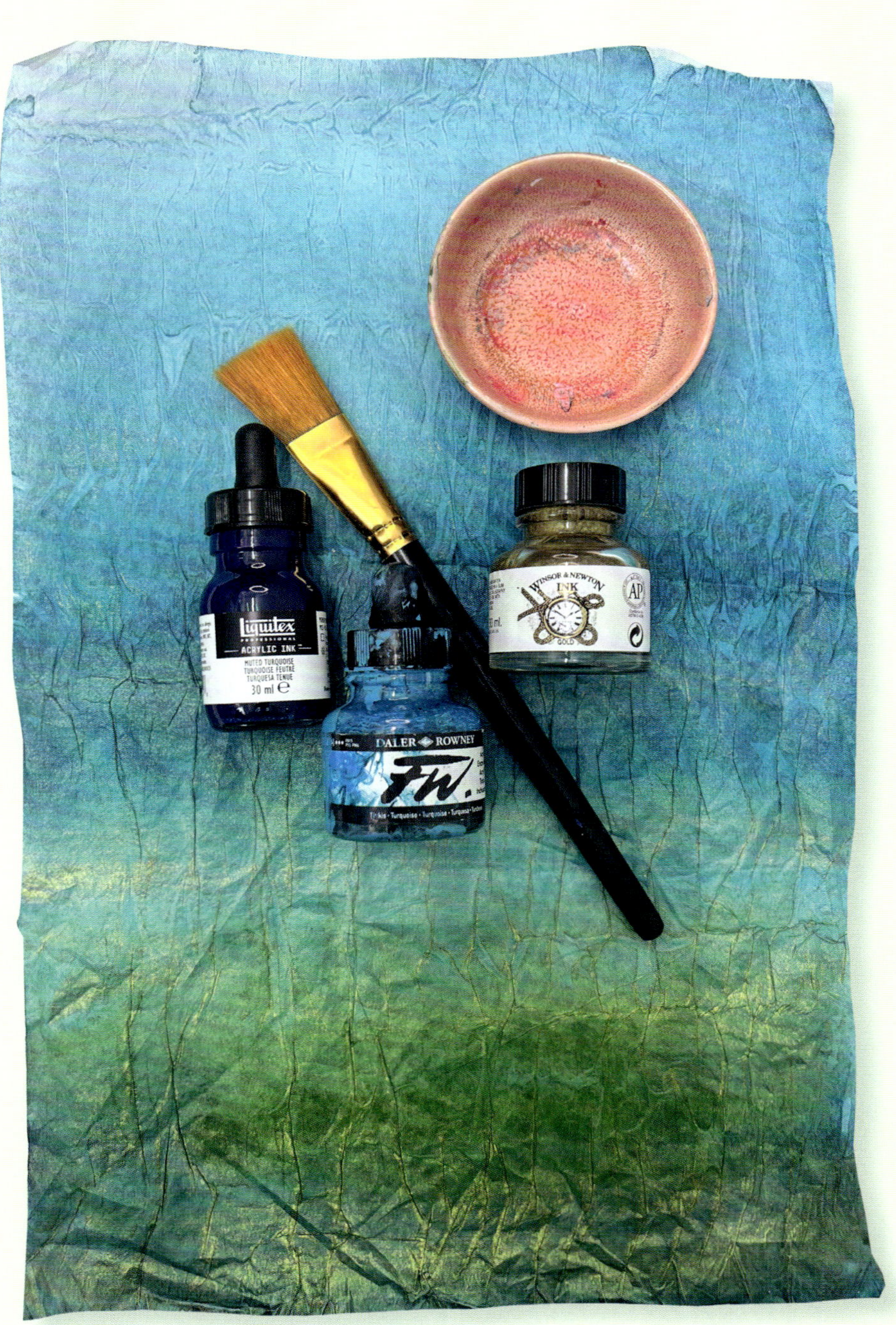

Preparing to bind the pages

Next, I'll show you how to attach the pages to the cover using a simple binding stitch. Make sure all the pages are facing the right way, especially if you have any with text. I used two bulldog clips to hold the pages in place while I stitched.

Start by measuring the centre of the page and marking it with a pencil. Then, make two more marks, 2cm (¾in) in from the edge of the page, on both sides (b).

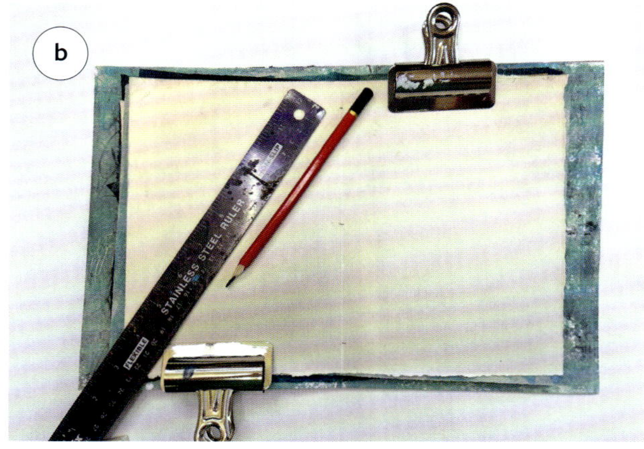

Marking the holes

Next, I place an eraser under the journal and carefully use an awl to push through the pencil marks (c). The eraser helps protect the table – and my finger! – from getting damaged. I do this for all three marks to create holes for the stitching.

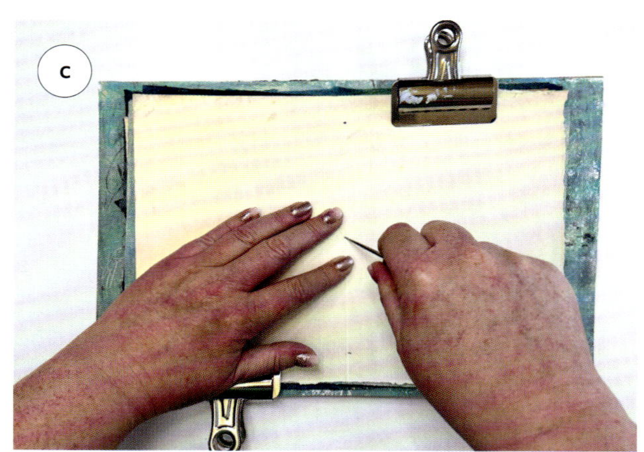

Threading the needle using a needle threader

A needle threader makes it easier to thread embroidery thread onto your needle.

First, cut a piece of thread about 140cm (55in) long. Tie a knot at the end, but don't double the thread or separate it (d).

Hold the needle with the hole (eye) facing you, then push the threader's wire hook into this hole (e). Using the unknotted end of your thread, bring a small amount through the wire hole in the threader, making sure the end is easy to catch (f). Pull the threader (with the thread) back out of the needle's eye and once you have got hold of it, pull the thread out of the threader (g)

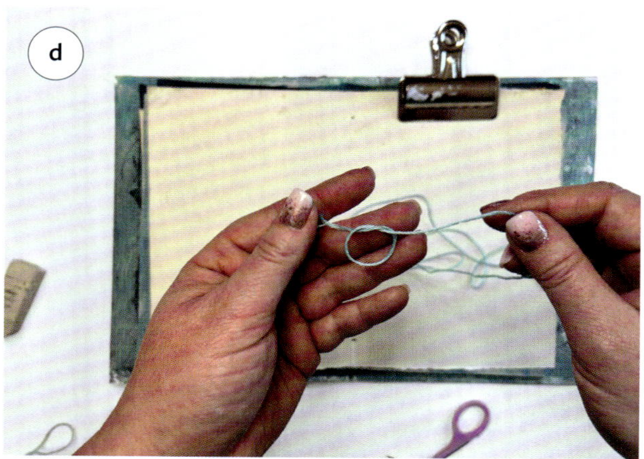

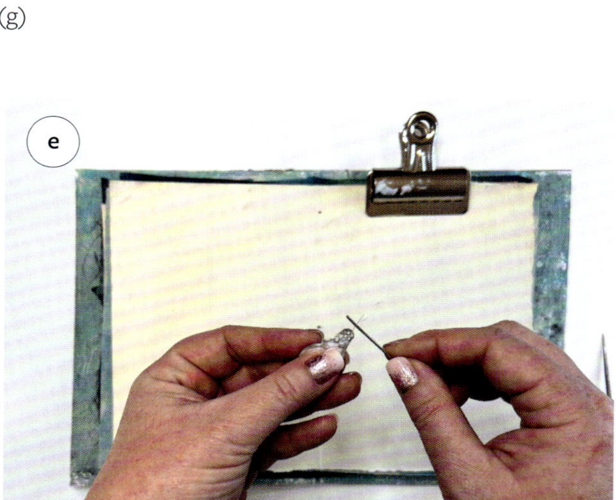

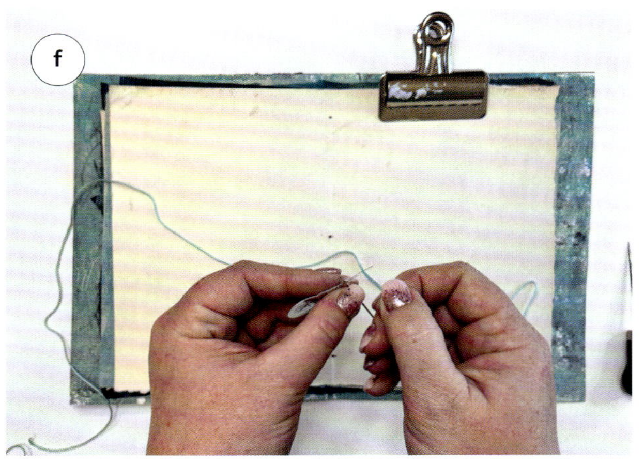

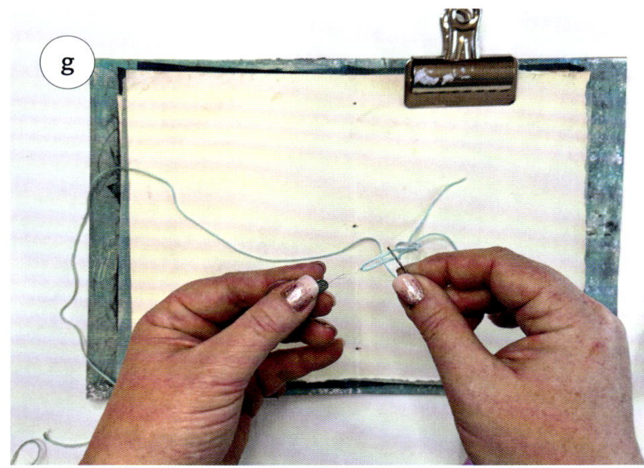

Binding the journal together

Push the needle through the middle hole all the way through the papers and cover (h), leaving a 10cm (4in) tail to tie off later. Flip the book over and insert the needle through the top hole, all the way back through to your centre page (i).

Next, bring the thread through the bottom hole on the inside of the book (j), flip the book over and go back through the middle hole (k).

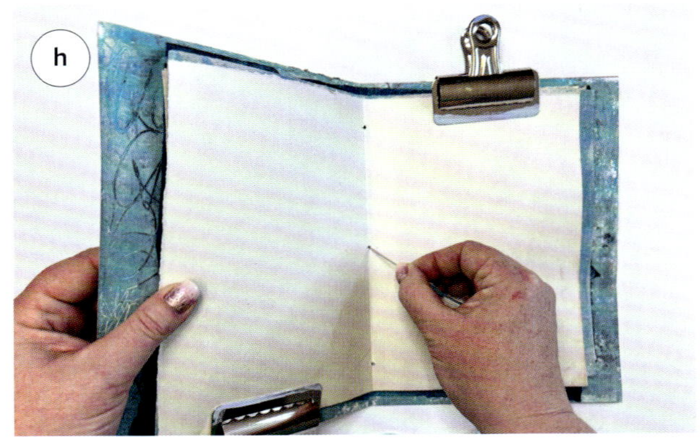

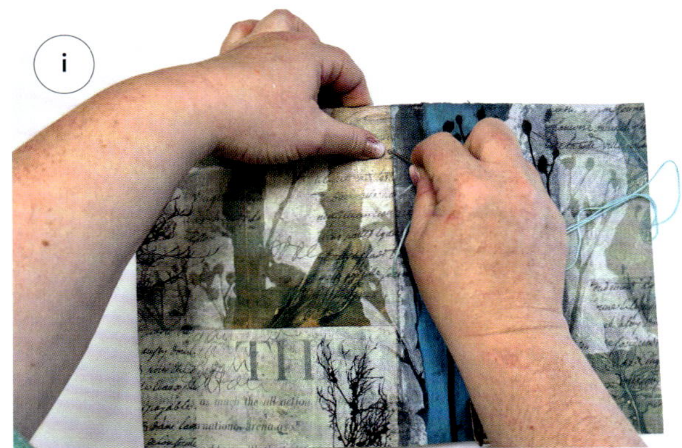

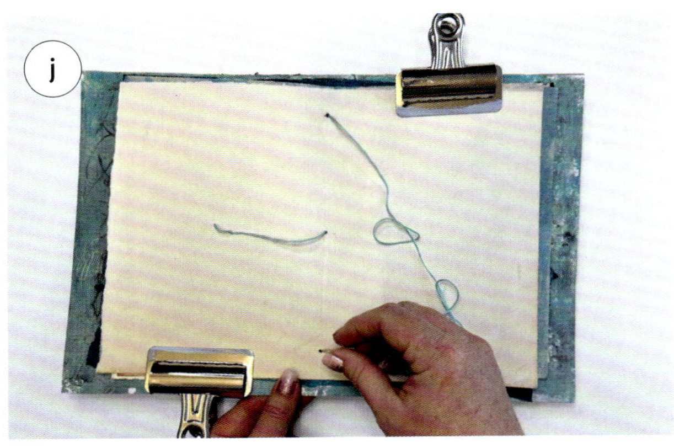

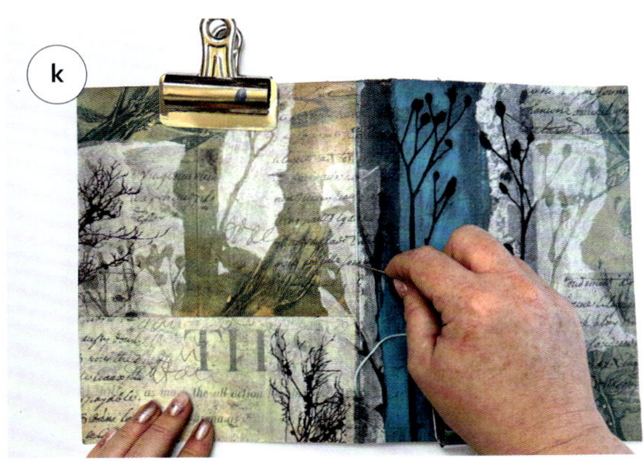

Snip the thread, then tie a double knot with the first tail to secure the threads in the centre of the book (l).

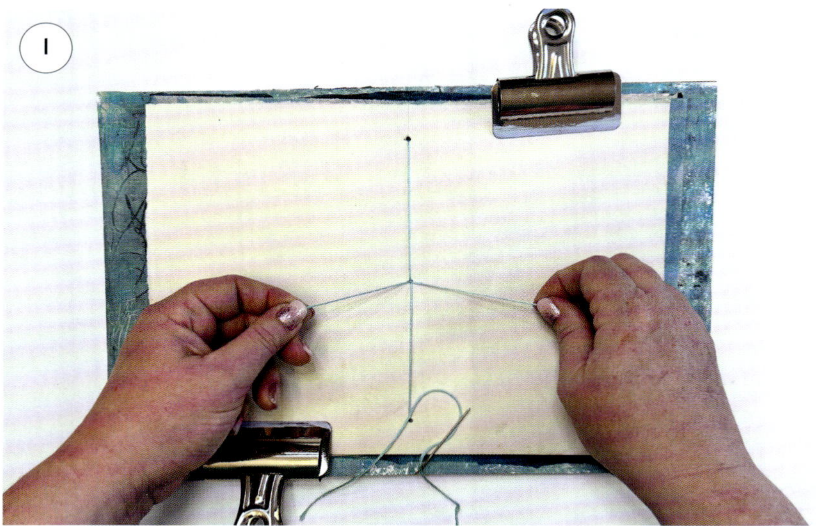

Adding the button

To close the book, I attach a button to the cover. To match the button with the journal's theme, I use découpage or glue collage paper onto a plain wooden button. If you don't have a wooden button, vintage buttons work well too.

Using découpage on a button

First, I pick out some collage paper for the button. I find that thinner paper is easier to work with. Next, I draw around the button on a piece of scrap paper or cardboard to create a template. Then, I cut out the circle with a craft knife to make a little viewfinder (a). This helps me decide which part of the paper I want to use. Once I've marked the areas I need, I'm ready to cut (b) and start decorating the button.

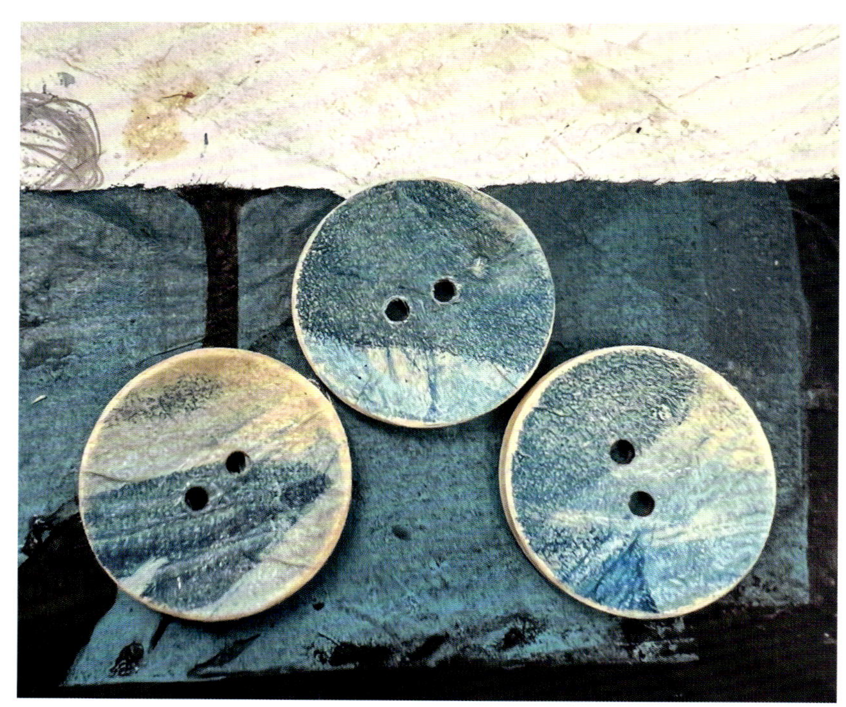

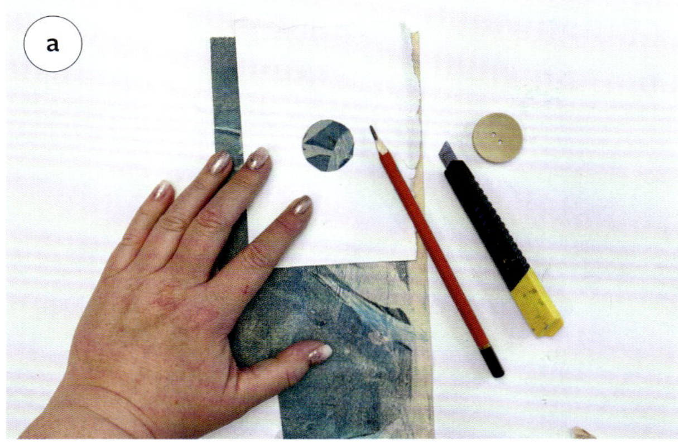

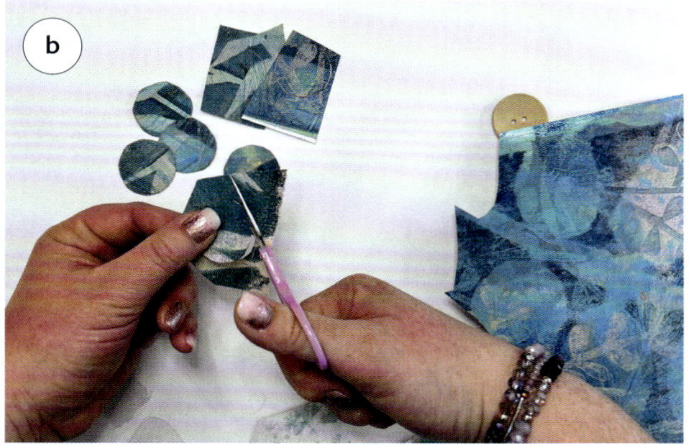

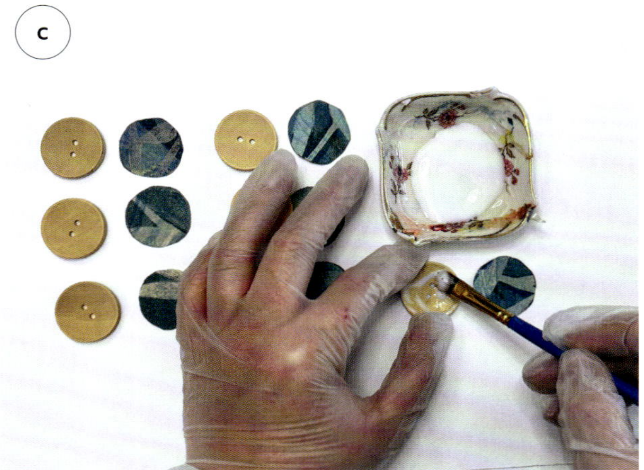

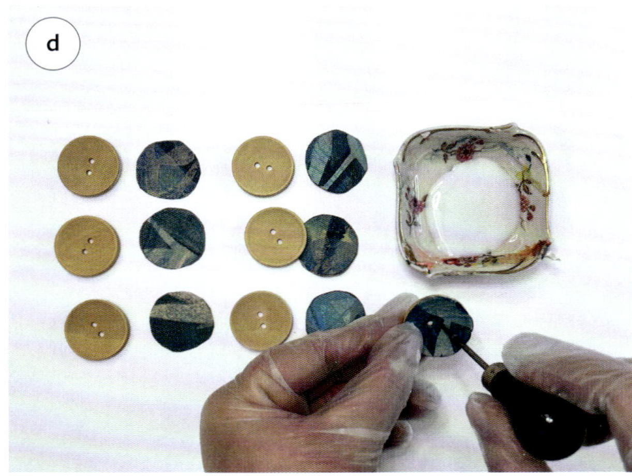

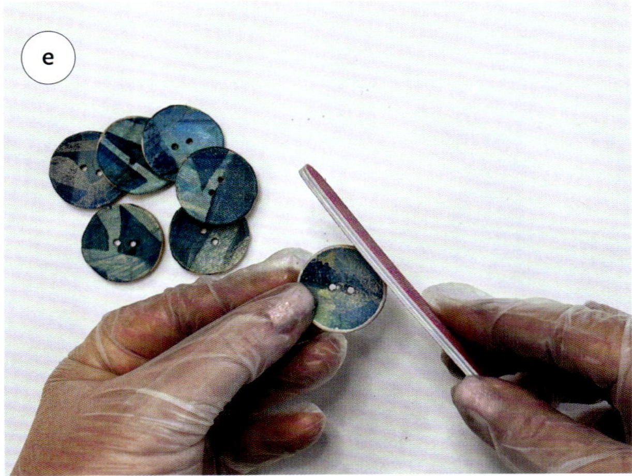

Gluing the button to the paper

Next, I use matte medium glue to stick the paper onto the button. I make sure to press it down evenly using both my fingers and a brush so there are no wrinkles (c). I then use an awl to push through the holes in the button (d).

Once the paper is completely dry, I smooth the edges. For this, I use an emery board, which works well on rounded objects like buttons (e). I gently file around the edges until they feel smooth and look neat to give the button a nice finished look.

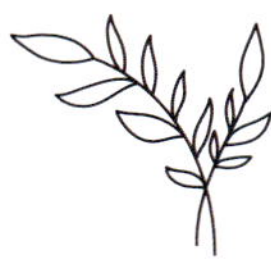

Tip

I like to make a few buttons at once. It's handy to have them ready for the next time I want to make a journal. Plus, they look so pretty sitting in a little dish in my studio – they add a nice decorative touch and spark inspiration!

Attaching the button and fabric to the journal

To attach the button, I measure halfway down the journal cover and 2.5cm (1in) in from the edge. Then, I sew the button in place using embroidery thread, making sure it's secure. On the inside cover, I tie off the thread and secure the knot (f, g).

To make the inside cover look nice, you can cover the knot with a small piece of collage paper glued on top. On this occasion, I use an envelope with a dried plant inside instead. It adds a beautiful touch and makes the inside cover more interesting. I use a glue stick to attach the envelope on the inside cover. Since the dried leaf inside was very delicate, I carefully used a few glue dots to position and secure the leaf in place, keeping it stable without damaging its fragile texture (h).

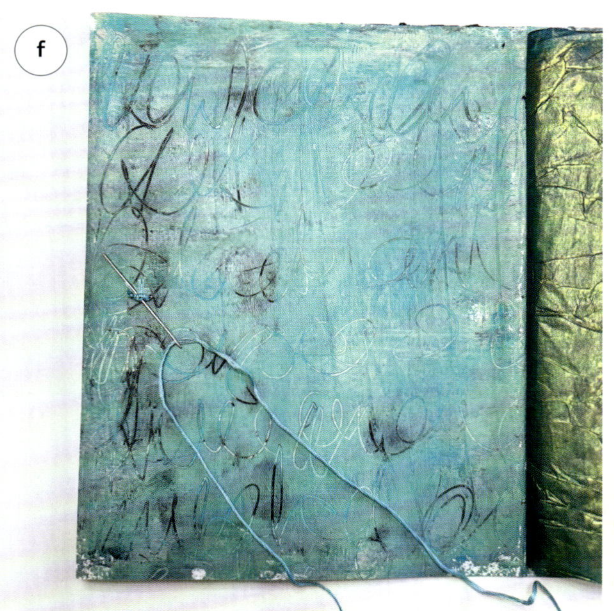

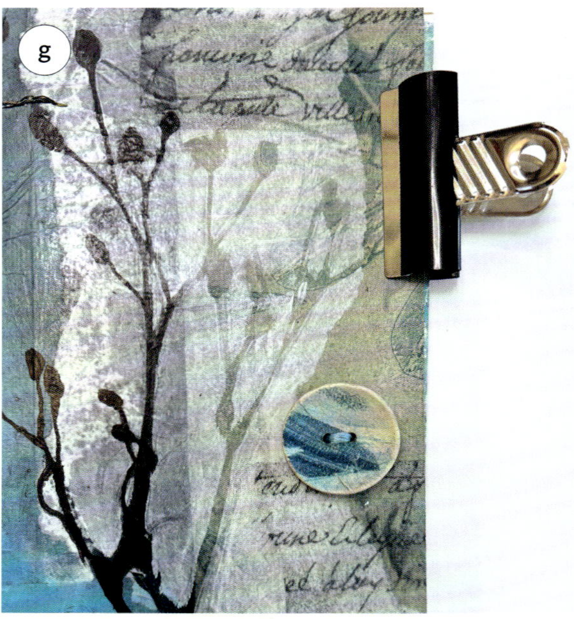

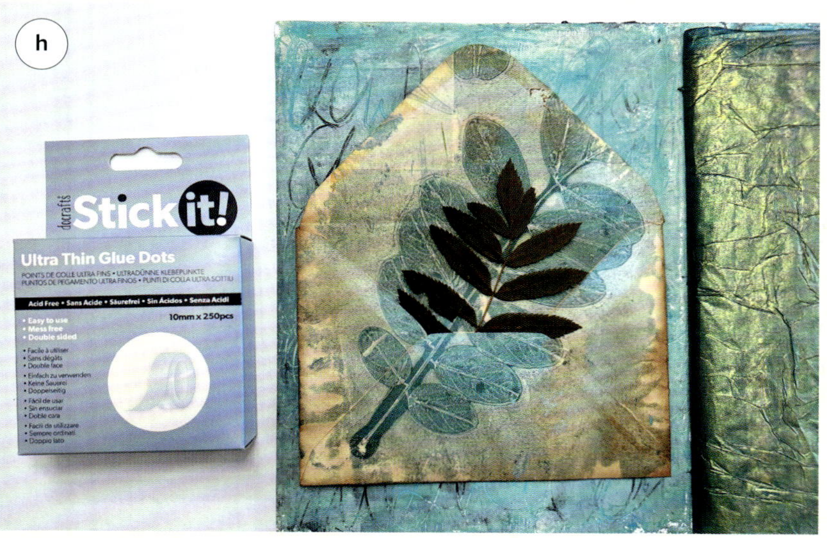

Attaching the closure

For the closure, I used a ripped piece of sari fabric that matches the journal's colour scheme. Lace is another great option if you want a softer, more delicate look. The fabric I chose is 90cm (35in) long.

To attach it, I stitched one end of the fabric to a small piece of paper (a) and then glued the paper to the journal cover with a glue stick (b). This method keeps the fabric secure and tidy.

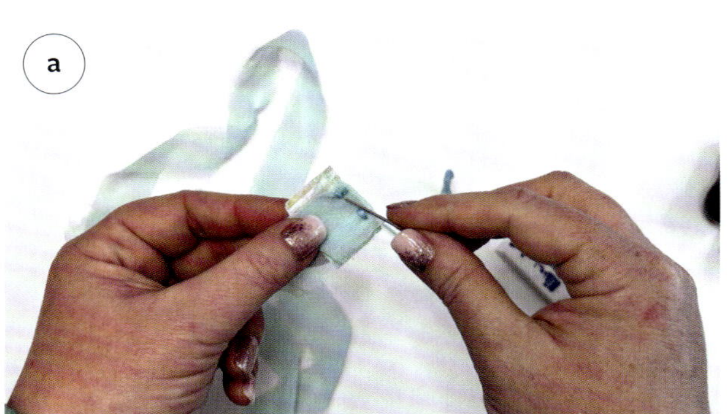

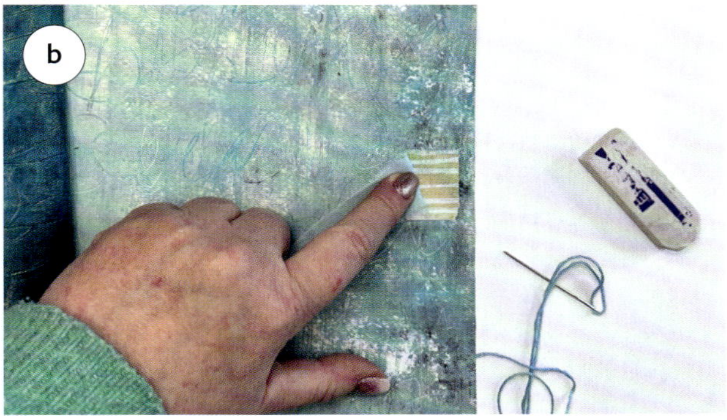

Securing the closure with collage

To ensure the closure stays in place, I use heavy gel medium, which works well with heavier papers, to glue a piece of collage paper over the fabric where it's attached to the journal (c, d). This keeps everything secure while adding another layer of decoration.

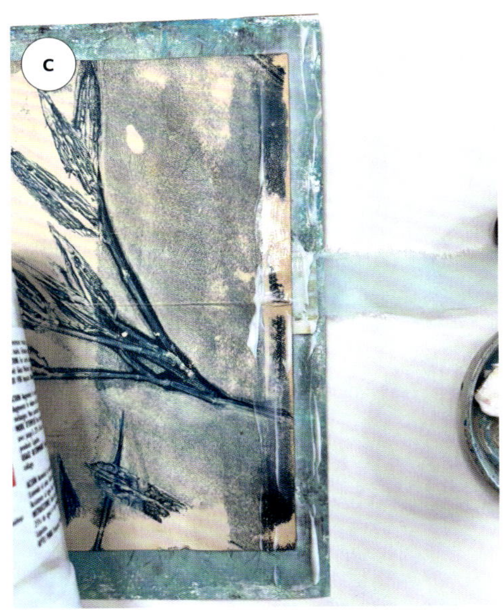

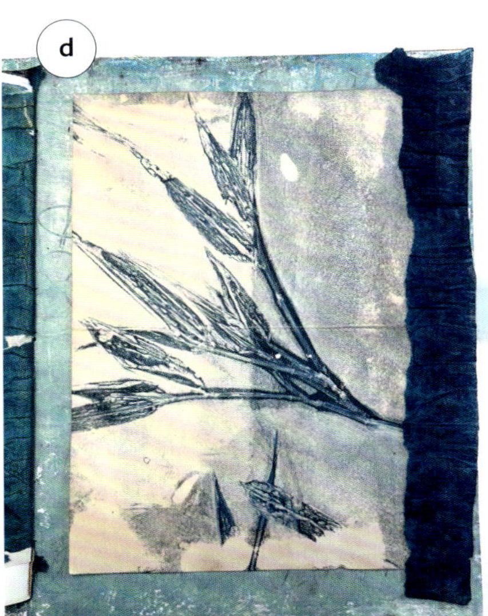

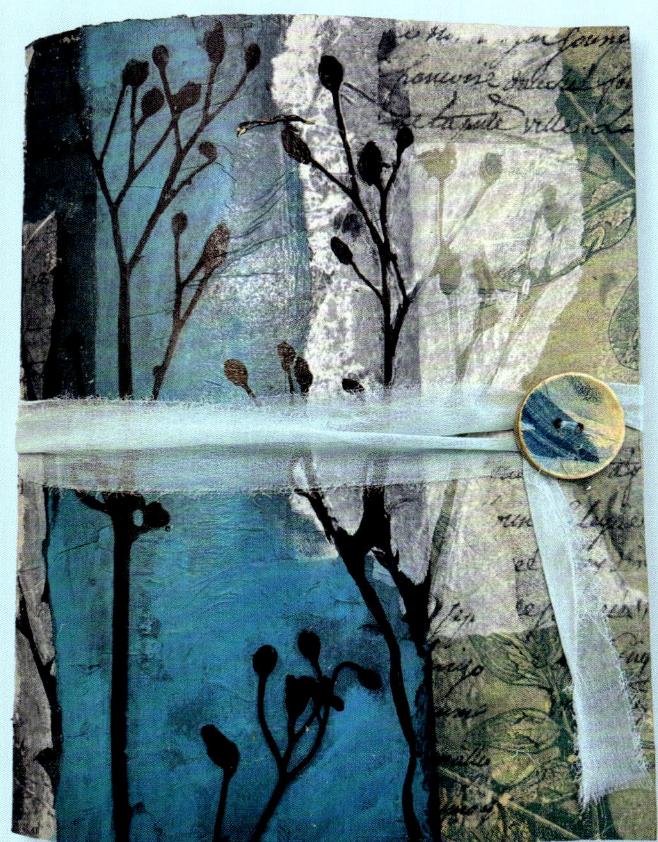

The finished closure, front and back. Your art journal is now ready to fill with collage papers, drawings, patterns or stitching.

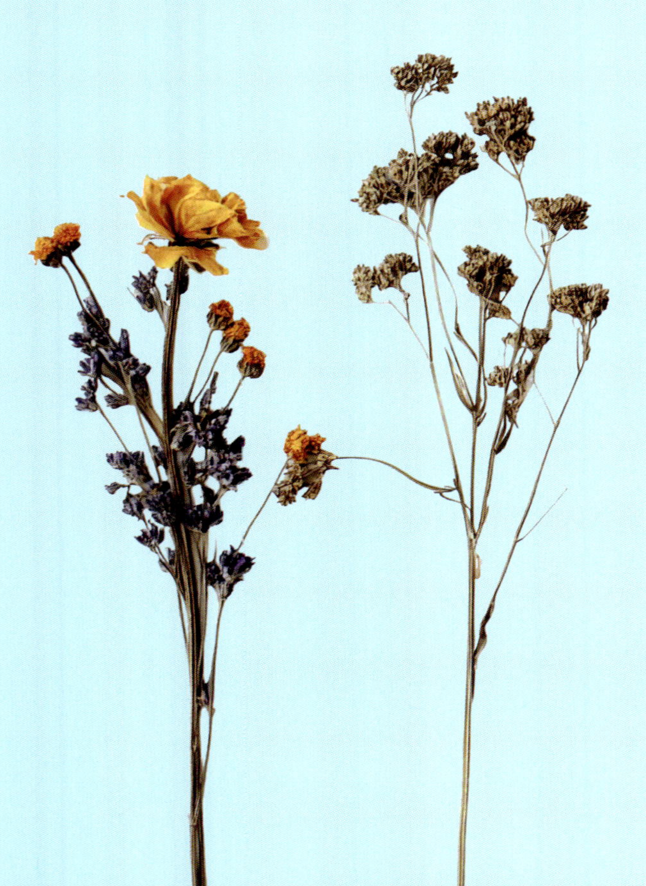

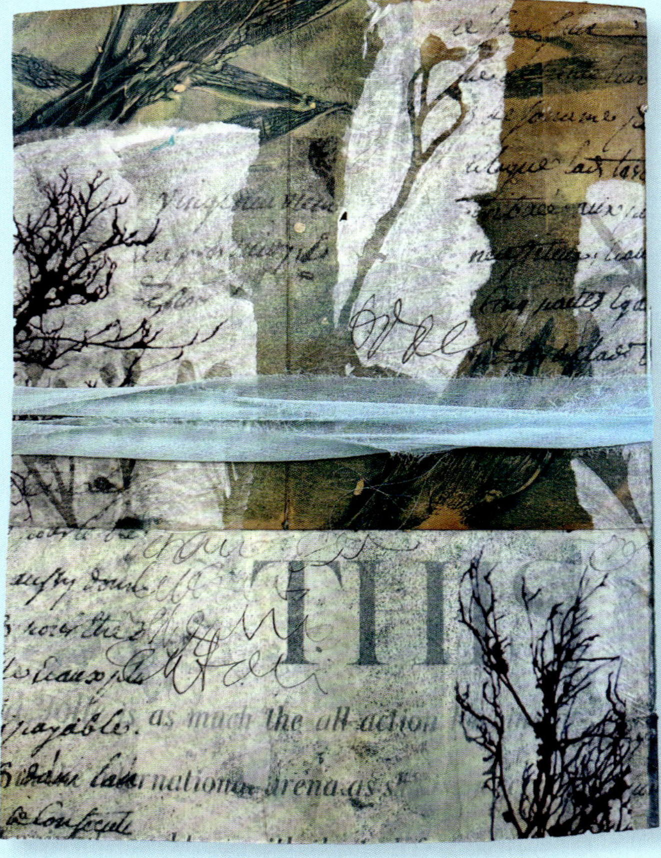

Adding secret pockets

I love printing on hand-dyed envelopes. They make great pockets in the journal to hold delicate prints or leaves, keeping them safe while adding a special touch.

I add a piece of collage to the inside flap of the envelope to make it more interesting when it's folded over. To do this, I draw around the flap onto the collage paper (a), then cut around it with scissors. I use a glue stick to stick it down onto the envelope flap (b), then I glue the envelope to a page in the journal.

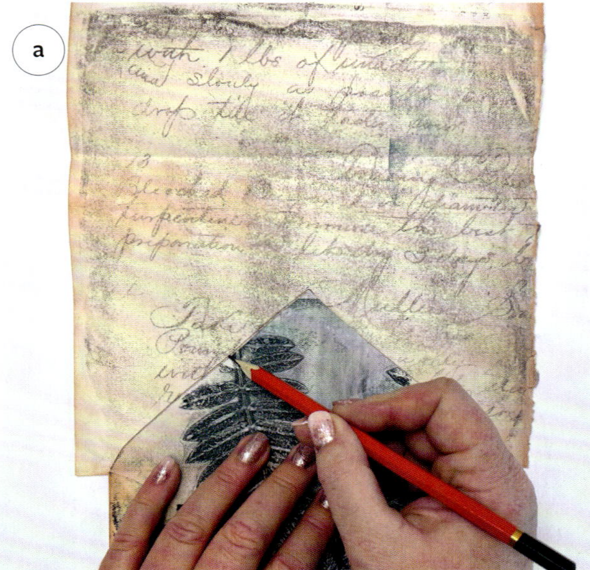

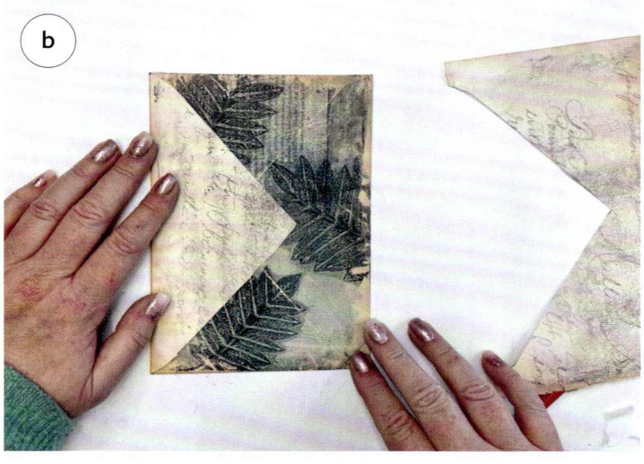

I had a leftover print from the Sapphire Blue Blooms project (see page 73) and thought it looked beautiful peeking out of the envelope.

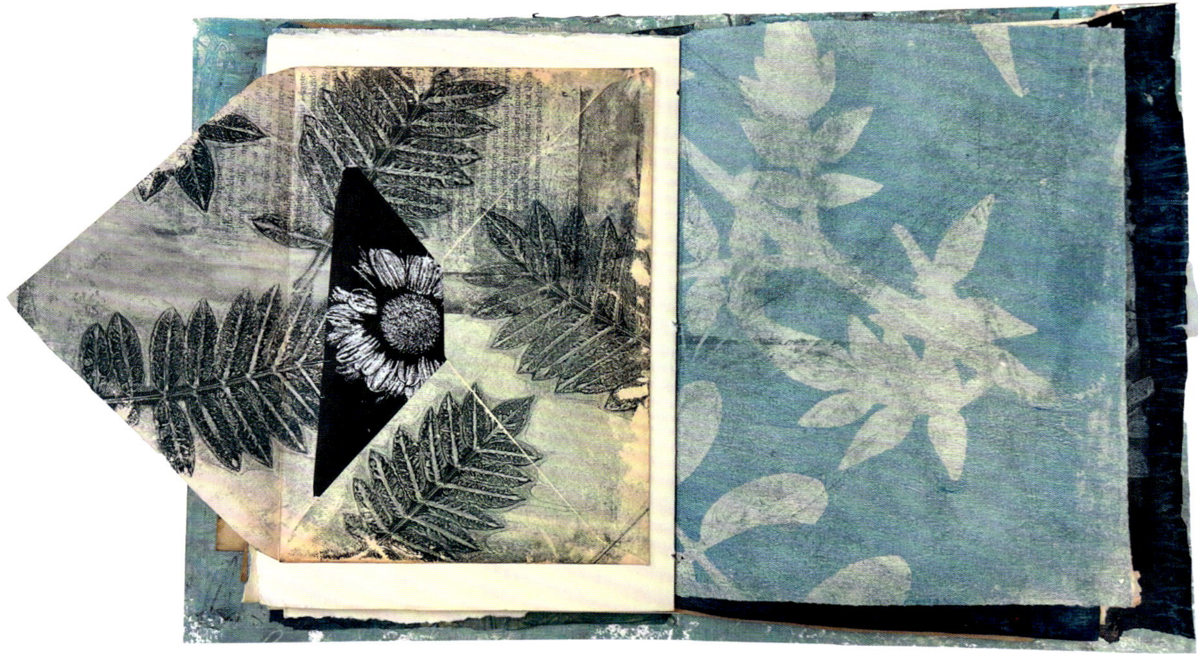

Monochrome composition

For one spread inside, I explored composition using different shades of blue. It's a great way to practise colour composition before working on a larger painting. I decided to combine a ghost print I made on wet-strength tissue paper with a page I created by spraying water on the gel plate when there was only a small amount of paint left. This gave the page a grungy effect (a).

The edge of the botanical print had some solid lines from the gel plate, and I really liked this detail, so I used it to create a blockier composition (b). The small leaf print fits perfectly in the top-left corner. I felt something was missing in the block at the bottom, so I added a linear botanical leaf drawing to pull everything together. These pencil lines were a little faint, so I went over them with a darker coloured pencil to make them stand out more (c).

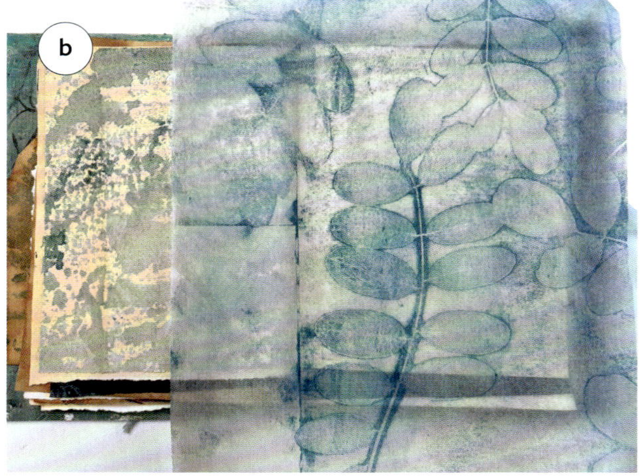

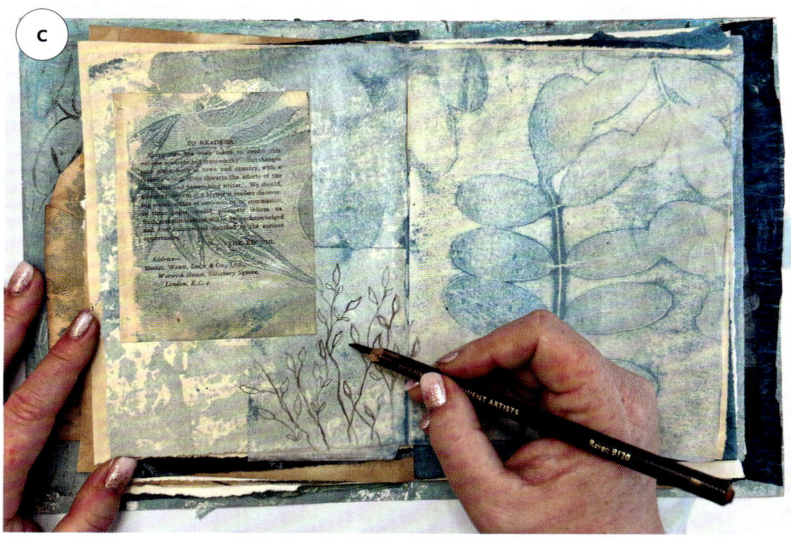

Tip

Place sheets of greaseproof paper behind the pages when you're gluing to prevent them from sticking together. Leave the page open for 24 hours to let the glue or paint dry fully. You can also rub a white candle over the pages to prevent them from sticking.

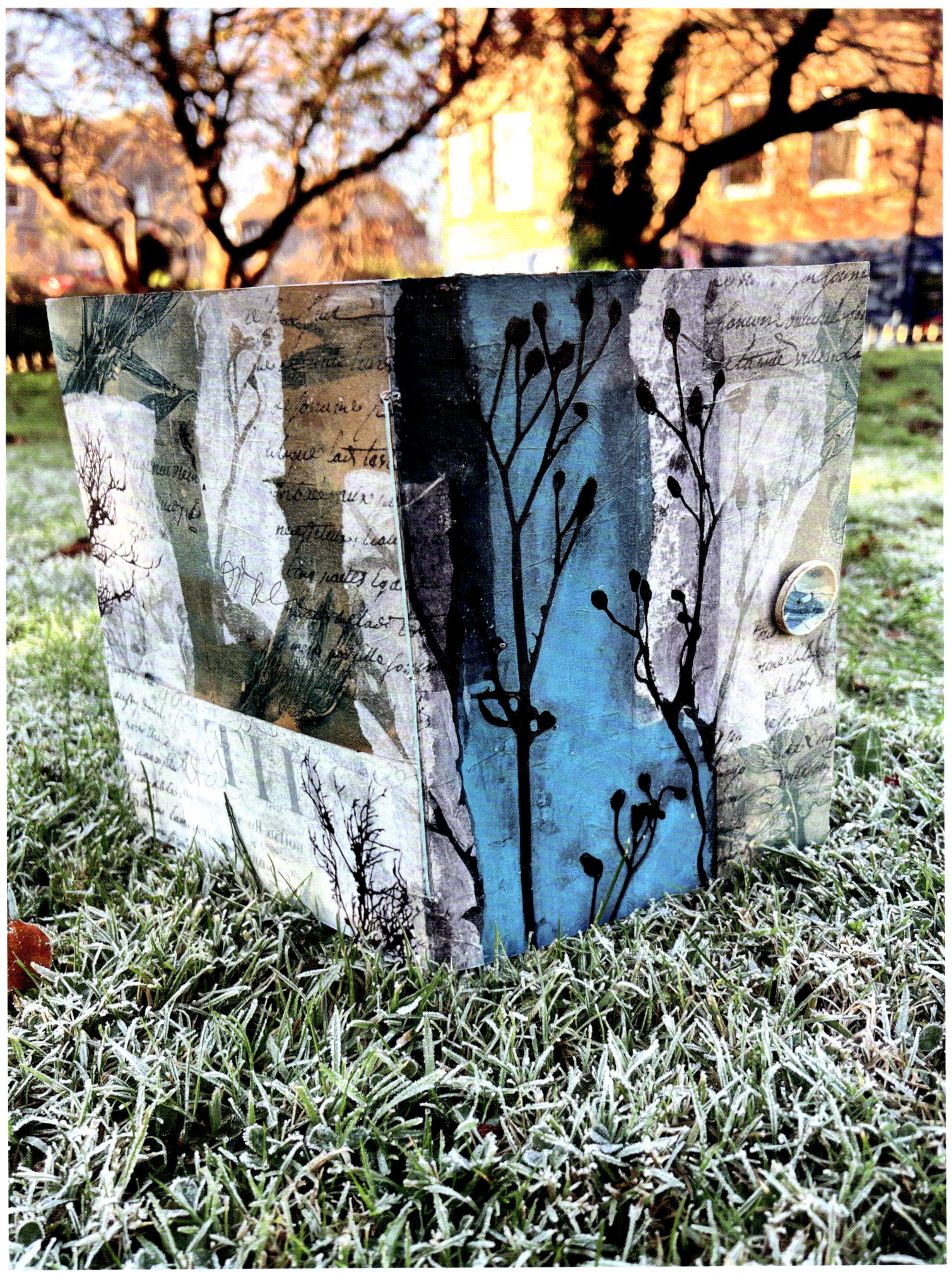

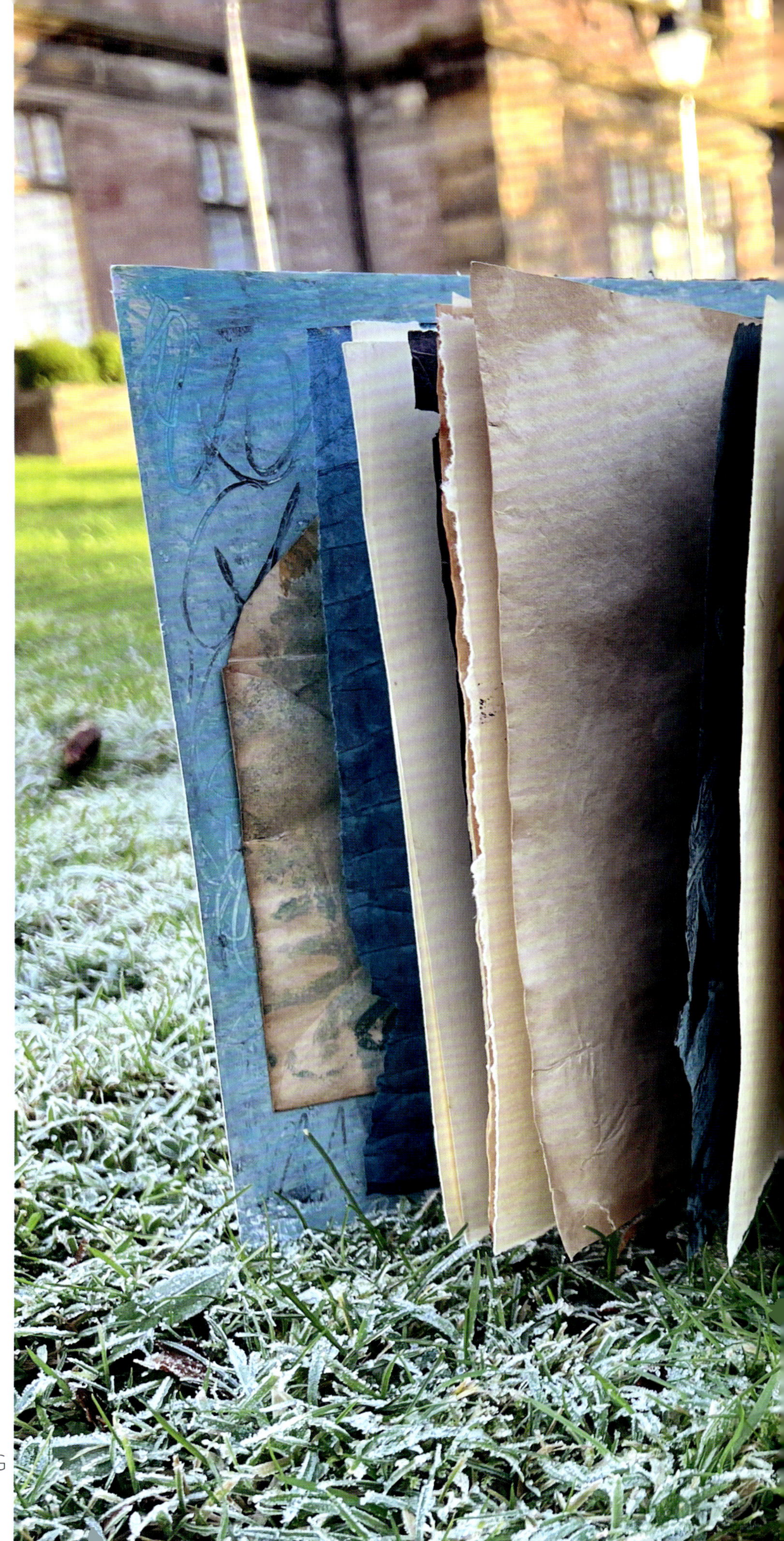

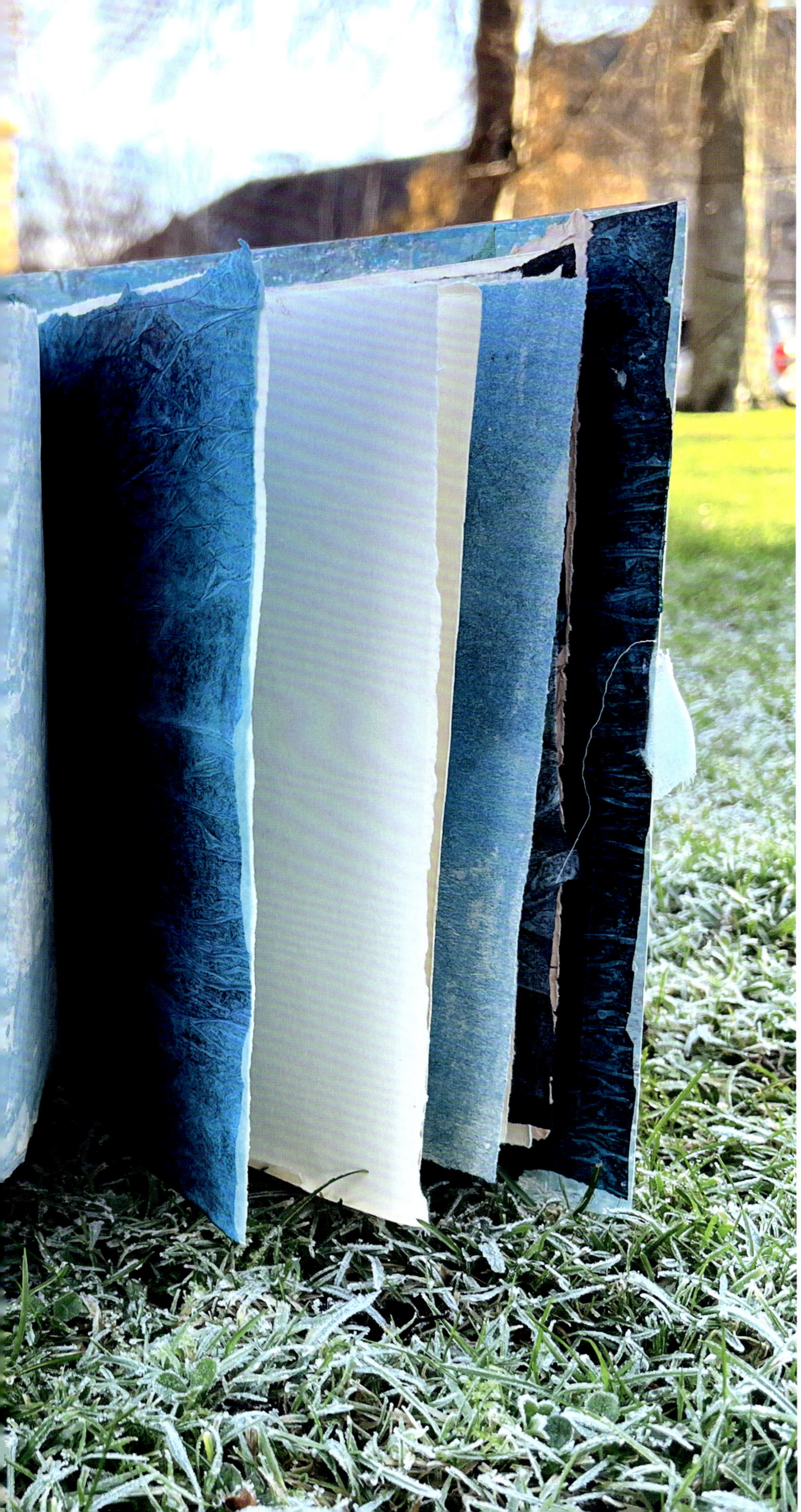

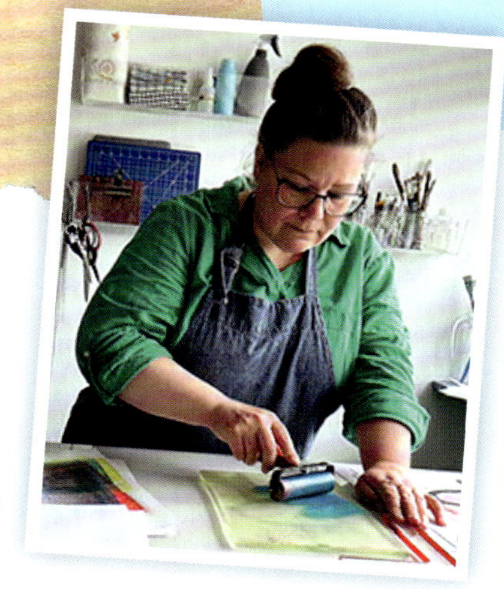

Q **Can you share a little about your background and how you discovered gel printing?**

A I'm a Dutch printmaker and creator. I don't have a formal art degree; however, I grew up in a family of makers and crafts(wo)men, so someone was always busy making something, and there was never a lack of art or craft supplies at my house.

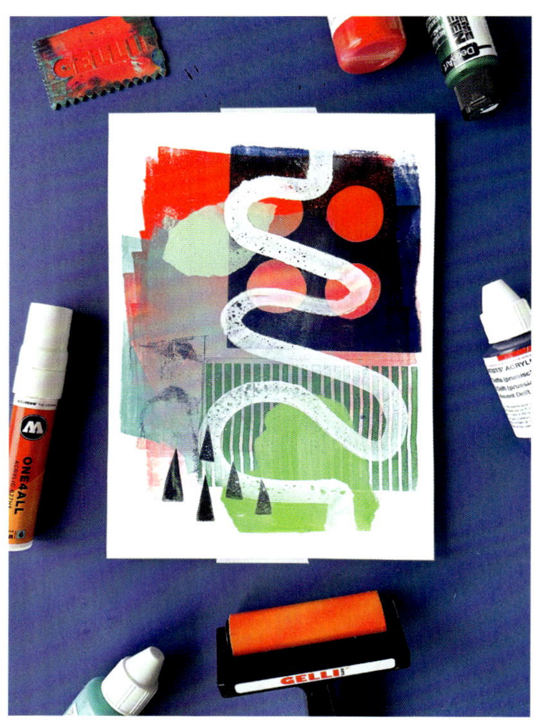

The Road, patchwork print

In 2003, I discovered scrapbooking, which led me to mixed media and eventually to gel printing in 2014. This paved the way for me to try other printmaking techniques, too.

I learnt about the gel plate not long after it was introduced. Friends who attended the Craft & Hobby Association show in the US came back raving about this new soft, flexible plate that allowed them to create prints.

The plate seemed expensive and wasn't easy to find in the Netherlands. Furthermore, I wanted to try it first before I ordered. In April 2014, I finally got my first chance to attend a gel printing class. It was memorable on many accounts. The teacher only had two plates, and the students had to take turns to pull their prints. But that's all I needed. I bought my first gel plate that afternoon and never looked back. I became a Gelli Arts brand ambassador in 2016.

Q **What drew you to using a gel plate in your artwork?**

A I feel I've always been drawn to printmaking. I remember creating a collagraph plate and watching it being printed on a huge press when I was only seven or eight. I also loved creating linocuts in art class. When I discovered gel printing, I was already a few years into mixed-media art journalling; however, I wasn't into the tactile heavy texture. I preferred flat colour and smooth texture. The gel plate was my missing link.

Q **Who or what are your main influences in your art practice?**

A My main influences are anything and everything. They can change at any moment because I follow my curiosity. At the moment, I'm heavily influenced by befriended illustrators. However, my always present influences are modern and contemporary art, films, photography, fashion, textiles and, of course, (Japanese) printmaking. Museums are my happy place.

Q **How do you see the role of gel printing in the broader context of contemporary art?**

A Monoprinting is the quickest and easiest way to enter the world of printmaking. The gel plate is suitable and accessible for printers of all ages and skill levels. Even without prior knowledge, it allows you to create fabulous and satisfying prints. This might blind some critics to the fact that it's a tool, not a toy. We are only just beginning to see the full potential of this tool in the hands of a skilled artist.

Q **What projects or directions are you excited about exploring in the future?**

A I'm currently at a pivotal point. I've been teaching gel printing for a long time and am used to jumping from one project to the next. So, I'm looking forward to exploring new ways of working and perhaps spending more time on one project instead of working on one and thinking about the next all the time.

Q **What advice would you give to beginners who are just starting with gel printing?**

A Give yourself time to get to know the plate. You will learn faster by printing lots, paying attention to what happens and being open to experimenting. Ask yourself lots of questions: What happens if I do this? Do I like that? What if I try that? You don't need to know everything before you start. Begin and learn by doing!

In short: less paint is usually better, and wait until the paint and the paper are dry before you pull your print.

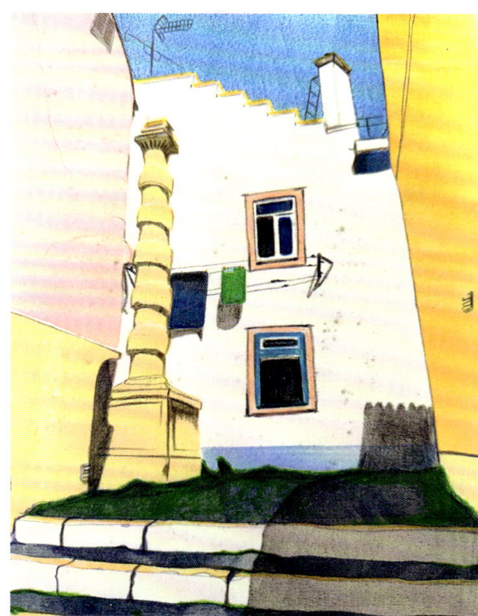

Bélam, **stencil print and coloured pencil**

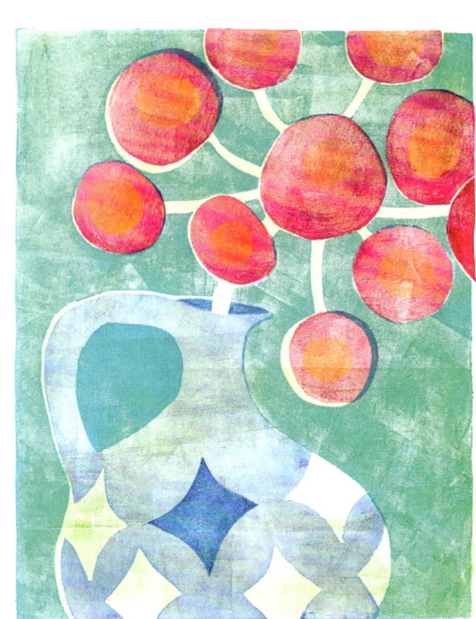

Vase with flowers, **stencil print**

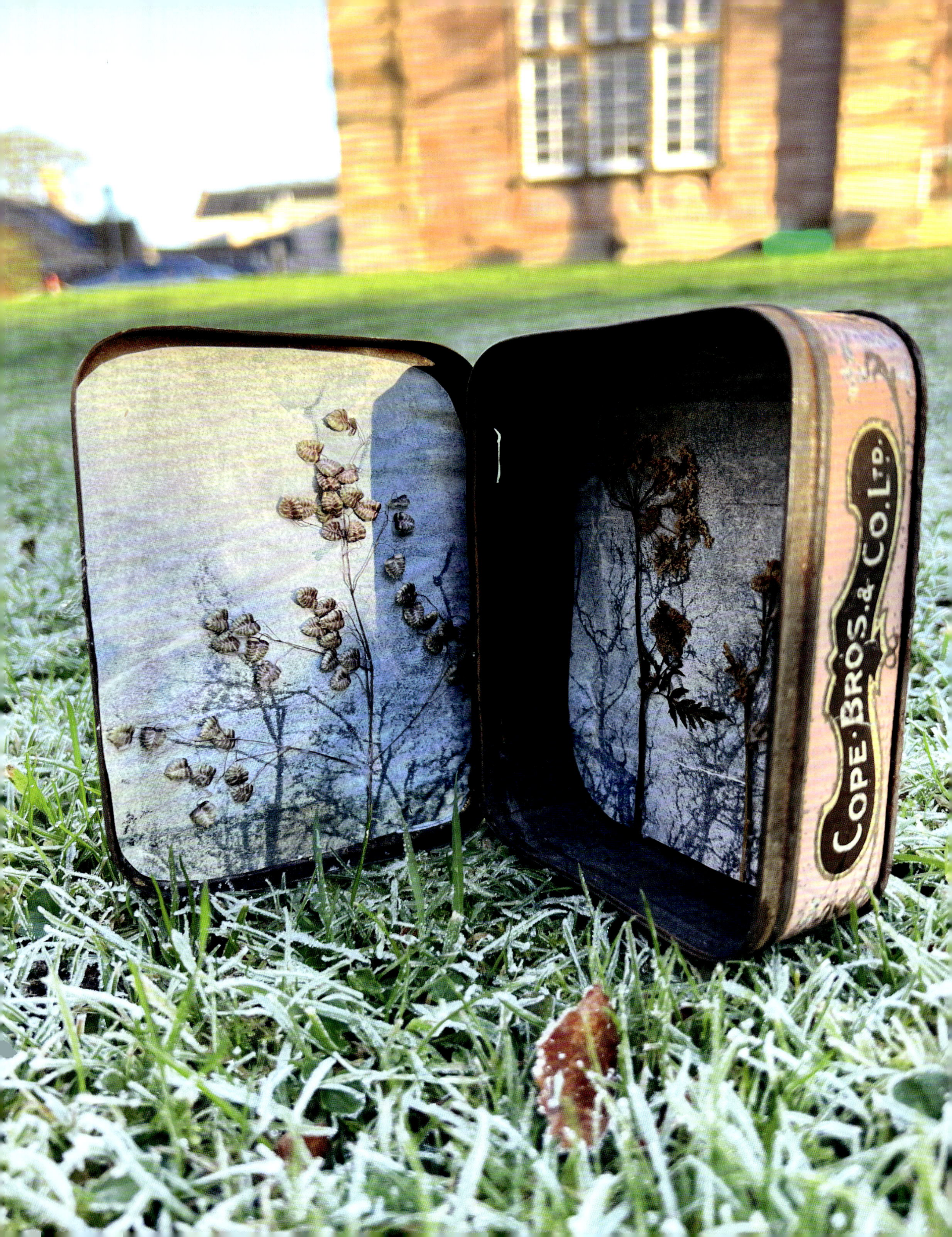

COPE·BROS.& CO.LTD.

MIXED-MEDIA ASSEMBLAGE TIN

For this final project, we'll explore mixed-media assemblage art – a creative way to combine different materials into one artwork. We'll use a tin container as the base, which could be an old can, box or decorative tin with a weathered look. The tin might have rust or patina, adding character and texture to the piece.

In mixed-media assemblage, artists use materials such as wood, fabric, paper, metal, found objects, glass, wire and natural items. These are creatively arranged and often glued or wired together to give the piece depth and dimension.

This art form is fun because it can tell a story or express a theme. The tin itself can be part of that story, and you can use image transfer techniques to add your own personal touch. The final piece is visually striking, with contrasting textures that invite deeper exploration. It's a way to turn everyday objects into something thought-provoking.

I love searching for the perfect tin. Junkyards, like Steptoe's Yard in Montrose, Scotland, as well as eBay, second-hand shops, car boot sales and vintage shops are ideal for finding old tins, books, fabric and ceramics that can spark new ideas for art projects and studio decoration. Sometimes there are shapes I can't use, but to avoid waste I offer them to fellow artists in my shared studio space. We use a WhatsApp group to sell items cheaply or leave them on the pigeonhole shelves marked 'Free stuff', which is a great way to recycle within our community. If you're after specific sizes, you can message the seller directly to ask if they have what you need.

MATERIALS
Refer back to the master list on page 18 for the essential items.

- Old tin
- Collage papers, with image transfers of tree silhouettes or other prints from previous projects
- Glue dots or craft foam pads
- Dried plants
- Heavy gel medium
- Toothpick
- Matte medium glue

I found my tin in a job lot on eBay. The dimensions are 9 x 12cm (3½ x 4¾in), depth 4cm (1¾in).

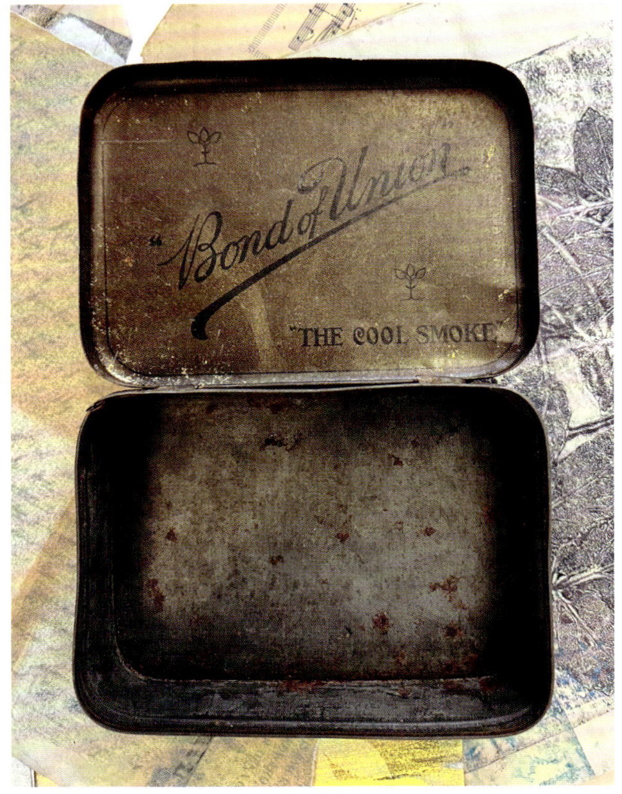

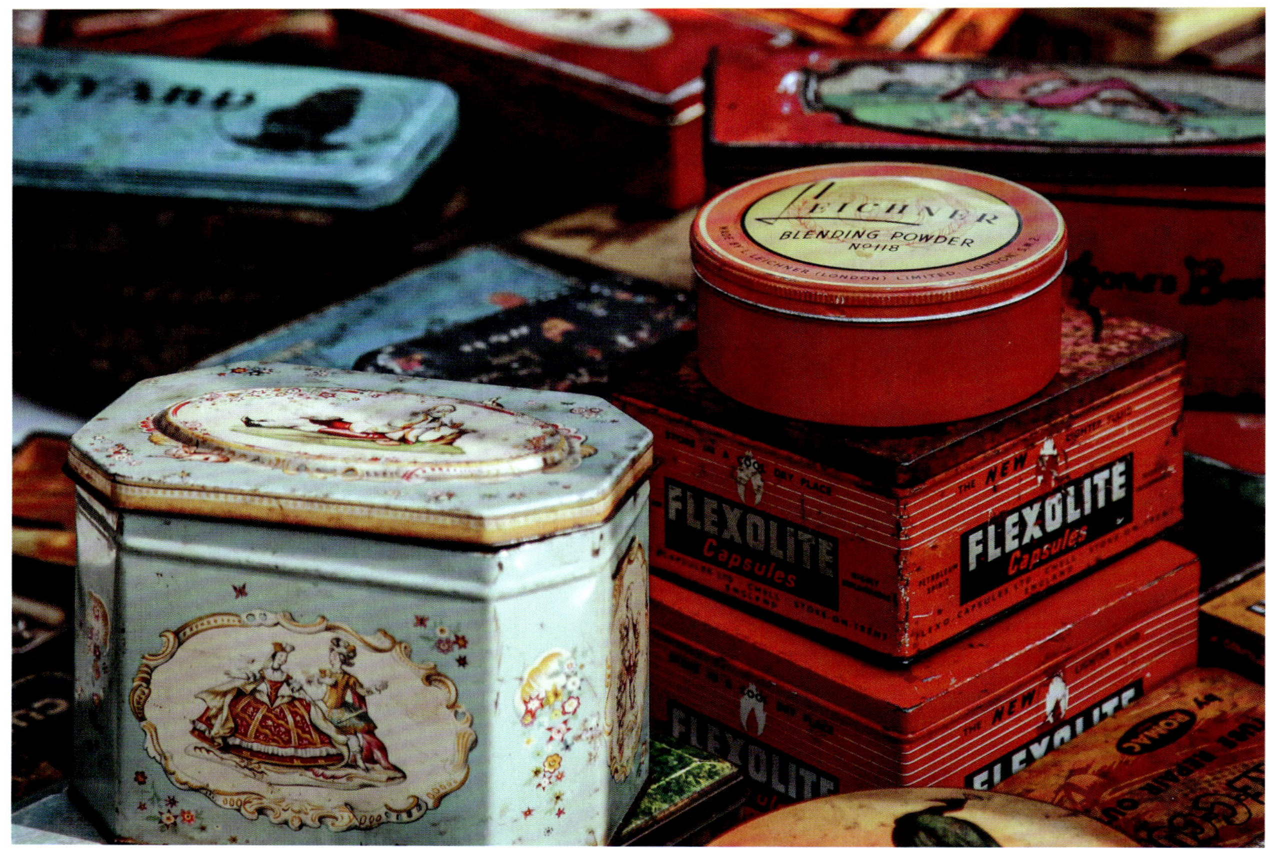

Using trial and error

Trial and error is one of the best parts of collage – you can experiment with different combinations before deciding on a final design. I tested various papers and 3D elements before choosing the tree silhouette background. When I first printed that paper, I knew it was special and wanted to use it in the right place. I'm so happy with how these assemblages turned out, and I hope you'll give it a try too!

Selecting your background paper

Select a few papers to try for your backgrounds. Draw around the base of the tin to get the correct shape for your collage paper (a, b). If you have a few different papers to test out, you could make a template (as shown on page 29). This also makes it easier to find the perfect composition for your piece.

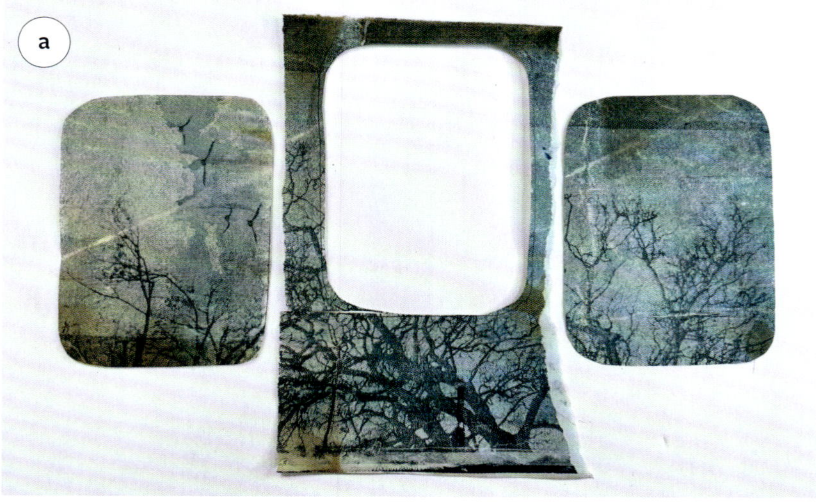

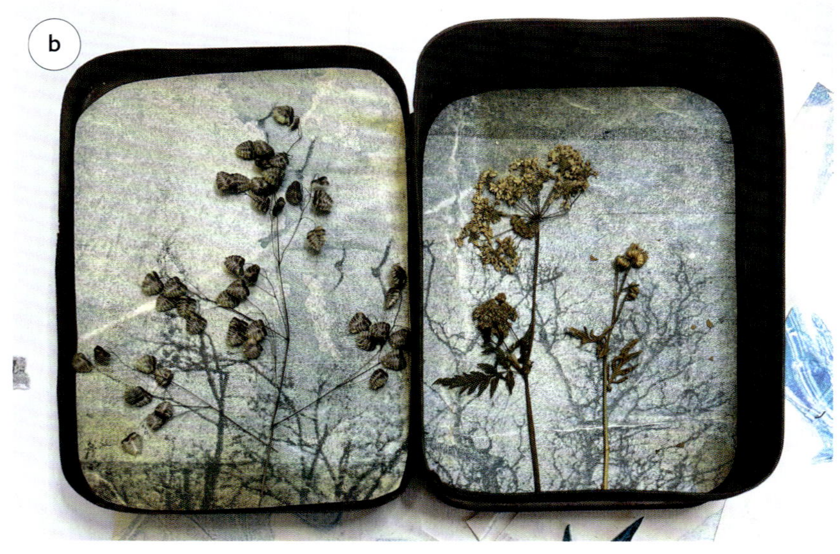

Finding extra materials for collaging

It is worth looking through your prints from previous projects for this collage as you might find some interesting small details or shapes, which will work well on your tin. I had some leftover blue Acer leaves on black tissue paper so I glued these to some firmer paper to make them easier to cut out (c).

Dried flowers will also collage well and will add a 3D texture to your project. I found I had pressed some delicate dried flowers, which would complement the blues and soft silhouettes on the background paper (d).

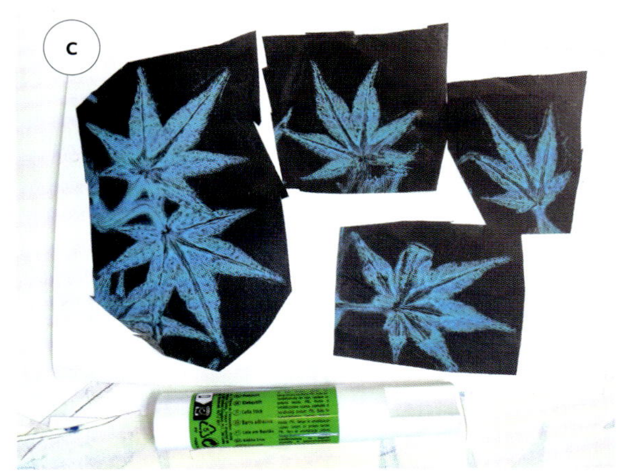

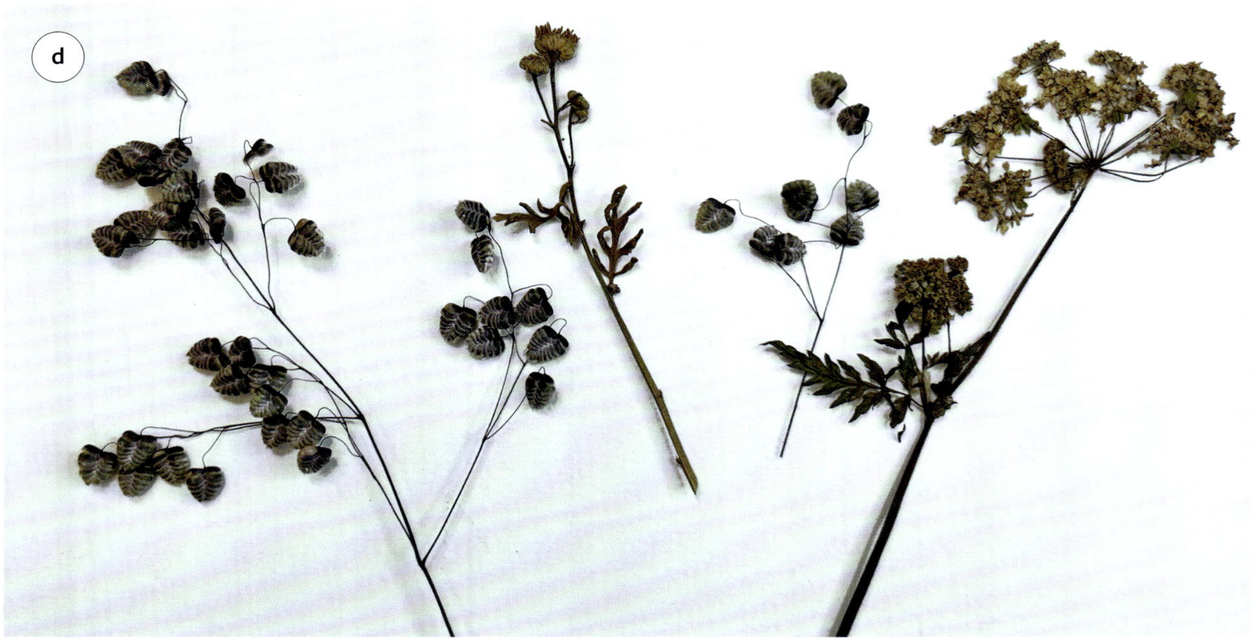

Preparing the tin

Look at the tin's surface before you begin collaging. If your tin is new, apply a coat of white gesso and let it dry before using matte medium glue to stick your papers. If the tin is old or rusty, use glue dots or foam pads, as rust can seep through and stain the collage paper (e).

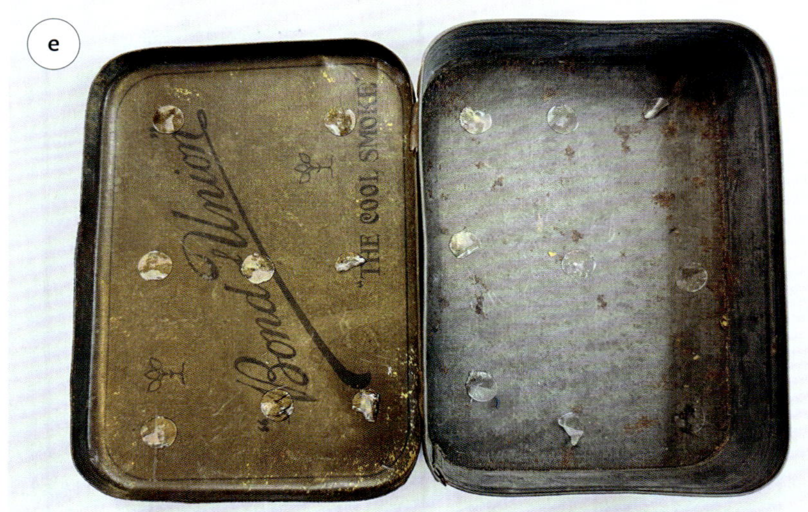

Final touches

I wanted to use the subtle tree silhouette print for the background paper in my tin and the hand-pressed flowers worked well with this. I applied heavy gel medium to the plant and used a toothpick for the more delicate leaves (f).

I was happy with the simple pairing of these two elements on my project so the blue Acer leaves will be saved for another time. Try out different combinations to see what works best in the tin you are using.

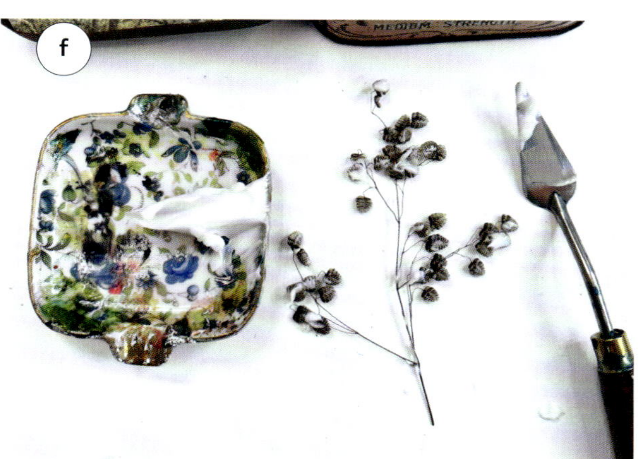

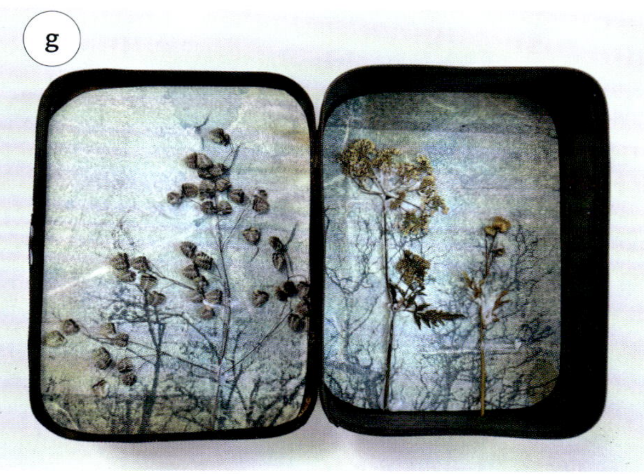

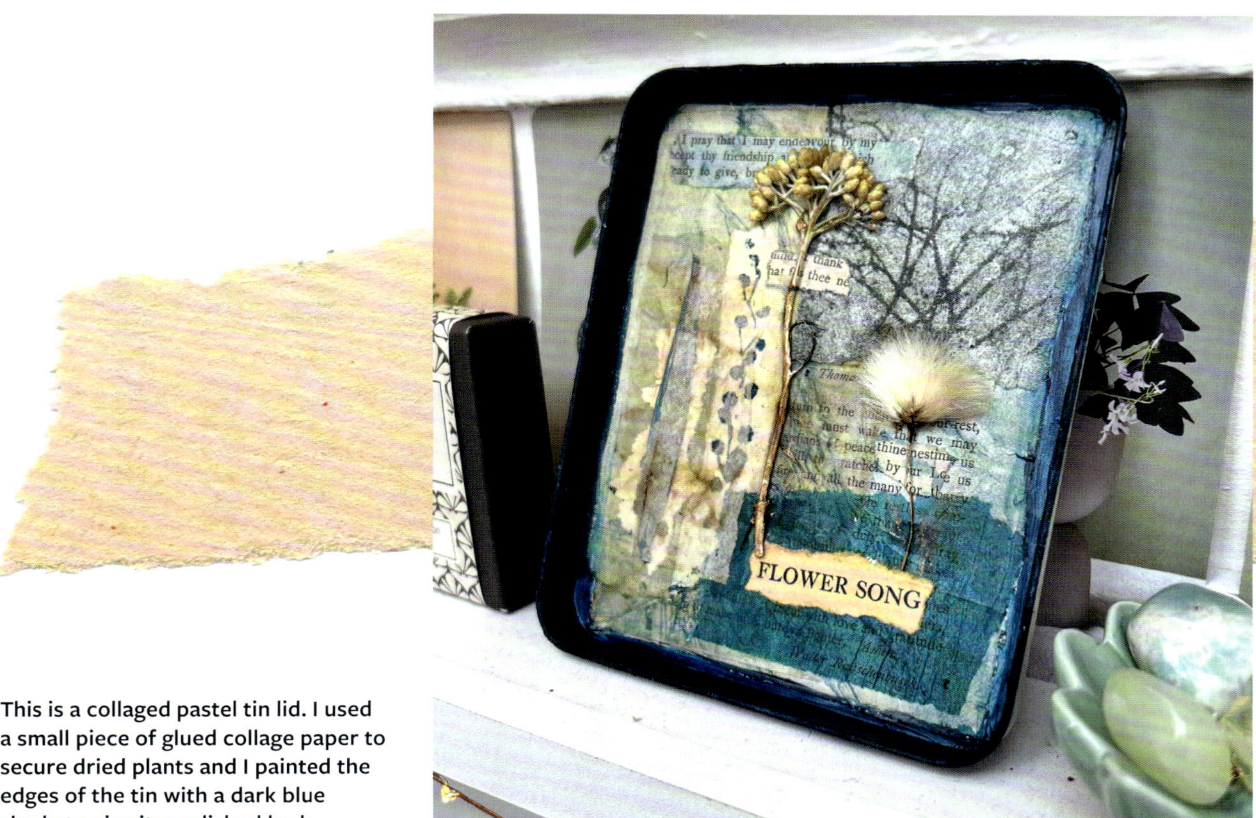

This is a collaged pastel tin lid. I used a small piece of glued collage paper to secure dried plants and I painted the edges of the tin with a dark blue shade to give it a polished look.

FRAMING AND PROTECTING YOUR PRINTS

In this section, I'll show you easy ways to display your prints. I'll also give you tips to make them more UV-resistant and archival, helping them to last longer.

There are many ways to display prints. For example, I've shared how to create a 3D accordion book, which can be displayed on a shelf. You can also frame prints behind glass to protect them from dust and light. Ready-made frames are an affordable option and can be assembled at home, making them perfect for displaying your work around your home or selling small pieces at craft fairs, while keeping costs low.

If you're selling finished artwork in a gallery, having your work professionally framed with non-reflective, UV-resistant glass can elevate its presentation and quality. However, this adds to your costs, so you'll need to price your work accordingly. Keep in mind that galleries typically take a 50% commission for their role in selling and displaying your art professionally.

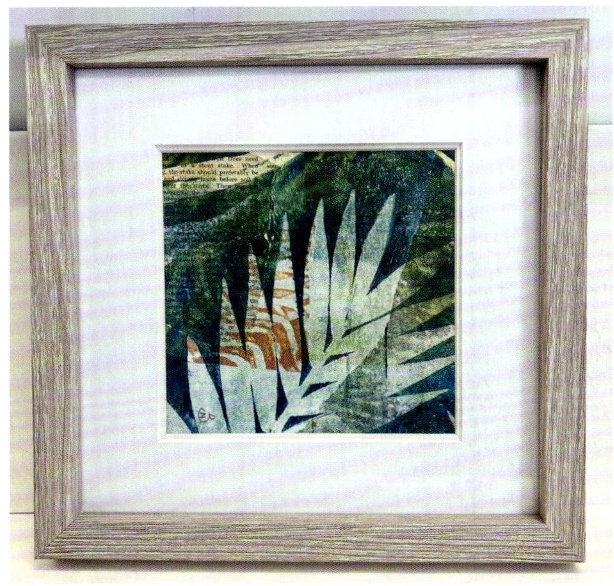

Here, I framed a print using a ready-made frame with a mount. To enhance its appearance, I added an extra mount to the print. Ready-made frame mounts can sometimes be quite thin, so I occasionally have a custom mount cut to fit the frame. This gives the piece a more professional finish.

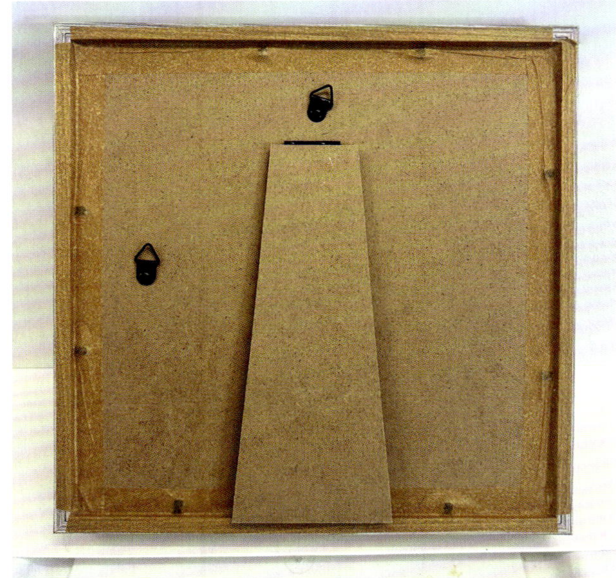

To secure the print to the mount, I use professional framer's tape, which is acid-free and offers better adhesion than masking tape. I also seal the back of the frame with framer's tape and sometimes attach a hanging string. Many galleries accept ready-made frames, provided they are of good quality and include a securely attached hanging string.

Here is an example of how to surface mount a print. I particularly like the torn edges of this print. To attach the print, I use double-sided sticky tape and mount it onto a piece of watercolour paper. I then frame it under glass. You can wrap a print around a canvas, but I only use prints on tissue paper or thin copy paper for this technique. For thicker papers, I prefer attaching them to a wooden cradleboard.

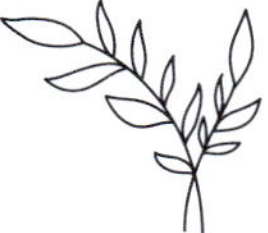

Tip

Depending on the frame you choose, leaving a small space between the print and the glass enhances the print.

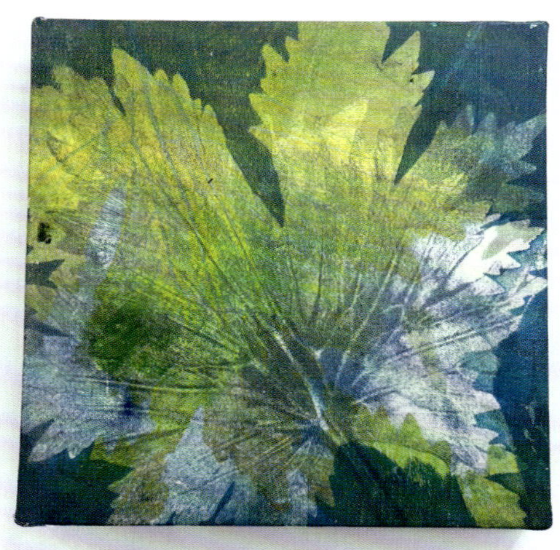

You can see here how the paper is wrapped around the canvas.

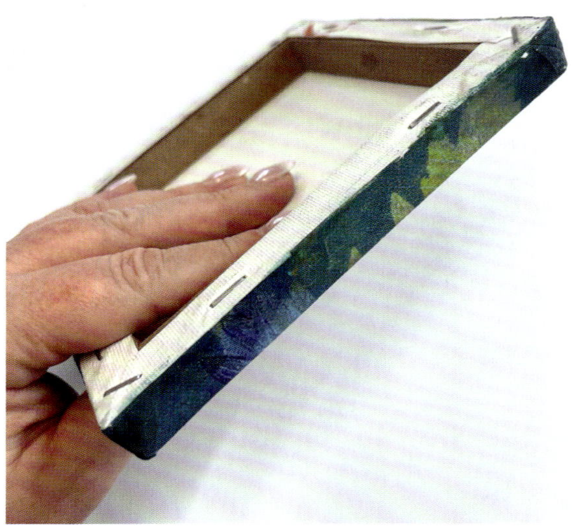

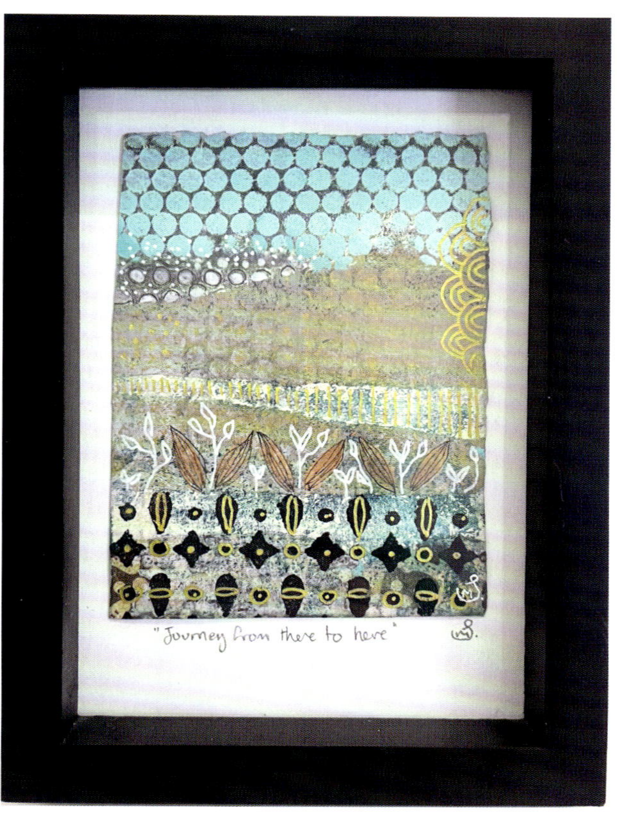

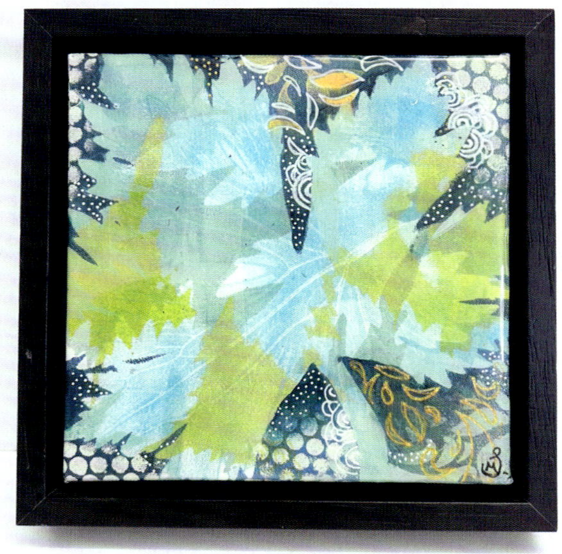

Examples of prints wrapped around a small canvas and placed inside a floating frame. These floating frames were made to order, as I've found it difficult to source this style in a ready-made frame. (The company I used, The Picture Gallery, is listed on page 172.) I've added a resin topcoat to the gel print, which gives it a more professional finish and enhances the depth of the print.

MATERIALS
Refer back to the master list on page 18 for the essential items.

- Canvas – 15 x 15cm (6 x 6in)
- Card or paper for a viewfinder
- Matte and gloss mediums
- Catalyst wedge
- Mountboard or thick paper
- Double-sided heavy-duty stick-on Velcro
- Wooden panels
- Heavy gel medium (optional)

- Wax paper
- Fixative
- Damp cloth or baby wipe
- Emery board
- UV varnish – matte, satin or gloss finishes
- Soft flat brush or sponge
- Ikea's 'SANNAHED' 25 x 25cm (10 x 10in) or Nicola Spring box frames
- Framer's tape
- ArtResin

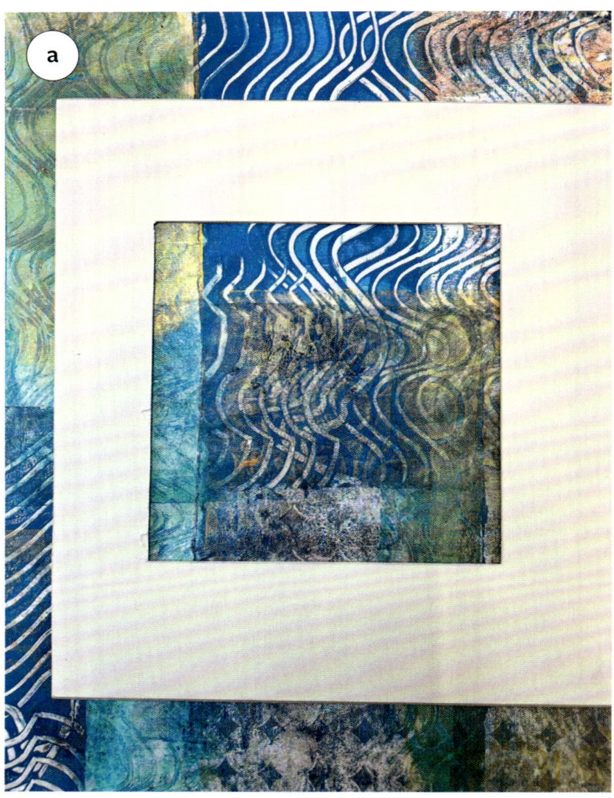

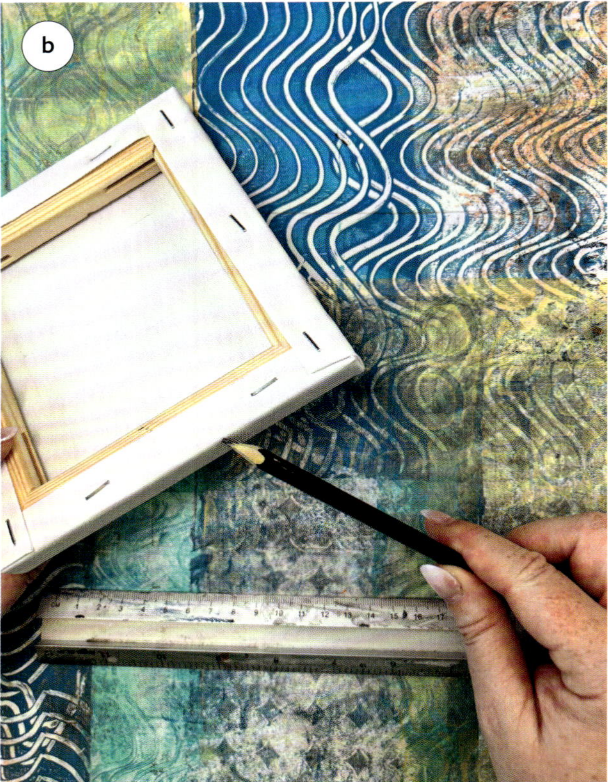

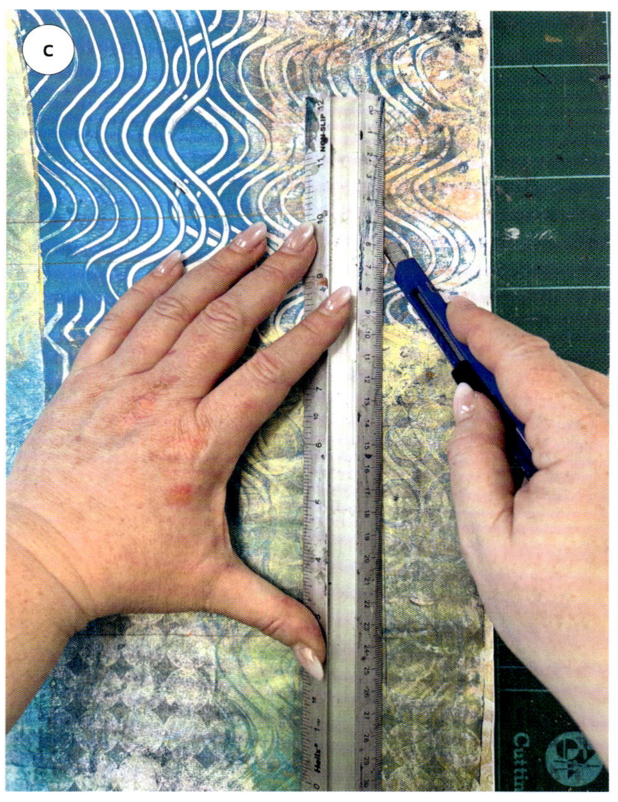

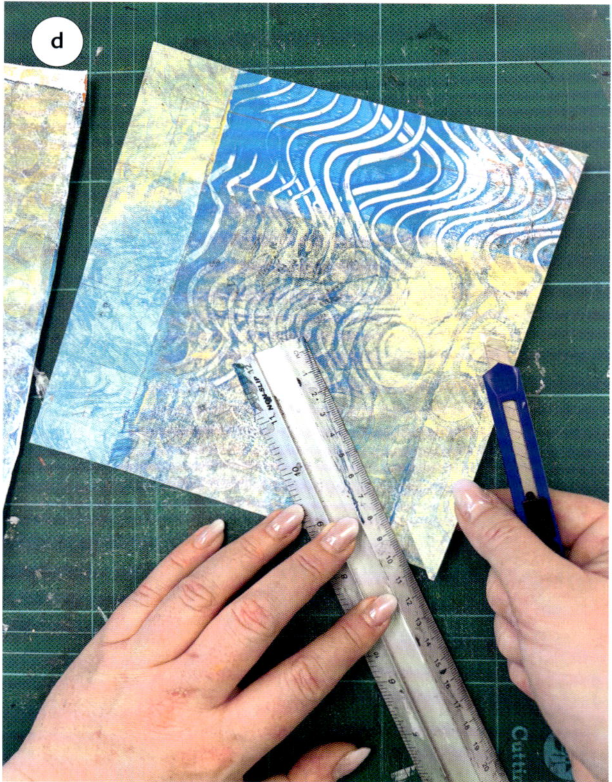

How to wrap a print around a canvas

Cut a viewfinder to match the size of your canvas (a). The canvas I'm using is 15 x 15cm (6 x 6in).

Allow extra paper to wrap around the edges. Since this canvas is 1.5cm (½in) deep, I measure an additional 2cm (¾in) to ensure there's enough paper to wrap comfortably around (b).

Cut out the paper (c) and trim the corners into triangles (d) to make it easier to fold around the edges. If there are any pencil marks, erase them now before gluing (e), as the matte medium will seal the pencil marks and make them impossible to remove once it dries.

Apply matte medium to both the substrate and the paper (f), then use a catalyst wedge to smooth out any bubbles (g).

Trim off any excess paper at the corners (h, i). Be cautious, as the paper can tear easily when wet. If this happens, you can easily fix it by touching up with paint once it's dry or by adding more collage pieces to the composition.

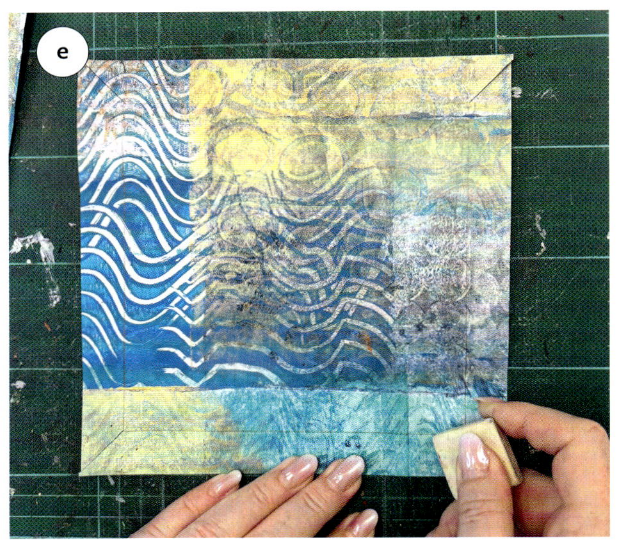

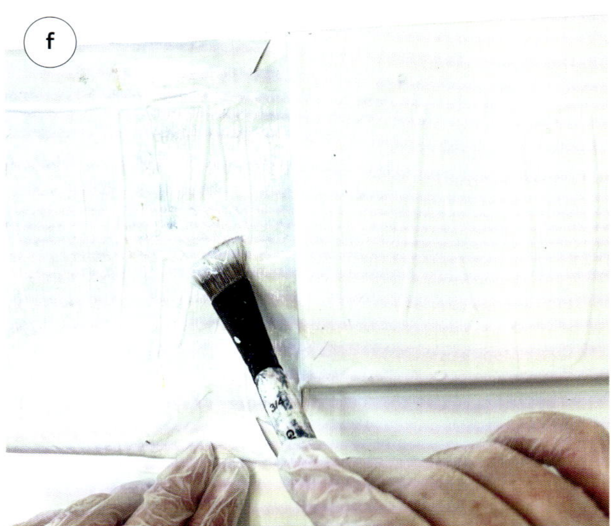

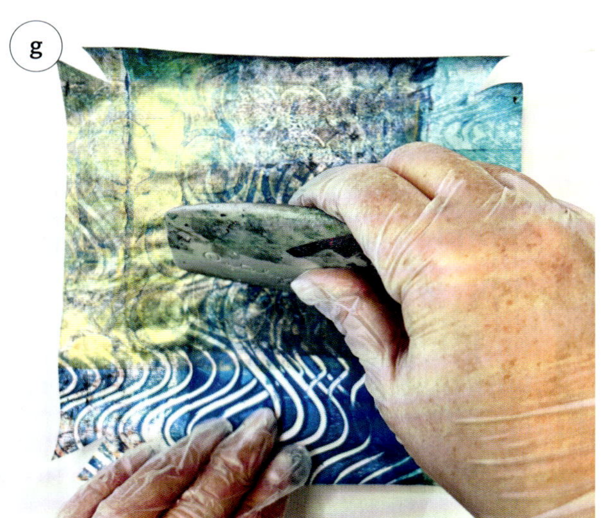

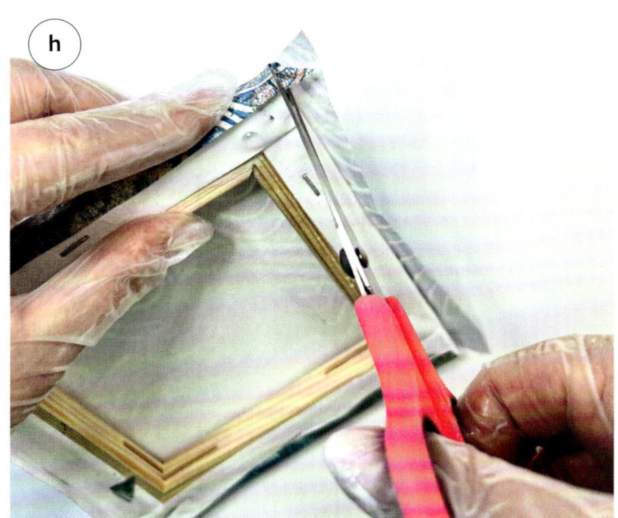

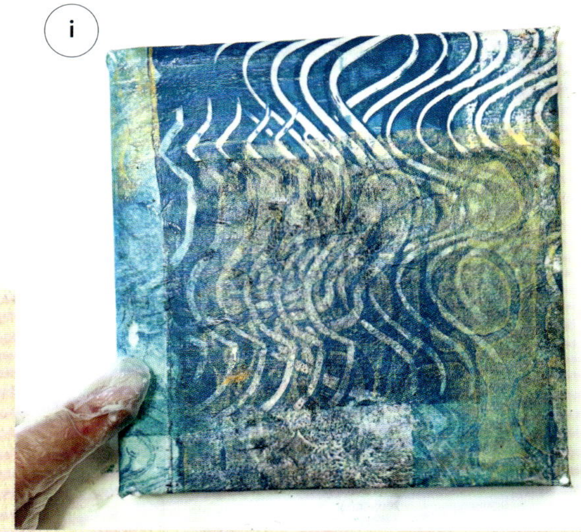

Attaching a print to a wooden cradleboard panel

If you're using wooden panels to display your prints, it's important to prevent sap or resin from the wood transferring onto the prints. Apply a couple of coats of Gloss Medium or Golden Gac 100 (a) to the wooden substrate before gluing the papers on. This acts as a barrier and helps protect the print from any unwanted residue.

Use a viewfinder to find a composition you're happy with, then cut the print to the size of the wooden cradleboard (b).

Glue both the paper and the substrate (c). The paper I'm using here is from the warm-up project (see page 21). If you're gluing heavier paper or mountboard to the wooden cradleboard, I recommend using a heavy gel medium for better adhesion. Place a sheet of wax paper on top, then apply heavy weights and leave it to dry overnight. This will ensure a strong, even bond.

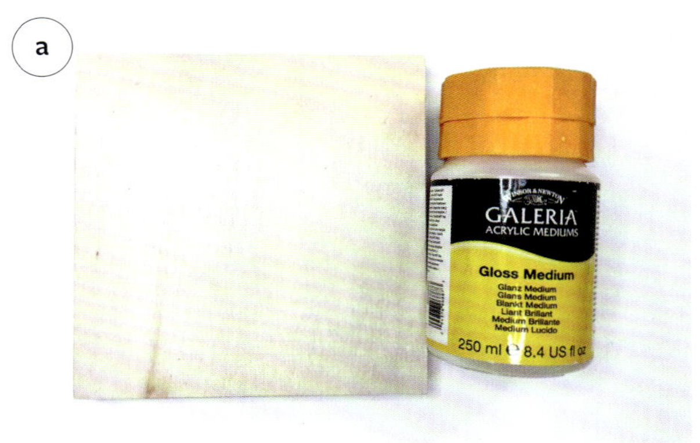

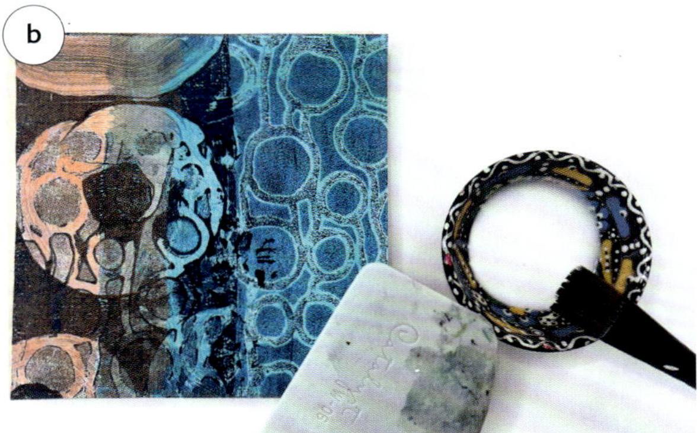

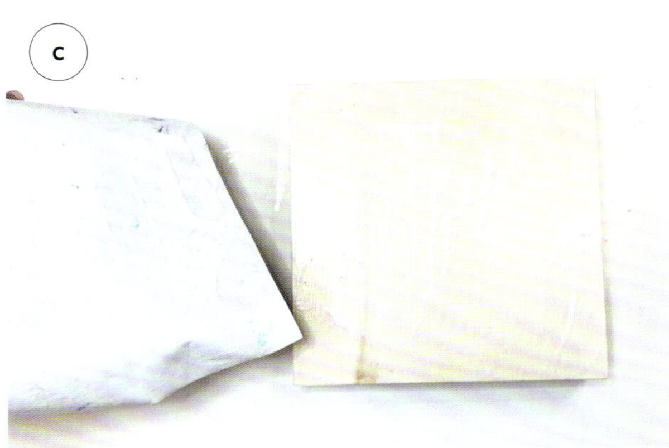

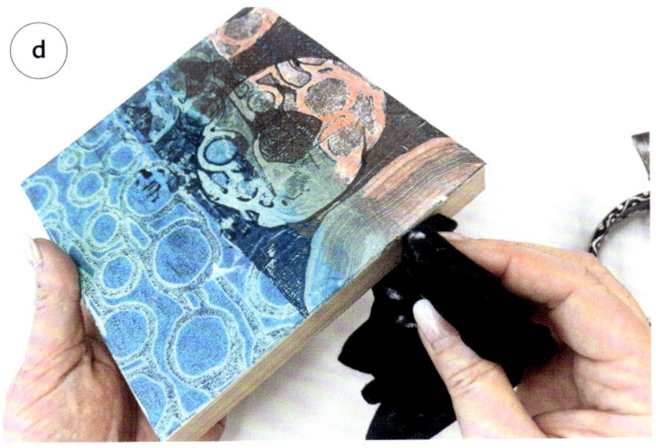

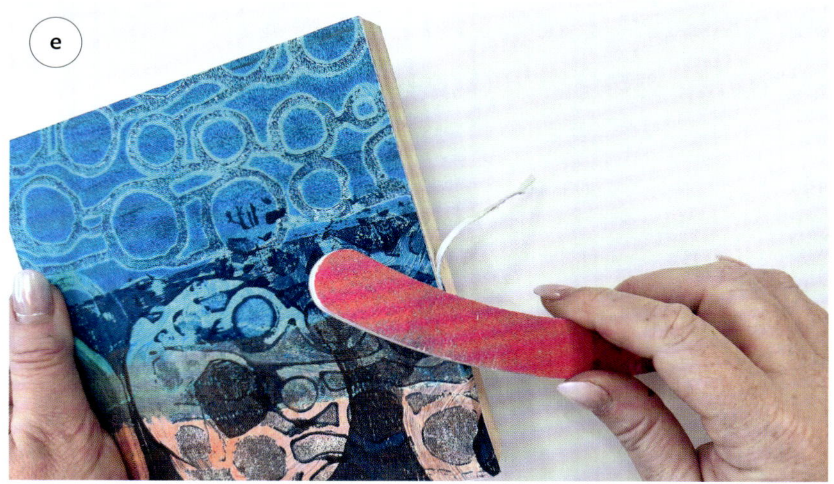

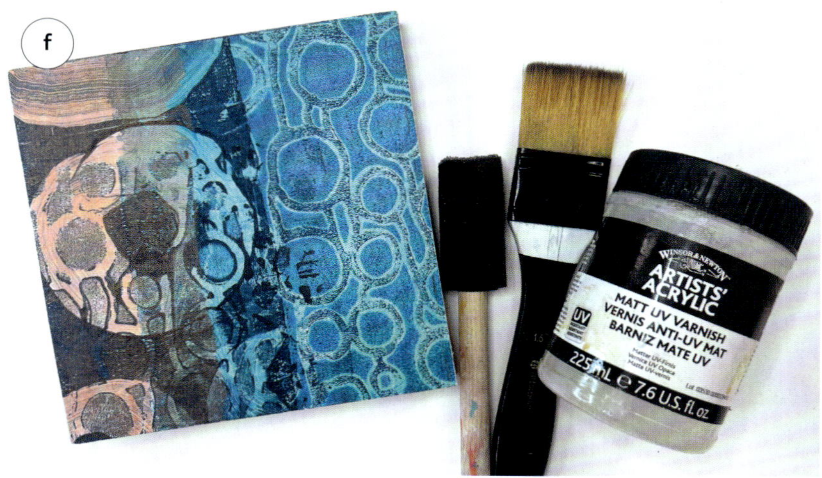

If your artwork includes lots of collaged elements, once you're finished, spray any water-soluble details like Posca pen-drawn elements with two layers of professional fixative. Then coat the entire artwork with gloss medium. This helps ensure that any small collage pieces will stay securely in place over time and won't lift.

Remove any excess glue from the edges of the cradleboard using a damp cloth or a baby wipe (d). This helps keep the edges clean and ensures a neat finish. Once dry, file off any excess paper using an emery board for a smooth, professional edge (e).

Apply two thin coats of UV varnish (f). This product comes in matte, satin or gloss finishes, so you can choose the one that best suits your preference. Use a soft flat brush or a sponge to apply the varnish. I recommend pouring a small amount into a separate container rather than using it directly from the original bottle to avoid contamination. Be sure to follow the directions on the container, as the instructions for use may vary depending on the brand you're using.

Framing mounted prints in ready-made box frames

One of my favourite ways to frame small prints mounted on wood squares or wooden cradleboards is by using Ikea's 'SANNAHED' 25 x 25cm (10 x 10in) box frames (a). What I love about these frames is that I can easily remove the Perspex film and mount the wood on paper inside the box. I also found another supplier – Nicola Spring – that offers frames where you can remove the glass, which is essential for framing in this way. I've listed a few suggestions in the References and Resources (see page 172).

Remove the packaging and keep the mount and Perspex. Replace the mount and Perspex with a solid piece of mountboard or thick paper. Draw around the original cut mount to get the correct size.

Use a sharp craft knife and cutting mat to carefully cut it to size, ensuring it matches the same thickness as the original mount and Perspex. This ensures the frame stays packed properly and prevents it from sliding around when reassembled. Sometimes, I reuse the Perspex for other monoprinting projects or as a paint palette.

Cut small strips of double-sided heavy-duty stick-on Velcro. It comes in two rolls: one side is rough and the other is fluffy. Cut four pieces of each type (b, c). I find this Velcro works better than regular double-sided tape and gives me confidence that the painting will stay securely attached to the backing board without falling off.

Peel off the plastic to reveal the sticky surface, then stick the rough Velcro down first. I place it slightly away from the edge so it isn't visible when viewing the painting from the side. Next, stick the fluffy side to the rough side and peel off the remaining plastic. The sticky side should be facing towards you on all four corners (d).

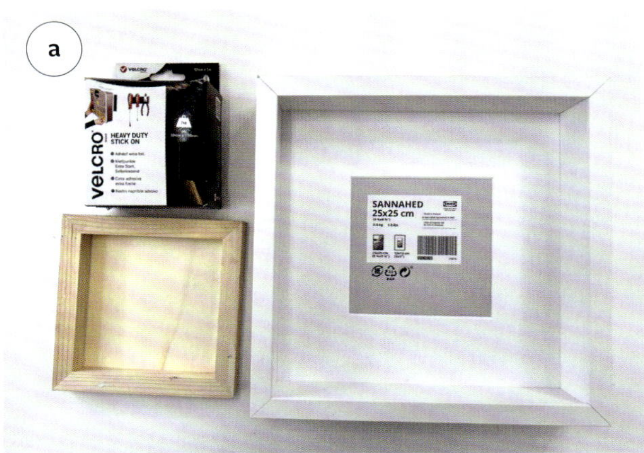

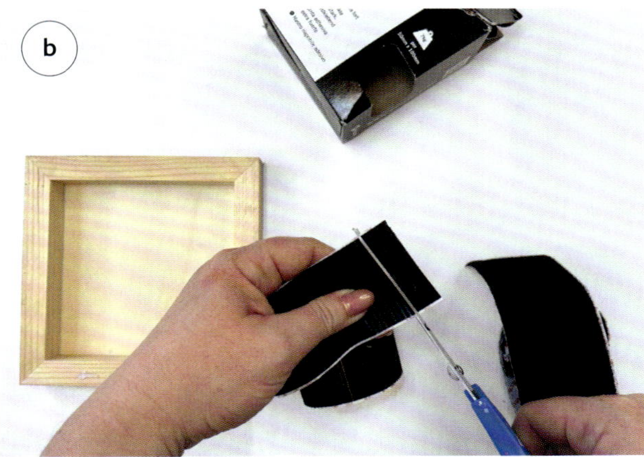

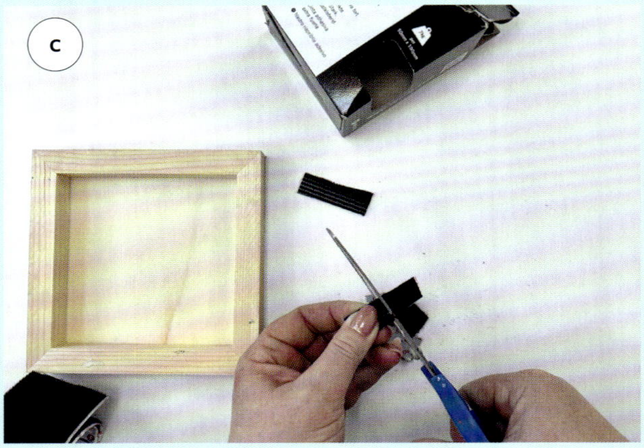

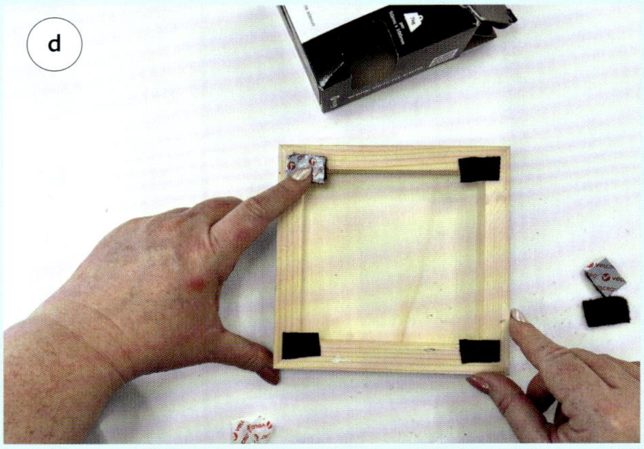

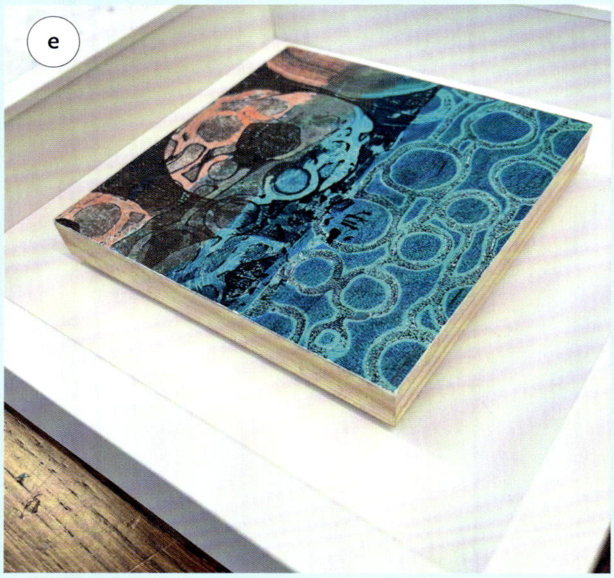

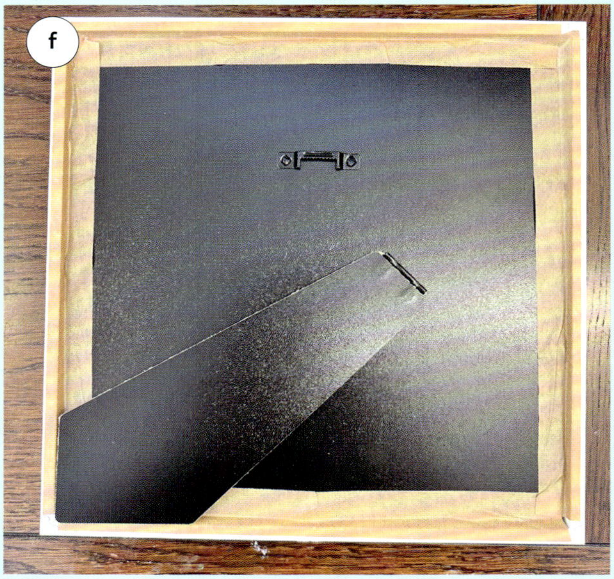

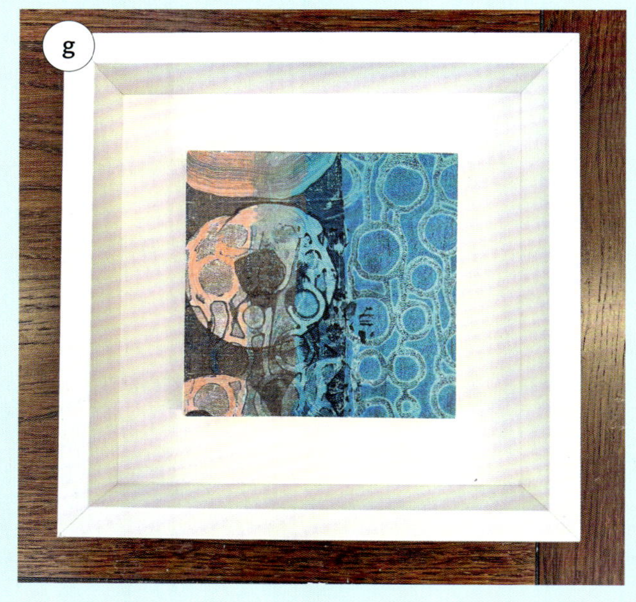

Carefully place the wooden cradleboard in the centre of the frame. I usually eyeball it, but if you're not confident doing it this way, you can measure and mark small dots to ensure precise placement (e). Turn the frame over and secure the back with framer's tape (f). This step helps give a more professional finish to a ready-made frame (g).

Below are some examples of wood square blanks that I attached gel prints to, added hand-drawn elements and then finished with ArtResin (any resin would work here). I've included detailed instructions in the Resources on page 172.

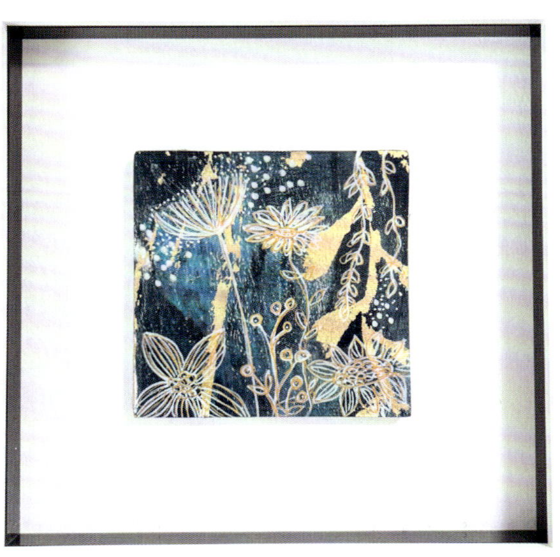

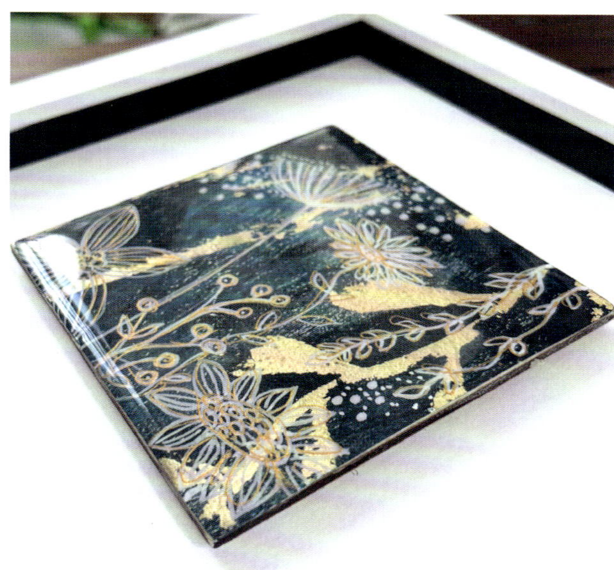

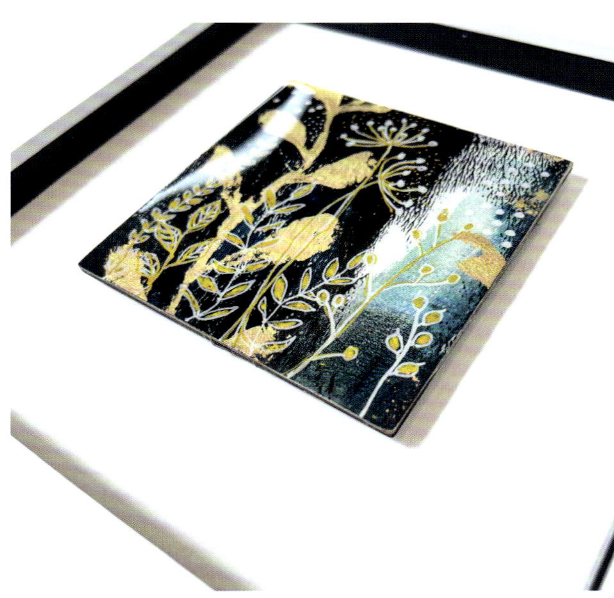

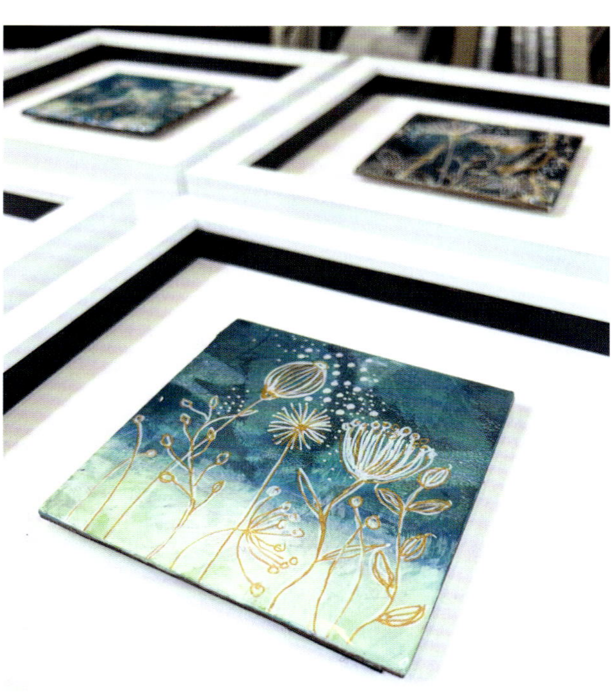

These pieces are framed in Nicola Spring 3D Shadow Box photo frames, which complement the artwork beautifully with their black edging detail.

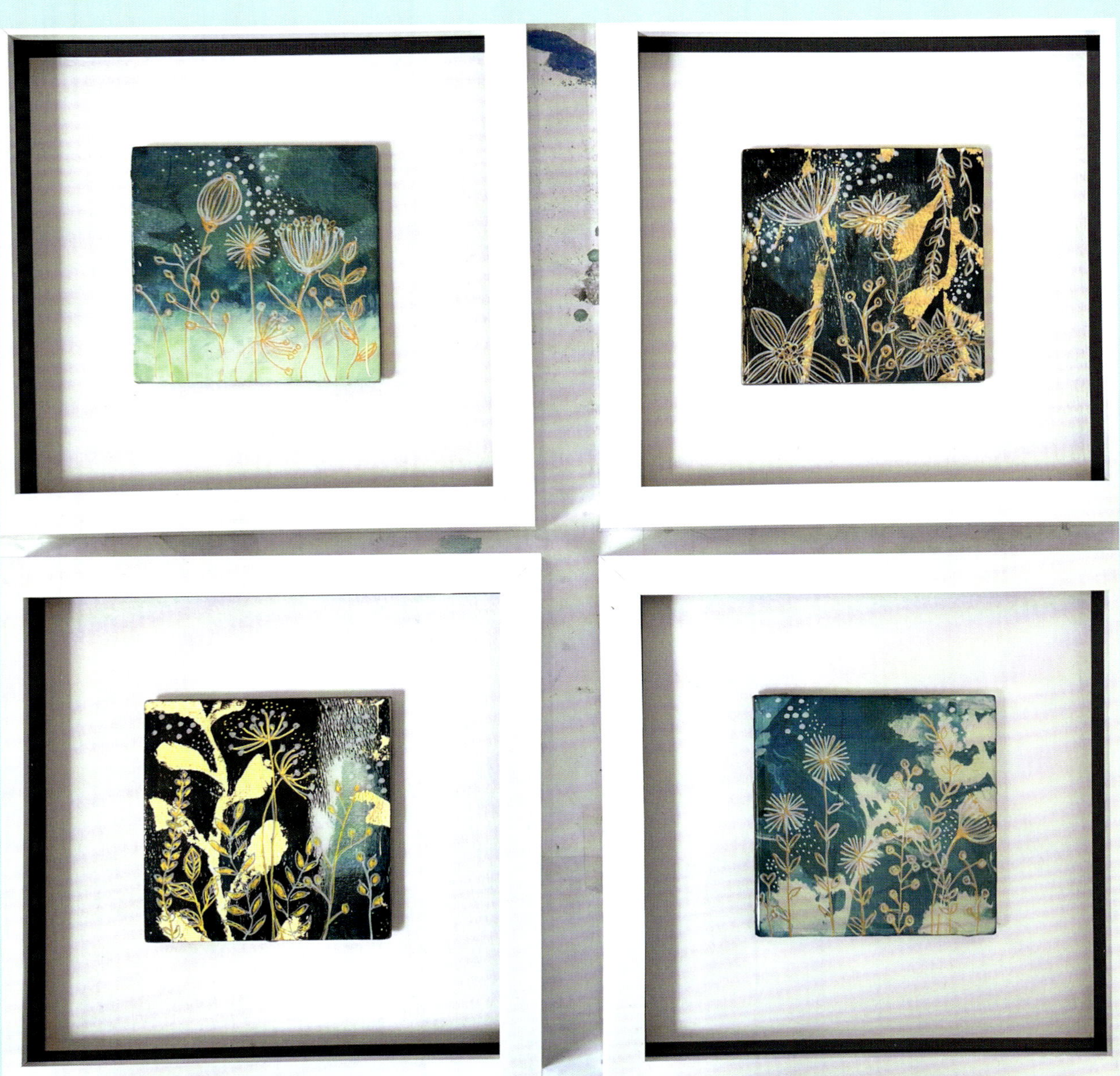

They can be hung individually or make a more striking impact when grouped together in a set of three or four.

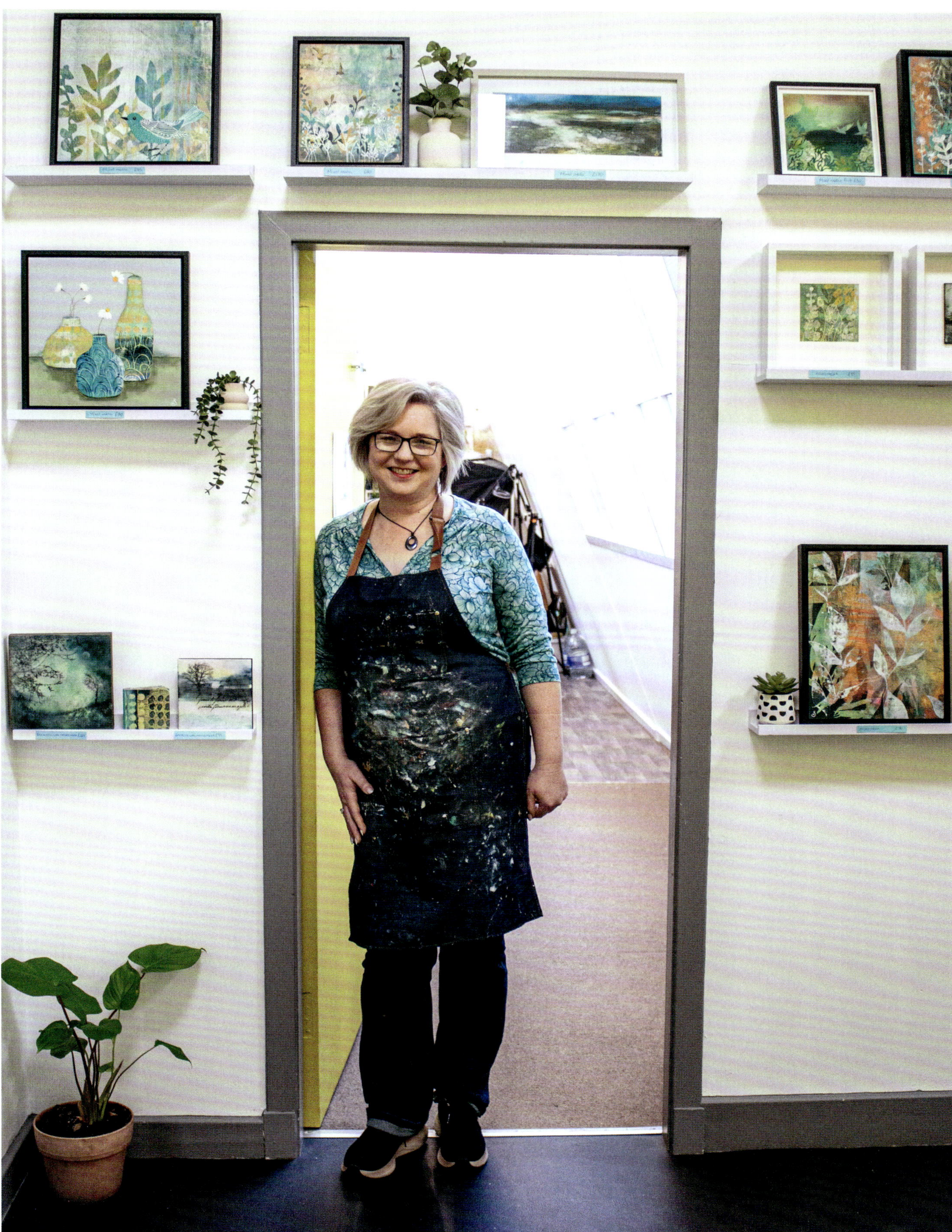

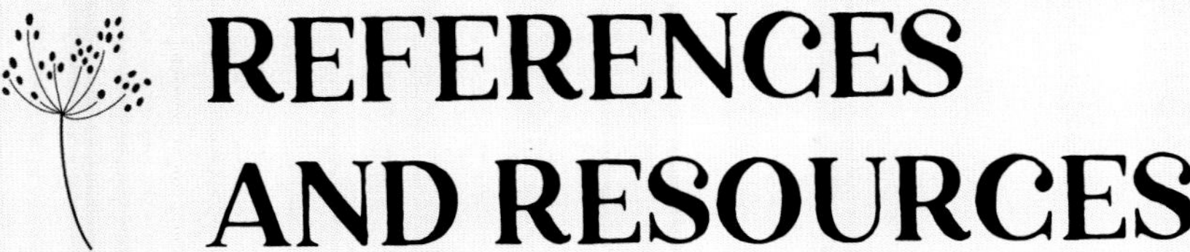

REFERENCES AND RESOURCES

Books and websites

ArtResin: artresin.co.uk/collections/artresin-epoxy-resin. For more information on how to use it on your gel prints, see susanmccreevy.com/how-to-resin-a-gelli-print

Cher, Barbara, *Refuse to Choose! Use all of your interests, passions, and hobbies to create the life and career of your dreams*, Rodale Press, New York, 2007

Colour: daler-rowney.com/resources/colour-charts – comprehensive reference guides for Daler Rowney acrylic paints, including clear indications of transparency and colour fastness

Shadow box frames: Nicola Spring, Hobbycraft, Ikea SANNAHED

Sutton, Tina, *The Pocket Complete Color Harmony*, Rockport Publishers, Gloucester, MA, 2020

The Picture Gallery, picturegalleryuk.com/canvas-floating-frames

Woods, Fleur, *The Untamed Thread: Slow stitch to soothe the soul and ignite creativity,* Koa Press Ltd, Christchurch, NZ, 2023

International page sizes

A1	33.1 x 23.4in
A2	23.4 x 16.5in
A3	16.5 x 11.7in
A4	11.7 x 8.3in
A5	8.3 x 5.8in
A6	5.8 x 4.1in

Videos

Susan McCreevy Artist, 'Adding Interest to Gelli Prints with Stencils and Hand-Drawn Details' [video], YouTube (uploaded 10 May 2023), youtube.com/watch?v=6HmJRIyNBdo, accessed 17 December 2024

Susan McCreevy Artist, 'Easy Gelli Plate warm-up | printing with everyday objects' [video], YouTube

Susan McCreevy Artist, 'Essential Paint Pens for Artists: Susan McCreevy's Top Picks and Tips' [video], YouTube (uploaded 19 July 2024), youtube.com/watch?v=ofCk_Lm3jf8, accessed 17 December 2024

Susan McCreevy Artist, 'How to add ArtResin to your gel prints' [video], YouTube (uploaded 26 July 2024), youtube.com/watch?v=iMSoOLbbsMw, accessed 31 January 2025

Susan McCreevy Artist, 'Halloween Pumpkin Decoration Tutorial' [video], YouTube (uploaded 25 October 2024), youtube.com/watch?v=VOhc6y5bTiM, accessed 17 December 2024

Susan McCreevy Artist, 'Layering Techniques with Collage Art' [video], YouTube (uploaded 23 February 2024), youtube.com/watch?v=uXtzX1izY4g, accessed 17 December 2024

Susan McCreevy Artist, 'Making Handmade Bookmarks: Gelli Prints, Stencils and Pen Detail' [video], YouTube (uploaded 22 June 2023), youtube.com/watch?v=tnIJCB7cDzw, accessed 31 January 2025

Susan McCreevy Artist, 'Stitching & Beading on Canvas | Easy 3D Mixed Media Techniques' [video], YouTube

Susan McCreevy Artist, 'Top tips for Perfect Gelli Plate Image transfers' [video], YouTube

Acknowledgements

Thank you to Clare Martelli and Natasha Collin at Herbert Press and Bloomsbury Publishing for giving me the opportunity to write this book and supporting my vision.

A heartfelt thank you to all the women who have supported me on my journey of growing my art business. Your encouragement and always being just a phone call away has meant so much to me. Special thanks to Jayne Emerson, Kjersti Lisbeth Matre, Sally Worsley, Heather Afrin and Anne Bryce.

Thank you to my family. To Norm, my lovely partner, who made all of this possible by helping me build an art studio in our garden. It gave me the space and freedom to create while being close to home to care for our girls, Niamh and Ella.

Thank you to my parents, Anna and Archie, for always supporting and being there for us all.

And many thanks to Edyta Wilczek for my beautiful gel nails that complement my artwork and for all the encouragement you've given me over the years.

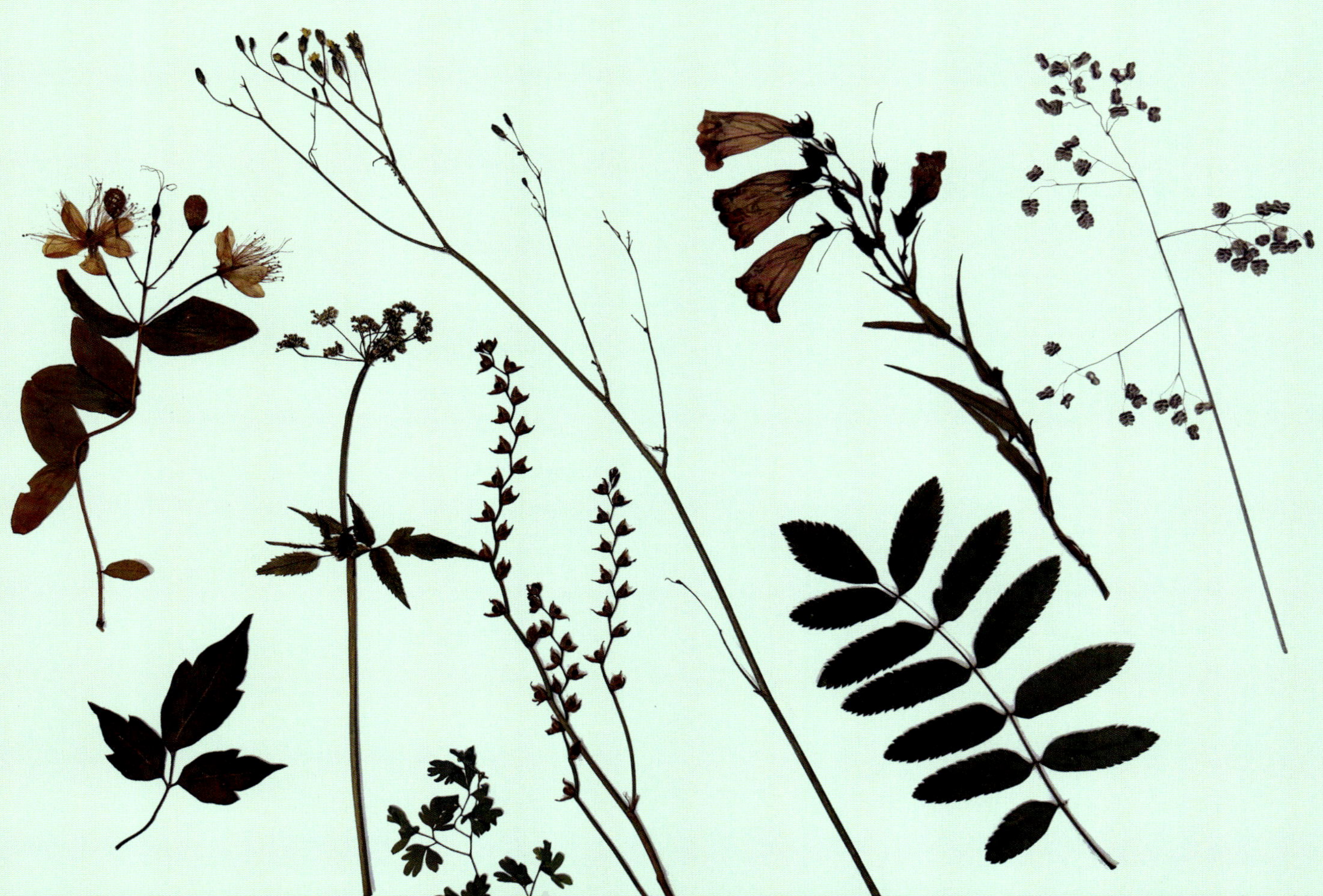

Suppliers

Australia

Art Store Online: artstoreonline.com.au

Art Supplies Australia: artsuppliesaustralia.com.au

Art Supplies Online: artsuppliesonline.com.au

Art to Art: arttoart.net

Craft Online: craftonline.com.au

Eckersley's Art & Craft: eckersleys.com.au

Jackson's: jacksonsart.com

Officeworks Art & Craft Supplies: officeworks.com.au

Oxlades Art Supplies: oxlades.com.au

Senior Art Supplies: seniorart.com.au

Spotlight Art Supplies: spotlightstores.com/art-craft

The Alchemist: thealchemist.net.au

The Art Shop: theartshop.com.au

The Sydney Art Store: thesydneyartstore.com.au

The Thread Studio: thethreadstudio.com

Canada

Michaels: Canada.Michaels.com

Denmark

Art-de-vinci.dk: art-de-vinci.dk

Hobbyboden: hobbyboden.dk

Kreatima: kreatima.com

Stelling: stellings.com

Germany

Gerstaecker, Eitorf: gerstaecker.de/eitorf

Ireland

Cork Art Supplies: corkartsupplies.com

Evans Art Supplies: store.evansartsupplies.ie

Netherlands

Gerstaecker: Gerstaecker.nl

Van Beek Art Supplies: Vanbeekart.nl

New Zealand

Gordon Harris: gordonharris.co.nz

Hobby Land NZ: hobbyland.co.nz

Spotlight Art Supplies: spotlightstores.com/nz/art-craft

The Drawing Room: thedrawingroom.co.nz

The Ribbon Rose: ribbonrose.co.nz

Warehouse Stationery: warehousestationery.co.nz

Norway

Panduro: Panduro.no

Tegne: Tegne.no

Torso: Torso.no

South Africa

Art Savings Club: artsavingsclub.co.za

Switzerland

Gerstaecker: Gerstaecker.ch

UK

ARTdiscount: artdiscount.co.uk

Art from the Heart: afth.co.uk

Art Van Go: vycombe-arts.co.uk

Bromley's Art Supplies: artsupplies.co.uk

Carnival Papers: carnivalpapers.com

Cass Art: cassart.co.uk

Cowling & Wilcox: cowlingandwilcox.com

Hobbycraft: hobbycraft.co.uk

Intaglio Printmaker: intaglioprintmaker.com

Jackson's: jacksonsart.com

The Range: therange.co.uk/arts-and-crafts/
art-supplies

The Works: theworks.co.uk/c/art-and-craft/
art-supplies

USA

Blick: dickblick.com

Cheap Joe's Art Stuff: cheapjoes.com

Jerry's Artarama: jerrysartarama.com

Joggles: joggles.com

Michaels: michaels.com

StencilGirl Products: stencilgirlproducts.com

Wet Paint: wetpaintart.com

Photo credits

Unless otherwise stated, all images copyright of the author. Photography by Chantal Macleod-Holdsworth (www.cmhphoto.co.uk)

10 (bottom), 11: © Gelli Arts Ltd, 2025

48: courtesy of Anne Bryce

70, 71: courtesy of Jessica Russo Scherr (@bluelavaart, bluelavaart.com)

88, 89: courtesy of Jane Faase (@janefaase, janefaasecreates.com)

108, 109: Jayne Emerson (@jayneemersontextiles, norulestextilesociety.com)

132, 133: Drew Steinbrecher (@drewsteinbrecher, andrewsteinbrecher.com)

152, 153: Marsha Valk (@marshavalk, marshavalk.com)

156 (bottom): Clem Onojeghuo on unsplash.com

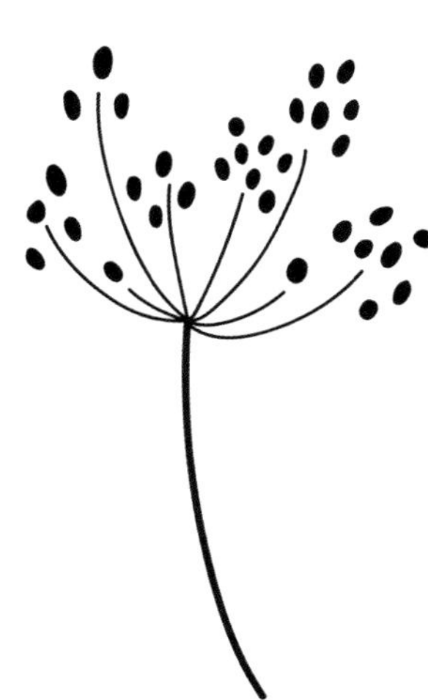

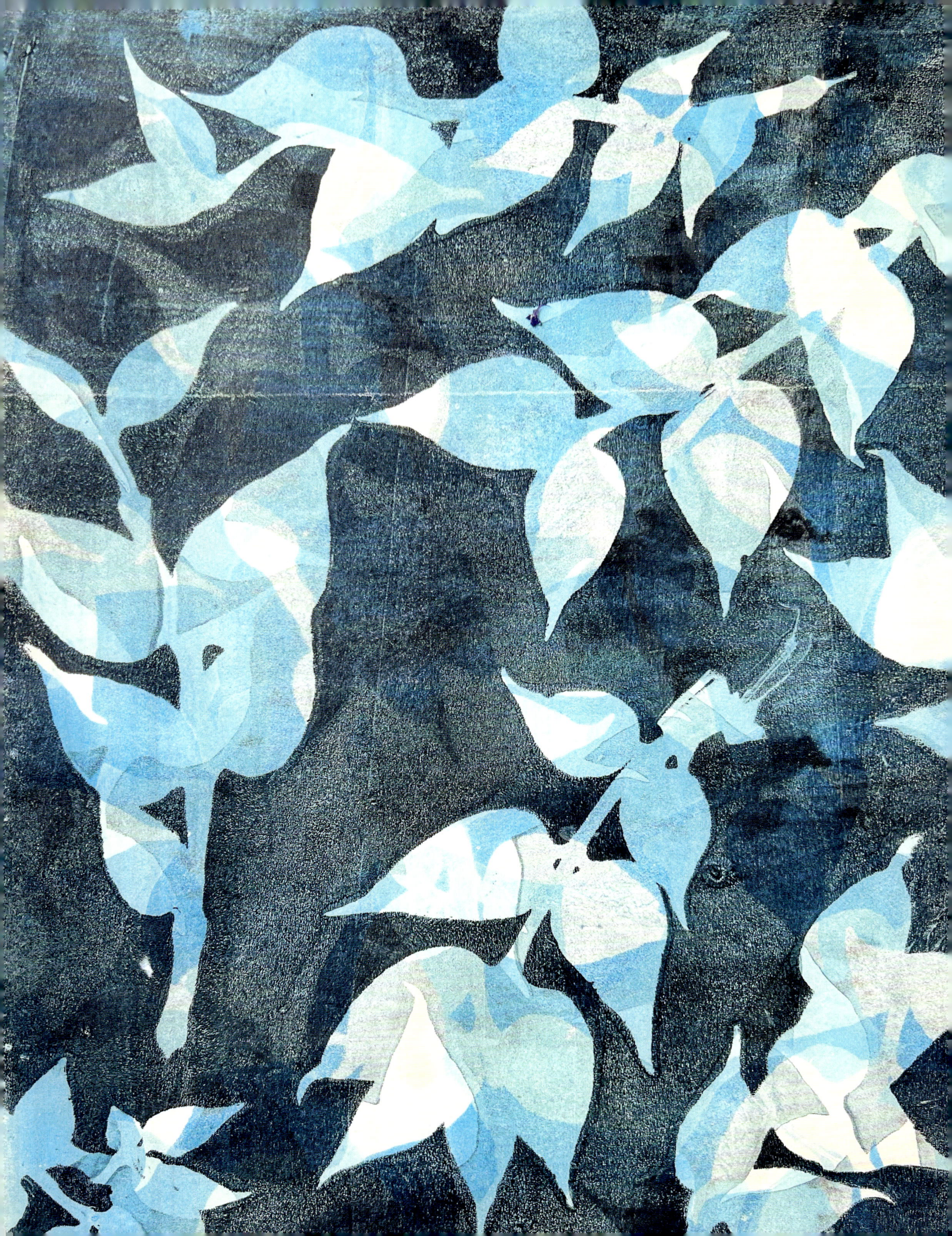